CRITICAL VISION

Random Essays & Tracts Concerning

SEX · RELIGION · DEATH

Edited By
David Kerekes & David Slater

- Critical Vision is an  imprint of Headpress -

A Critical Vision Book
First published in 1995
by Headpress

Headpress, PO Box 160
Stockport, Cheshire
SK1 4ET, Great Britain
Fax: 0161 796 1935

British Library Cataloguing in Publication Data

Critical Vision: Random Essays and Tracts Concerning Sex, Religion, Death
   I. Kerekes, David II. Slater, David
   082

   ISBN 0-9523288-0-1

CONTENTS

INTRODUCTION

This volume contains work, revised and updated, from the early, out-of-print issues of *Headpress* magazine and new material specially commissioned.

Headpress first appeared in the Summer of 1991. It was tagged a 'magazine of Sex Religion Death' as a means of maximising the scope of contents and consisted of a rather eclectic fusion of non-fiction writings. Not just articles, but slight episodes such as the painter and decorator who divulged over the telephone numerous work-related anecdotes, some life-threatening and each more preposterous than the last. Subsequent issues noted the paragraph in a text book which had spurred its reader to draw an analogy with love, and 'A Cup of Coffee in Downey', wherein the author leaves the writing of the piece for a short sojourn to his favourite coffeeshop down the road. (After its publication, the author, a retired mathematician, wrote to explain that he wouldn't be providing *Headpress* with any further work because his wife, "a Catholic nun, practically," forbade it.) Nuggets unquestionably, but those of a magazine yet to fully find its footing.

All revised and updated material has been taken from issues 1 through 5 and would not be out of place if published in *Headpress* today. It also adheres to the 'Sex Religion Death' motif in a much less ambiguous way than the original magazines were compiled. Of this reprinted work attention will be drawn here to 'Hookers For Jesus!', because attempts to contact Chris Mikul these past two years have proven unsuccessful (the update is a combination of material and letters Mikul supplied to *Headpress* back in 1993, and approximately three lines of text as provided by the *Critical Vision* editors).

The porn letters scattered throughout *Critical Vision* are taken, quite literally, from the wastebins of several British and US-based adult magazines who deemed them too extreme or too ridiculous for publication. They belong to the category of previously unpublished material (which constitutes approximately half the present volume). It might be judicious to note that the letters have been left exactly as they were originally written: misspelled and grammatically impaired.

Of course, preparation and completion of this book would have been so much more difficult, if not downright impossible, without the aid of certain individuals: Dogger for illustrating the porn letters; David Huxley, Stefan Jaworzyn and Roger Sabin for their assistance on 'Thrill to Stories of Graphic Lust!'; likewise Michael Butterworth and all at Savoy for 'Banned, Drawn and Quartered'; Douglas D.Clark, Kelly Keniston, Mark MacNamara and Richard Baylor for 'It's Fun To Kill People!'; for general maintenance and repair, Howard Lake, Stephen Whittle, Lesley Kerekes, Sue, Tim Buggie and Andrew Darlington. Thank you.

to a place we know not of

—Finis Farr

THRILL TO STORIES OF GRAPHIC LUST!
Two Decades of Pornographic Comic Books

David Kerekes

I N A BBC TV PROGRAMME FOR CHILDREN many years ago, a debate on comics and comic books prompted one erstwhile young man to deliberate that comix spelt with an 'x' were bad for you because the characters in them didn't walk around with a smile, nor were they happy all the day. Like they were in comics. That could frighten kids, he suggested.

Of course, by a children's TV definition of the term, 'comix' encompassed everything outside the likes of the *Beano* and the *Dandy* – stopping dead at Marvel and DC. Superhero stuff.

But to a lot of people, that superhero stuff *is* funny and happy all the day long.

Underground comics – comics spelt c-o-m-i-x, k-o-m-i-x, or plain old c-o-m-i-c-s – *they* laugh at superheroes. I too had a smile when, in a fleapit bookstore in the mid-1980s, in a stack of 'new' arrivals, I spotted one such underground: a pristine copy of Robert Crumb's notorious and rare *Snatch Comics*, issue No.2, dated January 1969. The woman at the counter said the owner had just nipped out, but, looking down at the cover and jolly Angelfood McSpade greeting the reader with "Hello '69!", guessed 69 pence would cover it.

In his *A History of Underground Comics*, Mark James Estren says "Some of the most basic things that make underground comics 'underground' are the great differences between the contents of these books and the contents of what are generally called 'comics'". In *Comix: A History of Comic Books in America*, Les Daniels claims underground comics to be "bent on inducing drastic change in America's state of mind". Roger Sabin, in *Adult Comics: An Introduction*, writes that they're a "product of the profound social divisions that racked the west in the 1960s and 1970s". While Reinhold Reitberger and Wolfgang Fuchs, in *Comics: Anatomy of a Mass Medium*, judge the undergrounds to be "rather less progressive, subversive or radical than generally supposed".[1] More frugal perhaps, speaking in the documentary film *Comic Book Confidential*, Robert Crumb defined the underground as "absolute freedom".

After almost 20 years of restriction imposed by the Comics Code Authority, a new generation of artists in the early-1960s broke free from the traditional confides of comic book creation and a fresh movement was born. That of the underground comic.

This piece isn't intended as a look at underground comics *per se*, but rather a look at a specific and dominant part of that underground: those comics given over primarily to the sex act. Porn comics, if you will (the metaphor in 'absolute freedom') and in particular the work of a much neglected British artist, Antonio Ghura.

> Undergrounds are more than just comic books to me. In fact many of the underground comix community have little interaction at all with the other comic books. Unlike many of the 'above-ground' comics, the undergrounds are truly an art form unto themselves in that they truly mirror – albeit distortedly – contemporary society as we know it.
> Bruce Sweeney, *Illustrated Checklist To Underground Comix*

The Spring of 1954 saw publication in America of *Seduction of the Innocent*, a scathing indictment of comic books by one Dr Fredric Wertham, Senior Psychiatrist for the New York Department of Hospitals (the book was released in Britain the following year). Wertham targeted 'crime comic books' – by Wertham's definition, most every comic was a crime book[2] – of leading its juvenile readership into delinquency. According to Wertham, these publications promoted murder (because a boy who killed his parents confessed to having read comic books), suicide (comic books having been found in the bedroom of a young suicide victim), and encouraged homosexuality (like Batman and Robin). More than that, so insidious were they, that each panel of each comic page was a veritable masterwork of subliminal sexual imagery (Wonder Woman's magic lasso is a vagina; women have breasts).[3]

1934 is generally regarded as the year in which the comic book was born: Reprints of newspaper cartoon strips, the 64 page all-colour *Famous Funnies* became the first title to be sold on US news-stands. Another three years and *Detective Comics*, the first all-original comic book, went on sale. There followed a steady proliferation of superhero showcase titles headed by Batman and Superman. Lev Gleason Publications introduced in 1942 *Crime Does Not Pay* – tough, factual tales of gun-totin' lawbreakers vs. the USA. The book was immensely popular and sported a whole genre, which included in its number such titles as *Crime Must Pay The Penalty*, *Lawbreakers Always Lose*, and *There Is No Escape For The Public Enemy* – the key words being of course CRIME, LAWBREAKERS, and PUBLIC ENEMY with the tag-line supplemented in suitably finer print.

The EC Comics Group went one further. They turned their *Crime Patrol* into *Tales From The Crypt*, *War Against Crime* into *The Vault of Horror*, and *Gunfighter* into *The Haunt of Fear*. Much more than simply initiating a new genre of horror comic, EC were to change the face of a medium. Here were stories that didn't necessarily have a happy ending, nor a good-guy who always came through in one piece. Intelligent and witty, EC were creating comics for a readership beyond that of children – a fact corroborated with the arrival of *Shock SuspenStories*, a kind of EC sampler featuring gritty tales of police corruption, racism, baby-napping, even the evils of fur-trapping (back in the 1950s!). Issue No.12, for instance, with its story 'The Monkey' and cover art by Al Feldstein, remains potent even today, by contemporary standards. It is not hard to imagine, in its tale of a high school dropout going cold turkey, that 'The Monkey' – and *Shock* itself – was harbinger to the 'adult comic'.[4] *"...It had taken me less than three months to move from blasting 'Jive-T' to popping 'H'. Sid provided me with 'the fit'... a 'spike' or 'hypo', a length of rubber hose to distend the vein, a spoon to heat the 'H' in, and a can of Sterno. I was on it..."*

The publication of Wertham's *Seduction of the Innocent* brought in its wake a huge upheaval in the comics industry. A clampdown. The major publishers in America gathered round to create the Comics Code Authority, a choking and not altogether clear set of guidelines to which all future comic titles ought to adhere. If they didn't, chances were news-stands wouldn't dare carry them. The Authority also saw that many smaller publishing houses – the competition – were pushed out of business. As part of its ruling, the Code demanded that

> Policemen, judges, government officials and respected institutions shall never be presented in such a way as to create disrespect for established authority... in every instance good shall triumph over evil... no comic magazine shall use the word horror and terror in its title... scenes dealing with, or instruments associated with walking dead, torture, vampires and vampirism, ghouls, cannibalism and werewolfism are prohibited... females shall be drawn realistically without exaggeration of physical qualities...

It was, however, possible to stay afloat in the comic business without resorting to stories about cuddly animals, goofy teenagers, or superheroes. EC again came to the fore, this time with a humour magazine. Advancing the attitude and philosophy of their crime, horror, and war books, *Mad* was another shrewd step for the publishing house. The same month the Comics Code Authority announced itself, the sixteenth issue of *Mad* had on its cover editor Harvey Kurtzman peddling his magazine to kids on a street corner. Above him was the header: COMICS GO UNDERGROUND*!*

Kurtzman is often cited as being the single, most important influence on the underground. After leaving *Mad*, he pursued similarly experimental and irreverential paths editing *Trump*, *Humbug*, and *Help!*. The latter, launched in 1960, featured work by fledgling underground artists Robert Crumb, Jay Lynch, Gilbert Shelton, and Skip Williamson.

THE GRABBIES ARE COMING

The underground comics tackled issues such as sex, drug-taking, racism, the sanity of the artist, the sanity of the reader, the sanity of the world. More than the actual themes themselves, however, it was the manner of the telling that was unique. Rather than recounting a violent situation, an underground artist might concentrate on the violence full-stop; no quarrel or consequence, just conflict. Then again, some strips might be given over to nothing in particular. Unlike conventional comics, in the underground there was no production-line environment with regard to the creating of a strip. There was no company of writers and artists, inkers and letterers working under the control of one editor. The underground artist controlled every facet of his or her individual creation.

Many underground titles were just one-shots. This because the publisher (often the artist, one and the same) couldn't afford a subsequent issue, or, *could* afford subsequent issues but would change the title anyway. If there exists a Golden Age of underground comic, then the Seventies and early-Eighties must be it. The height of expression and experimentation, several titles from this period are now regarded as classics of their type and are regularly reprinted. But for every underground comic book ever heard of – let alone still available – there are hundreds more relegated to obscurity. The print runs on these comics didn't always escape the three-figure mark. Smaller still would be their distribution.

The sex comic had a brief hiatus in the early years of the underground and, with the exception of a handful of titles, vaporised soon after. The San Francisco Comic Book Company issued *Mini-Lust Comics* and *More Comics* (1972). There was a *Cunt Coloring Book* (1975), a *Cunt Fart Funnies* (1973), at least two issues of *Good Jive Comix* (1972 and 73). Last Gasp published *Amputee Love* in 1974. The Print Mint and The Cartoonists Co-operative Press had, between them, two issues of *Manhunt* (1973 and 74). There was an *Amazing Adult Fantasies* (1974), *Good Old Lust* (1972), and *Sin City USA* (1972). But the first was *Snatch Comics* in 1968. The result of an association between Robert Crumb and S.Clay Wilson, the 800 pocket-sized copies sold out in no time at all.

A devotion to (explicit) sexual activity of all kinds, *Snatch* is the antithesis of everything the Comics Code stood for. In that respect it can be regarded as ground-breaking. But *Snatch* didn't create porn comics, merely relocated them. Illustrated pamphlets depicting penetrative sex date back to the 1920s. Eight pages in length, these pamphlets – or 'Tijuana Bibles' as they came to be known – are perhaps the earliest form of comic book. Personalities of the day, whether cartoon characters (like Popeye) or gangsters (like Al Capone), were depicted in a sexually compromising situation. The artist was always anonymous; so too the exact origins of the Tijuana Bibles (though it is pretty much accepted that they *didn't* come from Tijuana, more like Los Angeles or San Diego). Writing in the first volume of *Sex Comic Classics* [New York: Comic Classics, 1977], author Otis Raymond correlates the evolution of the Eight-Pagers with the Great Depression and Prohibition: "No job, no money: abject misery all about; no hopes for the future. Nirvana must come from someplace." Hundreds of separate titles were produced, some even extending to 16-pages and some in colour. The caricatures also went so far as to incorporate the likes of Winston Churchill and Mahatma Gandhi. When the resource of recognisable figures had been exhausted, the Tijuana artists set to inventing their own. But it was always straight sex between the players, no kinky stuff. By the mid-1930s the Tijuana Bibles were gone, replaced, come the 1940s, by the so-called 'Kinky Comics' which depicted bondage and mild SM scenarios.

Speaking in *Rolling Stone*, Crumb said that *Snatch Comics* "isn't regular pornography. It comes at it from another angle. It's a satire on itself; it makes fun of pornography." In *Snatch* No.2, Crank Collingwood (S.Clay Wilson under a pseudonym) kicks things off with 'Cunt Capers', a strip featuring two lesbians performing anal and vaginal sex with an "electric multi-purpose high-speed strap-on corkscrew dildo", which ultimately gets stuck at high speed. Crumb contributes 'Orgasm on Ice', 'Down on the Farm' ("Ya better make that th' last one, Ezry... We's

After years of utilising famous figures in sexual scenarios, the Tijuana Bibles hit upon the idea of creating their own characters. The first and most successful of these was the 'Fuller Brush Man'. 'Obliging Lady', the strip that follows, is typical of the Eight-Pagers. Artist unknown.

Opening pages to S.Clay Wilson's 'Cunt Capers'. Snatch Comics No.2

runnin' outa chickens!"), and the centre-spread 'The Family That Lays Together Stays Together!' Rick Griffin, who was to find fame in psychedelic Rock posters, delivers the obtuse panel 'The Secret of OXO'. Peppered throughout the issue are Rory Hayes' crude sight gags. 'The Adventures of the Mad Prickman' has a mad prickman bashing a girl on her head with his prick, "take that you fucki'n [sic] piece of cunt!!!" Hayes released his own title, *Cunt*, 'The Only Comix You Can Eat,' in 1969. As with *Snatch*, it was published by Apex Novelties, whose Don Donahue had a small printing press, hadn't been in the business long, and was willing to print what was deemed "too hot" for the larger companies. The comics, recollects Donahue in *Blab!* No.3, would be "printed and distributed in an atmosphere of secrecy and caution". Various hippies on a piecework basis, Donahue continues, "would come by with suitcases to pick up the pages and covers, and would return with completed comic books which were then sold to various entrepreneurs who came to my loft. Some of the books ended up under the counter at headshops, some were sold from under people's jackets on the street..."

Snatch lasted three issues. Crumb followed it with another one-shot sex title, *Jiz* (1969), and a couple of issues of – as much fetishtic as sex – *Big Ass Comics*. Despite furore surrounding all three – with *Snatch* being described as the most controversial of the undergrounds – it was another title altogether which attracted the authorities.

A BALL IN THE BUNG HOLE
God Nose in 1964 had marked the appearance of the first recognisable underground comic, but it was several years before the medium got itself together and a cultural

Panel taken from 'Joe Blow', Robert Crumb's controversial incest strip. Zap Comix No.4

hub for the cartoonists manifested itself in San Francisco. Even then, titles such as *Bijou Funnies* and *Feds 'n' Heads Comics* consisted of strips reprinted from underground newspapers of the day. *Zap Comix*, in 1967, was an exception. Conceived by Robert Crumb, with its skits aimed at middle-class America, *Zap* was a product and a dig at the permissiveness of the age. In August 1969, an issue of *Zap* was deemed obscene and removed from retail outlets across America. Although at least one store had been busted previously for selling *Zap Comix* No.2 (because of an S.Clay Wilson story wherein one pirate cuts off another pirate's penis), it was with issue No.4 that the publishers themselves were taken to court.

Zap Comix was never really a porn title. The debut number featured throughout the work of its originator, Crumb, while No.2 pulled in work from other contributors and ignited in *Zap* a volatility that would come to a head two years and two issues later. Despite the presence of S.Clay Wilson – whose strips rarely failed to conjure some sexual or anatomical anomaly – there was little to prepare the *Zap* reader for the sudden focus of ideas in issue No.4. All at once and for one issue only, the theme was sex. Unlike Crumb's foray with *Snatch Comics*, and possibly in light of *Zap*'s greater circulation, here sex was tackled in an altogether different way. That is, more comment and sexual politics as opposed to base sex scenarios. Sex in *Zap* No.4 is occasionally abstract, frequently self-conscious. Gilbert Shelton's 'Wonder Wart-Hog' strip goes so far as to parody Crumb and level at him the criticism that his work be sexist. Clay Wilson returns with his pirates, some of whom have not a hook in place of a hand but a hook in place of their penis; Victor Moscoso engages his distinguished front cover characters, Mr Peanut and Mr Penis, in a psychedelic sex orgy; Robert Williams conjures his own 'Big Bang Theory'; Spain Rodriguez has a cat-fighting space mistress; and Crumb has 'Horny Harriet', for whom a liberal sprinkling of salt onto genitalia draws the attentions of Bossy the cow.

When *Zap* No.4 went on trial at the Criminal Court in the City of New York, it was another Crumb strip that dominated the proceedings. The Print Mint, the publishers of *Zap*, heard how Crumb's 'Joe Blow' – a story incorporating the theme of incest – was not the satire on family and Middle America that the expert witnesses said it was, but instead was without value, hence obscene. As indeed was the verdict on *Zap* No.4 as a whole.

ARTIFICIAL PENIS IN 30 SECONDS

> *Young Lust...* may be parody sex to the adults, but it's as good as the real thing for kids who want to see what goes into what and who does what to who and how.
>
> Clay Geerdes, *Graphixus* No.2

One of the few sex titles to survive the Seventies, even making it into the Nineties, is *Young Lust* from Last Gasp, the first issue of which appeared in 1971. Bill Griffith – later to pen *Zippy Stories* – and Jay Kinney, the artists responsible, inaugurated in *Young Lust* the Teen Romance take-off. The sexual connotations implicit in popular titles of the Forties and Fifties – such as *Young Romance* and *True Confessions* – were taken to a dripping and not-so predictable conclusion. It is a genre of comic that opens itself wonderfully to the machinations of the underground artist's mind. Bill Griffith's 'They Called Our Young Love Pornographic*!* But We Don't Care' opens to a panel typical of the Romance strips – that of an attractive white girl locked in a kiss with a handsome white man. She even has a pensive thought-balloon, only here it isn't some love-lorn hesitancy, but a big, bold, underground, "Oh, James*!* I'm **dripping** with love juice*!!*" (The presence of tongues is a bit of a give-away, too.) The strip tells how, one day, Brenda goes to "one of those '42nd Street' type movies", only to see up on the screen her teenage crush, Jimmy Nesbitt. That night she falls in love with him all over again and cannot help but give him a call. "I had no idea you were so... sexually alluring," she tells him. In no time at all, Brenda has become a porn actress herself (starring in *Sex Kittens of Vietnam*) and the two of them are married (their wedding night recorded for posterity). Turning their back on the criticisms of family and friends, the couple move to the countryside. Brenda conceives and Jimmy Jr is born. Porn stars that they are, on the slippery slope and all, Jimmy Jr is seen as the subject of another of the couple's films in the closing panel. Art Spiegelman – later to pen *Maus* – contributes 'Love's Body' in which lonely Normal O'Brown finds a dead girl on his doorstep. He takes the body in and keeps it for

'Red Guard Romance.' Young Lust No.1. Art: Jay Kinney

several months before neighbours complain about a stench and the police arrive. "Look Sam*!* A stiff... and come spots*!!* Dis slimey pervert must of bin ballin' da corpse*!!!*" The story closes with Mr Brown in prison, quoting Tennyson: 'Tis better to have loved and lost than never to have loved at all.

Later issues concentrated less on the Teen Romance formula. *Young Lust* No.5, for instance, had more quirky fair with the likes of Paul Mavrides' 'Mutant Smut' and Jay Kinney's 'Red Guard Romance' (also the subject of the great cover painting). Somewhat unusual for the underground, the latter was a pointed jibe at Revolutionary Communism (a theme to which Kinney and Mavrides would later return, however, in *Young Lust* No.7). It had a counterpoint in another strip that issue, Guy Colwell's 'They Can't See Us Here', which expounded freedom from the constraints of class and sex – a philosophy common to Colwell's own comic series, *Inner City Romance*,

A personal ad for a couple bored with their sex life results in 'Love-Nest For Three!' Young Lust No.1. Art: Bill Griffith

discussed in greater detail later.

Young Lust met with general favour within the underground, even with those opposed to *Snatch Comics* and the sexual content of *Zap*. "The fact is," wrote Estren in his *A History of Underground Comics* "sex in the underground comics does not have to degrading to women, and in some cases isn't. *Young Lust* by Bill Griffith and Jay Kinney is a case in point." Clay Geerdes, founder of 'Comix World', the first newspaper column devoted to underground comicdom, came in for some *Young Lust* rebuttal when he wrote one time of himself, that comic and a juvenile. Geerdes reiterated the incident for *Graphixus*, a British monthly graphics review.

> I watched a 13 year old girl read all the way from cover to cover an issue of *Young Lust*. She read it standing up. I was working in a comic store in Berkeley at the time, the Summer of 73 as I recall. I didn't say, "Hey, kid, get away from those undergrounds." I suppose I should have played the oppressor, but I didn't. I thought it was interesting and I wrote about the incident in a 'Comix World' column. The following week I got a postcard from Bill Griffith attacking me for saying that underaged kids read the comic. Did I want everyone to get busted? Well, busts don't work that way and I thought Griffith's uptight reaction was as funny as that girl avidly reading the comic from cover to cover. It was routine in the store for the kids to try to score undergrounds and sneak them back into the back issue section of the store where they could read the stories with no clerk the wiser. I would tell them to stay out of the underground section, but I wasn't going to spend all day doing it and the braver ones usually got to read the ones they wanted.

In 1990, *Young Lust* reached it's 'Twentieth Anniversary Blowout*!*' issue – seven issues in nearly twenty years. A No.8 appeared in 1993. As a mark of *Young Lust*'s endurance, alongside that of their peers, it includes work by a new generation of hot and hip artists. Daniel Clowes and Charles Burns, for instance. Perhaps not truly definable as underground, but of the spirit nonetheless.[5]

THE BRITISH SCENE

> The major thing I wanted to say to the defendants was, "You're arguing *Nasty Tales* is in the public good – that's irrelevant because they [the jurors] think it's just a comic."
>
> > A juror at the *Nasty Tales* trial supportive
> > of the comic, speaking to *Oz*

In Britain, in 1970, the Children and Young Persons (Harmful Publications) Act of 1955 – implemented during the campaign instigated by Wertham and his *Seduction of the Innocent* – was brought into effect for the first time against one L.Miller & Co. The prosecution didn't pertain to the new politicised and permissive comics emerging, but to the publication and distribution of several horror titles, in the main US reprints from the 1950s.[6] Although there had already been short-lived British edition reprints of *Yarrowstalks* and *Zap* (in 1967 and 1969, respectively), it was the publication of a tabloid by the name of *Cyclops* in 1970 which nudged into motion the precarious underground comics scene in Britain. As in the US in the Sixties, these first comics came courtesy of the alternative newspapers (as indeed had 'straight' comics from newspapers before that). The difference being that instead of evolving through the

When Oz 28 went to court, much time was spent deliberating on a strip which amalgamated Rupert Bear with Robert Crumb's 'Eggs Ackley', a strip to originally appear in Big Ass Comics No.1. Shown here is the opening panel.

RUPERT FINDS GIPSY GRANNY

1 *" It looks just like a ball to me,"*
" Open it and see."

popularity of the small press as they had done in the States, here the comics were an attempt to rekindle *It* and *Oz* – the first underground newspapers to appear in Britain and, following an hiatus with the likes of *Frendz*, *Ink*, and *Idiot International*, the only two remaining come 1972. *It* was responsible for *Nasty Tales*, which ran for seven issues from 1971 to 1973, while *Oz* was more prolific producing various incarnations of their *Cozmic Comics* from 1972 through to 1975.[7]

The early British undergrounds were dominated by the work of US artists and reprints of material first to appear in the States. This wasn't the case for every title, but those comics with an entirely British line-up were few and far between. The pages of *Nasty Tales* No.1 were given over to Crumb, Gilbert Shelton, and Spain – American artists. Needless to say, when the British mainstream press picked up on this new development in the comics medium – the arrival of adult comics – it was to a knee-jerk condemnation. The story was 'the American sex-comics'. And they had to be stopped.

Not dissimilar to the American crime and horror comics scare of the 1950s, HM Customs attempted to halt the import of American comic books into Britain. In January of 1973, homegrown product came under attack when the creators of *Nasty Tales* found themselves at the Old Bailey charged with obscenity. Here it was determined that isolated panels depicting flaccid male members, occasional usage of the word 'fuck', drug-taking Furry Freak Brothers, and a reproduction of Robert Crumb's centrespread from *Snatch Comics* No.1, 'Grand Opening Of The Great Intercontinental Fuck-In and Orgy-Riot', were not obscene by law, and *Nasty Tales* was let off with a caution. The case was lampooned in *The Trials of Nasty Tales*, a (fantasy) window on the nine-day hearing by various artists, which depicted a prosecution with paedophiliac tendencies and the defendants themselves as barely legible, witless, profit-mongers. The issue closes on a courtroom orgy scene; a montage made up in the main of Crumb's 'Intercontinental Fuck-In', and through which the jury pass their verdict of 'Not Guilty'.

But it was a loaded victory. *Nasty Tales* may not have been obscene – official – but the trial pretty much killed it. Like L.Miller & Co., fined all of £25 for their horror comic reprints, *Nasty Tales* weathered the storm only to go under soon after. Indeed, *It*, the alternative newspaper responsible for the comic, had been successfully prosecuted previous to *Nasty Tales* for carrying small ads of a sexual nature.

But it wasn't just *It*. For a time, the whole of the British underground seemed to have its collective antlers locked with those champions of the status quo. The 'Schoolkids' edition of *Oz* – issue No.28 in which editorial powers were given over to a group of under-18s – found itself embroiled in what was to become the longest obscenity hearing in a British court. Elsewhere, in Barnsley, police were threatening *Styng* with the Obscene Publications Act for its reporting of instances of police brutality. A copy of *Ink* found itself in the lap of the Director of Public Prosecutions after moral guardian, Mary Whitehouse, took offence at being depicted as part of a Gerald Scarfe cartoon on one of its covers. According to Whitehouse's book *Whatever Happened To Sex?*, a Vice Squad officer at New Scotland Yard described the caricature as "the most obscene attack ever published on living people". No official charges were brought against the paper, unlike the *Little Red Schoolbook* – "a children's charter exhorting independence from authority," according to Richard Michael in his *The ABZ of Pornography* [London: Panther, 1972] – whose publishers were tried and prosecuted for obscenity in 1971.

Underground newspapers introduced to the public stark images of the naked female form. A maverick gesture designed to upset the establishment, but which also managed to create a backlash in the form of the feminist movement. As public interest would eventually drift away from the politicism of the underground newspapers, feminist conflicts from within only helped spur their demise. "The underground supposedly liked comics," wrote Nigel Fountain in his book, *Underground: The London Alternative Press 1966-74* [London: Routledge, 1988], "even if it didn't seem to want papers with words any more."[8] Issue No.4 of *Cozmic Comics* (dated December 1972) had on its cover a wide-eyed, salivating British policeman peering under the dress of a young girl. Only on closer inspection, it wasn't a dress but the pages of a book. The accusation being made and to whom it was being levelled was obvious, but the comic itself never quite managed the bite nor the pedigree the publishers strove toward. The top-heavy American content wouldn't abate until the following year and publication of *Sin City*, whose bevy of artists dealt with urban paranoia and class conflict from a wholly British viewpoint. Part of the Cozmic Comics stable of off-shoots, this first and only issue of *Sin City* featured the likes of Bill Sanderson's 'Mrs Higgins–Char', who, flashed at on the bus, mugged in the street, witness to a murder and raped, sits herself down in the evening and bemoans the level of sex and violence on television. 'Underground Madness' by Edward Barker has the breakdown of a micro-society when commuters are thrown together on a delayed tube train. Paul Simmons is responsible for the *noir* 'No Hiding Place', which has Duggie, a small time hood in Soho, on the run following some transgression of 'the underworld's unwritten code'. His mistake is to go to the police for protection, where too late he discovers that the men wanting him dead *are* the police.[9]

At the tail end of 1973, from Gemsanders Publications Ltd, came the sixth and –

contrary to its assurances of a new, regular monthly schedule – final issue of *Its All Lies* [sic]. Next to *Sin City*, the standard of work in *Its All Lies* is poor. Several pages are completely wasted on the puerile and inflated sight gag of 'The Adventures of Little Raymond and his Little Car', while the technical competence of 'Thong–Hero of Yesteryear' suffers from an overplay of the artist's own influences (*Mad* magazine by way of Jack Kirby). There is a spark of originality that overshadows all else in *Its All Lies* No.6, however, and that is the opening strip, 'Santa Comes Visiting'. Late one Christmas Eve, Santa Claus drops down a chimney and into the bedroom of a shrieking girl. "Look, you stupid old man," the girl tells Jolly Jack, "I'm 22 years old." She doesn't believe he's for real, but, so as not to break the festive tradition, tells him to leave a present anyway. The present consists of sexy lingerie. Santa gets excited and pounces on the girl while she's trying it on for size. Enter a second Santa who wrestles the impostor to the ground and reveals him to be 'Uncle Tom'. Sobs the girl, "I... I... can't believe it. My own uncle tried to rape me." The second Santa consoles the girl, tucks her into bed, then leaps upon her himself with a "Ho*!* Ho*!* Ho*!*" Hollers the girl: "Gran'dad*!!!* You really fooled me, you old devil..."

The artist is one Antonio Ghura. He remains unknown in the States and not that familiar in Britain. Yet he went on to single-handedly produce the funniest, most outrageous porn comic titles ever to grace the underground. That's transatlantic, worldwide underground. In the great sadly neglected scheme of things, Ghura is right up there at the top. To him we shall later return. But for British underground comics in general, while they may have absorbed the readership once given over to the underground newspapers, it was to be an equally transient popularity. By the close of the Seventies, as with the newspapers a half-decade before, the British underground comics scene, if not dead, was past its prime and fast fading out.[10]

Panels from 'Santa Comes Visiting', Its All Lies No.6. Art: Antonio Ghura

Sisters move in to take over the planet. 'You Got A Point There, Pop!' from
Deviant Slice No.2. Art: Greg Irons & Tom Veitch

DETESTABLE BUMPS, FESTERIN' SORES

Over in the US, a collection of female artists headed by Trina Robbins rallied against
the sex comics and produced *It Ain't Me, Babe*, in 1970. The following year came the
successful *Wimmins Comix* series, issue No.7 of which was advertised as being 'a
bit more brutal than previous issues, with some almost S.Clay Wilson overtones'.
'Women's Erotic Fantasies' were divulged in *Wet Satin*, and ranged from dreamy
encounters with man-animals to a call to arms for sisters everywhere. Joey Epstein's
strip 'Nifty Ways To Cleave Your Lover', set to the tune of the popular Paul Simon
number of a similar-sounding title, disclosed ideas on how to detach the penis from
the man: *'Slash it with a knife, wife!... Pull it out by the roots, Toots!... Put it in the
shredda, Hedda!... Break a glass tube in his crotch, Ilsa Koch!'*. *Tits & Clits*, on the
other hand, was never quite the unadulterated romp its title implied.

While the backlash and insurgence of women artists heralded the end of the
underground as a male stronghold, the reverse sexism and violence inherent in the
first feminist comics soon mellowed into them becoming comics of a "typically sweet"
nature (to coin a phrase Trina Robbins uses in *Blab!* No.3 to describe Crumb's early,
pre-porn work). Very often these comics would hold a mirror to the life of the artist,
her family, her friends and her relationships. Sex would be depicted but not
necessarily in a graphically up-close way. Emphasis was on dialogue and situations.
But the change in women's comics didn't change the porn titles. While women
advocated a revolutionary sex, the men forged on regardless. Theirs was a

The Snatch Sampler. Title page by Spain.

reactionary sex: full-on fucking. Such was the second issue of *Tales of Sex and Death* (1975), a generally lacklustre collection of work but containing a couple of notable sexual transgressions. 'Nocturnal Rendezvous' by Rory Hayes and Spain – two of the chief protagonists in the eyes of the feminist lobby – has the mother of recently deceased Lorreta returning unexpectedly to the funeral home and finding its director with his penis in the dead girl's mouth. (Hayes' contribution to the strip isn't difficult to spot; so primitive is his style that he has to label the expression on the arresting officer's face: 'SHEER NAUSEA'.) 'Pills In M' Pussy' by Dave Geisher has Alotta Box, the anatomical equivalent of a toilet, having her vagina stuffed with drugs when the police are heard to be raiding the party she's at. Also from the Print Mint came a Geisher solo project, *Demented Pervert*. Issue No.2 (1972) featured 'Billy Barstool', a sniffer of girls' bicycle seats who, after being granted a wish by Jesus, becomes a bicycle seat himself. Not entirely satisfied with the lack of young hippie butt coming his way, Billy takes another wish, becomes a barstool and ends up flattened by Rotunda Blivet, a slightly mad, massively overweight, quim dribbling wench over at Rat's Nest Beer & Eats. Geisher has a penchant for drawing oversize women with vagina's that envelop their male partner. More often than not, Geisher paints himself as the luckless victim (he did a comic in 1977 called *Pain*, the first 50 copies of which were signed in the artist's blood). 'North Beach Blanket Bingo' sees Geisher being picked up in a bar by a dominatrix, taken to The Reek Hotel and forced into sex. "Yikes, it's like being fucked by a super Hoover," he cries. "Eek, I'm being sucked in…" The artist disappears into the bushy ecliptic blackness, only to be spat back out again when it suits the lady. If not sucked in or sat upon, men in *Demented Pervert* are running away. Another oversexed female, her thighs rich in "creamy drippin's" after spotting the big balls on Chinese immigrant, Hung Low, laments "I'm gettin' one hell of a **wide on** over this*!* My poozel's barkin' nationalist love songs*!*" The Chinaman is chased through the streets by an increasing number of prick-hungry chicks, who, mid-stride, switch to becoming knife wielding feminists hungry for prick-blood. Hung Low heads back to his homeland. *'American women take heed!'* the strip concludes.

Dave Geisher wasn't the only artist compelled to respond to the feminist voice. But while many attempted to kick holes in its logic, many others artists, rather than denounce accusations of misogynism, played on the arguments as a means to fuel their own stories. In *Big Ass Comics* No.2, Crumb delivers 'A Word To You Feminist Women', a lengthy and articulate discourse which ultimately concludes with a plain old "FUCK YOU!!" Greg Irons and Tom Veitch in *Deviant Slice* No.2 dedicate the strip 'You Got A Point There, Pop!', to "all you women's libbers". It details how the last war is fought not between nations or race, but between sexes. Opening to two lone enemy soldiers in battle, it has Lem Peters losing out to the stealth and agility of Ruth O'Leary, bare breasted tigress of the Fighting 51st. (She's black and he's white to add extra *frisson*.) When Lem comes round, he finds himself tied to a tree with a fire burning between his legs, dangerously close to his testicles. Man-hate fills Ruth's eyes. But she stamps out the fire, climbs onto Lem's now erect penis and tells him, "I know you're young and you're fighting this war just 'cause some old men told you to." Jumping off again with a SLUP and an ejaculation, Ruth then explains how the physical struggle between the sexes is all down to the masculine ego, and stabs a dagger into Lem's mouth. She slices off his dick and balls, leaves his testicles to fry over a fire, and kills him. "Real tasty, white boy! You got a righteous set of jewels here! Yum yum!" The last panel has the tigress feeding on her pickings.

Work by S.Clay Wilson, which originally appeared in *Snatch Comics*, was collected and released as *Pork* in 1974. Three years later, the strips were again printed as part of *The Snatch Sampler*. Published by Keith Green in 1977, the *Snatch Sampler* amassed material from the three issues of *Snatch*, as well as some new work by James Osborne (his 'The Hard Man' concerns a repair man who cuts off an old woman's head, sodomises her, contracts festering cock rot and as a result is brought to justice). For some unknown reason several pages of the *Sampler* are given over to *Felch Comics*, which originally appeared in 1975.

'True tales of human folly' promised Facts o' Life Funnies (1972). A truce was called as male and female artists pulled together to offer the hippie community sexual advice in comic form. Ironically, while the female artists tend to deal with issues of unwanted pregnancy and abortion, the male artists tackle the clap and how to help prevent it. Panels here are taken from 'Fat Freddy Gets The Clap' by Gilbert Shelton and Gary Frutkoff.

Title page to Tales From The Leather Nun. Art: Dave Sheridan

WHAT KIND OF HELL IS THIS, ANYWAY?

Tales From The Leather Nun (1973), from Last Gasp, was a one-shot devoted to sex madness with an ecclesiastic twist. Dave Sheridan's exquisite penmanship introduced the character of the Leather Nun herself: a shapely wench dressed in nothing but a wimple, who somehow manages to traverse dimensions and put to right clerical wrongs. In the same issue, Spain's 'The Leather Nun Gets Hers' has a more hostile character, one who administers physical harm to those who fall short of being a "perfect catholic". After one such day attempting to "stem the rising tide of permissiveness", the Leather Nun depresses a secret button and mounts the erection which pops out from the statue of Jesus on the Cross. "It's OK," she tells the reader, "we're married." (The pre-title page to this story – which has a young boy drawn from the guided tour of the monastery by the faint sound of chanting and screaming deep within the bowels of the building – is uncharacteristically dark and foreboding for a porn comic.) 'Tales Of The Leather Nun's Grandmother' by Jaxon (real name: Jack Jackson) is a pre-history diversion with Leather Nun the Elder, whose vagina, following an unfortunate mishap with a rhino horn dildo and a dwarf, has become a gateway to another dimension. The forces that inhabit the dark abyss are set to traverse the opening and crush mankind, but are thwarted in the last minute. It shouldn't be difficult to guess how – suffice to say a giant penis is involved, so too the only fuck scene ever to be viewed from *within*. Other contributors provided Leather Nun-free stories. In 'The Adventures of R.Crumb Himself', the bespectacled artist takes a walk only to be confronted by figures of authority who attempt to beat him into becoming "a decent member of society". With a nun poised over his penis, about to cleave it off with an axe and pronounce him a soldier of Christ, Crumb comes to his senses and retaliates. 'Confessions of a Teenage Confessor', by Pat Ryan, has Father Justin Thyme – as is usual on his Saturday afternoons – taking confession. Just when he thinks he has seen everybody for the day, into the confessional walks a young girl. She tells the priest how embarrassed and ashamed she is. "Uh... well... it's about sex." "Do not be afraid to tell the truth," consoles Father Thyme. The girl relates how she and her boyfriend, Arnold, got stoned at a party and started to make out. *"Then his cock started to swell till it seemed it was on fire. I mean it was pulsating and all. Oh Father! I could hardly fit it in my mouth!"* No detail is spared and it soon becomes too much for the good Father who, there and then, surreptitiously pummels himself to a climax.

    Tales From The Leather Nun has enjoyed several reprintings and it's a puzzle as to why the title never made a regular series: The Leather Nun character herself is strong and open to numerous interpretations, while an element of religion has rarely proven a stumbling block for underground artists. By comparison, *Pure Joy Comix* (1975), stories of 'sex and adventure to stagger the imagination' *wanted* to become a regular series but failed to make it beyond the first issue – that itself having now lapsed into obscurity. The artwork is consistently good and the strips are occasionally tasteless in all the right places. 'The Hole Story', by Jim Himes, has a doctor who, after hours, masturbates to his latest gynaecological acquisitions – a series of snapshots taken via the miniature camera he keeps concealed. ('Lookin' Like a Queen in a Sale-Or's Dream', another Himes strip, makes no sense whatsoever.) Rich Chidlaw's 'Valley of the Dildosaurs' features a group of people who crash their small aircraft on Pleasure Island and must fend off the oversize mammals that live there. Many-breasted, penis-headed, vagina-tentacled behemoths menace the survivors in the best B-movie tradition, while the Love Interest find time for sex in a clearing.

INTERGALACTIC STAG FILMS

The Krupp Comic Works produced *Bizarre Sex* No.1 in 1972, a reasonably prolific comic that managed 10 issues in two decades of publication. As its title implied, the copulative shenanigans featured were of a more indeterminate nature than most sex books, with some of the stories being genuinely unpleasant, bordering on the nauseating. *Bizarre Sex* collated work by a number of artists. It's debut number carried on the cover 'The Giant Penis That Invaded New York', art by Denis Kitchen (co-founder of Krupp, later Kitchen Sink Press), which unfortunately was not representative of any strip in the comic. The opening piece, 'Incest!' by Grass Green (real name: Richard Green), tells of one boy's education in the ways of the flesh courtesy of his 14-year-old sister. He and sister later get a beating at the hand of their father. Green's style is heavy on the facial paroxysms of his characters – a handful of goofy expressions which go by way of compensation for the general crudity of technique. The strip doesn't really get started, either, floundering at its conclusion for a twist or a punchline, a trait common to the work of Green. Far better are the contributions of Daniel Clyne and Tim Boxell. Clyne (whose characters all look to be genetically linked to the Blue Meanies of *Yellow Submarine*) has 'Dr Lum Bago's Creation'. When the monster rises in Dr Bago's laboratory, it turns out to be "queer" and invites all its friends round. "I need a **beer** so I don't get **queer** like them," pronounces the doctor, before driving all but his own creation out. A fight ensues in which the doctor is split down the middle with an axe and out pops a homosexual "young body... held prisoner by Bago's old mind and spirit". Boxell's 'The Grip of the Grave' is a homage to EC's horror tales of the Fifties, but, as tends to be the case with such homages from the underground,[11] dropping EC's penchant for humour and making the darker elements yet darker. After the death of their parents, Jim takes to protecting his sister from amorous advances of male admirers. This against her will; Sue has discovered sex and has a veritable convoy of men coming through her bedroom door. The men ultimately all go missing, feared dead by the police. Jim's gift to his sister and her husband on their wedding day is a bed. The unusual texture of the mattress is soon attributed to row upon row of fingers, which Jim has severed from Sue's past lovers and nailed upright into place.

Another equally unpleasant tale featured as the cover story to *Bizarre Sex* No.3 (1973). 'Love Is', by Mike Roberts, has a future in which mankind is forced to live beneath the surface of the planet, evading humanoid alien beings and their giant insect pets. The story is told by one man who is captured by the aliens, taken to a spacecraft and locked in a cage for observation. Months go by and he becomes hopelessly infatuated with his guard, Vanna. One night he manages to free himself from his cell and steal his way up to Vanna's living quarters. Once there, however, he spies the girl mating with Goliath, her giant insect companion. Disbelieving, he makes his way back to his cell. Some nights later, escaping once again, he kills a number of the male guards and inadvertently activates the ship's lift-off procedure. The ship leaves earth's orbit and crash-lands on an asteroid. Vanna keeps her distance from the prisoner before going into spasms and dying. Under her skin, movement manifests itself as a grub. It devours what remains of Vanna's body before burrowing its way into the asteroid. The prisoner has ample opportunity to kill it but chooses not to. The thing, he determines, is the spawn of Vanna's genuine love for Goliath and hence reason enough to let it live. At the close of the story, the man sits in solitude, resigned to the fact that when the thing does emerge it will be as a full-grown adult. *"While I sleep it will feed on my dreams... When it wakes... it will feed on me..."*

The twist at the end of 'The House of Ill Repute' (by Ferbh?), the same issue, is a little obvious in coming – being the essence of many a 'bad taste' story – but still manages to illicit a few groans. After visiting a brothel and opting for the "passive-type", being 10 dollars cheaper, Joe is a little bemused to find that the girl he has paid for doesn't move *at all*. What's more, when he actually gets down to sex and climaxes, she starts "dribbling like a baby". Joe tells the guy working there, pays his money and leaves. He doesn't hear the phone call to the city morgue the moment he's gone: "Hugo, you'd better send us a new stiff*!* This one's just 'bout brimming over*!*" Interesting to note is that *Bizarre Sex* No.3 gives the vendor the display option of two possible covers. The more outrageous Mike Roberts' *insect fucking girl*, back-to-back with the relatively innocuous *big-eyed girl with bottle and octopus*. No such option with the coarse homo-erotic cover of No.7 (1979). Its Warholian *handgun jutting from groin* is indicative of the obtuse nature of the issue in general. Richard Larson's 'Children of the Goat' is a lengthy and word-heavy satanic adventure yarn in the tradition of Marvel Comics' Code-free B&W line of titles. Precisely what it is doing in *Bizarre Sex* is a mystery. 'Arcane Love', the first of two strips by Steve Stiles, is annoyingly non-linear, set in the future for what it's worth. Indeed, the highlights of No.7 – Dan Steffan's 'The Deviate's Delight' and Aldo's 'Cliffy's Wedding Day' – are relatively lightweight affairs and would stand as mere peripherals in earlier, better issues.

Howard Cruse contributed work to *Bizarre Sex*. He later went on to edit *Gay Comix* for Kitchen Sink and Bazooka Joe strips for Topps Chewing Gum. Reed Waller and Kate Worley introduced the character Omaha, The Cat Dancer, in issue No.9, proving popular enough to warrant its own title (which, in turn, was busted for depicting some scenes of a sexual nature). Joe Coleman had his first comic work appear in *Bizarre Sex*. *Bizarre Sex* No.3 announced the launch of a comic and text title, *Weird Trips*, persuading readers to contribute their weirdest acid trip stories, draft evasion secrets and UFO sightings. Two issues appeared.

QUICKLY I HID BEHIND AN ODD COVER, **THERE**...BEFORE MY EYES, **VANNA**... **NUDE**....AND OVER HER THE HIDIOUS **GOLIATH** MADE **LOVE** TO **MY** VANNA . AND **ME**, THINKING SHE WAS UNLIKE THE WOMEN WHO EXISTED IN MY WORLD.

'Love Is', Bizarre Sex No.3. Art: Mike Roberts

IN LIVING COLOUR

Don't go another further! [sic] Not until I warn you! I wanna confirm
your suspicions and tell you that this is *White Whore Funnies* # two,
the dirtiest comic ever published! Topic: that most sensitive of subjects
– interracial sex!... So if you picked it up by mistake, put it down and
move on 'fo' you git your feelings hurt! Specially you jive ass white boys!
This book might knock you down, tear you up and make a nigger lover
out of your girl friend!

Introduction, *White Whore Funnies* No.2

White Whore Funnies has been published on an intermittent basis since 1975. This
author has seen the first three issues and is reliably informed that a fourth does
exist. The third is dated 1979. Although the utilisation of racial stereotypes is nothing
new to underground comics – Robert Crumb's character, Angelfood McSpade, springs
to mind – no title outside of *White Whore Funnies* has devoted itself entirely, and
quite so thoroughly, to black and white skinned prejudice. Here, all black men are at
their physical prime, well-hung, probably pimps, oversexed and constantly lusting
after white bitch. White men, by the same token, are either redneck and brainless or
overweight, bespectacled wimps. On the cover of issue No.1, a negligee-clad blonde
is sitting on a bed, seized by a panic-fit: *"My God!! What am I... a white girl... doing
here... naked... in this nigger's apartment!??"* In the closing story of that same issue,
Willie Lee Nogoodnik is in the pen, guilty, "like most nigger-roe mates", of indecent
assault. Typical S. Whytegurl (S. for Sweet) is the victim. When paroled, Nogoodnik
heads for Africa so that he might keep his nose clean and stay away from white
temptation. However, in the ironic twist, Shestuf, Queen of the Jungle, a vine-swinging
pearly amazon, grabs Nogoodnik as her own and the Mumbweebwee tribe –
Nogoodnik's hereditary cousins who have been hittin' on Shestuf's ass for d'las six
years with no hint of success – boil the both of them in a pot.

The unfavourable characterisation of the black man appears to be foremost on
the *White Whore Funnies* agenda. Evident on closer inspection, however, is the fact
that the comic draws its opinionated views from its unfavourable characterisation of
the *white man*. These are stereotypes-by-numbers. Exaggerated cut-outs. Whereby
the black characters might come unstuck because of some misfortune to befall them,
their white counterpart almost invariably suffer the brunt of their own bigotry. In
'Appalling Love Story', Bev, the most popular girl in school, strings Waldo along for
sex – until, that is, Waldo proposes and Bev drops him, explaining, "I just wanted to
be balled by a spade 'cause I'd never had the chance before!!" Some weeks later,
Bev meets the mysterious Purvis and falls in love for the first time in her life. On the
night they plan to announce their engagement, Purvis reveals himself to be Waldo's
brother and "the biggest pimp in five States... I know how to handle cunts like you!
So I came here to blow your mind like you did his, you dig? Revenge, baby, revenge!"
Come the close of the strip, Bev is alone and traumatised.

The majority of the artwork featured in *White Whore Funnies* No.1 is accredited
to 'Wiley Spade', who is also publisher, editor, and 'all around head nigger', Larry
Fuller. His penmanship is competent enough, given that all his women share more
than a passing resemblance to the buxom beauties of Bill Ward, and his penchant
for shading often leaves the page looking overworked. Depiction of graphic sex isn't
at the forefront of this first issue. Vaginal penetration is depicted in a number of the
strips – a couple of panels to spice up the story – but in the main, the strips

**Front covers for White Whore Funnies No.1 and No.2
Art: Wiley Spade and James Davis, respectively.**

concentrate on the conflict and connotations arising from overwrought interracial relationships.

Much different would be the second volume, a full three years later. Twice the page count of its predecessor, the striking cover left little room to doubt what direction *White Whore Funnies* No.2 was taking. It featured the lower torso of a tanned white women with a heavily veined Negro arm reaching into her delicate underwear. Inside, the contributions come from a larger variety of artists, all working to the same objective: to make this issue more visually extreme than the debut number. Indeed, 'The Wild Sex Fantasy of Mrs White' – penned by Larry Fuller and drawn by James Davis – is little more than an exact replica of a European sex mag set in pencil. Its panels depicting coitus close-up are so clinically accurate that it is inconceivable that they *weren't* lifted from actual still photographs. Open vagina shots with plenty of gristle. Not only is 'The Wild Sex Fantasy of Mrs White' unlike any of the other strips to be had in *White Whore Funnies*, it is also unique among the sex comic strips under discussion here. Its existence resides entirely on its emulating, as closely as possible, hardcore photographic images. The prose which accompany these images is hack erotica, pure and simple. There is an attempt made to give some credence to all of this by way of a tagged-on prologue and a comical conclusion, but they seem hurriedly executed and flat by comparison.

The story concerns Patina White, married to a man much older than she. Her husband doesn't have the stamina to satisfy her during lovemaking, and, in the office

White Whore
Funnies
No.3 cover
Art: Grass
Green

𝕎𝕙𝕚𝕥𝕖 𝕎𝕙𝕠𝕣𝕖 𝔽𝕦𝕟𝕟𝕚𝕖𝕤

SEXTRA!!
Read all about it!

"The Truth in Black and White"

The Inkwell Revealer

★ ★ ★ ★ FINAL ONLY $2.00

Black Maniac Assaults, Rapes Innocent Young White Lass

Community Members Outraged, Demand Action
You Must Be An Adult To Buy This!

White Women 'go for lusty, sexy' Blacks

SAN FRANCISCO, Ca. - According to a recent survey by the little known, hardly respected and definitely biased Jive Niggers of America (JNA), a recently formed lodge whose members are dedicated to, in the words of co-founder and *vice*-president Wiley Spade, "ketchin' all de White pussy we kin," all three members of the organization have done "sextremely well in their pursuit of that best of all possible things, White ass!" Spade himself was only just recently the proud recipient of "summa de best 17 year ole, blue-eyed, blonde haired stuff money kin buy!" He went on to say that the party in question had smooth, creamy skin, big hefty thighs and one of the finest 240 lb female figures he had ever seen.

While conceding that the JNA's present membership is still somewhat limited (consisting to date of two other members with the unlikely names of *Larry Fuller* and, even farther out, *Grass Green*), Spade maintains that they have already received inquiries from such diverse geographical opposites as Pocatello, Idaho, Rome, Georgia, Down Heah, Texas, and Kampala, Uganda. Of the last locale, Spade chuckles and says, "Man, they got some real jive niggers over theah."

The writer regrets being unable to finish this extremely interesting interview as some local police arrived with a warrant for Mr. Spade charging statutory rape. We will, however, keep (chuckle) abreast of the trial proceedings.

The Victim - "Sweet, innocent, wholesome, virginal"

The Suspect - "Mean, nasty, vicious, niggardly"

Police apprehend, kill rapist

FT. WAYNE, Ind. - Police today shot and killed one Willard Coon, notorious rape suspect who had escaped from the Fremont Sanitarium. According to William (Billy) de Liar, shyster mouthpiece for the national chain, the Blankety Blank Sanitoriums/Camps for Recalcitrant Negro Offenders, said Coon's escape wasn't discovered until the 8 pm bedcheck. Coon's long record of demented, sadistic, psychotic, homicidal behavior and sexual aberration included 16 cases of sexual slayings. Police were notified and at approximately 11:39:48:05½ pm last night, Coon was discovered leaving the scene of a suspected rape. "*Suspect some shit!*" says rookie policeman Marshall Law, first officer to arrive at the scene. "*I caught the fuc-er,* suspect, bare-ass--er, red-handed." When Coon disobeyed an order to "*HALT, ASSHOLE!*", Officer Law drew his service revolver and "blew the Black bastard to Kingdom Cum."

Police were apprised of the suspect's possible whereabouts by a young couple that was stopped for excessive speeding. They informed the officer who made the traffic stop that they had heard the radio reports about Coon's escape and were on their way to check the well being of a young female friend, the rape victim, who was working overtime and had no knowledge that a dangerous criminal had escaped custody.

of one distinguished Dr Sigmund Dumpsit, Patina recounts the fantasy she has formulated by way of compensation. Dumpsit is Caucasian; bespectacled and overweight. He demands that Mrs White spare no detail in the telling of her dream. She explains how, in an unfamiliar part of the house, she happens upon a room and finds inside "a coloured man, buck naked except for a metal collar on his neck. A thick chain connects the collar to a bolt in the floor". With the childhood recollection of watching a tiger in a cage at a zoo, Mrs White throws the prisoner a key. "I want to tease this naked black giant as I did that tiger," she determines. But, once free, the black man charges towards her. He starts to tear the clothes from the terrified girl and drops her, unceremoniously, onto a mattress. With the last vestige of her defence ripped away – her panties – Mrs White's terror suddenly becomes a yearning. "I want to– to suck the big black buck's big black dick!" she explains to Dumpsit. She is fucked in the face, fucked doggie-fashion, upside down, "from every angle and position humanly possible." With her calling obscenities and he snarling his unintelligible gibberish, the couple reach their climax – nothing short of cataclysmic. The good doctor draws his conclusions, deduces that Mrs White is in need of continued therapy, and drops his trousers so that he might convey his own fantasy. Before he can get started, however, the door kicks in and a bellow shakes the very walls. Into the office storms Petina's dream lover. "I thought she said that was a goddam fantasy!!" bemoans Dumpsit, lying beaten and dishevelled on the floor.

In 'Numbnut's Revenge', Numbnut, bitter at Whitey for having sent him to Korea to kill his Asian brothers, exacts sweet revenge when he fucks the wife of the KKK's Grand Dragon. 'Pardon Me!' has Dr Leeroy Bojangles giving a beautiful, but naïve farmer's daughter a treatment of "Concentrated Intercourse". From the waiting room, the girl's equally artless father deliberates, "From the sounds y'all wuz makin', I'da swore y'all wuz fuckin'!"

One artist to join *White Whore Funnies* with issue No.2 – lacking the penmanship of Mrs White's James Davis but more than making up for it in volume of output – was Areola Corona. His frequently disproportionate figures and clumsy comic book manner encourage a surrealist effect, perfectly in keeping with the general nastiness of his stories. Some of these are single page collages focused upon bondage and humiliation, and are not dissimilar to the outrages of Rory Hayes. In the curiously titled one-pager, 'Lets Oher Size', a number of white women are seen sucking and fucking Afro-Americans. All the speech bubbles are empty so that you, the reader, may FILL IN YOUR FAVOURITE SONG. Another page, 'It Hurts... So Good!', has two naked women strapped against a backdrop of SM imagery (and a picture of Patrick McGoohan!), they themselves joined together by a single, skilfully positioned dildo. In the strip 'Surprize!' [sic], two white girls turn up at an apartment, responding to a classified ad placed by "two black sisters". Instead of the heavy lesbian action the girls anticipate, their hosts reveal themselves to be guys in drag. "Oh no," cries Carol as she is anally penetrated. "Oh my God!" shrieks Lorrianne as her playmate pulls out a dick sheathed in a spiked metal condom. The punch line in Corona's story 'The Stroker' has it that the top agents working for the title character, the mysterious black man dressed in black, look very much like the three girls to appear in *Charlie's Angels* (that is, as best as Corona can replicate them). "Boss, it's so -oh -oh -oh -oh nice... finally meeting you- ooooo- ooooo... in the- uh- uh- uh flesh!" they gasp when eventually they get to drop their knickers for the Stroker.

Closer to its original page count with but two contributions from Areola Corona, *White Whore Funnies* No.3 was less an exercise in excess. However, it did open to several panels from James Davis accompanied by the worst rhyme in the world. Went the second verse:

> So he went to the City
> And he found hisself a pretty
> L'll White gal with nice legs and big tits
> Who saw his giant cock and threw three fits
> And she begged him to git some *tight White ass*

The title story of this issue, 'Maniac On The Loose', is particularly uninspired. While it may not at first seem out of place, 'Maniac', uncharacteristically, stands as being genuinely tasteless. The protracted rape of an office girl, the inane gags delivered by the victim, and Grass Green's typically giddy technique, fail to substantiate the

Panels from 'Appalling Love Story', White Whore Funnies No.1. Artist not known

strip one way or another. The rest of issue No.3 is taken up with several Wiley Spade strips, reading more than ever like the blue gags one might hear in a bar room. A guy warning his inexperienced date of the size of his tool, slips it in to the hilt only to have her request, "That's not bad – Now shove in the rest of it!" Applying for a job as a housekeeper, and accommodating the sexual advances of her would-be employer, another girl asks whether she has got the job. "Why don't you wait and speak to whoever lives here?" comes the reply. "I live down the hall!"

Editor and publisher, Larry Fuller, advertises several other titles within the pages of *White Whore Funnies*. These – 'the world's sexiest and dirtiest comix' – include *Gay Heartthrobs*, *Adults Only Original Sinful Tales*, and *Aroused*.

REDISTRIBUTE THE FREEDOM

At the other end of the spectrum lies Guy Colwell and *Inner City Romance* – a booklength strip per issue devoted to urban revolution and social imbalance. With this proviso, associating *Inner City Romance* with sex comics might appear somewhat tenuous. It certainly lacks the slapstick attitude of most other sex titles under discussion, but given that Colwell frequently forgoes his social commentary for

lengthy and detailed episodes of coitus, its inclusion here is a valid one.

Colwell took to the idea of writing comic books whilst in prison for draft refusal and war protest. This together with his experiences in the years following his release, manifested themselves in *The Inner City Romance Comic: "Choices"* – as was the title of the first issue. Published by Last Gasp in 1972, 'Choices' is the story of three buddies fresh out of prison who make their way to San Francisco. Paddy and Marvin are going to return to a life of pimping and drug-pushing, while James is set on getting a gun and joining a black militant group. The three of them pick up some girls. "Evah made it with black meat b'fo, sugah?" asks one hooker of Paddy, "No, ever been fucked by a dude who's loaded on acid and ain't had no pussy for three-and-a-half years?" Paddy replies. The two embark on a 12 page psychedelic lovemaking session. Marvin spends a couple of pages with a white chick. James walks out on his stoned companion and decides he needs to talk to someone. This he manages with a girl from the Black Defence Committee, who gets him a gun and convinces him that pimping and pushing might be breaking the Man's laws but it isn't helping the cause. James returns to his buddies and their whores. The choices facing him are: join in with the sex and drugs, or, shoot them all dead.

Colwell – whose employment previous to comic book work included toy design at Mattel and freelance courtroom quick life sketching – is a master at orchestrating panels. Despite the essentially block, woodcut nature of his characters, his strips are *fluent* in a manner quite unlike any other artist. With the exception of *Inner City Romance* No.4 ('Ramps': the story of a rundown high rise apartment block), the art in which has a craggy and hurried look, Colwell swaps his technique between panels meticulous in their detail, and those very isolated and sparse. His incorporation of dreams and psychological tomfoolery, never overbearing or self-indulgent, is particularly inspired.

While employing a 'free from prison' theme once again, issue No.3 of *Inner City Romance* is possibly Colwell's visual masterpiece. Alternating his differing artistic styles in equal measures (the first half of the book is over-detailed, while the latter half is clinical and clean), this issue puts Colwell's penchant for mind games to full use. An unidentified black man is seen traversing a series of underground passages after breaking out of prison, and emerging from a manhole cover in the city. His

Guy Colwell varied the intensity of his style, often to dramatic effect. This and the panel previous are taken from the opening and close of his Inner City Romance No.3

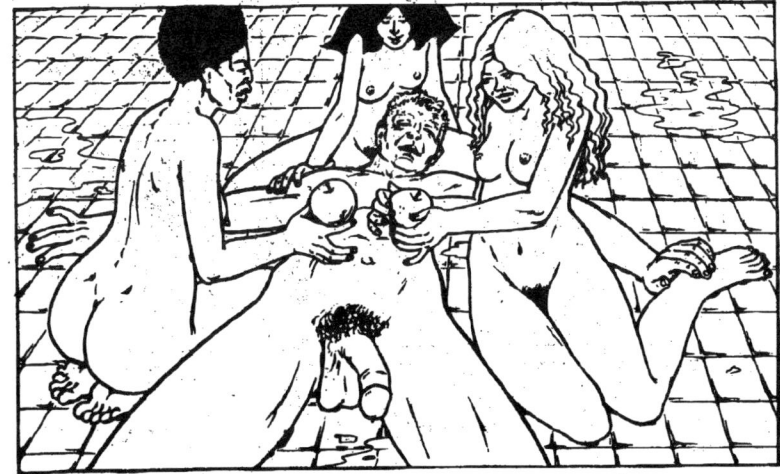

friends greet him. They bring him a joint, strawberry ice cream and a gun before making their move on prison to bust the rest of their people out. A bloodbath ensues. Our protagonist is eventually felled by the guards, and, a gun barrel levelled at his head... wakes up in his cell. His cell mate tells him to go back to sleep as he himself starts to dream. This one's more with nature than he is with revolution, breaking out of prison to be told by a girl on a beach that, "You got to go in to get out." Into the self. The resultant *sex-amid-giant-conch-shell* is interrupted by the warder's call to rise for breakfast. The third and final dreamer, ignoring the morning call, sees himself making his way to the shower stalls. Only there are no showers as such, but a pool inhabited by three curvaceous women with a single apple balancing on each of their heads. With a sudden erection, our dreamer makes his way over and engages in sex. When finally spent, and his erection subsiding, the girls start to giggle. Our dreamer opens his eyes to find, to his dismay, that he is indeed within the prison shower stalls. Other men around him are taking showers. In a corner, on all fours, however, he spies one of the girl's from the pool. He gets another hard-on and makes his way over, but on mounting her finds the girl's upper torso to be obscured. To one side two effeminate men play with themselves and suck each other off. The girl is gone. Our dreamer takes his hard-on to the two men and enters the nearest. Into the frame a punk is chased. The men chasing fight to bugger him, but their attentions soon turn elsewhere. Like some oversize Russian doll, a chain of men is created, each being raped by a man bigger and more grotesque than himself. Our dreamer is near the bottom of the rung. He is awoken by the cries of the guard.

There was no prison motif in the fifth edition of *Inner City Romance*. Nor was it given over to any one particular story. The opening piece, 'Good For You', is a dialogue-free observation of a couple making love (she inserting a diaphragm; he using spit for lubricant). In 'Sex Crime', a woman is attacked in a back alley at gunpoint. A passer-by attacks the would-be rapist, beats him senseless and himself attempts to rape the girl. The girl gets the gun and shoots him dead. On hearing shots, a third man arrives at the scene. "Stinking animals!" the woman calls out and blows a hole in the stranger's chest. "Whud I do?" croaks the dying man.[12] After *Inner City Romance*, Colwell left the medium of comics to concentrate on painting. He returned in the late-Eighties with the *Doll* from Rip Off Press. The series – four issues by 1990 – concerned a lifelike sex doll utilised by one Dr Lyle Gladmount to aid troubled males to 'readjust' ("The best thing you can do is screw, screw, screw!"). The comic was hailed by readers to be "fascinating" and "intellectually challenging" on the one hand, while "disgusting and sexist" on the other.

ONCE YOU GET PAST THE SMELL YOU'VE GOT IT LICKED

The phantasmagorical landscapes rendered by Wallace Wood in the EC science fiction stories are distinctive enough in themselves. A bigger give-away, however, is that they are rarely without a female 'interest' in the foreground, pointing her big breasts at the reader. These figure-hugging space-suited space gals are a recurring element in Wood's work. In the artist's more down-to-earth stories, the girls remain lascivious and magnificently proportioned as best the frills of a demure and tailored fashion will allow. But to outer space Wally would return and throw into the frame the comparatively less restrictive confines of a female space suit: the nearest thing to a naked body in 1950s comic books. An astro-bimbo reeling from a bug-eyed carnivore chomping on her fellow travellers, EC's *Weird Science* No.4 has one such lovely fixed upon its cover – one arm drawn toward her helmeted mouth as if to stifle a silent scream but better to show off her bosom.

Following on from his work at EC, Wood appeared sporadically in such mainstream publications as *Mad* and *Vampirella*. But his heart lay in the underground and, in the late-Sixties, Wood instigated his own title in an attempt to further liberalise the comics medium. *Witzend*, a non-profit making affair, was intended as a platform for new and established artists who couldn't or didn't want to sell their work to the major publishing houses. The major companies paid little per page and held a binding contract over any work they utilised; *Witzend* paid nothing, published a work only once, and had no hold over it. Contractual obligations aside – and more important to the *Witzend* ethic – Wood sought work that the major companies possibly saw as too outrageous or unsuitable. An admirable idea and most certainly a labour of love. But, according to its detractors, actually doing very little in its eight issues by way of expanding innovative horizons, and instead dallying on scantily clad girls. Some of whom had spacesuits. In the 1977 strip 'Super Cosmic Comic Creator Comix' (not published until 1992 in *Slow Death* No.11), Wood has a belittled comic artist suddenly capable of transforming himself into a Neanderthal sex monster, to feature in porn films by day and draw comics by night. Wood's affiliation with the underground was endorsed in 1980 with the publication of the now notorious *Gang Bang!* Reprinted and bootlegged[13] many times over, *Gang Bang!* is a large format comic book which parodies other strips and cartoon characters, placing each in a hardcore sex scenario. Here we have the sexual escapades of 'So White and the Six Dorks', 'Lil an' Abner', and 'Perry and the Privates'. In 'The Farmer's Daughter', a country girl is caught masturbating by a farmhand while her father is in town buying groceries. The boy takes the girl's virginity in the woods, aided by a group of boys who happen upon the scene. As with all the strips, and in true porno tradition, the essence of the story is not the plot but the vivid depiction of the sexual act. ('The Farmer's Daughter' does, however, conclude on a poignant and somewhat existential note. The closing caption addresses the reader: *'...It was a day like all days, full of the events that alter and illuminate our time... all things are as they were then, except **you were there!**'*) How *Gang Bang!*'s skit on Snow White and the Seven Dwarves evaded the legal department at Disney Studios is a mystery – Disney not exactly noted for letting it's characters suffer indignation lightly.[14] In the Wood version, on hearing that there is

So White and the Six Dorks

'So White and the Six Dorks.' Gang Bang! Art: Wally Wood

one more fair than she, the evil queen calls for a hunter to take So White into the woods and kill her. But So White is spared her life when she gives her would-be assassin a blow-job, only to be then raped. Spending the entirety of the story then wandering around with the bottom half of her dress and underclothes missing, So White happens upon a small house and falls asleep on the tiny beds therein. She awakes with a start surrounded by little folk. "Permit me to introduce myself," says the first dwarf. "I am Dork. The eager one eating you is called Retardo... And this is Slappy... and Sloppy... Peepy and Sleazy... and last but not least is Protozoa! Who nobody has ever been able to figure out." The story continues much as the original, but with a liberal sprinkling of So White servicing her hosts at every convenience. When one suggests a gang bang: *'So White tries... She takes Slappy. Then Sleazy enters by the back door... She takes Dork in her mouth, and gives hand-jobs to Sloppy and Groucho... which leaves Peepy and Retardo to wait, or find holes of their own.'*

Though the work throughout *Gang Bang!* is undeniable as being that of Wood, it is uncharacteristically sloppy on occasion, sparse, and perhaps even retouched. Chances are that the whole thing was only ever meant as a personal distraction on Wood's part; never a serious endeavour. Interesting, though, is how the concept of sexualising recognisable personalities harkens back to the days of the Tijuana Bibles, and the quirky parodies themselves are not unlike inflamed versions of those to grace the pages of *Mad* magazine – to which Wood had once contributed.

A second volume of *Gang Bang!* is said to exist (although this author has yet to see a copy). According to the *Amok Fourth Dispatch* catalogue, it features the sexploits of 'Prince Violate', 'Flasher Gordon', and 'Sally Forth'. The latter must have been a particular favourite of the artist. A sex-happy air-head who constantly gets herself into dishevelled mischief, Sally Forth is also featured in the first volume of *Gang Bang!*, and, printed after Wood's death, went on to further adventures under the Eros Comix imprint. The Eros series sees a much more conservative, less explicit *Sally Forth*. That is: no pubes or penetration. Furthermore, it also sees the penmanship and attention to detail expected of Wood, as if this indeed be a proper commission. Issue No.7 – despite a truly wretched cover courtesy of Jaime Hernandez – is typical of the series and places Sally in a Barbarella-inspired phantasmagorical landscape; lost in outer space and with no clothes.

THAT'S THE WAY TO CRAM FOR AN EXAM

> I remember thinking, as I was dreaming *Cherry* up, that for a comic book to call itself 'Underground' it should be dangerous in one way or another. If they even think it's dangerous, then it is. Showing explicit sex as if it was a fun, positive, wholesome, healthy thing could be considered dangerous by some people.
>
> Larry Welz, *The Gauntlet* No.4

The character of Cherry Poptart would seem a logical development given the style Larry Welz was adopting in *Tuff Shit* and *Bakersfield Kountry Komics* in the early Seventies. A buoyancy akin to the 'teenager' comics (that Grass Green in *White Whore Funnies* would later so badly misconstrue); an easy-on-the-eye, almost minimalist approach in which the befreckled, somewhat goofy, characters are struck by a look of perpetual large-eyed astonishment. Welz had moderate success previously with his *Captain Guts* comic book, a beer drinking superhero with an intestine emblazoned on his chest whose aim it was to rid the world of hippies. He also did work for *Kids Liberation Coloring Book* and *American Flyer Funnies*, but Cherry Poptart has to date proven his most famous and endearing creation. The tales of the bubbly blonde high school student – some might say bimbo, but she always holds a manipulative hand in any situation – were pulled together by Last Gasp for the debut issue of *Cherry Poptart* in 1982. A second issue appeared in 1985.

Cherry Poptart emulated the happy-go-lucky Teenager comics so well that a law firm representing the Archie Series demanded Welz cease and desist publication. Created in 1941, the red-haired Archie Andrews was the first and remains the most popular of the Teenager comic characters.[15] The initial grievance was over a story Larry Todd had contributed to the first issue, which openly lampooned actual Archie characters and presented them as coke snorting, pill-popping, hypersexual, blood lusting fiends.[16] 'Vampironica', the offending strip, was pulled for subsequent printings. With issue No.2, however, the law firm was noting further similarities and Cherry herself, her friends, even the design of the comic's cover came under scrutiny. Ultimately, the Archie group failed to put a stop to the comic. (In the Cherry strip, 'Best Friends', Welz gives a subtle, but irrefutable tip of the hat to Roland Topor's *Paysage Polonais*.)

Panels from 'Hot Rod Boogie'. Cherry Poptart No.1. Art: Larry Welz

Like a regular comic book, *Cherry Poptart* carries its own letters-cum-problem page and fictitious minutiae ads for novelty goods (ATOMIC SUBMARINE; POCKET SPY TELESCOPE; FAKE COLOSTOMY BAG; MIDGET CAMERA... *Guaranteed to take pictures. But only if you're a midget*; MANHOOD KIT; INSTANT UNDERGROUND ARTIST CARTOON COURSE... *Have fun as a highly-paid Social Satirist!*). The strips, as can be expected, focus on interpersonal teenage relationships but substitute Archie-type innuendo for actual sexual congress. In 'Hot Rod Boogie', Cherry goes for a ride in Ronnie's souped-up motor. They go to the outskirts of town with some booze, smoke a joint, and get into some heavy petting. "C'mon Cherry–" says Ronnie, unzipping his flies. "This is funsies – No pokey," is Cherry's rebuttal, pushing Ronnie's penis away. Cherry compromises and gives Ronnie a blow-job, so long as she gets to drive his cool car later. Full-throttle, crunching the gears, Cherry plows the vehicle through the countryside, demanding of the dumbstruck Ronnie, "Tickle my clit – I think I'm gonna come in my pants!" before wrapping it around another car. The cops arrive, denounce the boy a menace, handcuff him and drag him off. Other cops drive the "poor girl" home. The closing panel has Cherry in the back of a squad car, thwarting the advances of an amorous cop. "Uh-unh... No pokey," she tells him. Another strip, 'Scool Daze', has Cherry in the classroom, momentarily distracted and unable to answer the question directed at her. "Gosh, Mr Feeney, I... I really don't know!" she tells the tutor, thinking to herself, *"Oh, Jesus – He's got a hard-on!... I'll give 'im a little Beaver shot."* She spreads her legs under her desk. It goes without saying that Cherry is called to stay behind after class.

There is a disclaimer at the opening of issue No.2 which has it that 'All models are 18 yrs or older'. A word of caution precedes it: 'Possession and/or sale of this funny book may be a crime where you live!' Later the same issue, Welz has a one-page strip focused upon Cinnamon Poptart, Cherry's phantom kid sister. "They won't even let me exist around here!" Cinnamon informs the reader. "An' y'wanna know why? They're afraid that if I even show up in one of these books that someone's gonna start sayin' that it's kiddie porn – or child abuse or something!" When the girl, jealous of her older sister, pulls off her top and explains, "Look! I got titties, too! Well, kind of!", any offending appendage is suitably obscured with an apology from the editor. Writing in *The Gauntlet* (issue No.4 dated 1992), Welz explains the very serious issues behind the Cinnamon Poptart strip:

> There are certain things I don't mess with. The biggest one is Cherry's age. The idea is that she's a teenager, right. But if I depict her as being under 18, then she's a child, and it can or could be classified as child pornography, a "bustable offence" in my publisher's words. He wants me to have her be in "junior college" instead of high school. I take my original line of defence which is to be generic. It's just a school.

In over 10 years of publishing, Cherry Poptart has yet to age. She has always *just turned 18*. "As fresh as you can get, legally," Welz puts it. That may or may not be a contributing factor why the comic – now selling under the abbreviated title of *Cherry* (abbreviated purely for aesthetical reasons) – is the most popular sex comic ever. And, reaching No.15 in 1993, easily the most prolific.

ANTONIO GHURA

Not by any stretch of the imagination can the same be said of Antonio Ghura; success and longevity are not words that spring immediately to mind. Yet, simply put, Ghura's work – little of it as there is – stands as an example of the finest the underground can offer. Perhaps it has something to do with sex never appearing to be the motivating factor, more a concentrated bonus. Or that Ghura's stories are genuinely funny, and his art the most succinct parody yet of the True Romance titles so cherished by his contemporaries.

Apart from his own *Raw Purple* and *Bogey* and a handful of isolated appearances in other publications, Ghura is known primarily for the title *Truly Amazing Love Stories*, which managed two issues (1977 and 1983). They carried no outside contributions, possibly never made it beyond British shores, and pulled no punches. Together, they succeed in creating this insular little world: slightly mad; completely obscene. Ghura is not a name that springs readily to mind when conversations are attuned to comic books. He simply is not prolific enough (and his subject matter relegated his work to only the hardiest of retail outlets). Even those who have been 'employed' in underground comics themselves need an occasional pointer as to 'what did he do?'

In preparation for this piece, some effort was made to try and trace Antonio Ghura. Naturally it proved unsuccessful and it isn't known whether the artist is now alive or dead. He possibly was aquainted with Mike Matthews, an underground artist with whom he shares some affinity – Matthews too being sadly neglected, well-versed in the art of outrage, and self-publishing in order that he might make available his more 'progressive' work (his *Horrific Romance Comix* appeared in 1984; he went missing and was found dead in 1993). It is thought that Ghura and Matthews worked together on *Hot Nads*, published in the late-Seventies, but which this author has yet to see. Another possible lead was John Muir of Manchester's Babylon Books [see 'Banned, Drawn & Quartered' for more information], whose *The Complete Bootlegs Checklist & Discography*, published in 1978, carries original Ghura artwork championing the Babylon Books logo. Having attempted and had no success maintaining contact with Muir in the past, little was expected by way of this particular avenue. Knockabout Comics in London do recall Antonio Ghura. His is a name which rankles all who work there. One staff member has it that Ghura, "a mad hippie," broke into her flat and "threatened my life". This because the artist believed Knockabout to be responsible for reprinting his comics and ripping him off. David Huxley, a comic artist producing *Blood Sex & Terror Comics* in the Seventies, on the other hand, corresponded with Ghura (in 1990), met him once, and recalls him to be "charming".

Even tracing Ghura's published work is a not altogether satisfying, very often fruitless exercise. According to Mal Burns in his *Comix Index* [Brighton: John Noyce, 1978], Ghura contributed to *Sin City*, one of the Cozmic Comics. On examination of said title, however, there is no evidence of Ghura. It also associates the artist with occasional work for *Home Grown* and *Creem* magazine. Of more interest to us here

**Bogey cover. Art:
Antonio Ghura**

is the work Ghura did for *Libertine*, a journal of period erotica conceived in 1974, but later including humour, some contemporary sex matters and advice. *Libertine* was taken to court with issue No.7 charged with Obscenity. One item to have particularly galled the prosecution is 'Home On Leave', a Ghura strip in which a Regimental Sergeant-Major returns from Ulster, brags to his mother of his exploits there and engages in cunnilingus with her. "Melvin just loves his mum's hot crumpet", the wintry one sighs from atop the kitchen table. *Libertine* was acquitted. (An evidence copy of *Libertine*, when opened in court, was found to be missing its raunchy pin-up of co-editor Arabella Melville. The police were suspected.)

One title not listed in the *Comix Index* directory, but to which Ghura most certainly did contribute, is *Hot Gravy*. Perhaps Ghura's earliest work in print is that of the front and back covers for this, the one and only issue. Not particularly inspired, and aided not at all by the execrable two-colour overlay, the cover features a bedraggled hippie tucking into his sausage and mash, while on the back an aged grandad is seen doing likewise with a bowl of something – hot gravy, presumably. No publication details are listed, but the date of the strips themselves would place *Hot Gravy* sometime around 1972. The contents harbour no Ghura, only reprints of US material. It's impossible to say just how much of the reprinted material in British comics of the early-Seventies was authorised, but the variable reproduction qualities of the work included here (the usual crew: Crumb, Dave Sheridan, Richard Corben working as 'Gore'), the lack of publication details, and the fact that Ghura himself has failed to put his name to his cover art, deeply suggests that *Hot Gravy* is a pirate.

Following his work for *Libertine* and *Its All Lies*, discussed earlier, Ghura concentrated on producing his own comic titles. The first was *Bogey*. With assistance on some strips by one Michael Feldman (in a purely writing capacity, by the looks of it; the artwork is that of Ghura), *Bogey* was published in 1975 in a run of 3,000 copies.[17] In a chapter headed 'Political or Destabilising Pornography', Francis Bennion in his book *The Sex Code: Morals for Moderns* [London: Weidenfeld and Nicolson, 1992] has *Bogey* down as displaying "some of the best features of the underground magazines; predominantly, honesty about what society is perennially dishonest about". (When considering that works actually pertaining to the study of comics and their creators fail to even mention Antonio Ghura, it is nothing short of amazing that Bennion's book – a work *not* devoted to comics, but lending several of its 323 pages to the subject – should discuss the artist.) *Bogey* takes its title from the closing speech for the defence at the *Oz* trial, an analogy which drew on the prosecution's oft asked question of the witnesses: "Would you encourage it?" While picking one's nose may be discouraged, argued the defence, it doesn't actually do any harm. *Bogey* has on its cover Humphrey Bogart with a finger up a nostril, announcing "I'm picking it again, Sam!" The strips within concern themselves with sex and drugs. 'The Wedding Night' has a new bride awaiting her husband in the conjugal bed. "Don't switch on the light, Mack, dawling!" she says as the bedroom door swings open. In total blackness, creaks and groans and the sound of fucking issue forth. The door swings open once again and the husband walks in to find his wife has mistakenly given herself to his horse. (Although the newly weds are obviously of quality stock, there's nothing to suggest they're of Prussian descent, as *The Sex Code* has it.) Other strips include 'The Peyote Connection', a lengthy meditation on the conflicts between hippies and police, while 'Fatherly Love' delves into the theme of incest (incest being a popular theme with Ghura, rearing its head in 'Santa Comes Visiting', 'Home On Leave' and later in 'Love Conquers All!!'). 'Fatherly Love' has Vanessa's dad suddenly realising how his 16-

year-old daughter has grown. *Fuck, she's really filled out, look at them tits!* When mum goes to bingo, he makes his way up to the girl's room. The following day, Vanessa decides she just has to stay with her boyfriend at his flat. But a night of sex there leaves her tense and she heads for home again. *Will he ever forgive me for leaving him?* sobs Vanessa. *Oh!.. He's smiling... He's forgiven me! Yes!.. Yes! I'm sure now, he's the man I truly love!!* "Oh... Daddy!.. Daddy! I will never leave you... Never!!!" she exclaims on her return. Later, Vanessa and her father are indisposed on the settee. "Oh!.. Oooooh!! Come on Dad, shoot your load... Mum'll be back from shopping soon!.. Oooh!"

The sex in 'Fatherly Love' – as in 'The Wedding Night' before it – is inferred and not actually seen: it comes in the form of exhalations from behind closed doors, movement from under bedsheets, or a naked hairy buttock pointing at the reader. Referring to this, Bennion writes in *The Sex Code*, that, "It is one of the rules of the underground comics that you do not show gratuitous sexual images: the sex is aversive, not stimulative." Despite an empathy toward the comics, Bennion's statement is not wholly correct. While the majority of undergrounds do avoid gratuitous sexual imagery, the prospect of a court hearing should sex be tackled any other way makes aversion the more appealing option. As for Ghura himself, he wasn't playing by these rules anyway. His next comic venture was neither aversive nor stimulative, but a coy play-off between the two.

IT'S AT LEAST TWELVE INCHES, AND THICK TOO

> This comic book dares to go forward to the very precipitous edge of conventionality and by so doing expand it.
>
> Introductory blurb, *Truly Amazing Love Stories* No.1

> "Er... Debbie, it's been a long while since the last time... I haven't been getting it from your mother. I know I'd promised I wouldn't ask you again... but I'm desperate! And I am driving you all the way to Bristol. Er... could we? Would you? Er..."
>
> "Suck you off, Dad?!"
>
> 'Love Conquers All!!', *Truly Amazing Love Stories* No.2

With little exception, no one else in Britain before or since *Truly Amazing Love Stories* has dared to tackle such blatantly explicit tales. Fewer still have been willing to give whole comic books over to them. *Cozmic Comics* had imported material from *Young Lust* back in 1972, but the less explicit, more satirical work of Jay Kinney. Brian Bolland – later to find fame working at *2000AD* and in the US – would do a mock Fifties bondage strip called 'Little Nympho' which utterly outraged feminists. Mike Matthews, whose work in general contained an element of sexual activity, came closest to a fully fledged porn book with the previously mentioned *Horrific Romance Comix*. But even he concentrated more on updating EC than on a sexual assault of the senses.[18] Perhaps the most bizarre contender came, not from the underground, but via a British 'topshelf' magazine. For a short time, *Rustler* carried within its pages a digest-sized comic book supplement. As best as can be determined, these were European and hardcore in origin, but, so as not to place *Rustler* on the wrong side of British law, had all representation of genital contact erased and replaced erect male members with strategically positioned *flaccid* members.

Published by Beyond the Edge Publishing Co., *Truly Amazing Love Stories* ran

Double page spread. The inevitable truth in 'The Inevitable Truth!' Truly Amazing Love Stories No.1. Art: Antonio Ghura

for two issues and, as the title and cover illustrations implied, was a pastiche of the American Teen Romance titles. Issue No.1 appeared in 1977 (the year in which *Libertine* was taken to court) and had on its cover two young lovers stealing an embrace under moonlight. Their faces reflect their sudden and unexpected predicament. "Oh, Lord!" he says to her. "I've just come in my pants*!!*" THE AGONY AND ECSTASY OF LOVE, ran the blurb beneath. Common to all the stories within is the introspective, first person narrative. 'The Inevitable Truth!' has Madge musing over the fatal night she and Tom made love in his mini. *I remember a feeling of total relaxation overcame me... followed by the sudden realisation...* "Christ! Who's driving the car?*!!*"

> *In a mixed up kind of way I remember the skid...*
>
> "Aaaargh*!* Let go of me prick*!!* Let go*!!*"
>
> *and a world of light and sound that suddenly exploded...*
>
> "Holy fuck*!* I can't reach the steering wheel. My hand... It's caught in your knickers*!...* If only I can plow into that old faggot, his body might just slow me down enough*!...* Oh fuck*!* Missed him*!*"
>
> "I'm too pretty to die*!* Sob*!*"
>
> "Shut up you cun–" CRASH*!*

'Remember Rodney.' Truly Amazing Love Stories No.1. Art: Antonio Ghura

By a miracle Madge has been thrown clear, but all that remains of Tom is a half-burnt penis and ball sac. Beyond that she remembers nothing and the next we see of her is in a hospital bed. A doctor – whose name alternates between Fanny and Mabel – helps her to come to terms with the loss of Tom and start life afresh. *I'd come to depend on Fanny for everything... Her friendship, her comforting words, her help when memory clouded the sunshine of my new life.* Following an evening out together, returning home in the doctor's Volkswagen, Madge is presented with a sudden and unexpected request: "Look Madge, I er... don't know how to say it... CAN I KISS YOU GOODNIGHT?" The doctor thrusts a fumbling hand into the woman's knickers. "How can I possibly make love to you?" Madge protests, "I... I'm not a LESBIAN!" But she is, and in the end comes out of the closet to find true happiness.

In the strip, 'True Love', young Jonathan sets off to stay with his uncle and aunt on their farm for the summer. At an age when he is "experimenting with sex", Jonathan has sex with Bluebelle, his uncle's cow.

> *Well, there I was, by now getting a good deep rythmic [sic] action going, when who walks into the barn but my Aunty Jean...*
>
> "Jonathan*!!* You cunt faced toe-rag, what the fuck do you think you're doing?"
>
> "Blimey*!* Aunty Jean*!* I er... I came to milk the cow*!* Eh*!*...Eh*!*"
>
> *Christ, I almost shat myself.*
>
> "You dirty little sod, can't you find any girls? Jesus*!*... Hurry-up and shoot your load. Dinner is getting cold*!*"

Neither Jonathan nor his aunt bring the incident up again. A few days later, however, during a family reunion at the barn, the sound of giggling draws Jonathan to his aunt's bedroom. He peers in to discover... *Aunty Jean, standing in front of the mirror... masturbating!!!* So excited is the boy that he cannot help but toss himself off there and then. Naturally, his aunt spots him and calls the boy into the room. "C'mon

A Puff–A Party–A Tragedy! 'Marijuana Madness' title page. Raw Purple. Art: Antonio Ghura

Jonathan, I'm better than a cow*! Fuck me!*" The boy's 'first time' with a girl doesn't last long, but Jean presents him with more lessons and opportunities during the course of the next few days. Then comes the day Jonathan has to leave. He promises himself that he will return to the farm the following year.

> *Well, it was now the summer of 68 and I was coming back to Uncle Ben's farm... like I told myself I would. All that winter my thoughts would constantly turn to that previous summer spent at the farm, I just couldn't get her out of my mind. Then I saw her standing by the shade of a large Oak tree, surrounded by a field of wild flowers. I ran the last few yards... It had been a year... One year too long. Oh, Jesus Christ! How I'd missed her!!!*

"Bluebelle*!* Bluebelle, my dearest love*!!*"

The final tale of the first issue, 'Remember Rodney', concerns itself with a homosexual theme. Mr Alcock, a private music tutor, has moved to the country and become something of a recluse since his last love affair broke down. He's reluctant to take on any new pupils, but something about Rodney Brown, who turns up at his door for tuition one morning, catches his imagination. *His playing was good... But he was wonderful. So young so full of life, I wondered how his prick would taste in my mouth.* Mr Alcock becomes infatuated with the boy, cherishing those Wednesday piano lessons together, but resigned to the fact that he must never get physically involved with a pupil. His release comes in masturbating to thoughts of the boy. Particularly distracted one day, pants down and dick in hand, he doesn't notice Rodney arrive for his lesson. "Hello! Mr Alcock! Are you hom... Oh!" Rodney moves to comfort the humiliated tutor. *He came and sat beside me on my bed. I felt so ashamed... I wanted to die... Then Rodney reached across, cupped my heavy balls in his soft, warm hand and gently whispered...* "Don't cry, Mr Alcock... I er... understand how you must feel... Please let me help you... I love you!" Despite Alcock's reticence, he and Rodney become lovers. Months are spent engaged in all manner of sexual activity. But the day does indeed arrive when Rodney moves on to pastures new – notably those frequented by a young girl working at the local inn. While Rodney and his new found love make out in the grass, Mr Alcock watches unnoticed from behind a tree. A shell of his former self, he drives himself to try and forget by frequenting gay bars, cottaging in public toilets, offering sexual services to all and sundry. Then, one day, as suddenly as he had left, Rodney returns. "Oh, my darling... Can you forgive me?" he asks of his tutor. "I had to find out if I was truly gay..." Going on to form a renowned musical partnership, Alcock and Brown live happily ever after.

All the strips in *Truly Amazing Love Stories* interject their narrative with liberal helpings of graphic fornication. Coupling the naïveté of the subject, and the 'charm' of their recollection, with grotesque sexual displays in which erect male members are bulbous, throbbing, thickly-veined beasts, and vaginas, perhaps not so erect, but bulbous and misshapen nonetheless. Ejaculations fly in every direction leaving mottled residue suspended on walls, clothing, light-fittings... Indeed, the anticipation of procreation is enough to squeeze a multitudinous array of substances from every orifice with a give-away SQUIRK or a SQUIRCH. By way of contrast, in this hypersexualised world, everyone drives around in tiny, economical motorcars.

Truly Amazing Love Stories falls somewhere between *Snatch Comics* and *Gang Bang!* – beyond the experimentation of the former and not quite the out-and-out titillation of the latter. In many ways, *Amazing Love Stories* is too funny to be titillating. The sex, although depicted explicitly, is almost always victim to some indiscriminate nuance which cares not a jot about the 'serious' nature of the subject at hand. Whether it be the position of the legs during lovemaking, or a car horn going BEEP! when a knee inadvertently catches it, or the sudden mood-shifts of the characters ("Piss off, mate! Oh! It's you, Fanny!"), or the uncontrollable flood of emotions when love turns bad, particularly campy, gay love ("Nyeeaargh!.. *sob* Boo hoo!.. Hoo! Nyaaeergh... *sob* Rodney...*gasp* sputter..."), it is impossible not to laugh at the sex. (There is one exception to this as shall be discussed later.) To further adhere the reader into this insular little world, *Amazing Love Stories* has its own advertisements for the likes of BROWNHOLE VASELINE – THE SMOOTH ONE, and the POSTGRADUATE SCHOOL OF LEISURE AND EASY VIRTUES, PARIS. In a mock-up of cigarette advertising (no longer legal in Britain), Ghura substitutes tobacco for cannabis, for 'WHEN YOU REALLY REALLY WANT TO GET HIGH. £36OZ DEALER'S PRICE. GOVERNMENT WARNING: SMOKING CANNABIS CAN BE HAZARDOUS TO YOUR LIBERTY'.

Following on from *Truly Amazing Love Stories* No.1, Ghura, in 1978, unleashed another solo project: *Raw Purple*. The emphasis here was not on sex – though it too had its fair share – but on drugs. A little circle at the bottom of the front cover, under which read *'THIS SPOT is impregnated with d-Lysergic Acid Diethylamide 25. Licking it will make you dance, sing and see weird colours'*, actually prompted one person in the presence of this author to do just that. Lick the cover of a shop copy (well it *was* the Seventies...). The opening strip, 'Marijuana Madness' adhered to the format of *Truly Amazing Love Stories*, but putting its first-person narrative into a 'cautionary' tale of drug misuse. 'Oliver Jones and his Weird Penis' is a 'nitty gritty type story flagrantly reflecting on these troubled times' and concerns a man whose penis acquires the power of speech. An acid trip that, curiously, does end with a genuine fatality is depicted in 'Nightmare Journey' (unleashing several pages of cosmic self-indulgence along the way). There are other mordant moments in *Raw Purple*. For example, 'No Supper To-Night' has a child hanging by his neck from the light-fitting in his bedroom – not even a hint toward the circumstances or an explanation why. In 'Grandad, What did YOU do in the last War?', two children play in the company of an elderly gentleman sat in an armchair, his face, wrinkled and aged as it is, unmistakable as being that of Adolf Hitler.

For all its experimentation, *Raw Purple* isn't quite of the standard of *Truly Amazing Love Stories*. Indeed, it's best moments are those strips which harken back to that title ('Marijuana Madness', for instance). A second issue of *Raw Purple* was not to

The start of what is to become "a chocolate sandwich!!" in the strip, 'Love's For Sharing!'. Truly Amazing Love Stories No.2. Art: Antonio Ghura

appear. A second issue of *Truly Amazing Love Stories*, however, did – albeit a full five years after the first. Printed 'Somewhere in England', as if by way of compensation for the delay or by way of a swansong, Ghura plied *Truly Amazing Love Stories* No.2 (1983) with his most outrageous work to date. This is the pinnacle of porn comics. The title to be had after wading through the best of the rest. It's cover bares another young couple locked in an embrace under a night sky, exhibiting signs of anxiety. "Oh, Harry," she says to him, "I love you so much*!*" "Lord*!*" he muses to himself, "How can I tell her that I'm not a man but a woman?*!*" And, should there be any doubt as to what type of comic this might be, the opening panels of the first page have her sucking on his penis. *He doesn't have all that much... but what he has is rock hard!* 'Love Conquers All*!!*' tells the story of Debbie and Harry – her parents the owner of a small hotel just outside of Bristol, and he, their only guest. The wild relationship the young couple share is brought to an abrupt end when, one day, Harry has to leave for an appointment in Bristol. Their last night together they go to see the "new Village People movie" playing at the local Odeon. So engrossed in fucking, the couple stay on to watch the programme a second time, and a little old lady in the seat in front gets a liberal SQUIRT of Harry's semen down the back of her neck. The next morning Harry is gone. A note he has left sheds no light on the mysterious appointment in Bristol, but still Debbie manages to trace his whereabouts. He's in hospital, having undergone major surgery, and is allowed no visitors. Debbie returns home, heartbroken. A month passes with no news on Harry's condition or what ails him. Suddenly, having resigned herself to never seeing him again, a familiar voice rings through the hotel. "It's me, Debbie, Harry*!*" Indeed, the love of her life has returned. Complete with a change of sex. Harry – or rather, Hariette – expresses the same feelings for Debbie. So too Debbie for her/him. "Come to my room, Harriette, and I'll prove my love for you*!*" she tells the transsexual.

"B-Be gentle, Debbie, the stitches are still a bit tender*!*"

"I will be gentle, Harriette... I will*!*"

"Say, Debbie, won't you miss my hard cock thrusting into your warm, juicy cunt? If you do I could always use a dildo on you*!*"

"No, I'm alright on that count... Daddy will see to that*!*"

As the couple lick and suck their way to a climax, the story ponders

Will Debbie's Mum's twat ever thaw-out?
Will Debbie's Dad ever keep it up for long?
Will Harriette blackmail Debbie's Dad?
Now that Harry is a woman will Debbie become a man?

Homosexual rifts are the focus of 'I Lied For Love'. Nigel Willocks is a skinny, spotty, bespectacled Johnny Mathis fan who falls for a hunk by the name of Sebastian. In order to lure Sebastian away from his obnoxious mincing queen boyfriend, Nigel fabricates a story of infidelity. The ruse works and he and Sebastian become lovers. But it isn't long before Nigel is experiencing nagging pangs of guilt. "I think I must have a lot on my mind," he tells Sebastian one particularly limp and frustrating night. *If I tell him I lied to get him I may lose him!* But tell him Nigel does.

"Sebastian, listen... I must tell you that I made it up about Oscar going with that guy on the motorcycle... I said it to get you away from Oscar...

I'll understand if you don't ever want to see me again.'"

"I know all about that.'"

"You know? H-How?.. Who? Since when?"

"I asked Bryan... He told me Oscar did indeed go to the Gents... He hadn't stood me up.'"

"Oh, I'm so ashamed.'"

Sebastian forgives Nigel and the two of them – Nigel with his tiny pre-ejaculating penis, and Sebastian, hung like a stallion, with the presence of a Greek god – go on to live happily ever after. (Apparently, the only problem Ghura had with printers arose from the gay strips. Straight sex was fine; gay material they objected to.)

Truly Amazing Love Stories No.2 incorporated more ads of an improbable nature, and even a Babs Cartfart problem page, offering irresponsible advice to highly intimate questions. There is 'Tampon Tales', a one-page strip which unites a discarded used tampon and Bela Lugosi in the guise of Dracula. "Now, that's what I call a lollipop!" determines the Count in the last panel. Tasteless, most certainly, but not quite as reprehensible as 'I Loved a Sex Fiend!' touted as 'a truly nose blowing story!!' While having sex in the park, Emily thinks she spots a man hiding in the bushes. Her companion thinks not – but he would say that seeing as he's 'about to unload'. Someone has been molesting girls in the area. When Emily returns home and discovers that a flatmate is out walking her dog, she becomes concerned and rushes to try and find her. No cause for alarm, however, Emily bumps into Detective Sergeant Paul Rutcliffe of the Yard – the man she thought she saw in the bushes earlier. Rutcliffe explains how his search for the sex maniac isn't faring too well, that the police need a local girl to act as a decoy and flush out the attacker. Emily agrees to help after a classmate at the polytechnic falls victim. The following evening, behaving like starry-eyed lovers, she and the detective take to strolling around the park. On hearing a noise, Rutcliffe leaves the girl and goes to investigate. It is a vile creature who returns in his place, ugly, naked, and with an erection. Emily screams, but Rutcliffe is nowhere to be seen. The monster overpowers the girl, tears off her clothes and throws her to the ground. Not before Emily has been violated vaginally and anally do the police arrive and the nightmare ends. The identity of the maniac? None other than bogus detective Paul Rutcliffe, under a mask. "I'm sorry, Emily," he cries as the police haul him away. "I didn't want to hurt you!.. T-The voices in my head they commanded... forced me to hurt you!.. It wasn't me..."

RAPE IS NO FUN AT ALL*!* reads the note at the close of the story, which goes some way in explaining why Ghura makes so little headway toward humour in the strip. 'I Loved A Sex Fiend!' (the 'love' element constituting one kiss between Emily and the pre-bezerker Rutcliffe) is unlike Ghura's other work in that it *does* present the sexual act as out-and-out pornography, no risible quips or visual tomfoolery, a half of the strip's page count given over to Emily's subjugation. Emily struggles hard not to orgasm during her ordeal, "but he made me come..." In the end, Emily resigns herself to not caring *to what dephts [sic] of pervertion [sic] he submitted me to... for I felt like a lifeless rag doll... to be used and abused... to do with as he pleased...* If all of this is particularly loveless and uncharacteristic of the artist, then the Paul Rutcliffe character being an obvious take-off of Peter Sutcliffe, the Yorkshire Ripper, should further complicate matters. 'I Loved A Sex Fiend!' was published not two years after Sutcliffe was apprehended for the sex-murder of at least 13 women; the date Ghura

Previous. Title page to 'I Loved A Sex Fiend!'. *Above.* Emily is victim to the Weirdo when Sergeant Paul Rutcliffe goes to investigate a noise in the woods. 'I Loved A Sex Fiend!' Truly Amazing Love Stories No.2. Art: Antonio Ghura

has actually given the strip suggests he was working on it only months after Sutcliffe's arrest. It is difficult to imagine to what ends Ghura was directing the strip. He cannot have failed to comprehend the magnitude of *even insinuating* Sutcliffe in a 'funny' book, let alone in a rape scenario, given the grip the Ripper had held for so long over the north of England. Perhaps in there lies the answer? "If they even think it's dangerous," said Larry Welz, "then it is."

The sum of Ghura's solo output in the Eighties would seem to amount to *Truly Amazing Love Stories* No.2. According to one source, a second issue of *Bogey* appeared in 1984, but this has proven impossible to track down. (It strikes this author as unusual that Ghura should return to an earlier, not as good nor as popular a title like *Bogey* when there was *Amazing Love Stories* and *Raw Purple*.) *The Laid-Back Adventures of Suzie and Jonnie*, a Ghura project published in 1981, in a print run of

5,000 remains equally as elusive. *Snow Queen*, 'Startling confessions of a high society dope dealer', a Ghura title announced as forthcoming, did not make it into print.

THIS LAXATIVE OUGHT TO FLUSH THEM OUT

> Well I didn't really think of them in terms of comics, I thought of them as pornography.
>
> Daniel Clowes on the early underground, *Blab!* No.4

Ghura's work is not typical of the British underground. What he was doing with *Truly Amazing Love Stories* was far removed from that of the 'scene' around him. Furthermore, he had talent. While the British comics did nurture some great artists, for every Angus McKie, Brian Bolland or Bryan Talbot there were countless others seemingly grasping for the rudiments of the art... but making it into print, nonetheless. For all their good intentions, providing an open arena in which anyone could participate, underground publishers in Britain would have done well to exercise *some* discretion. Or, perhaps they were only too grateful for any homegrown work, seeing as most all comics openly requested submissions? The problem lay in that, unlike their US counterparts (who were able to draw upon sophisticated drawing styles dating back to newspaper strips at the turn of the century), British artists were often searching for a style they could apply to the medium. The result was either awkwardly contrived or an inferior imitation of US work. As to making so little headway once artists had found their niche, John Sutherland raises the point, in referring to the *Nasty Tales* trial in his book *Offensive Literature* [New Jersey: Barnes & Noble, 1983], that the main reason it was cleared was that, by 1973, its kind of protest was "out of date and irrelevant". Despite times a-changing, many underground artists were locked in a preoccupation with their own counter-cultural lifestyle, increasingly removed from that of the world outside comics. They were the Furry Freak Brothers, but in real life, writing comics for other comic artists. What progress was made in British underground by the likes of *Brainstorm Comix* and *Near Myths* towards the end of the Seventies, was negated come 1980 with the arrival of *Knockabout* No.1. *Knockabout* not only brought a return to reprints of US material, but also a trading of the traditional British comic size for the smaller, more compact American standard. Formerly bookshop owners before changing to distributors and ultimately publishers, Knockabout Comics were subject to a police raid in 1982. Among the 75 book and comic titles seized, primarily drug related, was Ghura's *Truly Amazing Love Stories*. Knockabout changed their policy thereafter. In order to survive they had to conform.

While underground comics in the US might not have attained the glories that artist Jack Jaxon predicted in 1971 – that they would turn the straight comics industry upside down[19] – neither did they cease (like they did in Britain).[20] In France and Italy, however, adult comics weren't relegated to the underground but made it onto most every news-stand in the form of quality graphic magazines (such as *Pilote*), or sleazy little booklets (known as *fumetti per adulti*). A crossover was made when, in 1977, National Lampoon introduced to the US a selection of European comic artists. As might be expected by way of *National Lampoon Presents: French Comics (The Kind Men Like)*, this introduction featured cartoon strips of a frivolous nature. However, its itinerary did stretch to include some salient morsels. A pre-*Heavy Metal* Moebius strip, 'Mom's Apple Pie', is a story about Little Lili whose big biker brother inspires in her strange desires. 'Hellzapoppet' by Buzzelli is a sketchbook of outrageous SM and necrophiliac imagery. In the first Buzzelli spread, a vampire's party sees the guests sucking on the blood of naked (except for sexy lingerie) females: one draws on a tube inserted into the vagina of a victim; others tip their glasses in gore dripping from victims suspended above their heads. A double-page spread has a graveyard in which the widows of the recently deceased wander seemingly oblivious to the madness around them: devils with pitchforks squabble with angels on tombstones; naked women cavort with the dead rising from the ground; Frankenstein's monster lumbers by. The last scenario is that of a homicidal backpacker whose trail down a country lane is littered with the dead and the dying. Girls whose limbs have been hacked off lie by the wayside. Others have their upper torso buried in sacks, their lower halves mutilated with darts. Some bodies hang battered and bloody out of car windows, while others are stacked naked in a heap, a fuse wire burning its way toward them.

Despite shifting attitudes towards sex over the years – some liberalisation and a political correctness – pornography still has the capacity to shock and intimidate. Similarly, comic books given over to depicting the sexual act are no more acceptable today than they were 20 years ago. Certainly more of them are *available* now, but that they are more common doesn't grant that they are generally desirable. Kitchen Sink Press, one of the few original underground publishers to make it through the Eighties – now a 'respectable' company – continue to publish the work of Larry Welz and the occasional sex comic. Specialist outlets and mail order cater for a sex comics market in which porn movies and novels are adapted into comic books (*Debbie Does Dallas*, *The Story of O*, *Fanny Hill*); porn personalities are given their own comic adventures (Annie Sprinkle, Cicciolina, Sarah-Jane Hamilton); and whole publishing houses concentrate on the steamier side of comics reading. Eros Comix in Seattle carry a whole range of material from big-breasted fantasy to explicit hardcore encounters. Their catalogue includes the titles: *Time Wankers*, *Big Top Bondage*, and *Wendy Whitebread: Undercover Slut*. BD Adultes in Paris utilise a variety of internationally renowned artists for their pocket-size edition sex comics. Forbidden Fruit in Minneapolis publish adult 'adventure, fun and fantasy' in the form of Bill Ward's *Scorchy*, Nicola Cuti's *Moon Child* and Vic Martin's *Puntella Primm: The Sexy Superspy*. But neither company can truly be considered as underground – as indeed one must question whether a comics underground exists at all today. Certainly comics are still being produced on a purely fan basis, friends together, and without major collateral, but these are few and far between and they miss the networking of their Seventies counterparts. Likewise, the capacity to break new grounds has diminished.

With noted exceptions, many of the original underground artists still working today, once frowned upon, have turned their hand to dealing with family issues and 'cute' politics. Their work and that of artists appearing daily in syndicated newspaper strips are growing increasingly alike. It cannot be mere coincidence that the most adamantine approximation of the spirit of the underground in recent years is *Screw Comics*, a porn title. The result of a team-up between Al Goldstein and Eros Comix in 1992, *Screw Comics* has George Bush fucking, literally, his fellow Americans while detailing all the famous cocks he's blown (they include Gorbachev's mottled member and a hefty bell-end belonging to Maggie Thatcher); a hardcore lampooning of *Calvin and Hobbes* (which doesn't even bother to change the name of Bill Watterson's original syndicated strip); and Goldstein himself as the unstoppable 'Juden-creature', Adolf Hitler's worse nightmare.

There is a strip Howard Cruse did for *Bizarre Sex* No.4, 'Unfinished Pictures', in which the artist reminisces on the "high-voltage horniness of youth". While most boys have it tough with puberty, 13-year-old artists are fortunate in that they can draw dirty pictures any time they want. This leads to another quandary for the young Cruse, however: The act of drawing *itself* becomes hopelessly stimulating*!* Each time he so much as looks at pencil and paper he ejaculates. With the passing of time the artist manages to overcome the problem. Satisfaction comes now from a job well done and Cruse contemplates going back and finishing those first pictures. Too late*!* When he does go back, he finds he has forgotten what it was he had hoped to draw.

This piece is not intended as a concise roundup of porn titles to have emerged from the underground, but hopefully provides an equitable representation of its more notorious and more obscure artefacts. The underground never came close to overturning the straight comics industry, yet unquestionably was a primary mover in helping to shape it. As to what shaped the underground, credit for the porn comic is long overdue. Lost in the satisfaction of a job well done. Comics have ceased to be driven by the vitality and the innocence which made the underground so stimulating. Now it's a grown-up world; no time for squalid, little, limited print-run comics with pictures of sex in them.

"You dirty little sod," Ghura would say, *"can't you find any girls?"* No, but I came from Alpha Centauri looking for love.

SELECTED BIBLIOGRAPHY

There aren't many books devoted specifically to the study of underground comics. To be exact, three: Mark James Estren's *A History of Underground Comics* [California: Ronin, 1993], Abe Peck's *Uncovering the Sixties: The Life and Times of the Underground Press* [New York: Pantheon, 1985], and Patrick Rosenkrantz and Hugo van Baren's *Artsy Fartsy Funnies* [publisher unknown]. Estren's volume is the only one still readily available, yet, despite its recent reprinting, stops dead at 1974 – the year it was first published. Neither book provides coverage of the 'British scene'. *Kitchen Sink Press: The First 25 Years* [Mass: KSP, 1994] is a colourful and informative insider's perspective on the most successful underground publishing house. Les Daniels' *Comix: A History of Comic Books in America* [London: Wildwood House, 1973] and Reinhold Reitberger & Wolfgang Fuchs' *Comics: Anatomy of a Mass Medium* [London: Studio Vista, 1972], both stand as general histories of the comic book and devote some space to the US underground. The *Illustrated Checklist To Underground Comix: Preliminary Edition*, edited by Robert K. Wiener [Mass: Archival Press Inc., 1979], may prove difficult to track down but is a good indicator of the sheer volume of underground titles to emerge (in the US) since the late-Sixties. The only book that delves into British underground comics to any discernible degree is Roger Sabin's *Adult Comics: An Introduction* [London: Routledge, 1993]. Further information on this dark area was gleaned from a PhD paper by David Huxley, entitled, *The Growth and Development of British Underground and Alternative Comics, 1966–1986*. For more on Dr Fredric Wertham's comic campaign in the Fifties, Martin Barker's *A Haunt of Fears: The Strange History of the British Horror Comics Campaign* [London: Pluto Press, 1984] is also recommended.

KEY TITLES DISCUSSED IN THE TEXT

United States
Bizarre Sex No.1 [Wisconsin: Kitchen Sink, 1972]
Bizarre Sex No.3 [Wisconsin: Kitchen Sink, 1973]

Bizarre Sex No.5 [Wisconsin: Kitchen Sink, 1975]
Cherry Poptart No.1 [California: Last Gasp, 1982]
Cherry Poptart No.2 [California: Last Gasp, 1985]
Demented Pervert No.2 [California: The Print Mint, 1972]
Deviant Slice No.2 [California: The Print Mint, 1973]
Gang Bang! [California: Nuance Inc., 1980]
Incredible Facts o' Life Sex Education Funnies [California: Rip Off Press, 1972]
The Inner City Romance Comic: "Choices" No.1 [California: Last Gasp, 1972]
Inner City Romance No.3 [California: Last Gasp, 1977]
Inner City Romance No.5 [California: Last Gasp, 1978]
National Lampoon Presents: French Comics (The Kind Men Like) [New York: National Lampoon, 1977]
Pork [California: Co-op Press, 1974]
Pure Joy Comix [California: Pooo Bear, 1975]
Snatch Comics No.1 [California: Apex Novelties, 1968]
Snatch Comics No.2 [California: Apex Novelties, 1969]
The Snatch Sampler [California: Keith Green, 1977]
Tales From The Leather Nun [California: Last Gasp, 1973]
Tales of Sex and Death No.2 [California: The Print Mint, 1975]
Wet Satin No.2 [California: Last Gasp, 1978]
White Whore Funnies No.1 [California: Ful-Horne, 1975]
White Whore Funnies No.2 [California: Larry Fuller, 1978]
White Whore Funnies No.3 [California: Inkwell, 1979]
Young Lust No.1 [California: Last Gasp, 1971]
Young Lust No.5 [California: Last Gasp, 1977]
Zap Comix No.4 [California: Apex Novelties/Last Gasp, 1969]

Great Britain
Bogey [The Vicar's Raw Balls, 1975]
Its All Lies No.6 [London: Gemsanders, 1973]
Napalm Kiss, No.2 [Birmingham: Arts Lab Press, 1978]
Nasty Tales No.1 [London: Bloom, 1971]
Raw Purple [Beyond The Edge, 1977]
Sin City [London: H.Bunch, 1973]
The Trials of Nasty Tales [London: H.Bunch/Bloom, 1973]
Truly Amazing Love Stories No.1 [Beyond The Edge, 1977]
Truly Amazing Love Stories No.2 [Antonio A.Ghura, 1983]

NOTES

1. Which is funny because the 1972 Studio Vista edition of *Comics: Anatomy of a Mass Medium*, sports a cover painting by Reitberger himself, in which Superman – surrounded by the likes of Batman, Dick Tracy, and Donald Duck – can be seen about to snip the shorts from a rather anxious-looking Thing, Marvel Comics' stoneman member of The Fantastic Four. Entitled *The Anatomy Lesson of Dr Tulp*, the picture epitomises the attitude, irreverence and – as is sometimes the case – crudeness of style common to many of the underground comics.

2. "In our clinical research on crime comic books we came to the conclusion that crime comic-books are comic books which depict crime, whether the setting is Western, science-fiction, jungle, adventure, or the realm of superman, 'horror' or supernatural beings." *Seduction of the Innocent*, pg 20. Wertham's crusade actually dates back to 1948. Prior to Wertham, in 1940, Sterling North, a writer of children's books, denounced comics in the pages of the *Chicago Daily News* as being "a strain on young eyes and nervous systems". They were an "hypodermic injection of sex and murder", he wrote. J.Edgar Hoover, several years later, declared crime comic books harmful to the "American way of life".

3. Prior to *Seduction of the Innocent*, Wertham compiled the case histories of several

murderers he had examined and treated as psychiatrist, publishing them under the title *Show of Violence*. "The kind of book," Les Daniels notes, "bored psychology students pray for, exciting if not exactly edifying." Similar, from what can be determined, is Wertham's other book *Dark Legends*.

4. Though comic books were read by a proportionate number of adults anyway, they were still regarded as a juvenile medium. (Like they are today.) Unlike other publishers of the day, however, EC often addressed issues they themselves, as adults, felt strongly about and tackled themes they were interested in. Their war comics, for instance, are anti-war.

5. The back page of *Young Lust* No.1 carried an ad for other '... "now" comics for young moderns'. Unfortunately, its itinerary of titles – *Mutant Love, Rape Fantasies, Just Laid, Galactic Romance, Lib Love* and *Queen Diary* – were pure fabrication.

6. *Tales from the Tomb, Weird, Tales of Voodoo, Horror Tales* and *Witches Tales*, according to Martin Barker in his *A Haunt of Fears*.

7. To be more specific, it was Felix Dennis, part of the original *Oz* team, who moved into underground comics publication. Unable to retain the name *Oz* and unable to relaunch the paper as a quarterly journal, Dennis ensured that there was no mistaking the link between his COZMIC COMICS and that influential paper. After comics, Dennis went to achieve phenomenal success with *Kung Fu Monthly* and other personality/ film tie-in poster magazines.

8. Given the detail with which Fountain retraces the newspapers of the day, *Underground*'s coverage of comics is horribly shallow and smacks of some disdain. That and the fact that *Cozmic Comics* is misspelled throughout.

9. *Sin City* carries an announcement for the final, belated issue of *Oz*, 'in the shops on 12th November 1973.'

10. In at least one instance in recent years, the British Library is known to have purchased from a private collection back numbers of several British underground comics. But try to actually locate them or find an employee who can...

11. While many titles belie an EC influence, many others openly ascribe themselves to the EC tradition: *Two Fisted Zombies, Insect Fear, Fantagor, Skull, Slow Death, Deviant Slice, Death Rattle, Dr Wirtham's [sic] Comix & Stories*, are to name but a few. Greg Irons and Tom Veitch are involved in many of them, so too Richard Corben.

12. The concept reappeared in *Hot Box*, a short-lived British comic whose first issue (published in 1986) carried a 'rape strip' and garnered much negative feedback because of it. Here, three men attack a girl with intent to rape. His conscience suddenly getting the better of him, one man turns on his buddies, kills them, only to then be stabbed himself by the girl.

13. The copy of *Gang Bang!* this author procured in the early-Eighties is obviously a pirate. The biggest give-away is the cover: a horribly murky combination of black, white and greys – exactly what you'd expect from a monochrome lift of a colour original.

14. In 1973, the Disney Studios took to court the underground title *Mickey Mouse Meets The Air Pirates Funnies* for portraying in its pages a pot-smoking, sexually active Mickey Mouse. Accused of "defiling Mickey's innocent delightfulness", the cartoonists – a group of young artists from Seattle headed by Dan O'Neill and calling themselves the Air Pirates – found themselves stung in excess of a million dollars.

15. So popular in fact that 'America's top teenager' has a whole gamut of interrelated titles. These include: *Archie Comics, Laugh Comics, Archie's Girls Betty and Veronica, Josie and the Pussycats, Archie's Pals 'n' Gals, L'il Jinx*, and *Archie's Pal Jughead*. Apart from the comics, Archie has had his own animated TV series, a radio show, and range of merchandise.

16. Then again, even in the equable study, *Comics: An Illustrated History* [London: Green

Wood, 1991] authors Alan and Laurel Clark have Archie's pal Jughead down as a misogynist. And in the 1973 *Zap Comix* trial, there was some discussion on *Archie* comics arousing the sexual interest of its teenage readers.

17. A reasonable quantity. Print runs for small press endeavours of the time tended to be around the 1,000 mark, but could be as low as 60 units. Knockabout, a proper company, would be printing in the region of 10,000 per title. Bryan Talbot, with *Brainstorm Comix* No.1, hit 14,000. But such high quantities were exceptional.

18. A typical example is Matthews' story 'Slutrot' for *Napalm Kiss* No.2 (1978). When a young man by the name of Colin Wilston [sic] turns up to assist the old alchemist Marlin, he finds himself the focus of the ancient one's voluptuous wife. Before too long she and Colin are scheming against Marlin. "He has me under his spell!" she tells her new love. "I can never leave him whilst he lives!" That night, Colin murders Marlin. The spell over the girl is broken, but as a result Colin finds himself having sex with a stinking, rotten, living corpse. *"Hhhckolllinn!!! Sssstay withhh meeeeeee!!!"* it cries, legs wrapped around his waist.

19. Jaxon's 'Comics Or Comix?' appeared in a small press publication by the name of *Infinity* in 1971. It was reprinted in *Blab!* No.4 in 1989, with a follow-up piece by Jaxon lamenting on the little change the underground has actually brought about in almost 20 years.

20. The only small press title to have ever made any headway in Britain – not itself definable as 'underground' – is *Viz*. The first issue was published in 1979 with a print run of 150. By the late-Eighties, with backing from Virgin, sales were in excess of 500,000. *Viz* is an adult variant on the likes of the *Beano* and the *Dandy*, in as much as it mimics their style but subverts the traditional children's comic with toilet humour and coarse language. It has spawned many imitations. Most outrageous of these is *Top Banana* whose issue No.5 carries 'Ad Land', a curious diatribe on the legalities of sodomy (or, "Rogering your Missus up the bottom" as the strip has it). Elsewhere is 'Rudebear', a take-off of the popular children's character Rupert Bear (most contentious in the *Oz* trial was the strip that juxtaposed Rupert with Crumb), and 'Herpés Adventures of Tinker'. While some retail outlets fail to differentiate between these adult comics and children's books, it is worth noting that *Oink!*, a genuine kids title, flopped when outlets came to associate it with *Viz*. Any attempt at an adult comic with adult themes – such as *Pssst!* in 1982 – seems doomed to failure.

WHEN YOU KNOW WHAT GUYS LIKE
Alternative Viewpoints on the Masculine Sexual Role

A Miscellany of Correspondence to Various Porn Magazines, Pt I

DEAREST: C——— A——,
I am a white male, who's been a Slave/servent since the age of 10yrs., Old and made to dress like a female and do what my Mother, and sisters, order me to, know matter what it is they went to do.

Or be wip, or spank, till I am black and blue, and at all times I must, Be dress in women's Bra's, pantie's, pantiehose, Blouse and dress. And makeup*!*

As a slave, my job is to do the cooking, cleaning, washing clothes, And any thing us they order me to do, to there satisfaction.

Also I must wait on all guest, and see that they are kept happy, And have what they need Food, drank's, anything*!* even Sex. (Oral) You, see most of my mom's and older Sister's friends are gay like my Mother and all my sisters.

my mother raise all my sisters up to be gay, cause she hats men. Because she, was rape by a man, who is my father, who I never met. In a way I am glad I never met him and I don't went too because, Of all the hell I went throught cause of him.

Some-times I wish I was born as a female, because I love so much, Dressing up in womens clothes, That I just cum in my panties before I even get finish putting every-thing on.

Maybe my mom and sisters are right that I will be better off being a woman, then a man. Some-times my mom and sisters take me shopping with them, to buy new clothes and they make me try the new clothes on in the womens dressing room. Last week I try on some new bra's, body-shapers, panties, slips, Garter-belts, and corsets, Dresses, blouses, and slacks, womens-shoes...

You might be wondering why iam writing and telling you this*!*

Like me, my mother, wents so much to have (Oral-Sex) with you because she loves your body so much that she plays with her-self till climax. why, she think's of you. she also says that only a woman knows how to please another woman. Not a one inch wimp like me. So I made a deal with her because for a year my Mother has been wenting me to get a sex-change into a Woman, so I told her I will, cause I went too not only make her happy but to make me happy as well, cause I Love dressing up as a woman. and went so much to be a real woman, so we agree that you will make the Decidion for Us.

The reason. We would like you to make the desideion is because my mom knows how much I went to be a slave/servent to you no matter what*!!!* As your slave/servent I will do anything that you order me to do. At any time no matter what to your amazing satisfaction or you may punish me any way you see fit.

As your slave/servent All work by me will be Free of charge, at all times.

Thats if you deside to let me be your slave/servent if you dont I will understant and I wont be up set, and I still want you to make the desideion.

Here's how the desideion will be made on my Sex-change as follows*!*

ONE–If you send us just a old bra of yours*!* I get a SEX-Change from the waist up. TWO–If you send us just a old pair of panties, I get a SEX-CHANGE from the waist down, BUT IF YOU SEND THE FOLLOWING THINGS I MUST GET A FULL SEX-CHANGE

1#–USED OLD BODY-BRIEFER

2#–USED OLD TEDDY

3#–OLD FULL SLIP

4#–OLD PAIR OF LEOTARDS

ALL ITEMS MUST BE SIGN BY YOU SO WE KNOW THEY ARE FROM YOU*!* IF AT ANY TIME, YOU DO NOT WENT ME AS YOUR SLAVE/SERVENT, YOU WILL STILL OWN ME FOR ONE YEAR AND MAY ORDER ME TO BE A SLAVE-SERVENT TO ANY FEMALE YOU WISH ME TO SERVE, YOU CAN ALSO HAVE MY MOTHER AS SEX-SLAVE FOR ONE MONTH IF YOU ARE GAME TO IT*!* SHE WILL DO ANY-THING YOU WENT HER TO DO TO YOUR SATISFACTION.

TILL I HEAR FROM YOU*!* KEEP COOL, STAY SEXEY,

WE LOVE YOU ALWAYS

J——— A——— C—— (son)
B———— M—— C—— (mother)

Dear Sirs,

I'm a changed man, mentally I've accepted the female thought of performing good head for men. I only do men, they are now my reality and women are my fantasy. I've had several experiences with men, I just love cock and the sperm that I've eaten in the past has only made me more willing to become a female in body as well as in mind. I bought ——— magazine and I masturbated for some of the pictures.

I also collect social security benefits. I'm 44 years of age, 6'2" in length and thin to medium build. The main reason I'm writing you is I'm ready to become a woman physically, but I don't have much money. I've heard that it's a very expensive operation etc, plus hormone injections. Please help me if you can and I'd pose for pictures, give good head, fucks, etc.

D——— T———

PS: I will also do pornography videos as well. Once again please help me become a woman and I'll work for you for free.

Dear ———,

I want to tell you that you are not an "all-action" magazine do to the fact that you do not have any male bi-sexual stories. Which I feel is just as hot as the female bi-sexual stories. I am writing to tell you this because I have seen ads. on top of your magazine saying that you are an "all-action" magazine. Now don't get me wronge, I love your magazine. In fact it is the only one I buy.

To tell you a little about myself. I am a 25 year old male. Who has never had a bi-sexual experience. But, I do rent and own videos of it. I have fantasys of sucking cock. And beat off constantly to the thought of haveing sex with a man. I think the best would be fucking pussy while sucking my dick or getting fucked up the ass while fucking pussy, or any other combo. And I think I would blow my biggest wad when the guy cums on my balls or down my throght. (I've tasted my own cum and loved it!)

Another thing I do is shave my cock & balls and put in a video and get out a huge container of lube and a dilldo grease up my ass and fuck myself blind. It feels so good that I cum and cum. Some times I cum so much that it squirts on and in my mouth. Some day I would like to experiance the real thing, but I'm afrade I would be found out and my life would be over. So I thought I'd write you in hopes that you would do a bi-sexual pictorial or something. It might even bost your sales.

Dear Editor,

I think ———— is a fantastic magazine, but for not the reasons most of your readers buy it monthly. I am a 28-year-old male and for many years I have longed to be sexually a woman. That is to be fucked as a woman and feel being fucked as those women in ———— feel.

Am I blowing your mind? I often dress myself in a similar way to the women in your magazine. I wear nylons, garter-belts bras and high heels (I know a store where you can get large size shoes) wigs and make-up and pull my cock back between my legs so it is like I have a cunt instead of a cock. Then I amuse myself with games that use a variety of dildoes and other toys like putting a dildoe in my ass when I lie on all fours on the bed and pretend I am getting fucked in the ass by one of the studs in your magazine. Wearing femenine lingerie makes it all the better when I put a mirror in front of me so I can see myself being a slut and getting it in the ass.

This turns me on. It is sometimes hard to come with my dick between my legs when it is hard. I can have it in the ass for a long time before I come. I imagine my sperm is cunt-juice which goes into the panties I am wearing. I imagine the sensation to be very much like the women feel when they are getting fucked by your studs.

Other times I beat off on to a dildoe and then lick the sperm off of it like it was a cock. I get close to the mirror when I do this and it looks real and like you see in films when stud's come on her face. I find that very exciting and can do this for hours at a time without stopping.

I hope you print my letter. I am very happy just reading ———— magazine and have had many succesful female relationships but what I really want is to be fucked as a woman.

Yours,

C.F., Phoenix

Dear Sir:

I am a married male in my twenties, and never thought I would be writing a sexual fantasy letter to a porno magazine. Your magazine is probably the best dirty book on the shelves today. The colors, the layouts, the almost-sex on every page makes me start dripping pre-ejaculatory juice (PEJ). I especially like the graphic depictions of blow jobs, without actually showing penetration, it leaves more up to the imagination. These layouts are the fuel for my fantasies.

Like I said, I am married, but I have a weakness– I love to give head to big dicks. I don't consider myself gay, maybe bi, but I don't have any romantic or emotional attractions to men. The only part of their body I like is their penis. As a man I know what men like, they want to be able to pursue intellectual interests, hang out with other guys, drink beer, and whenever they get a raging hard-on, they want a mouth to relieve it. Most men say they would only take it from a female, but I would be willing to bet that any mouth would do if given the right circumstances. Think about it men: a mouth that's willing to take your log into its orifice, roll its tongue around your head, slide up and down on your shaft (particularly that little place on the underside of your dick just below the head), and let you blast your cum down its throat! All that and not interrupt your good book, your pool game, or have to worry about being romantic, or buying flowers. What difference does it make its a female mouth or a male mouth? None to me. I like to give a nice clean BJ so the guy doesn't have to go back into the office with wet stains on his pants, or still dripping cum in his underwear.

Now don't get me wrong, I feel we have entered a new era with AIDS, but there are ways to overcum that problem. If didn't know a guy like me and he wanted me to suck his cock, all I would require is that he abstain from ANY sexual contact for three months, then go to the Health Department, get an HIV test and bring me the results. If he got a clean bill of health I'd suck him on the spot. However, there is a life-long friend of mine who I suck off every chance I get. Let me tell you about it and see if this doesn't sound like an ideal set up for men.

My friend has had a steady girl friend for about five years and she is really devoted to him, and my wife to me. We both like having relationships with our females. Whenever I go over to his place, though, I always hope his girlfriend isn't there. We usually sit around for a while and catch up on times, smoke, and maybe have a beer. Invariably, I always ask him if he has any new porno movies or magazines, this usually is the clue. He always wears these sweat pants that make his dick bulge in the front. It spurs me on to see it sticking out there and needing to be sucked. Most times I wait until the movie or magazine is at a blow job scene (usually the first one we cum to), then I'll say, "That's what I want to do," or "You want that don't you?" A chuckle of confirmation. I ask him if he wants to do it in any particular position or chair. The last time this happened he wanted to do it naked on the bed. He quickly took off those tight sweat pants and already had a stiff boner. Keep in mind I was only there about 30 minutes by this time– he doesn't have to do any long drawn-out foreplay, or say the right things, or do anything. Men just want some mouth to show up and suck their dick. We got onto his waterbed and began to suck each other, slowly licking up and down on each other's dicks. I don't get to do this often so I was enjoying it, however, it was uncomfortable. So I said,

"Can I offer a kinky suggestion?"

He said, "Sure."

So I got off the bed and on my knees on the floor and asked him to stand in front of me. I told him to shove it in and out of my mouth like he was fucking some pussy and I would be still. As he did this I jacked myself off. I always do the sucking– he would suck me but men don't want to suck, they want to be sucked. This went on forever, but I was so turned on I found myself wanting to bob up and down his shaft. I wanted him to work up a heavy cum load so it would fill my mouth. I wanted him to feel ecstacy with no committment. Harder and harder, I bobbed, he fucked. Occasionally I would get choked on his big cock, but hey, occupational hazard. His PEJ was oozing down my throat mixed with my saliva. Several times I would pull back, lick him all around, get us both cleaned up, and resume bobbing and letting myself be fucked in the mouth like all men want to do to somebody. Finally, I couldn't take it any more, so I got a hand in the action around his thick shaft, and this got him worked up. He exploded his great-tasting (less-filling), hot, sticky cum in my burning hot mouth. I know I felt three solid jolts of cum hit me in the very back of my mouth, which was gagging, but hey... what the hell, men hate to pull out. These gobs of goup were sliding down my throat like raw oysters. He just kept shooting and shooting, and I took it all. By this time I had my lips tightly around his midshaft and was bobbing and jacking with my left hand, trying to contain the eruption in my mouth. My right hand was busy working up a wad for myself. I had laid out a towel on his carpet below me so I wouldn't get my jizz all over his floor. As he was getting toward the end of his orgasm, I shot my wad all over the towel. I could have sucked another ten guys at that point.

Now the big question, do I shallow? I don't mind loads of cum shooting and streaming down my throat, it cums with the job, but intentionally drinking every drop? Up until this latest blow/mouth fuck job I hadn't, but that attitude is changing. I did drink a different friend of mine's once when we were teenagers. The next time I suck my friend (or any male who's willing to put aside gender hangups, and who is clean), I'm going to drink it as they cum, I'm going to swallow each time their dick flexes with a spurt. Men want somebody to do this to, believe me I'm one of them.

Do I do other things like take it in the ass? The situation and person would have to be on my own terms, and even then with a rubber, but I never have.

How about two guys at once? For blow jobs, abso-fucking-lutely. I've never tried it but I would. Two dicks so thick and long that they can put them both in my mouth and cum at the same time. That would be a lot of jizz to swallow.

How big would I go? You name it, but I do get gaged. I would make sure to treat every inch of it though. A big dick deserves to have a mouth around it all the time to relieve those hard-ons.

Blow jobs in public places? Yes, but its got to be clean. I have a fantasy, and I know men would love to be able to do this, of my friend walking up to a hole in the stall door and putting his hard, bulging cock through and me bobbing on it 'til he shoots his wad. Then he just leaves while I jack off.

In conclusion, I would like to say that men should learn to enjoy a suck job from other men, and take it for what it's worth. We could sit around and do men things– like darts, pool, work on cars, suck each other off– then go home to the wives. Giving a big, rock-solid, raging, throbbing, shapely, clean, smooth, AIDS-free, dick a complete from A-Z blow job makes my marriage all that more exciting.

Signed,

Happily married

Publisher–Please do not publish my name, address, or other real information.

HITTING BELOW THE BELT
Sex, Pain and Gender

Simon Whitechapel

EOPLE SOMETIMES COMPLAIN ABOUT SEX and violence being so often linked, as though the two things were equally bad or equally damaging to immature minds or equally disgusting to all right-thinking people. Because, of course, they aren't. Sex is good, violence is bad. Violent sex is good too, if there's consent; sexual violence, when there isn't, is bad. Sex and violence do not go together like fish and chips or black and blue or dumb and bimbo.

True enough – for some people. False for plenty of others. For plenty of people, sex and violence do go together, always have and perhaps always will. But very few people have had the courage or the perversity to claim openly that this is a good thing. Sexual pleasure from the suffering of other people good? Rape good? Sexual torture good? The Marquis de Sade said so, and the Marquis de Sade went to prison for it.

But he isn't, perhaps, the supreme advocate of sexual freedom for the strong at the expense of the weak that he seems. In his works he was fantasizing, seeking stronger and stronger stimuli for his jaded sense of the forbidden, and whether he would have been capable of carrying out what he drew up minutely detailed instruction manuals for isn't at all certain. Suggestive bones were once found at one of his country houses, but there was never any evidence that he had had anything to do with their appearance there.[1] On the other hand, evidence of a humanitarian side to his nature is definite. During the Revolution, after he secured release from imprisonment, he "served on a commission which recommended humanitarian reforms in the hospitals of the capital" and he "was horrified by the September massacres of 1792".[2] He did not take the opportunity to have his revenge on his mother-in-law, whose scheming had been largely responsible for his prolonged stay in prison, when a simple denunciation of her as an *aristo* would very likely have brought her to the guillotine. A conceivable, if doubtful, reading of his character is that he was a sensitive man who overcame his horror at the evil and suffering of the world by teaching himself to take pleasure from them rather than pain. If evil is inevitable, impossible to prevent, learn to see it as good. Under this reading, de Sade is a kind of perverted Benthamite. The greatest happiness for the greatest number can only be a greatest happiness for a Sadean few.

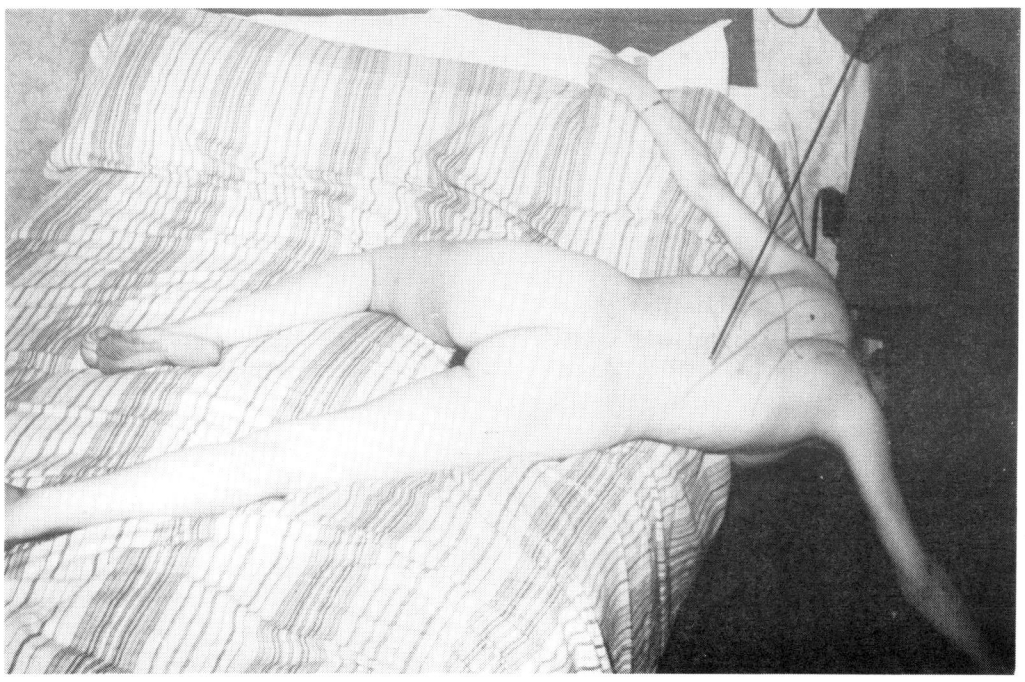

However he arrived at the formula, de Sade certainly believed in it, as a pornographic fantasy at least. One of the clearest expressions of it in his work is the sex-slave camp overseen by four libertine monks in his *Justine, or the Misfortunes of Virtue*.[3] *Justine* is a deeply anti-romantic work. The heroine escapes madman after madman, always seeking to do good, always seeking to resist temptation, and always suffering pain and sexual abuse because of it. At one point she arrives at a woodland shrine to the Virgin Mary to offer up thanks for her latest escape, and falls into the hands of four monks who have imprisoned dozens of beautiful aristocratic women in escape-proof dungeons. The penises she has encountered during her misadventures have been growing steadily bigger, and she is buggered by the biggest so far, which belongs to the chief monk, then vaginally raped by another monk, then forced to defecate into the mouth of a third. Then she watches the torture of her fellow captives. A pregnant woman is forced to balance one-legged on a narrow platform above a heaping of thorns; she falls off the platform, is whipped mercilessly, then ejaculated on.

The horrors continue in similar vein during the remainder of Justine's imprisonment. Each of her adventures so far has involved her listening to long lectures from her abusers justifying such things as anal intercourse, child-murder, and rape; after he has lashed blood from her buttocks, breasts and genitals with a whip, one of the monks delivers yet another, and Justine manages to forget the pain of her wounds sufficiently to put forward counter-arguments that are contemptuously swept aside by the monk. The monk then falls asleep and she continues her discussion of her prison with the woman who has shared her whipping, learning more of the "retirement" into which one by one the sex-slaves are forced. This is one of the few subtle touches in the book. We never learn precisely what "retirement" is, other than that it involves a departure from the sex-slave quarters. Each sex-slave forced into it has promised her comrades that she will do all in her power to escape and have them rescued when she is in the outside world, but none ever has. Almost certainly, "retirement" means death, and death in some peculiarly horrible fashion. The excesses of the monks with those they wish to preserve for further rape and torture are very great, and their sexual stamina is enormous. What do they do that carries sex beyond the point of death, and leaves them exhausted for a day afterwards?

Justine, of course, does not find out. Although hundreds of women have passed through the monks' hands and none has ever managed to escape, when de Sade finds it necessary to set her on her way to yet more misadventures and yet bigger penises she escapes with relative ease. The motif of the sex-slave camp is repeated later in the book when she is imprisoned by a coin-forger who owns a remote mountain castle and keeps women in kennels when he is not whipping them, buggering them, or using them to power his machinery.

Justine is an absurd book, but then it was certainly meant to be by de Sade. It's a satire on and complete inversion of the virtue-rewarded, vice-punished novel of his era. Nonetheless it presents the arguments for sexual violence very clearly. Men and women should pursue their own pleasure at any cost, and the greatest pleasures are found in the sexual torture and exploitation of the weak. One cannot always be certain of being able to give pleasure to one's sexual partner, but one can always be certain of being able to give pain. A reluctant orifice is preferable to a compliant: it will be tighter, hotter, and give a greater sense of achievement to the one who penetrates it. De Sade goes further and creates a metaphysic of sexual violence and selfishness: he does not recognise a more-than-human God, but he does recognise a more-than-human Nature. Those who conduct their lives according to Her principles of violence and creation-in-destruction are rewarded in abundance. Those who, like Justine, refuse to do so will suffer nothing but pain.

But Justine is also pornography and like most pornography it isn't realistic. The four libertine monks have raped and tortured their way through hundreds of beautiful women. In reality, given the strenuousness of their sexual demands, it would be thousands. The victims in Justine recover from their beatings and rapes almost as readily as the anti-heroes from their orgasms, and are always ready to present milk-white buttocks and almost-virginal orifices for fresh outrages. In reality they would be scarred physically for years, if not for life. Justine herself endures day after day of anal rape and whippings, escapes, endures day after day of anal rape and blood-letting, escapes, endures day after day of anal rape and near strangulation. By the end of the book, she is still beautiful, still youthful, still faithful to Good. In reality, she would be prematurely aged and at least half insane.[4]

In reality, so too perhaps would be some of the book's anti-heroes. One of de Sade's most devout disciples in this century has been the Moors Murderer Ian Brady. Brady now is half-insane, but this fact probably has little to do directly with his crimes. He is half-insane because of his imprisonment.[5] He undoubtedly gained great pleasure from his crimes and undoubtedly would have gone on to commit and gain great pleasure from more if he had not been caught. He can still be used as indirect evidence for the potential dangers of de Sade's philosophy for the active practitioner, however. Brady's crimes were on a limited scale. He had to plan them carefully and conceal them carefully. They were difficult, and because they were difficult they were more enjoyable. But what if Brady had been able, like the anti-heroes of Justine, to indulge his sexual tastes more or less at will?

An example of what might then have happened is provided by the Second World War. Brady, like many people with his sexual tastes, was fascinated by the Nazis. In 1941, the Nazis launched Operation Barbarossa, the invasion of the USSR. As Soviet territory was overrun, huge numbers of people were deliberately and systematically killed by special extermination squads called the *Einsatzgruppen*. Members of the Einsatzgruppen took great delight in their work, which involved such things as the machine-gunning of entire villages lined up in front of graves that the villagers themselves had just been forced to dig. However, it's reported that as time went by attitudes amongst the Einsatzgruppen changed, and there were suicides from remorse. Significantly, the remorse is said to have been caused by the fact that they had been murdering women and children. As the editor of *Gory Comix* pointed out inelegantly but insightfully in *Headpress* 4,

> ... violence against men originates from an entirely different spectrum
> of human interactions (property dispute) than violence to women (sex).[6]

Violence against men was and still is backed up by millennia of tradition. Wars have always been fought by men against men: for the most part women and children suffered only indirectly, if not necessarily to a smaller extent, through the economic and demographic after-effects of battles in which men practised fatal violence against each other. When men killed not only other men but also women and children, the justification provided by a dozen years of Nazi ideology and the personal pleasure they experienced in their task were not strong enough. One might imagine one will take pleasure in something, and consciously want to do it, but there are sometimes forces in the mind stronger than anything that appears in the conscious. In this way, then, the disciple of de Sade who achieves the Sadean paradise – limitless sexual power over limitless victims – may risk madness. Einsatzgruppen members

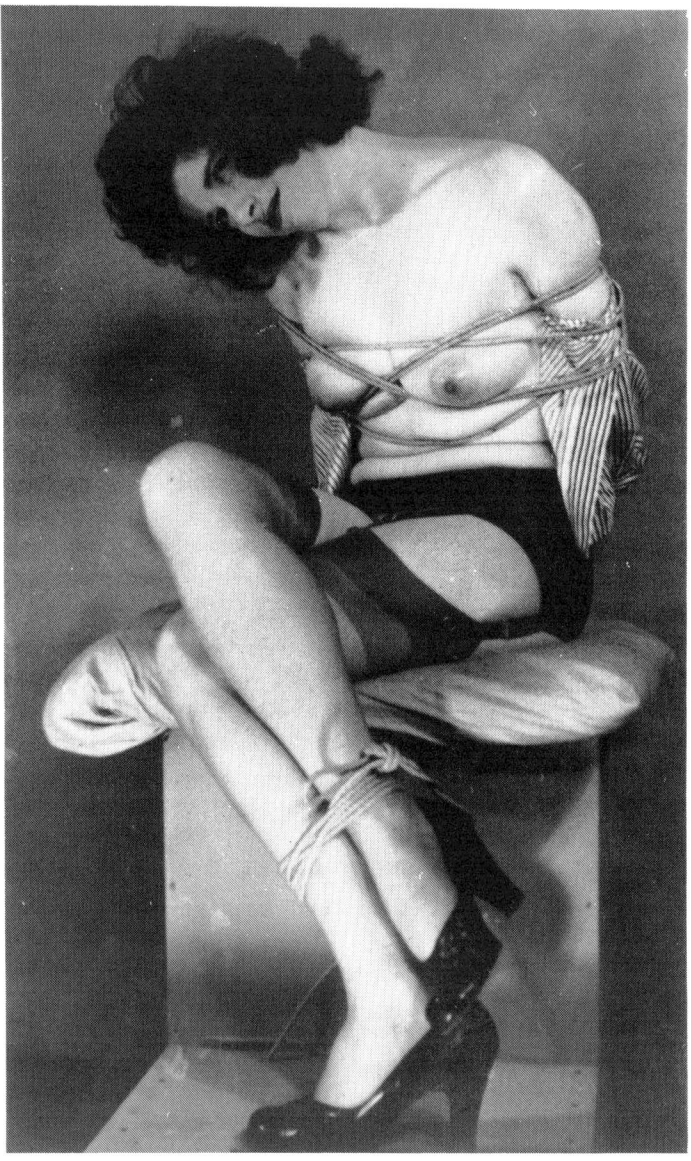

committed suicide because they weren't really conditioned to kill women and children, whatever they may have felt consciously.

It's true that in the Second World War military activity on both sides expanded to involve civilians, men, women and children, but it's significant that the killing carried out by "respectable" Allied and German agencies was second-hand. An individual Lancaster or B-17 or Heinkel 111 bomber crew might have been responsible for many more deaths in far more painful ways than an Einsatzgrup section, but a bomber crew did not see the faces of those they were responsible for killing, and didn't suffer the psychological consequences – as long as they were able to keep their imaginations under control:

> You drop a load of bombs and if you're cursed with any imagination at
> all, you have a least one quick horrid glimpse of a child lying in bed
> with a whole ton of masonry tumbling down on top of him; or a three-
> year-old girl wailing for *Mutter... Mutter...* because she has been burned.
> Then you have to turn away from the picture if you intend to retain
> your sanity.[7]

By some definitions, the bombing of some Axis cities in the Second World War was
a war crime on an enormous scale, but the Axis didn't win the War and those
responsible neither regarded themselves nor were regarded by others as war
criminals. This question of responsibility and motive is very important, at least to the
perpetrator, though to the victim it makes very little difference. Compare, for example,
the horrific fictional sex-tableaux of de Sade's *120 Days of Sodom* with what
happened to those seeking to escape from the fire-storm caused by the conventional
bombing of Tokyo on March 10th, 1945:

> [t]housands submerged themselves in stagnant, foul-smelling canals with
> their mouths just above the surface, but many died from smoke-
> inhalation, anoxia, or carbon monoxide poisoning, or were submerged
> by masses of people who tumbled in on top of them, or boiled to death
> when the fire-storm heated the water.[8]

If those responsible for these things had been able to see and take pleasure in what
they did, perhaps their psychological health would have been in danger just as that
of the Einsatzgruppen was in their far more limited but far more affecting – because
face-to-face – massacres of civilians.

Further illustrations can be drawn from World War Two and the history of the
Nazi extermination machine. Ivan Demjanjuk was a very small part of this, but his
crimes were almost uniquely revolting ones. His job was to conduct Jews into the
giant gas-chamber of the Treblinka *Vernichtungslager*, or extermination camp, and
then oversee the clearing of the corpses after the gassing had taken effect. The
testimony of the very few prisoner-workers who survived the camp was that he used
to delight in maltreating those queuing for the gas-chamber, whipping them or
slashing them with a knife – which could involve slicing off the nipples of women.
One small girl, by a millions-to-one-against chance, is reported to have survived the
gassing process and emerged, screaming with fear and covered in faeces, from the
gas-chamber exit. Demjanjuk reportedly ordered one of the male Jewish workers who
removed the corpses to rape the girl. The worker was unable to, so Demjanjuk beat
her to death with a shovel and sent her body off to the burial pits.[9] Paradoxically or
not, the same regime that had ensured its citizens were unable to obtain de Sade's
works had enabled some of the same citizens to enact de Sade's fantasies of sex
and murder in reality.

But was Demjanjuk an ultra-intelligent ultimate sensualist, wringing every last
synapse's-worth of pleasure from his powers of life and death over thousands, tens
of thousands, *hundreds* of thousands of naked victims? No. According to the same
testimony of the prisoner-workers, he spent most of his time drunk, and he was drunk
when he carried out his attacks on the prisoners queuing for the gas-chamber. He
needed to lower his inhibitions and deaden his senses in order to do what he did.[10]
He was not an intelligent man. On the contrary, he was brutal and stupid. Undoubtedly
he enjoyed what he did, but he didn't enjoy it in the clear-eyed, philosophically

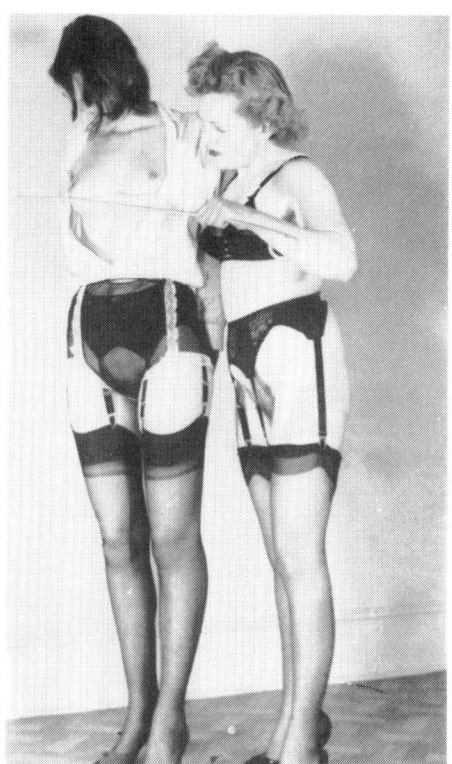

rationalized fashion of the Sadean anti-hero. He was given the power and he used it and he enjoyed using it, but he had to drink heavily to do so.[11]

And he also, perhaps, had to be brought up as a Catholic. The responsibility borne by the Catholic Church for the Holocaust has never been recognized to the necessary extent. *All* the highest Nazis were brought up as Catholics, as were half or more of those who actually worked in or ran the concentration camps. According to Gitta Sereny's biography of Ernst Stangl,[12] the commandant of Treblinka (and an Austrian Catholic), the Pope during the Second World War, Pius XII, did as little as he did to protest about the Nazi extermination programme because it was aimed at Jews and civilians from the communist and Orthodox Christian East, to which the Catholic Church was hostile. For hundreds of years the Church had justified and encouraged anti-Semitism, and when the Nazis based their politics on it and went on to practise what they and the Church had preached, the Church did very little about it.

But then the Church had also, in the past, practised what it preached. The Crusades, intended to wrest the Holy Land from the enemies of Christ abroad, often started off with attacks on the enemies of Christ at home. The enemies of Christ at home were, of course, the Jews. The claims made by present-day Christians about Satanic Ritual Abuse are the direct descendants of claims made in the Middle Ages about ritual murder by the Jews, who were said to cut the throats of Christian children and drain off their blood into vats for mixing into matzos, the unleavened bread biscuits eaten during Passover. This kind of anti-Semitic libel even entered Catholic hagiography:

Hugh (Little) (St) M.   Aug. 18

d. 1255 A boy of Lincoln, aged nine, who was said to have been put to death by Jews. Henry III conducted the judicial investigations which unfortunately resulted in eighteen Jews being hanged for the crime. Little Hugh is shown as a boy bound with cords, often kneeling before Our Lady. This feast is not now kept, being an example of popular anti-semitism rather than the result of individual sanctity.[13]

The lack of evidence for such stories, then just as now, did not stop mob hysteria, and there were executions and massacres of Jews all over Europe. That these involved such sex acts as rape is at least possible, but those who recorded them would doubtless not have mentioned such shameful features. In those days a Christian could feel proud of having killed a member of the race that murdered Christ, but not of having had sex with him or her.

The same hysteria and refusal to allow the facts to get in the way of a good prejudice were seen in the Witch Crazes, and here there was an openly sexual element. Two of the most important strands in the history of Christianity have been anti-Semitism and misogyny: the Witch Crazes were among the greatest manifestations of the latter. They began in the 14th Century, when the Church began to accuse people, very largely women but also some men, of making pacts with the Devil for the power to be able to fly, make animals barren, and curdle milk. Various theories have been advanced as to what caused them: some historians say that the accusations of devil-worship were entirely unfounded, others that they reflected a final death-struggle between Christianity and an ancient folk-religion that had survived underground after Christianity's political triumph toward the end of Roman rule. However they are explained, the Crazes were undeniably misogynistic, and the scope they offered for the exercise of sadistic sexual power in the name of purity and truth was very great. A manual on the detection and interrogation of witches was published by two Catholic monks in 1489. It was called the *Malleus Maleficarum*, which can be translated into English as the *Hammer of Evil-Doers*. Something's lost in this translation, however: the Latin word "maleficarum" means specifically *female* evil-doers. According to the book women are sex-crazed, very easily corrupted by Satan, and very dangerous to men. When they have sold their souls to Satan, they are capable of any enormity. One story told by the monks was that of a witch who kidnapped the penises of men in her district and kept them hidden in a box up a tree. When she was found out and the box was opened, she was asked who one particularly large penis belonged to, and said that it was the local priest's.

It is not very likely this was meant as a joke. *Malleus Maleficarum* saw many editions and the fact that it was written by Catholics did not stop its being used by Protestants in the following century as guidance in their persecutions. One recognised sign of Satanic affiliation at the time was the possession somewhere on the body of a supernumerary teat, with which a witch was thought to feed her diabolic familiars. This might be a genuine extra nipple, which is a well-documented if rare medical phenomenon, or simply a mole or oversized wart. It also seems likely that some women were convicted of witchcraft for possession of a "supernumerary teat" in their private parts – in other words, for possession of a clitoris. Men who had remained ignorant of the female body because nakedness and sexual pleasure were sinful made such startling discoveries because the gang strip-searching of women was not merely acceptable but even holy when carried out in Jesus' name as part of the

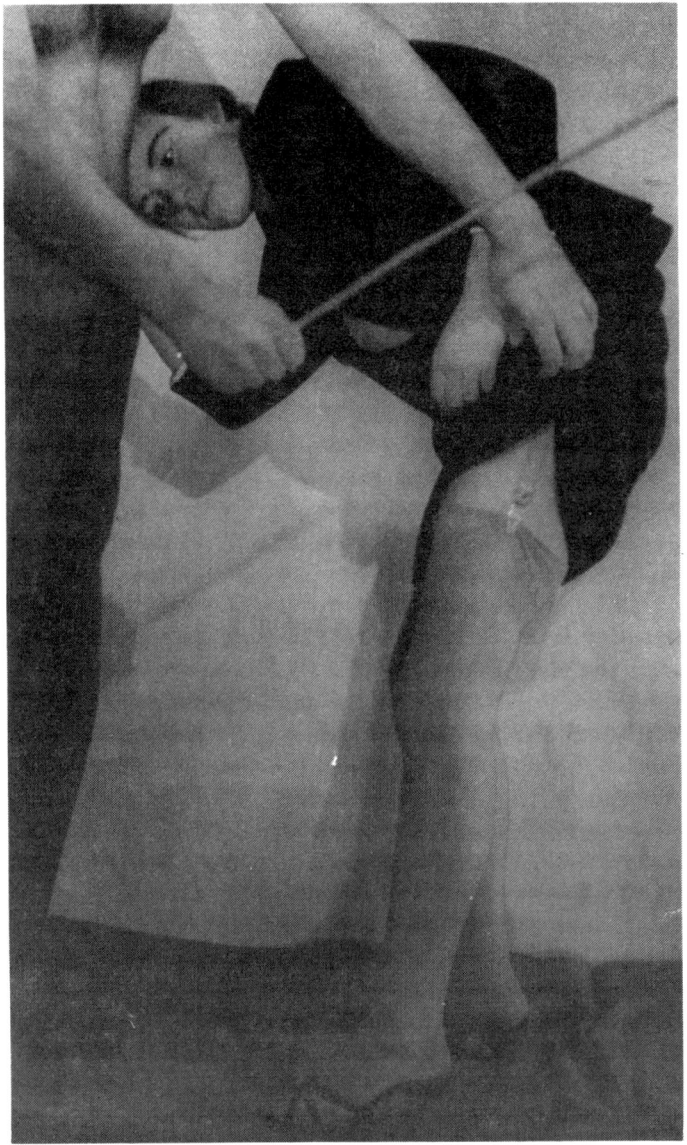

battle against Satan. And strip-searching may not have been the full extent of men's power. According to Barbara G. Walker's *Women's Encyclopedia of Myths & Secrets*, in some areas it was possible for any respectable male to visit a woman imprisoned under accusation of witchcraft and "interview" her in private.[14]

The picture painted by this claim – of a state that rounds up and imprisons young women in thick-walled stone cells for any male to visit and rape – is typically Sadean.[15] Again there's the apparent paradox of a system under which de Sade's theories of sex could not be recognised, actually creating opportunities for their practical application. In the name of goodness, women were stripped naked, flogged, roasted, branded, racked, had limbs broken, joints dislocated, fingers and toes crushed, and were finally burnt alive. This was a Sadean paradise created by a religion for which de Sade felt the deepest contempt and hatred.

This certainly *seems* paradoxical. De Sade was an extreme advocate of the rights of the individual, yet an individual is only likely to be given an opportunity to follow the Sadean life-style under an authoritarian, anti-individualistic system like Roman Catholicism or Nazism – or Stalinism. Stalin's head of secret police was Lavrenti Pavlovich Beria (1899–1953), a man who had very cruel sexual tastes, and more than enough power to indulge them. Horrifying as the stories that circulated during his life-time were,[16] they may have reflected only part of the truth: excavations in the cellar of his former house in Moscow are said to have uncovered several female skeletons. The citizens of Stalin's police state might not have had the remotest opportunity of reading de Sade's descriptions of extreme sexual violence, but if they were young, female and nubile, they might have had the opportunity of experiencing their literal enactment.

The same is true of many, perhaps most or even all authoritarian systems. On signing his first death-warrant, the Emperor Nero is said to have expressed sorrow that he had ever learnt to write. In time he came not only accept such power but to rejoice in it and be so inventive with it that he has established himself as an archetypical sexual despot – he was, after all, one of de Sade's greatest heroes. The possession of power is in fact too little regarded as a factor in morality. The question is often not whether people are capable, but whether they are able. If the Nazis had invaded and conquered the United Kingdom, they would undoubtedly have found recruits to help them run their concentration and extermination camp system, as they found recruits to a greater or lesser extent everywhere in occupied Europe. If you were born in Europe, you could become actually guilty of war-crimes; if you were in the UK, only potentially. It's obvious that many of the members of today's Conservative Government would be very happy to serve or exercise power in a totalitarian system: witness, for example, the arse-licking they gave to Saddam Hussein in the days when profit could be made from him, and the support still given by certain of them to the mass-murderers of Indonesia.[17] The same is undoubtedly true, though nowadays probably to a lesser extent, of many Labour politicians. In reality and on a more general level, the fact that sexual violence is directed overwhelmingly by men against women reflects the power balance between the sexes. Men are physically more powerful than women, and through most of history have been financially and socially more powerful as well.

Or is it quite so simple as that? Perhaps it is. But this is not to deny that women are also capable of sexual violence, because they very certainly are. It's likely that cases of sexual violence perpetrated by women against other women and against children and men are largely under-reported. Society doesn't expect women to be violent or to be sexually predatory, and it even less expects them to be sexually violent, and what is not expected is very often ignored or overlooked. Some feminists in fact deny completely the possibility that women could, for example, be involved in the sexual abuse of children: for them, this is very decidedly a man's job. But women can and do abuse, and women can and do carry out rape. Battered "wives" are not always in heterosexual relationships; reporting, at least, of them is rare, but there are instances of lesbian gang rapes in all-female institutions like military training colleges, prisons and schools.[18]

And female sexual violence seems likely to become more widespread as more women gain power and begin to explore the opportunities power gives them. Even this seemingly ultra-modern development was anticipated by de Sade, at length in

Juliette, more concisely in his unlikely-ever-to-be-fully-performed play *Philosophy in the Boudoir*, which describes a young woman who is introduced to the Sadean catechism by a wealthy libertine called Dolmancé. In less than a day she is converted from conventional morality to a position of such extreme sexual libertarianism that she is able to take great pleasure in raping her own mother with a dildo. She then supervises her mother's vaginal and anal rape by a syphilitic manservant, and the sewing-up with thick thread of her mother's anus and vagina to ensure that his semen infects her.

Psychologically, in so far as any of de Sade's characters are credible, she is credible. She has hated her mother before she is introduced to Sadism, and when her mother is in her power after the introduction, she applies Sadean precepts in full measure. Similarly, one would expect some of the women who accept feminist ideas about such things as patriarchal oppression and men's inherent wickedness, and who achieve power over men, to exercise their power in sexually violent ways.

Rumblings of this are already heard in the Western *kulturkampf*. In 1991 a woman called Helen Zahavi had a book called *Dirty Weekend* published. It is "The story of Bella, who woke up one morning and realised that she'd had enough".[19] What she has had enough of is being sexually victimized by men. First she takes a hammer to the skull of a man who has been threatening her with rape. Next she suffocates a lecturer called Norman with a polythene bag after he has hit her for laughing at his failure to achieve an erection. Next she rams a dentist's Mercedes into the legs of the dentist, who is urinating against a car-park wall after forcing her to fellate him. Next she shoots dead three Clockwork-Orangean young men, who have cornered and stripped and readied for incineration an old bag-lady. Finally, beneath a pier on Brighton Beach, she turns the tables on a Geordie serial killer by stabbing him to death before he can strangle her.

Dirty Weekend isn't a very well written book, but it is in places surprisingly (and intentionally) funny. It would be interesting to know whether Zahavi had ever read *Justine*, because *Dirty Weekend* reads very much like it in some ways. The female protagonist in each book only has to meet a man for her to be sexually abused or threatened by him, but whereas de Sade's heroine has to grimace and bear it, Zahavi's grimaces and then kills the man. In neither book is this constant stream of encounters with sexual madmen credible, and *Dirty Weekend* is in its own way just as much as a wish-fulfilment fantasy as *Justine*. However, where de Sade's fantasies centre on sexual violence against women, particularly where this involves anal rape, Zahavi's centre on the violent death of men. The problem is that, though doubtless intended to be, the violence in *Dirty Weekend* isn't very shocking. There's a simple reason for this: violence against men isn't a shocking thing. On the contrary, it's a perfectly familiar and acceptable thing. Entire genres of literature and film are based on it. 'Sports' like boxing and American football exploit it and earn billions of pounds every year from it perfectly legally. As already mentioned, millennia of military tradition sanction it. Reading about men's skulls being cracked, faces smashed, legs broken and livers punctured isn't shocking. Reading about women's skulls being cracked, faces smashed, legs broken and livers punctured would be, as I think I've probably just demonstrated.

Inadvertently, then, Zahavi may have made an additional point quite different from the point she was trying to make. However, her book might well have become as shocking as she intended it to be if the scenes of violence in the book had not simply been preceded by sex, but had actually incorporated them. A woman castrating her way through an assortment of males or anally raping them with a strap-on dildo, or both, might have had some of the shock-value attributed to the book in the hype that accompanied its appearance, because *sexual* violence against men isn't a familiar part of our culture. Subconsciously, Zahavi may be hinting at this more disturbing sex-with-violence. She talks about penis-envy only once in the book: as Bella stands on a hotel balcony listening to the sexual boasts of three yobs walking

> beneath her, she experienced, for the first time in her life, a stab of purest penis-envy. She knew... a willy would indeed have been wonderful. For she was unable, anatomically incapable of, expressing herself in the way that she wished.

Which was to piss on the yobs. However, penis-envy may be more of a motif than the book openly admits. One man is killed with a hammer, one with a Mercedes, one with a knife, three with a gun. All these men were either sexually threatening to Bella or had actually sexually abused her, and all the weapons could be seen as substitute phalluses. The man killed by being suffocated with a polythene bag, which isn't a substitute phallus, was impotent. In other words, he wasn't a sexual threat. Unlike the others, he doesn't threaten rape and so, unlike the others, he doesn't have to be 'raped' to death in return.

On the back cover of *Dirty Weekend*, feminist sex-kitten Andrea Dworkin is recorded as having said of the book

> Poor Martin Amis, poor D.M.Thomas. The game's over, boys – literary terrorism and the fun on the streets. Will the "objective" reviewers appreciate Helen Zahavi's mordant wit, her hair-trigger timing of her comedic narrative, her steady, calm, trenchant narrative? No, but you will. Read it. It's good – it may even be beautiful – and it's true.

It would be necessary to read the full review to reach a final conclusion, but it looks very much as though Dworkin distinctly likes the idea of women dishing out to men what men have always traditionally dished out to women. Well, you can't really blame her. It's been pretty obvious for a long time that people like her are less concerned about the abuse of power than about the fact that it's not them abusing it. As for me, I'll predict that an alliance between radical pro-censorship feminists, fundamentalist Christians and fundamentalist Muslims will be sweeping all before it by early in the coming century. They'll ban and they'll burn, and perhaps they won't do the latter just to books, but they won't alter the simple fact that regimes that do what the Marquis de Sade approved of do not approve of the Marquis de Sade. Sexual violence is probably here to stay, and the more authoritarian the state, the more likely it is to flourish in its grossest forms. But just try telling that to Andrea Dworkin and her sisters. They'll rip your balls out.

NOTES

1. As even Robert del Quiaro's hostile *The Marquis de Sade: A Biography & A Note of Hope* [Messidor, 1994] has to admit.

2. Pgs xiii-xiv of the introduction to *The Misfortunes of Virtue and other Early Tales*, trans. David Coward, OUP, Oxford, 1992. See also *Marquis de Sade: A Biography*, Maurice Lever, trans. Arthur Goldhammer.

3. A greatly expanded and pornographified version of *The Misfortunes of Virtue*.

4. And very badly anally incontinent. One of the Hillside Stranglers' victims, who was subjected to a real-life Sadean regime of buggery, had to keep a tampon permanently in her anus.

5. De Sade himself died imprisoned in a lunatic asylum at Charenton. Unlike Brady, however, he remained sane to the end.

6. pg 42.

7. The words of an American air-force officer quoted on pg 63 of *Wings of Judgment: American Bombing during World War Two*, Ronald Schaffer, OUP, New York, 1985.

8. Op. cit., pg 134.

9. I suspect that some of the worst stories about individual acts of brutality and sadism in the concentration and extermination camps are exaggerated or even apocryphal: this may be amongst them. Saying this, though, I bear in mind first the certainty that some of the worst things that happened were never recorded, and second a remark made by Robert Jay Lifton in his *The Nazi Doctors: A Study in the Psychology of Evil*. In expressing doubts about some Auschwitz horror stories, Lifton points out that the moral nihilism of the camp was such that anything was regarded as possible, and so anything was credible.

10. See *Ivan the Terrible: The Trial of John Demjanjuk*, by Tom Teicholz.

11. See the wider discussion of the role of alcohol in violent sex-crime in Brian Masters' *Killing for Company*.

12. *Into that Darkness*, Gitta Sereny, London, 1974.

13. *The Book of Saints: A Dictionary of the Servants of God canonized by the Catholic Church*, compiled by the Benedictine monks of St Augustine's Abbey Ramsgate, A.C. & Black, London, 1989. The delicate hypocrisy of that "popular anti-semitism" is almost beautiful, but mention should be made of another St Hugh (1140–1200), a Bishop of Lincoln who "died, aged sixty, lamented by all, especially by the Jews, whom he had always defended and befriended." (ibid.)

14. This book is very entertaining to read on the subject of Christianity, toward which it takes a jocularly hostile line, but I'm not sure how historically reliable it is.

15. See, for example, the manifesto included in his *Philosophy in the Boudoir*. Rape-factories that exist in reality, as in the American prison system, have understandably attracted less attention and condemnation from feminists and their allies than de Sade's fictions.

16. A flavour of these is provided by the anecdote of a ballerina who rejected Beria's advances and was then sent flowers by him. On her saying thank-you-but-the-answer-is-still-no she was told that they weren't intended as a second invitation but as a wreath for her funeral. But see note 9 above

17. Our would-be Führer John Tyndall, leader of the British National Party, recognises this fact in his autobiography-cum-manifesto *The Eleventh Hour*, in which he says that part of the hatred he feels for the Tory party is founded in the fact that it siphons off potential fascist recruits.

18. For a wider discussion of female violence of all kinds, with plenty of gruesome case-histories, see Alix Kirsta's *Deadlier than the Male: Violence and Aggression in Women*, HarperCollins, London, 1994.

19. The opening line of *Dirty Weekend* by Helen Zahavi, Macmillan, London, 1991.

DREAMS JUST DREAMS ARE
The Libido and Morale of the Incarcerated

A Miscellany of Correspondence to Various Porn Magazines, Pt II

DEAR SIR
First of all as you already know for the address on the envelope I am writing from the F——— S—— P—— in which I am reclused since 1988. I am a black Latino (from Colombia) and what you may call a real sex fiend. I've been really hot about those babes in your magazine though before I come to prison I didn't bother myself on buy a magazine (there were the real thing plus videos) but few months after being encarselated I started getting on loan (from fellow inmates) a few publications such as ———, —— and of course the best one —— magazine which I began enjoying without buying any one. Well sir the thing is that the delightfulness of joy of reading your mag and seem all these wonderful and incredible very beautiful and senxual girls (I can't believe there are so many fantastic women al over this country and how do you guys find them so easy) are all them professional models or dancer do they show up in night clubs around the country or in their locations? Of one thing I am sure no everyone of them is a porno starlet. Well, coming back to the point – the enjoyment of your mag has managed to raise my temperature all these years and also give me a little trouble due to the facts that every time I remember those babes featured in your mag I began rubbing my little nine and a half inch piece of meat of love no matter where I was and don't giving a damn who were around. So then the female staff (officers) started writing me disciplinary reports on profane acts and when that happened – me being a rebellious bastard and nasty pervert just improve the damn filthy behavior and started going right at fifty feet from under the gun towers occupaid by female officers and right in front of her withdraw my 44 mannung special and started shooting at her do you believed me? Jerking my pole off in front of a lady officer. Well sir these acts which I did repeated several times in three years in this camp (my initial institution) gain me besides several disciplinary actions even getting a few beatings from security staff members the lost of a hell of a lotta gain time which enlarged my prison time for about three more years and transfer to a maximum security camp and close management status, the nicknames of Billy the Kid, Jacky-Jacky and Gun Slinger the best and wild one in the West. Well sir the true is that by now I am not proud of this anyhow so don't get me wrong I am neither blaming your publication for none of my disgrace it was all

stuff of my own ill-mind. Anyway sir the punishment I've received teached me that I gotta kept my mind together and clean my acts that what I was doing by being a horny filthy macho Latino but I've come to realized that in my actual sircustancia and situation all sexual practice must be forbidden and that in any other sircustance public masturbation is an obscene and profane act; and that if I be catch in the act I could be santione; so though it give me a hell of a thrilled and fun it does not worth the price of more prison time. Well lately I've thrilled only by ———— magazine it's totally constant pleasure and happiness month after month to the point that I've made the effort of buy me three issues for $4.00 a piece from this dude that got a full year subscription of ————, ———— and ———— and do let me check them often. I know I ought to buy me a subscription and you may think it is a better choice but my economic situation do not permit it to be. I did already spend $12.00 but I can't spend $50.00. Well the issues I choose are the ones I myself considered the better even though all of them are pretty good.

I've bought first Holiday 1993. Damn if it ain't got me going on there is where I first see a little flick of the great black beauty C———— laying on the bed holding those monumental lucious tits that look like two chocolate pie with a grapefruit on top of each one waiting to be licked sucked and nibbled, then that angelical face with a perfect nose beatiful eyebrows a very kissable mouth as her whole body is she gotta the fines skin I've ever seem color and texture well anything more that I could say about this god-dess would be unnecessary for anyone who bough the Holiday 1993 issued of ———— or any other one in which she appeared and what I would do to her is by luck one day I had the blessing of have her I only gotta say she is a chocolate bombon a sweet candy from head to toe a divine nectar for Gods in olimpus and that the way she should be treated. Then there is that baby name of S———— Oh man she is so fine so pretty with that round ass long legs firm tits with bite hard nipples pointing to the sky beautiful blue eyes very senxual mouth that tell wonderful tales say something 'bout her pussy? Man it looks like a Big McD hamburger waiting to be eated and eated good. Man let me tell you what that's the kind of my dream girl. If I was to make love to her I tell you that I don't really know where to start but everything will come naturally and if she wanna hear my fantasy she just gotta let me know. So well sirs is about time to finish this long letter but before so I got to tell you that I really love to make love to D————, E———— and J– I really got one for each of them now keep me dreaming in the very end dreams just dreams are and I did never heard that dreaming was a sin. At the end I got a little suggestion; it's as follow why don't you start an amateur photo contest like they got in ———— and ———— this way you could show the world that there are millions of beautiful women in our country not just the professionals and I bet you anything that there are thousands of women begging for an opportunity to show up in ———— mag and many many husbands and boyfriends wanting to show other people what they felt they owned because they are proud of what they are enjoying at home and want to share a little bit of enjoyment because they are not selfish because they get thrille by that kind of situation or just because they want the prize. Well many men and women also be delighted if you set aside couples pages for pen-pal service, just like you got the sizzling hot personals that is maneuvered by phone it's a lot more economic write a letter and buy a 25¢ stamp and this way you are doing something really good for your customer here in prison. I believed there are many horny women and men who want to communicate with their peers throughout a friendly conversations printed in paper. Well sir I would like to talk a little bit more about the beauties featured in your Holiday 93 and July 94 which are the issues that I've actually acquired. Specially about that baby A——— in June 94, T—— same issue; S——, A———, B—— etc. And in the July 94 you guys almost killed me with that Goddess A—— C——— man she's so fantastic with that innocence looks yes she looks like a little school goer teenager girl and at the same time exotic, exuberant, mysterious and savage beauty and senxuality that that made just the right contrast with the continent for which she was named and a real perfect contrast with the landscape where she was photographed she is actually my fantasy girl, the woman of my dreams. Well sir I hope you continue you good job and may God bless America, women and ——— mag.

WD

PS: I may be writing you again real soon.

Full thanks and appreciation goes out to you for your efforts to continue bringing these lovely ladies together in your magazines. The enclosed letter is for one of those special ladies in the April-May double issue: S———.

Your problem finding someone to satisfy your every need to have your cunt licked is understandable, but it's something I personally take great pride in. Everyone can't do it, it's an act that takes a lot of practice. I often had trouble finding a woman who can appreciate it or stand it.

I once had to pay for a headboard to be remounted to the wall of a New York hotel room. I lived there for about seven years after I was discharged from the Marine Corp.

I'm going to sit here and describe a scene that you may be able to appreciate.

We take a hot shower together. Afterward, I'd carry you to the bedroom and rub you down with hot oil, your shoulders and arms, then your stomach, massaging the oil into your pert breasts, gently squeezing you nipples then briefly bending down and kissing your beautiful lips. Then turning you on your stomach I'd straddle you, kneeling, and massage the warm oil into your neck, shoulders and back, just to relieve the tension of a long day.

Sliding down between your slender legs, still kneeling, I'd squirt the oil on your ass, making sure a few drops find their way between the outer lips of your pussy, then knead the oil into your cheeks with my large strong hands. Now rolling you onto your back, I would massage your thighs with the same strength only gentler, one at a time, being very careful to get as close as possible without touching your thick juicy pussy lips.

Now kissing, licking and nibbling my way from your knee to your hot cunt along the inside of your thigh, I'd spread your luscious lips apart only far enough to have your swollen clit poke out at me, flicking at it with my tongue, gently sucking it between my teeth, nibbling and licking at it. Then, taking your lips into my mouth, sucking at them in an attempt to eat you alive, then licking the length of your pussy up and down, occasionally going past the boundaries of your pussy to lick your g-spot, then to thrust my tongue into your love-hole, probing as deep as possible to lick all the juice flowing from your soaked pussy, again finding your clit, licking and sucking it, squeezing your nipples between my fingers, you holding my head in place and rolling your hips as wave after wave of bone shattering climaxes come over you.

S———, the rest is fundamental. I hope you would be very pleased, out of your time, or both.

I was only concerned because I've always figured if I can't please a woman then I don't deserve to be pleased.

Dear ——— magazine,

Would it please you to know that its only because of ——— magazine I can make it through the days here? I am G——— and I have been in prison since 1988 after I killed a man in a fight in Detroit. I have no idea when I will be paroled and the time here is very hard sometimes. Last week a man died through a fight in the head and we were locked down for two days. Thank god I had the copy of ——— magazine!

It is very hard here because of sex. When I was free I was a man who loved nothing better than having sex with a woman and women were always there for me when I needed it. Because I have a big cock I was always crazy to get laid and the women I had sex with liked it very much on account of my size. Here the only sex is with your hand or with a queer. I have done this out of need but only head because you can always imagine it is a woman when your getting head. Some guys get fucked or raped but that scene isnt for me. I feel bad for some of them but in prison theres very little else to satisfy so I would say it happens just about every day. But thanks to your mag I can handle it without needing to be a fag!

I liked C——— plenty in your June issue and got off looking at her pictures a whole lot. D——— and H——— were hot too and I would really like to have sex with them.

"Pantysniffer"

fantasies

my fantasie is to have sex with two weman I would like to see them fuck each other untill I cant take it anymore the I would like to have one set on my face while Im eating her pussy the other one sucking my dick then when she about to come she set on my dick while I like the other ones pussy and just fuck them over and over all in the ass, mouth, and pussy.

#2 I all ways wonted to get in a sex book or a movie making hot sex with some of the sexey weman I see in theas books

#3 Ive all ways wonted to woman to rite me a talk about fucking me to teth when I get out of jail I can do theas things to her and I would like pitcher of her in all kinds of poses

What I wont from you

#1 I wont to know hoe I could get in one of your books and maby one or mor movies This have ben my dream

#2 I wont to know if one of your workers could make my fantasie #3 come true or mor then one

#3 Could you send me anything to keep me going this little time like something from a woman

What you need to know about me

Im 21 years old all most 22
I get out of jail in about 9 months
Im 5/9 178 pounds
Brown eyes, Brown skin, Small wast, Very hairy, Medium chest
Body parts N/medium lenth 8½

Dear Sir:

I would like to take a lil time out to try and explain the situation, sorry for my sloppy writing and misspelled words I don't have much of a education but I try my best. Now I am doing a lil time in a state prison & I don't have much access to your magazine in here due to new laws & such in prisons so when I came across a fellow convict who was selling a december '94' issue I bought it for a can of tobacco and let me tell you it was a good buy.

I looked through the pages quickly at first in my cell, then I let my cellie take a peek & gander at it. He was about due to go to work so I had the cell & all your beautiful women to pass my time by. And I sat on my toliet shorts down to my ankles & my lil bottle of vaseline body lotion next to my feet. I started to go through the pages slowly as my 7½ cock started to get hard as a piece of penitentary steel when I saw C——— on page 58 to 63 I had to squirt a lil lotion on my hard cock and slowly work it up and down very slow. I didn't want to shoot my load of nut juice so quick.

The way her lips are all puffy and wet & moist looking made my mouth start to water and the way it's all shaved and clean when she is on all fours I just had to slide my hand faster up & down the whole length of my cock I was ready to shoot my load but I stopped my movements on my throbbing cock.

But all the while my mind was on page 61 with her nice firm ass in the air I would love to just sit there behind her with my face between those cheeks I wouldn't want to leave I would suck that pussy & ass hole til she begged me to stop. And when I turned the page and saw her with her legs up spreading those pretty pink lips I just had to grab my cock with a lil more lotion and once again sliding my hand up to the

swollen head and give a lil twist of my hand then all the way back down for a few minutes then it was count time so I stopped put my shorts back up cleaned my hands & cock with a wet cloth.

About 10 minutes passed and so did the officer on the tier so back to my seat put some fresh new lotion on my cock it was soft at first so I had to work it a lil. I have to get my cock hard when it's soft so it didn't take so long to get back into the swing of things again I could just imagine C——— on her knees and elbows with me stark nakid with my hard on in hand rubbing it up & down her slit getting it all wet and ready for me. I would slide it all the way in til my nuts hit lips slowly at first I would pull all the way out then put the head in & pull it out then I would do real short quick thrusts then when she wasn't expecting it I would shove it all in real hard.

And all the while I'm wishing I could do you like that I'm slamming my fist up & down up twist down then it hit me all of a sudden I could feel my nuts tingling about ready to cum & cum hard so I picture me pulling my cock out and sliding up that tight hairless asshole all the way to the nuts and cumming all up in there all the while your ass hole tightens & loosens in quick spasms.

And at that moment I start to release my heavy load of nut juice all in the toilet spurt after spurt of thick white gobs of cum & now that is my situation. But I'm due to get out in Feb 95 so I can make up for some lost time. I would like to know if I can get a response or an address to write to where I will get a letter in return a nice nasty one so I can jack off to it.

If you would print this I hope you could fix my errors in writing & don't use my real name use Scrooge.

Much thanks and respect.

Mr C.B.

sign the letter San Quentin Scrooge

Dear ———: My greatest fantasy is to get fucked one of your models Get suck in cabin in the middle of the winter in a place where no one has ever heard of. I want to get stranded in this cabin with only one room with only one bed. And I wish it was so cold that we had to fuck night and day just to keep warm. But every night we would have some fun with it. She will suck my dick and I would tie her up to the bed post and lick her pussy and suck her Tits and when I really want to be mean, I will fuck her up the ass so hard that she will start to cry of so much pain. And when she don't want to fuck for a while then she can just suck my big dick till she chokes, or I will suck her pussy. And when she is ready again I will fuck her so hard that she will be screaming "stop, stop, please it hurts" but I won't I'll just fuck her harder and harder till she is so much in pain that she do anything to stop.

CABIN HOUSE MASSACHUSETTS

Dear C———

I was looking through the Sept issue and I saw your picture and you have a beautiful pussy. My problem is this. My wife's little sister stayed with us for a week befor I went to prison., when her sister stayed for the week she got out of the shower one night wrapped in a very little towel and got on the couch to relaxe, I jumped in the shower and when I was finished I was dressed in shorts but as I walked out her sister had her leg on the back of the couch to where I could see her pussy and then she said, Do you see something you want, I dident know what to say, at that moment, she said she has been watching my wife and I have sex. She told me that she has never seen a cock as big as mine but in a magazine for I have 9 inches for a love muscle very thick.

Her sister is 15 years old and I'm 27 and she shows her pussy everytime my wife turns her back and that makes my dick hard all the time because I love the natural look and aroma of pussy, one night my wife cought her with her pussy open to me. shit hit the fan if you know what I mean. Her little sister told her that she was watching us for a few nights haveing sex that no has ever eaten her pussy and she wants me to be the first for she is a virgin, my wife told her that no man has the same size and that she could not handle me. her sister asked her to let us try and my wife said no way because she would get hurt because of my size. C———— I want to eat her virgin pussy because I havent had a virgin in ten years when I met my wife when she was young. My wife is 24 now we have been together since we first met 10 years ago. I would love to eat my wife's pussy it has only my smell from me only. No other man has ever had or ever will get the pleasure of my wife. She is faithful to me and I have been the same to her, every place we go, girl's, and women staire at me because of the bludge in my tight jeans like she wants to show me off to the world. when we go to the beach I cant go to the bar to get a drink for us alone because of what I have between my legs, you can hear the ladies talk about me and how much they would like the chance to get me in bed.

This happens everyplace and I dont know what to do. If you were my wife what would you do let me fuck your sister – or tell her to keep her virgin hand's off. It took a long time for my wife to get use to me. I dont like to brag about but I was gifted and there is nothing I can do about it. Being well endowed has it's problems so would you write me and tell me what I should do, if you could send me a autographed picture of your self in the position you would want me to enter your love canal or tell me witch one to enter first, for I am starving for sex and I need a woman now or two of the best life can give, you wont be disappointed if I ever got ahold of you I would love to eat you until you cum all over my face and then we would really get started for pussy cum is my energy for real love making, how many hours can you go, I bet you will quit befor I do. just ask my wife gotta go but not for long be good or be good at it.

Love you in prison

J. T.

P.s. please write me and let me know what I should do and send <u>a picture</u>

To ———— mag

The cunts in ———— are the hottest. I got a copy a week ago and had a great time jacking off and blasting hot wads of cum over each and every one of those whores. J—— has to be the best in the mag. She is one mighty fine whore that I would dearly love to screw in her tight little butt. I have fisted my dick to each of her pictures and cum on every one. J——'s look tells me that is what she wants and the way that she holds apart her butt to proudly display her tight puckered shit hole is saying to every man to screw her in the ass and pound her hot butt until shit cums out of her mouth. She is ONE HOT WHORE*!!!*

I have always loved to fuck whores. They don't give a man any bullshit or headgames. They just take the money and fuck like a whore should. When I was making big money in Florida I could have a whore every night and I knew if I paid them right they would let me screw them in the butt as hard as I liked. Whores do anything for money. I wonder how much $ you pay the ones in ——— mag. Do you fuck them after you take the pictures? Just thinking of that has gotten me thinking nasty. I would jack off onto J——— again if the mag wasn't already caked with my wad from the times I have jerked over that whore's tight ass and hot cunt. Right now I am midway thru 10 yrs of time and all I have to do is think of whores like I used to have and the ones in mags like ———. I lay on my cot and fantasize about screwing them in their tight hot butts and hearing them wimper and cry out as my hard dick forces all the way into their shit hole. Screwing whores in the ass is THE BEST. I love it when it hurts them and they beg me to stop. I never do and just screw them harder. That way whores know who is the boss and they can't do shit about it. I love seeing what whores will do for money. In Tampa there was this guy I knew who ran 4 whores all were junkies and when one whore got him mad one time he had her fetch her fetch over her 17 yr old sister who got screwed in the ass by three of us while the whore licked her innocent teenaged snatch. That teenager had a raw ass afterward you can be sure of it. That's why I like ——— mag Your whores always look young and fresh. Thats the way I like my meat. If they have never gotten screwed in the ass before that's even better. When I see a girl mag I always like to fantasize it is me who gets to screw their juicy shit hole the first and make them scream as I bust their innocent virgin butts. I have many hot fantasies but one of my favorites is when I meet a teenaged hitch hiker who looks like a high school cheerleader on her way back from practice. She is juicy young and pretty hair in pony tail and I look at her sweet teenaged tits under a sweater and her fresh white legs and it makes my dick get hard as an iron bar. She sees this and it makes her hot as she has never seen a dick as big as this before. She asks me what I do with my big hard dick. I tell her I screw whores with it. By this point she has unzipped my pants and is slowly stroking my huge dick. I want to screw this innocent teenager bad so we drive somewhere quiet then I tell her to take my big fucking dick in her mouth. This she does and as I fuck her pretty mouth I look at her tight firm teenaged ass and know I am going to screw it. My dick is so big it chokes her but she likes sucking men's dicks so much she can't stop. I know I am going to shoot my wad and tell her she is going to eat all my sperm. With my hands either side of her head she can't break free and I force my dick all the way in her mouth and blast my wad deep in her throat. She has to swallow it all. Now I tell her she is going to get screwed in the ass. She leans up against the car hood and I pull apart the cheeks of her innocent virgin ass. I spit on her tight butt shit hole and then force my dick inside. She cries out in pain as I get into that tight puckered hole but no one hears and there is nothing she can do. I fuck her shit as hard as I can and deep in that teenaged butt. It is so tight and hot I love it and pound away as hard as I can. All the time she is begging me to stop but now she knows what its like to get screwed in the ass by a real man. In time I fire the biggest wad I have ever done right inside her ass and then make her lick my dirty dick clean. I give her $50 for being such a good teenage whore and she suggests I meet her mom. Her mom is ripe for screwing in the ass as well and by the end of the night mom and daughter are my whores and have left their old man and are living with me. They cook and clean for me and their tight hot butts are mine for fucking any time I want.

I would like for you to send me pictures of your whores, prefferably them showing their butt holes to me. I am sending you this fantasy free of charge on the condition you send me some hot pictures of J——— and her sweet young ass.

Yours Sincerely,

L. T.

MR PUNCH: SEX-KILLER PUPPET
Traditional Sadean Atrocities for Children

David Slater

ARE THE BIZARRE AND VIOLENT ANTICS of the timeless Punch and Judy shows really suitable for children? Is Mr Punch himself as harmless as Rupert Bear or Peter Pan? Or is he a homicidal misogamist, more akin to Gilles de Rais than the aforementioned children's characters?

In essence, the basic story could have been conceived by no less a deviant than de Sade. Numerous murders, including infanticide, various sexual innuendoes, and a final satanic twist are intrinsic elements in this atavistic tale of a lecherous assassin.

The first recorded script was penned in 1827 and it derived from Giovanni Piccini's show which he touted around the London streets. Over the decades, the story has evolved and mutated to the whims and desires of individual puppeteers, but the same fundamental theme has stayed throughout. Characters have appeared and disappeared and others have slowly metamorphosed. For instance, it seems that the Devil has evolved into the contemporary crocodile familiar to most people today. However, despite such acute alterations, Punch's voice is something that has remained unchanged. A frightening falsetto buzz pitched to make you hear even if you don't listen.

Piccini's version runs as follows.

Punch introduces himself to the audience, then calls his wife. Instead of Judy appearing, a dog named Toby trots on stage and attacks Punch, biting his nose. Punch beats the dog off and summons its owner, Scaramouche, who promptly enters carrying a slap-stick. He wants to know what Punch has been doing to his dog. Punch ignores the query and asks about the stick he holds. Scaramouche explains it is a fiddle. Punch asks if he may play the fiddle and, on taking the stick, he beats Scaramouche to death. He dances and sings in ecstasy until Judy arrives. He takes her in his arms and attempts to kiss her, but receives a slap in the face instead. He asks her to bring their child which she obediently does. Judy then leaves father and offspring together.

Punch plays with the baby in a violent manner, and when it begins to cry he murders it. Judy returns and sees what he has done, but Punch comments that they could quite easily have another. Judy takes the stick and attacks him, but he snatches the weapon back and beats her to death too. He disposes of the bodies and Pretty

Polly arrives. They dance and cavort in each others arms then leave the stage.

At this point a mysterious character appears and begins to sing. He removes his hat and his neck elongates, eventually shrinking back to his shoulders before departing.

Punch returns and wishes to pay another visit to Polly. He mounts his horse but is soon thrown to the ground, injured. He summons the doctor who promptly examines him. "Where does it hurt?" he inquires with his hand on Punch's head. "Lower," insists Punch. The doctor touches his belly. "Lower," says Punch again. He touches his legs. "Higher," Punch demands. The doctor fetches the stick to beat him, but again Punch wrestles it from him and murders him.

Now he entertains himself with a bell and a black servant arrives to complain about the noise. They argue and a fight ensues, culminating in the death of the servant. "Is that the kind of music you like?" Punch shouts at the battered corpse.

A blind beggar knocks at the door requesting a donation. Punch refuses alms and the beggar accidentally sneezes in his face. Punch kills him. A policeman arrives and accuses Punch of the murder of Scaramouche. Punch thumps him to the ground. Another policeman turns up and charges him with the murders of his wife and child. He too is knocked senseless. Jack Ketch, the hangman, arrives and accuses him of killing the doctor. They fight, but the two officers recover and Punch is restrained and taken to jail. Punch is in a cell sliding his nose between the bars. Jack Ketch is erecting a gibbet, and two men arrive with a coffin. Ketch leads Punch to the scaffold. Punch thrusts his head to one side of the noose. "The other side," says Ketch. Punch places his head on the other side. "Like this?" he asks. "No, like this," demonstrates Ketch, placing his head in the noose. Punch quickly yanks the rope and strangles him. He places the corpse in the coffin and hides. The bearers come in and take the box away. Punch dances and sings, claiming even the Devil cannot scare him now. The Devil appears and advances on Punch. They fight, and the show concludes with Punch raising the dead Devil on his stick.

Physiognomy reveals much about Punch's character. His physical attributes have hardly altered since his conception centuries ago. His eyes, bulging and usually divergent, protrude like those of a chameleon. This, coupled with a permanent grimace, lend him the semblance of acute psychosis. Several sexual connotations are detected in his features also. His monstrous red-tipped nose and chin are both blatantly phallic, as are his hump, bell-tipped hat and staff. These five symbolic representations of the penis signify his satyric affinity.

Punch: *a drink concocted of five ingredients, the word itself deriving from the Hindi 'panch', meaning 'five'.*

Analysis of the story discloses Punch's progressive decline from sexual misfit to murderer.

Punch has discovered that wedlock has provided him with an unwanted detriment: the new-born baby and, therefore, responsibility. This overrides the singular benefit of his marriage: regular accommodative sex. The recent birth has effectively terminated sexual activity between Punch and Judy, and Punch, being a violent erotomaniac, is having problems adjusting to the situation. He is like a heroin addict midway through rehabilitation by means of deprivation. In effect, he is suffering a condition of libidinous cold turkey. With this carnal starvation in mind, his antics with the dog Toby, in the opening scene, must be looked upon with a depraved ambiguity.

SLATER '91

Punch's penetration of the dog is discretely intimated with his nose sliding into its mouth.

Scaramouche, the dog's owner, discovers Punch interfering with Toby, and Punch feels he has to murder the man to keep him quiet. He revels in the frenzied attack, his erotic urges suddenly transformed into sadistic brutality. Scaramouche is an essential character used to inaugurate Punch to the proclivity of violence. 'Scaramouche' is correlated to the word 'skirmish', defined as unpremeditated fighting. Punch has discovered something almost as potent as sex: sadism.

Punch: *to beat or strike, a shortening of the word 'punish'.*

The sexual purge is only temporary. The adrenaline rush he received during the murder soon evaporates and his testosterone level peaks again. He makes a pass at his wife but she slaps away his passionate advances. Still sexually unsatisfied, and lacking any willing partner, he turns his attention to the baby. The child is plainly distressed by the violation and, fearing its crying will attract unwanted attention, he beats the infant to death. When Judy discovers his crime, Punch simply suggests they can easily conceive another. This indicates Punch's deranged state of mind. The murder of his own child is utterly insignificant in comparison with the desire in his loins. Appalled by what he has done, Judy attacks him, but she too is overpowered and despatched in a similar manner to his previous victims. Punch is determined to fuck, no matter what.

Punch: *to perforate or pierce with an implement.*

Eventually he succeeds by surrendering his carnal yearning to the flirtations of Pretty Polly the local whore. Punch's achievement is parodied by the dancer with the elongating neck. However, Polly's original gender is somewhat ambiguous. 'Poll' could be taken as an alternative to 'moll', a prostitute, or 'molly' being an effeminate boy or man. Furthermore 'poll' means to cut the horns from an animal. In other words, to deprive it of its masculinity, a kind of symbolic castration, making male appear female. This indicates that Polly was in fact Punch's catamite.

Punch's satisfaction is only short-lived. When the urge returns, he attempts to visit Polly again but is thrown from his horse. As the doctor examines him, Punch verbally directs the healing hands to his groin. The doctor is aware of his patient's intentions and produces a stick which he calls 'physic', meaning a cure or remedy. He proceeds to beat the arousal out of Punch. Whipping and beating was a well known cure for promiscuous thoughts in the confines of a convent or monastery. When Punch realises the doctor is reluctant to indulge in his inverted activity, his sex drive switches off and the violent self takes over, resulting again in murder.

Punch's desires now seem solely directed towards killing rather than attaining sexual gratification. However, his dancing around and interfering with the corpses could indicate some form of stylised necrophilia. He twists any innocent event into a reason for murder. The black servant is killed simply for complaining about the noise. And the slaughter of the blind beggar is further evidence of Punch's maturing misogamy. So twisted has he become that he believes himself immortal and able to do whatever he wishes regardless of the obvious injustices. He simply feels no guilt over his crimes, an attitude very reminiscent of the do-as-you-please philosophy promoted by such infamous persons as de Sade and Aleister Crowley.

When Punch is finally confronted with the hangman's noose, he says to Jack Ketch, "You would not be so cruel." Ketch replies, "Why were you so cruel to kill those people?" Punch evades answering directly and says, "Is that reason for you to be cruel and murder me?" Unable to argue such a point, Ketch orders him to put his head in the noose. Yet even at this late stage Punch triumphs and strangles the hangman with his own rope. This only adds to his delusions of immortality, and his rantings and ravings encourage the appearance of the Devil who is also summarily dispatched.

Tracing the story back to its roots would be a virtually impossible task. Speculation, then, can offer some plausible theory towards its origins. Perhaps the tale is autobiographical, stemming from the crimes of a medieval serial killer. He 'confesses' his sins to the outside world through puppetry to allay the feelings of guilt. To distance himself from the crime scene he becomes itinerant, and thus the show migrates and evolves through imitation. The judicial characters are used to emphasise the fact that he has escaped the law, and the confrontation with the Devil shows he fears no-one save God. He models his character on his inner self and disguises his voice to create a disparity between himself and the puppet as it re-enacts his crimes. Punch doesn't look or sound like him, yet it is him, and, like the puppet, he believes himself immortal as he exposes his atrocities to the unknowing audience.

And, indeed, Punch is truly immortal, for he is still here today, on every beach and promenade: still killing; still fucking; still entertaining the children.

MORE PERFECT THAN WORDS
Subjugation of the Self in Pursuit of Gratification

A Miscellany of Correspondence to Various Porn Magazines, Pt III

D EAR T——
I saw your picture in —— magazine and had to jerk off four times, I was so
horny. I'm a 32-year-old submissive white male who now fantasizes constantly
about being your slave.

I see you in those black boots you posed in, standing before me, taunting me with
your red lips and eyes. In broad daylight in a public place you force me to drop to my
knees and crawl to you. You laughingly tell me that if I want it I will have to beg for it.
Before a gathering crowd of astonished onlookers you make me beg to lick your
boots and kiss your ass.

Once you feel you have me sufficiently crushed you have me tag along and crawl
into the passenger seat of your car. On the way to your place you continue to taunt
me with a view of your thighs until I am begging to kiss them. Soon you have me
stroking my cock at traffic lights and promising to do anything for you.

Once back in your apartment you force me to do a sexy strip-tease while you
reach under your skirt and finger your soaking clit! When I'm completely naked you
mount me like a stallion and force me to crawl around your apartment while you ride
me bareback. All the while you grind your pussy into my back and spank my ass and
squeeze my balls to get me to go faster. Eventually I collapse with your laughter
ringing in my ears. You then crush me beneath your heels, impaling my rock hard
cock and making me worship your boots.

My fantasy ends with you lying spreadeagled to your bed and me tongueing out
your luscious asshole and eating your pussy.

Please write back with your feelings on this fantasy.

Yours in submission,

R——

I had to jerk off again!

PS: Enclosed is a stamp to pay for postage. If you would like more stamps or
have photos or personal items for sale please let me know as I am very generous.

Dear E—

Madam, I'm Adam!

That's a palindrome (a phrase which is the same letters backwards and forwards) and how much I want to make love to you – backwards, forwards, inside out and upside down! I want to eat you up!

You're soooooooo tantalizingly beautifully blonde. I could be soooooo gentle and tender with you – and sooooo passionately, worshipfully obedient to your every need.

I was turned on watching you unfold the many faces of E— through May, June, August and September. At first I thought you were shy and cuddly, parting your pussy lips and raising your firm proud breasts only in clean lingerie on satin sheets. Then you wrote how much you liked to be told how to pose and loved being fucked backwards and forwards out in the open for all to see and how much you hoped your legion of fans would be jerking off reading you writing them. Next August showed a dominant side of you with a riding crop in hand, electricity in your eyes, as you slowly shuffled off your white pants and crawled naked on the floor! But September, with milk spraying and spurting all over you and K——— as you worshipped his cock all over your face and pussy made me rewrite that milk ad jingle. You know, the one that goes:

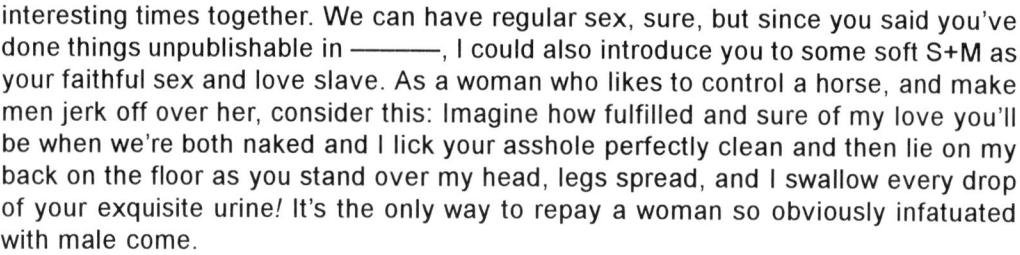

> She likes milk and it shows–
> She's got strong healthy bones!

To sing instead:

> She likes milk and it shows–
> She makes long, sexy moans!

How much I'd like those pictures of you in ecstacy, moaning, eyes closed, to be really you, lying under me.

If you choose me as one of your lovers, I guarantee we can have great fun and interesting times together. We can have regular sex, sure, but since you said you've done things unpublishable in ———, I could also introduce you to some soft S+M as your faithful sex and love slave. As a woman who likes to control a horse, and make men jerk off over her, consider this: Imagine how fulfilled and sure of my love you'll be when we're both naked and I lick your asshole perfectly clean and then lie on my back on the floor as you stand over my head, legs spread, and I swallow every drop of your exquisite urine! It's the only way to repay a woman so obviously infatuated with male come.

But more! When I'm in NYC on business (and I can make business in NYC if you want a wild hotel weekend), we can go to a sex shop and fit you in a black dominatrix outfit with a cock ring and leash for me. There can be nothing more striking than a sultry blonde bombshell like you, decked out in black! I was reminded of this by seeing you, standing in white, holding the riding crop like a whip. Once, in an S+M club, I saw a dominatrix with a riding crop put 5 men through their paces and then line them up onstage, on knees, hands, cuffed behind them, cocks erect. Then, when the men could stand it no longer, she touched each one in turn on the shaft of the cock with the riding crop, like a magic wand, saying, "Come for me now, slave!" It didn't take much touch for each man to come and when they did it was like a 21-gun salute to the dominatrix! I can just see us going to some S+M clubs with slaves saluting you! How jealous the others would be knowing you'd be taking <u>me</u> home.

If you're not interested in S+M in NYC, I'd be delighted to have you visit me here. I'm good-looking (can send pic). At my expense. You're a woman to treasure. You know what the bumper stickers say: Virginia is for horses and Virginia is for lovers. How much I'd love to affix my lips to your beautiful rear bumper permanently! If you don't feel in the mood for riding, we could go dining, dancing, movies, theater – hell, let's do bocce or snorkelling or crochet or the lawn, whatever turns you on! Can't you tell I'm crazy about you?

At any rate, please write me back. I'll be on my knees jerking off in tribute to you till you do, wondering what you'll come up with for pictures next and hoping I can do it with you!

Love,

S——

Dear J——

My name is S—— from Fayetteville, NC. I hope what I am going to say does not shock you, but you indicated when you appeared in —— that you were very unshockable. I am hoping you do not think my words offensive.

Ever since I seen your picture in —— magazine I have dreamed of my perfect fantasy involving YOU. What it is would be for you to tie me up and mistreat me crulely for days on end. I want for you to be wearing 5 inch red patent leather pumps with very sharp heels that you would stamp all over my hard 7 and ½ inch cock until it would bleed. Then you bend me over till I must lick my blood from my bleeding cock. It would hurt very much but I would be delighted to have this done from the beautiful J——. You would then make me lick your 5 inch red heels clean. But the best part is still to come.

I am laying on my front over a chair with heavy weights attached to my cock and balls hanging down. My ass is completely exposed. You take your 5 inch red patent leather pumps and crulely put the spike heel as deep in my asshole as it would go. You are fucking me with it. My cock gets hard but the weights pull it down. Then you take the spike heel out of my asshole and have me lick the blood and shit off it till it is clean. I feel the blood from my bleeding asshole on my balls. I want to cum and tell you so. You laugh and bend me over till my mouth is near to my swelled cock then you beat my cock with your heels. I cum and my own sperm goes in my mouth. I must eat all of it.

But J—— the best part of my fantasy is for you to shit and piss on my face and in my mouth. To swallow one of YOUR turds would be heaven to me and more perfect than words.

Please reply and tell me what you think about my fantasy.

Dear ——

I am R—— and I am writing you to tell you how it is for a 24 yrs slut who is completely submissive to her man. His name is J— and he is a biker 218lbs 6'5" and 36yrs with a cock of 10". I want you to print this in —— to let him know how much his slut is submissive to him.

When I met J— he told me I was a slut and then said a slut should live in complete submission to her man if she wanted to be free. I soon realized it was right what he said as I'm happy now more than ever before. The guys I used to fool around with were all wimps compared to J— and always afraid to get what they wanted from me. When your with a slut like me you must treat her like one or what you don't ask you don't get!

I always dress sexy and my nipples and labia are pierced. I don't wear pantys at all because I'm a slut and always ready to be fucked 24hrs. When I'm bad I need to be punished and J— will beat me in many ways. Sometimes it is his bare hand on my tush or sometimes a paddle or a strap or even a whip. I get off on this because I am a nasty slut and love being told whos the boss. After I have been punished I have to apologize for being a bad slut and this is even better! Sometimes I have to do myself with a dildo in my pussy or asshole while J— watches. When his brothers are here I still must do it with them watching. This is something drives me crazy and I let them all see this nasty slut pumping her cunt with the rubber cock in my hand. They even suggest other stuff I can use like: deoderant cans, bottles or banana. I do this with them all watching and telling me I'm a slut then we'll go to a bar in the neighbourhood to drink beer and shoot pool. I once had to blow this old guy of 68yrs because J— told me and like a proper submissive slut I agreed and made him cumm all on my face while they all watched.

Before I found J— and realized I was a slut my life was very bad. I was fucked by a boyfriend of my mom when I was 14yrs and left home soon after. I was a hooker for 5yrs taking drugs: coke, smack, PCP. Now I only smoke weed. I tried to kill my self 3 times with pills and jumped in front of a car, 6 months in hospital. I even was in porno pictures (photographs) with three guys in all my holes so it's obvious what a nasty slut I always am. J— is the best thing in my life right now and I call him my daddy. I don't care what people think about me because I am happy with J—. The other night one of his brothers brought around this girl he knew called M———. She is 25yrs, ½ Asian and likes to party with girls. She is very into S/M and we did a scene together. M——— whipped me good then hung weights from my nipples and labia. There were 5 brothers there all watching. M——— then screwed me with a very large dildo in the cunt and ass and it hurt and I was enjoying it. I even had to open my mouth and lay on the floor when M——— pissed on me. To end it all M——— – placed a studded collar and leash around my neck and made me crawl on the floor as she led me around all of the brothers to suck their cocks in turn and have them each cumm on my face. It was my best night ever as I was completely submissive and a complete slut.

My brother (who I never see) lives in Macon where he is an insurance broker. It would sure blow his yuppy mind if he knew what a nasty slut his sister was! I hope he reads ——— and sees me saying it. So I must tell all of you women out there to become submissive and find out what you really are. Nasty sluts who must serve your men right.

R———, Trenton, NJ

Sir: I don't suppose you get many fan letters from feminists, but here goes...

I used to disapprove of girly magazines, but over the years I've changed my mind. My husband G——— has always bought them and finds the sexy girls irresistible. I found his collection about a year ago and decided to make his masturbation part of our own sex life together, devising a method that would ensure he showed a proper respect for the models.

First he strips naked and asks me rather sheepishly if he may 'do it'. I always have two or three current magazines which he hasn't seen yet so I bring them out and show him the covers. Then he lies face down on the bed with several pairs of my knickers covering the area his penis would spurt over – partly to protect the duvet but mainly because G——— is a bit of a panty fanatic. I put the mags wherever he can get a close look and start turning the pages.

By the way, I like the fact that you always give the girls' names, so they're not just anonymous flesh but real people.

When we reach a photo set of a girl called, let's say, S———, he groans and says "Oh S———, you're so lovely. May I wank over you, please?"

I reply on S———'s behalf. "Yes you may, you naughty man," or something like that, and he starts to thrust his rock hard penis into my knickers.

I like to think the girls who pose for ——— would appreciate his asking their permission before enjoying them in this way. If they would hear those helpless, almost desperate, moans and sees how intensely he stares at their gorgeous faces, breasts and bottoms – well, I'm sure they would be pleased.

I can always tell when a particular set of photos turns him on. He lets out such a deep groan and wriggles himself so frantically over my knickers with "Oh, B——— darling," or "Oh T———, baby," and "Thank you. Oh thank you!!"

When he reaches the point of no return I turn back quickly to the spread which brought the deepest groan and allow him to finish, concentrating on that girl with all his might until he spurts with a loud cry of sheer bliss.

This may not be politically correct, but after all so many men are simply compelled to masturbate over pretty girls in sexy poses and at least G——— does so respectfully and with a deep gratitude which I find very touching.

Mrs. D.L., Whitby

I read ——— magazine because its the nastiest mag around but how can I find women who are nasty as in your mag??

I want a big tit slut who will be nasty to me because I deserve it.

I want a woman who makes me do every thing she wants and sucks me till I cum on her face. Then she beats me. She can do any thing to me. I want it.

My fantasy is for two big women to hold me captive in their house. I am naked and chained to a wall. My cock is hard just writing about it. All the time my cock is hard and these sluts walk about in nasty clothes all the time. One is blonde the other maybe black or latino. They are both big women and also lesbian. They fuck and screw each other as I am tied up and my cock hurts to watch them but I can do nothing about it being tied. The colored slut whips my cock till it is red then whips her girlfriend ass. I see how sore and red it gets and my raw cock aches more. I want to cum but I cant. I want these two nasty bitches to abuse me some more. That is what I get. I am untied and made to kneel on all fours. My ass is greased then I am penetrated by both women who force dildos into my ass. As this happens the colored slut is whipping my back and ass and whipping her white girlfriends tits as well. My balls are full with semen but the studded cock ring I wear stops me from shooting my load even though that is all I want to do. The pain of my asshole being torn is a lot. I scream for mercy, but the colored bitch just laughs and calls me a useless slave.

In my fantasy it is always two women from my office where I work. The colored one is called R——— and she has very big tits. She is 36. I want to suck and lick on her big brown titties and would like it even better if she said yes I can but first she

wants to abuse me like this. D——— is the white woman and I know she is a slut because she is always showing off her big tits. When I think about R——— whipping D———'s ass and tits I gets me so excited I have to beat off my cock. I want these women to be nasty to me and hurt my cock and balls and screw me in the ass with out letting me cum.

This is my fantasy and I have been masturbating all the time.

S.L., Sacramento

When I married A——— three years ago it was the best thing to ever happen to me. All my life I have desired strong, forceful ladies who will be sexually dominant with me. A——— was everything I wanted, being six foot tall and having an Amazonian 42-28-38 figure. In bed she was delighted to take the upper hand and our sexy sessions were out of this world. She would call me weakling and a wimp and deride my five-inch cock as not being big enough to satisfy her. However, she can have as many orgasms as she wishes through making use of my tongue. She has trained me to give her head to perfection and in any position, although I prefer it when she straddles my head and closes her strong muscular thighs around my face and forces her cunt into my mouth, all the while abusing me with insults and slaps. A——— has a very ripe sexual vocabulary and makes good use of it when mistreating me like the worm I am. She will say things like: "I should piss in your eyes, you useless piece of shit," or "Your dick is so pathetic I ought to cut it off." All of this makes my tiny cock squirm in pleasure and eager for as much punishment as she can deliver. A——— will regularly chain my dick and balls in a padlock to which only she has the key. This happens in the morning and I am forced to spend the day at work in excruciating agony until she decides to release me when I return home. Once when I had annoyed her, she made me wear a condom with chillis inside it for a day. Come the evening my cock was so red and raw it needed ice cubes to bring down the swelling.

A——— takes great pride in her humiliating me and recently she has found a way of making my punishment even more intense. What happens is this:

A——— will dress me as her slave maid. I am forced to wear sheer stockings, pumps, and a frilly apron. I have a blonde wig to wear and A——— makes up my face like a girls. She then cuffs me to a wall-mounted light fitting in our front room so my arms are over my head and my dick is exposed. Giving my cock and balls a severe beating for good measure she then leaves me standing there while she goes out.

What happens then is that she will presently return with a hooker she has picked up from the Strip. Not ever having witnessed her doing this I don't know how she achieves this, but with A——— anything is possible. I can only presume the girl is briefed on what is required of her on the way home. A——— is always careful to ensure the hooker is as sluttish as she can find, either skinny or fat. On a couple of occasions she has brought home a transvestite or transsexual. These occasions have been particularly memorable.

Of course, I am still in bondage in the front room when A——— and her guest arrive. I make a pathetic and humiliating sight for the hooker and they always laugh when they see me dressed like this and chained to the wall. A——— then invites her to take a seat and mixes the slut a drink. They sit in the chairs and A——— encourages the hooker to deride me, mocking my tiny penis and how ridiculous I look. They come over and abuse me. I get my face slapped and my dick and balls come in for a rough treatment.

Thereafter, events can vary but my humiliation is always the chief concern. Sometimes A——— will produce a plastic tie-on cock and suggest the hooker wears it. I'm made to kneel and 'give head' to the dildo. I believe the girls always derive great pleasure from seeing a man squirm like me. It must make a great change to not be on the receiving end for once. We have an extensive collection of whips, paddles, canes, riding crops etc and A——— will tell the girl to use them on my ass, balls and thighs as hard as they like. I am very tolerant to pain and can take a lot, so the girl has no worries about going too far. While this happens A——— will be using her foul tongue to deride me, saying: "I hope you are not thinking of getting a hard-on, E———. Even a hooker wouldn't be interested in your dick." Of course this gives me a hard-on, for which I am instantly punished.

I am always fascinated how street girls react when invited to abuse a middle-class, well-off man like myself. Most react with enthusiasm and eagerly carry out A———'s every instruction. Some become very excited and want to abuse me in ways that not even A——— has suggested. Several have urinated on me. One even wanted to take a dump on my chest, but A——— told her that was not what she wanted.

After I have been abused for long enough, I will be forced to give the girl head. We use a dental dam for this in case of diseases. Finally, I am forced to crawl to a table where the girl's payment is waiting, pick up the money in my teeth, crawl back to her and without using my hands, insert the money into her cunt. Afterward I am again chained as before while A——— drives the girl back. She always leaves one hand free, however. This is because she knows I will have the urge to masturbate, even though this is strictly forbidden. It is a terrible struggle to resist and I do not always succeed. If A——— returns to find I have relieved myself, she will punish me extremely rigorously.

I find all of this very exciting and a sexual dream come true. We are now discussing further ways to heighten our excitement. I would dearly love to watch A——— get screwed by a stud with a huge dick, but she does not seem that interested. Instead we are planning a trip to Los Angeles to visit some of the S/M clubs there. A——— says she wants to parade me on a chain in front of everyone there and allow other mistresses to humiliate and ashame me. I must confess I find the prospect daunting, but very exciting.

Sincerely,

R.H., Tacoma

'AND I SHALL BE HEALED'
Visit to a Miracle Crusade

David Kerekes

O NE EVENING DURING SEPTEMBER OF 1991 a leaflet was pushed through my door. Normally, they go straight in the wastebin, being the latest special offer for pizza or wood chopping done cheap. But this was a little different. Here was a free invitation to a Miracle Healing Crusade. The bible says 'Believe on [sic] the Lord Jesus Christ and you shall be saved'.

I put the leaflet to one side. In case.

A day or so later, fly posters for the wondrous crusade began to appear around town, so too advertisements in the local press. Big, bold headers addressed the reader: ARE YOU LOOKING FOR CONTENTMENT?... DO YOU SOMETIMES SUFFER WITH DEPRESSION OR DESPAIR? ARE YOU SOMETIMES ANXIOUS, FRUSTRATED, WORRIED AND HARASSED? While hardly bleating "*Yes!*" and dropping to my knees on the spot, there was something strangely compelling about the messages. BRING THE SICK, they cried. SPECIAL HEALING FOR THE SICK.

Special healing? Apparently so. I could just pop along to the New Life Church down the road, join in with the 'music, bright happy singing', meet a Reverend Melvin Banks in person and 'be cured'. On the posters, the Rev Banks – thinning grey hair, suit and tie – has a glint in his eye. He is saying:

> Lives have been changed by the power of God... The blind have seen...
> the deaf have heard... the lame and crippled have walked after prayer
> in these services.

Indeed, on the reverse of my free invitation was a montage of newspaper clippings deliberating how, over the years, the Rev Melvin Banks and Jesus had seen to it that a Mr R.Palmer of Norfolk was healed of stroke; how Pauline of Clevedon, who had been mostly confined to bed and could only get around the house holding furniture, had a miracle and is now well and started a job last week; how invalid Mrs Jenkins, stuck in a wheelchair for 17 years, is since cured and can bend down and touch her toes; and that 17 years of mental illness was dashed overnight for Mrs Joan Bibby of Heaton Chapel following a visit to the Melvin Banks crusade of 1968.

What manner of power did this mystery man, 'Britain's renowned healing evangelist', have? Was he really about to cure the lame and enable the blind to see?

Here? I took to my Miracle Healing Crusade flyer and noted the time of the next 'happy and marvellous uplifting evening'. My mind was made. I was to be uplifted*!* Slipping into my euphoric trapdoor shoes, I braved the September cold and made my way to church.

The New Life Church (formerly the Full Gospel Tabernacle) might be tiny and unobtrusive by day, but the aquamarine neon crucifix on its roof gives it a distinguished advantage by night. For miles, the neon of the New Life can be seen glowing. *Jesus is in*, I suspect it signals.

A dozen stone steps lead to the door of the church. It's going on for 7.30 PM, so I make my way up toward the building and in. Once inside, a gangling young man extends a hand of welcome. I accept his limp and sweaty handshake. By the gangling man's side is an attractive woman in her mid-twenties. She, too, bids me welcome. I'm reaching out for her hand but she offers me a card instead. "Would you like a healing request?" she asks. I figure my expression betrays my bemusement. "A healing request card?" she confirms, allowing me to peruse one of the blue slips of paper extended before me.

For a moment my mind trips into the vacuous reaches of a deep, deep space, where only the most distant of stars pulse. For a moment there is nothing but emptiness and the implication and logic of a 'healing request card', and the logic itself is... a deep, deep vacuous space. Then I'm back in the New Life Church with a multitude of possible healing requests.

I almost take a card. It's at my fingertips. I note there is an empty space on the card in which to write *Your Ailment*, followed by another space for *Your Name and Address*. I'm seeing the Reverend Melvin Banks' face on catching 'Impotent' or 'Piss-head' or 'Right fucking twat' scrawled within *Your Ailment*. Then I let the card slip away as quickly as I would the dreaded parchment in Jacques Tourneur's *Night of the Demon*. I get the impression I've been standing there for quite some time before delivering my Healing Request "no thanks".

"Please take a seat," says the woman. "At the front there."

The New Life Church has the look of pine, with a light sepia staining running from the wooden floorboards up the walls to the rafters. Here, several stretches of flex hold the modest lampshades in place. There are some windows, but they're all above head height and will offer no distraction in the hours that follow.

A short aisle leads to a pulpit, emblazoned over which is the inscription JESUS CHRIST IS LORD. On the right of the pulpit is a musical ensemble (cheap drums, cheap bass, cheap guitar and a tambourine). On the left is a overhead projector and a door. I get to the front and my suggested seat. If I'm to sit here, I realise, the Reverend would be no more than an arm's length away, and the band – which do not look anything short of dreadful – will be blasting straight into my face. I wander back down the aisle to a less lucid position.

More people are arriving. Next to me sits an old guy. He looks over and smiles. "Awright?" he says, then shows me his left hand. "I've come about me hand. If he can make me hand right, I'll be right." He relates how for years he has suffered from poor blood circulation. He also claims never to have been to this church before and, leaning closer, confides, "I'd go to my own church for help but you don't like to, do you?"

Then the band start up. The tambourine swings twenty to the dozen while a girl

'MIRACLE HEALING CRUSADE,' announced the flyers. 'Come and hear Melvin Banks, Britain's renowned healing evangelist.'

sings – what sounds like – "He's a Miracle Working God". A man steps from the door on the left and takes to the pulpit. With the music completed, he begins to speak. Whatever this small man is preaching is lost to the severity of his gesticulation. Whenever he says "God" or "Lord", his arms pivot mechanically into the air like a cosmic reflex. I'm wondering whether someone hasn't shown him how to do that.

Next, a lady member of the congregation takes to the stand. She doesn't gesticulate at all but gives a solo rendition of 'The Old Rugged Cross' in that time honoured Amateur Operatic tradition. It's awful but gets ecstatic applause and a round of "Beautiful!" and "Praise God!" when it's over.

The Reverend Melvin Banks is introduced next, Britain's renowned healing evangelist. No puff of smoke and materialization, just walks in through the door like everybody else. He takes to the pulpit and immediately goes on at some length about his new book, soon to be published. It's out in February and costs £6.00, but if you fill in a form now it will be forwarded to *Your Address* at half the price. Forms are quickly circulated by the Gangling Man and The Woman who greeted me earlier.

This Reverend is no clown. Banks is eager to establish a pace and work up momentum. The forms aren't left to idly circulate among the congregation, to be taken home and put to one side, forgotten; Banks instigates – quite literally – a countdown for filling the forms in. No sooner have they been distributed then they are being collected again. No forms leave the building. Don't hesitate – either you fill one out now or you don't get the book. It's what is commonly known as a pressure sales technique.

"10... 9... 8..." calls Banks, "half-price if you do it now... 7... lady at the back hasn't got a form... 6... wonderful... 5... 4... we need to get the formalities out of the way, don't we!... 3... 2...1... wonderful!"

More forms are to follow later.

JESUS CHRIST IS LORD and the Reverend Melvin Banks has written 14 books in total (most of which are available at the back, on a makeshift stall tended by Mrs Banks). The Reverend woos the New Life Church full house. He has the gift of the gab and never lets up for a minute. When he takes a breather, the band shift into another song.

The words of this next number are projected onto the wall. The band are playing a more up tempo ditty, and the congregation appear to be getting into the spirit of things. The guy with the bad circulation next to me attempts to join in with the 'bright happy' clapping, but his dodgy hand gets the better of him and he quickly gives up. Looking around, I see one manic gentleman hopping arithmetically from foot to foot, arms sweeping in circles, his bottom jaw plunging in mock singalong. It's very nearly funny, but then others everywhere are getting to their feet, rejoicing wildly, their hands banging together. What's wrong with them? Chad Valley manage a better drum sound.

"Forgiveness," says the Reverend. "We are going to talk about *for-give-a-ness*."

Banks is a natural. He enunciates and gesticulates with confidence. He also punctuates every other line with a "Hallelujah" or a "Praise God". But the neologism isn't all of classic denomination. Like a gameshow host on TV, Melvin Banks has his very own key phrases. He cries "Marvellous" and "Isn't that wonderful!" at every turn, triggers for the audience to 'affirm' their faith with the response "Praise God", or "Thanks be". Banks' catchphrases instil into the proceedings a certain virtue, as if by continual enumeration he does indeed make it wonderful and marvellous.

"Computers? I'm not one for all that technical stuff." So Banks opens his sermon, going on about how he'd much rather write with a good old pen and paper than with a computer keyboard (prompting an immediate affinity with the older element present). The sermon centres around a book Banks was working on several years ago, one that he was writing and storing on computer, except that the computer crashed and erased the lot. "Don't trust computers. Praise God."

After the New Life Church band have taken to the podium once again, striking up (or *off*, as the case may be) another number, Gangling Man takes to the aisle to distribute more stuff. This time it is yellow 'Prayer Cards'. Over the microphone, during an instrumental break(down), the Reverend Banks announces that "Only those who have filled in the yellow card can receive prayer." The said item is held aloft for all to see. On it is yet another space for *Your Name and Address*. Is the Good Lord compiling a directory?

Britain's renowned healing evangelist has some nerve. Not enough that this temple be infiltrated with money-lenders – with Mrs Banks and the Healing Crusade stall at the back, and Mr Banks flogging his new book at a special price at the front – but now only the privileged can receive prayer.

"Who wants to be saved?" yells Melvin Banks, hands in the air. Mumbled approval from the assembly. Again, "Who wants to be saved?" A few people raise a hand. "Who wants to be saved? *Everyone!*" prompts the Reverend. "Everyone!" Maybe I should have filled in a yellow Prayer Privilege card after all. "Come on. Everyone in this room tonight is going to be saved by our Lord Jesus Christ. *Who wants to be saved!*" It isn't so much a question anymore. Hands are being raised left and right. Bad Circulation next to me lifts one hand, then the other instead. *"Everyone in this room tonight is going to be saved! Isn't that wonderful!"* I allow my hands to slide off my knees in a bid to get closer to the floor. "EVERYONE!" hollers Banks. Lower, my hands are going lower. "EVERYONE!" He means me! There isn't a solitary hand in the house bar mine not reaching skyward! People are even getting to their feet to have their hands higher. Shit, you either want to be saved or you don't – I can't imagine it's possible to be saved any *higher* than anyone else. But, by now it's a living hell. All those around me are swaying, yelling, leaping, while the Reverend's words blast through the speaker system. "EVERYONE!... *EVERYONE!*"

Don't wanna be saved by Melvin Banks, don't wanna be saved. My hands continue their slide.

"*EVER-REE-ONE!*"

The congregation respond by leaping at the very syllables, thrashing and howling. Among the turmoil I'm certain I catch sight of the Wicker Man. It's unbelievably hot. Can I stand my ground or do I have to submit and raise my hands? My spirit – it's beginning to buckle. I reason that if I am to raise my hands it will be on the pretext of being *safe* as opposed to *saved*. Gangling Man and The Woman are about to pounce and raise them up for me anyway, I'm certain.

Then, quite suddenly, the room goes quiet. Composure returns. "Isn't that wonderful*!*"

There follows a collection. I drop a 50p coin into the basket. Gangling Man looks at me as if I'm about to make off with the money. Should that be the case then God Wills It, I smile back at him.

There is an announcement that those people who have filled in a yellow prayer card should make their way to the annex, the room beyond the projector. Elderly folk get up, clutching their card and edging through the crowd. With them go a young couple, newly weds it appears. An Asian guy holding his son in his arms tails behind them, the all-important yellow slip ready. But it's mostly elderly people. A song breaks out.

By the time the band have got to the end of the song, in those few short minutes, the group that left for the annex are returning and making their way back to their seats. Some meagre counselling session that was*!* Neither is there a yellow card anywhere in sight.

It's 9 PM by my watch. For a terrible moment I think it's all been a scam to get us into church; that there isn't going to be any healing at all... or, worse still, there is, but it has just taken place behind closed doors. But no, those who filled out a Healing Request card earlier in the evening are called to the front of the church. A queue forms down the aisle in front of the Reverend. Bad Circulation next to me is visibly flustered. "I haven't filled me card in. I haven't got a pen." His eyes flit from side to side, as those around him get up to join the growing queue. He is starting to panic. He is being left behind, but won't ask anyone or do anything about it. Body and soul he is with Banks, and body and soul he can see it all slipping away for wont of a ballpoint pen. For a moment I'm desperately saddened by it all. For a moment I want everyone *EVERYONE* to snap out of it – not just the guy next to me. But I reach into my pocket and hand him a pen.

At the front of the queue, on the Reverend's right hand side, stands The Woman. From each person as they step forward she takes their card, shows it to Banks, then places it to one side in a neat pile. Banks notes *Your Ailment*. He puts his hand upon a forehead.

"Trapped nerve in your leg..." he softly tells the lady before him, "*vanish*." Then, jerking his hand free from her temple, bellows, "JESUS!" The lady moves away

Where it happened. Photo: Gino Kerekes

healed.

Next, a man on crutches hobbles cautiously over. Polio. Banks places one hand upon the guy's head, the other behind the guy's back. With this support, the man eases the grip on his crutches and his body appears to relax. Again Banks hollers "JESUS!", and flicks his hand away from the temple as if yanking the very polio free. "How do you feel?" Banks asks. With barely pause for a reply, he has the guy cast off his crutches and headed down the aisle. "Somebody walk along side him – don't hold him, let him walk by himself. Isn't that wonderful!" Without his crutches, the man deliberates each step through clenched teeth. His face is an expanse of wide-eyed agony, beads of sweat rolling from his forehead. Grim determination gets him halfway down the aisle and back again without toppling over. Making it to the pulpit, resounding applause greets the achievement. "Praise be," one woman calls out, tears rolling down her cheeks. "Marvellous!" cries Banks. And the next in line steps forward.

A blind woman, assisted, holds her card out. A few words of comfort from the Reverend and then his hand is upon her. Her face is serene, trance-like. Banks sways very gently, his other hand upon her shoulder. A few moments of this, then he labours over the word "blindness". Suddenly, both hands are whipped free and a word rings out. "*SEE!*"

The woman pops open both her eyes.

But for Banks' last ejaculation looping round the walls, the church stands silent for several long minutes. Slowly, precisely, the woman begins to speak.

"*Clouds... moving in... I see... clouds... moving together – A form... a face... I see a face.*" (Banks' smiling face.) She continues to sob, "A face – eyes, nose, mouth... I CAN SEE*!*"

The Reverend then takes a hold of both her shoulders. "What colour are my eyes?"

"B-brown," the woman stammers.

"Brown, ladies and gentlemen. Isn't that wonderful*!*"

Hooray*!*

At 9.20 PM, I get up and leave the New Life Church. On my way down the steps outside, I catch the strains of the Reverend's "*Jesus!*" one last time. The joyous yelp of the congregation lingers a while longer, then that too is gone.

The 'happy and marvellous uplifting evening', as promised by my free invitation flyer, has been somewhat lacking. I had gone to the New Life with an open mind and come away a sceptic. There is a great tragedy at play in this Healing Crusade – a putrefying manipulation that is more cunning, much more wicked than the so-called tasteless spectacles local councils see fit to have run out of town. But the Miracle Crusade *is* just another freakshow, and Melvin Banks its ecclesiastical Jim Rose. It is of that tradition: peddling sensationalism and showmanship and stinging a gullible public.

But at least all Barnum took was your money.

The Reverend Melvin Banks can't channel faith. Not mine, not anybody's. He can be a friend to the people and claim to spread the Word and be able to heal, but *faith*? Faith cannot be made or truly broken, yet Banks demands that "everyone in this room tonight" *believe*. Believe what? That Banks is truly right? That faith in Jesus (and the purchase of a book) is the path by which we are to reach the big pay-off: the miracle?

Many tonight have been betrayed. They had come here under a shadow of desperation, only to find that not even the Lord can help them. Banks proffered hope. He was the possible saviour for those who could not be saved. The one last, desperate chance.

Modesty eludes Banks, this renowned healing evangelist. I fail to accept that any god would dress such an 'important' ambassador so sanctimoniously and endow him with the power to "forgive" those who are crippled, or deaf, or blind.

And so it is that as I make my way from the church, I'm warmed by a truly marvellous and wonderful searching of the soul. I feel a demon this night has been cast out. I've taken up serpents and not been bitten. The Reverend Melvin Banks is wrong. Faith? What more do I need but to believe I'm right?

POSTSCRIPT

Two days following the Miracle Crusade, those who attended and had filled out a Prayer or Healing Request Card were recipient to a knock on the front door, more chat, and more literature.

JUST THOUGHT YOU'D BE INTERESTED
A Melee of Masturbation

A Miscellany of Correspondence to Various Porn Magazines, Pt IV

IT'S END OF ANOTHER LONG DAY of California floods, earthquakes, crime and slime. The clock strikes midnight and my cock is 'straight up' twelve o'clock high as I whip out the February issue of ——— to masturbate and blow my brains out squirting hot come all over your magazine – as I have done for weeks now ever since my girlfriend has been away.

Cum to think of it, I've been having orgasms courtesy of ——— magazine for twelve years now. I've never written before, but tonight as I pulled out the mag I said, 'I want to try something different tonight.' The nastiest thought I could think of was sharing my masturbation with all of America!

I use lubricating oil, jelly or vaseline and twist my slippery hand as I go up and down on my raging hard dick while I sit up on the bed with my legs spread and —— — magazine on the bed between my legs. This allows me to 'give' my cum to the model I've chosen for the night. I have a talent of always hitting the girl right on the cunt when I squirt my jizz. That way, it's the most like she's with me. This is why I like the shots of them from the front with their legs spread.

This week I have probably shot twenty cumloads on your photos (usually about three times a day). In the February issue I have squirted hot jizz all over N—— on page 75 – her beautiful blonde hair looks so sweet and pretty there.

Yesterday, I played with myself and got off on the picture of D——— on page 54 where she's reaching up to suck 'N———'. She's all wet and her tits are soft, warm and round as she looks like an old girlfriend of mine who used to fuck me like there was no tomorrow.

As I masturbate to that pic of D——— I can see her beautiful legs spread open in my mind. I can see her gorgeous soft dark brown pubic hair and hot pussy as I thrust my naked cock in and out of her pussy, which is so incredibly eager. My ex- would hold my face in her hands and plead with me to 'cum in (her) cunt' and, being the generous guy that I am, I always obliged. Trust me, you would have too.

My page 9 of February is all rippled from the dried cum on that picture of C——— – A—— with her legs spread. That got me really horny because right below it she says, 'I love it that all these guys are going to get hot looking at my body' – I interpreted that to mean: 'I know you're masturbating right now, and it's okay … Feel good …

make yourself cum, especially if it makes you happy ... stroke your dick, do the forbidden*!'* I always dig through ——— looking for anything that refers to the fact that I'm masturbating because this causes the magazine to become a sexual experience. I love it and now the whole world knows*!* I would jack off and cum a hundred times if I even saw this letter in ———. And now, once again, I put down the pen to 'grab the rod'. Tonight, I think the big picture of A——— on page 23 gets it. Thanks for getting me off*!!*

Dearest be loved ———

I need your mag on and off and on. Sometimes. And I find it pretty entertaining what with the stile of humour and the wit of the caption writers.

And of course not forgetting the girls, all of them with their fair share of beauty in all manner of places, and again of course, "not forgetting their looks", Very nice.

Nice camera work, lighting, so on and so forth.

BUT TELL ME QUITE HONESTLY*!*

"How come there's never a splash or drip or glint or even a sniff of femanin lube near or around or in the tube. How come you never show even the slightest afectionet arousal of a swollen fanny lip, or even clit?"

Most men, and most wimen them selves, find the sight of fresh juice excitingly stimulating. Not to mention lip smacking or even lip licking.

So what's happening to your girls?

"BIG QUESTION."

Perhaps your phot, ogers have lost their touch, and only are bothered about possessive perspective positioning of take*!* "And I my self, might add, very good too and in all of your other pubelick, ations. 'Tis one of the reasons I buy them. Being an artist of no reenoun, except to me self. Buy them for sexual porno positions for the characters "squeeze me" in the cartoon books I draw. I may send you a cartoon or two, sometime in the near future. I know very well you'd publish them "simply for the craft of my analogy." Or I should say, craftness of my anatomical fruition. Not to mention "..............", so I wont. "And don't let me hear you say it! We just might meet some day*!!!* But, back to the girls, same as ever.

'The poor lovelies never seem to be showing any arousal in faceal eye expreshon,

or in their pussies. I know that they do act with faceal reasemblance as if ravenous, but the eyes gives it away. =NON, or, if very little stimulation. The art work's fine, and they look to be enjoying that. Thank God no complaints there looking at it from that angle. "And it look very nice, to, love." O.K. set does look sharp _ _ NEXT*!*

Infact this is "not" a letter of complaint... only a question, big question? O.K. Two*!*

And that is:-

"Where is the look of arousal, in the eye. And where is the sweetness of showing its self on the sensuously saductive part of a sensual woman?*!*

"It ain't no use without the juice, rips the foreskin in shreds"

It's like going to the swimming baths and forgetting yer trunks, and also finding out its closed, owing to the fact there's no water to splash about in.

O.K.*!* So I'll use my imagination*!*

Watch out, here I come, oh*!* oh*!* – Oh no

– CRASH –

Is it possible that you would not consider of these lovely women sensualy and joyusly spreding them? With the real look of pleasure?*!*

Juicing up fondly of them selves?*!*

Copiously showing of it?*!*

With the true exitement of spontnewity?*!* Mesmerized in true inward feelings? Showing it in the sparkle of the eye? And the sparkle on their smiling pussy*!!*

It is after all us oglers who ogale, men and wimen alike.

'Tis like looking into a bag of proones*!*

You know that they'll do you good.

But they've gone and lost their sweetness...

To look at a woman like so many of your readers "seems" to do (from the letters) they are ogling at them with thoughts of possession, and not how it should be. That is:- joining in with them and enjoying them selves together. Lovely provocative posess, face smiling at camera, strip off...*.*!*

Then what? Corr, I don't half fancy shagging that. POP*!* Spunk all over.

"Corr*!* That piece got my blood up"

"I held back for two hours then blue me balls off."

So, so, so well and good, nothing wrong with that. "Come hear my darling, let me shag yer," Corrrrr...

See my point?

"IF"... ("And how it should be") the sensuality of the woman her self was showing through that of actually and truly showing to us her feelings, the real concept would show through of her actually being a human being willing and wanting to share her body, to actually share the experience of exposure with the audience who even it is who was ogling.

This can only come through the woman "IS" sensually aroused.

Of course not to point of a wide gapping hole skwishing out sweetnes all over the place. But yet? . . . we see this in other mags.

Most of your girls admitadly 'are' beautiful. But then again I've seen quite a few well and truly enjoying them selves with vibes jamed up tight in front, and sometime back hole too, very arousing.

Of course there's art and there's porn.

"Now, you can't tell me that ——— is a family mag, and that you dernt show the female in passonat extraction. In other words. Blowing a sticky bubble or two from between the folds of her nicely rippening lips. "Oh no*!* The children might see." This children have already seen from their own genitalia again in other words."

"If you show the woman in the true natural instinctive involvment she instinctively becomes involved with the camera in a more open natural way." As if to say.

"Look at me, this "IS" me. I'm wet... Share it with me*!*"

I've seen J–, your fantasy lovely doing just that. And one or two others. J– "IS" instinctive. That's why she "IS" the fantasy girl.

So come on, you lot, open up. Get with the times.

Show a bit of pink, a splash of juice. Not just the strip, show a woman for what she is. Sensual, sharing, wet and wanting to share. It does not have to be porno nor does it have to be just posing. Look*!* I'll get me camera and pop down. I'll have a word with J– telling her to spred the message about (and a few other things). Use a crystal sparkle lends to catch the shimmer of the soft lighting on the puss. Let the modle run SEXUALY RAMPENT in her own way.

Have a cup of tea then edit your mag. And to fuck with the prudes.

The eyes "will" be showing "true" sharing with the oglers, lips acimbo, and a splash of sweetness glistening out as if to say, "Don't just fuck me, but be with me."

"Corr! I held back five and a half hours, didn't want to spole the effect of us together. By she's a cracker, I would love for us to make love together, she's something else."

"Warm and sensual" "Open and showing it."

Ha! Ha! Is it that your trying to show us that at least.

"Our women don't touch them selves. Their not like that! Oh! Shame on you, just the thought of it, they wouldn't do a thing like that."

Oh! Before I forget, let's see more of C————, October issue, page 72.

Their all lovely girls in your mags of course but I do seem to have an affinity with C————. Now there's sensuality in the making, a shared glansss, of passionate feeling. And not just a poser. Keep her in mind for your next fantasy girl, or in fact set her up in a collem of her own and see the letters rolling in.

They won't just be letters of... "Come hear! I want to shag yer" more on the lines of, "I would love to spend an evening or two with you."

Try her out and see!

Oh! And send her my love too while yer doing it. She is sensuality, it self.

"The eye "IS" the windo to the heart and soul."

Anyway, must fly...

"I've got a bit of wanking to catch up on." I can fair taste the sweetness on both pears of C————'s parted lips. Hope they've put the plug back in the swimming pool?!!

So come on. Men and wimen alike, let's see the sensuasness of your girls in natural exurerance.

In other words.

"Show us what you are realy made of. Are we a slave to the prudes, or are we man and woman enough to open up to them.

QUESTION? <u>BIG</u> QUESTION?

"Oh! But we don't want the standerd of our name slanderd about."

"Were not like that you know!" We cater for the oglers of nice standerds 'the come here let me shag you lot.' Not the open minded knowledgeable sensuas dripping cock lot, with their eye for naturalissm.

Anyway, don't forget C————. Which ever way you want to put it she'll have your readers creaming in their pants before the get home from the shop. If, if you truly show what she is made of. She's a wet one, whach her, she's slippy, she'll have them eating out of her love box in no time.

"Let her spred em! Sway them, and bed em."

Your onto a winner there and no! I'm not her mannager, if that's wat's tha thinking. As just a reader yer sees.

Oh! By the way... What's that J– doing tonight. Oh well, just a thought. Give me them both for a week, some hot sparks would effervess from the three of us. "Fingers flashing everywhere bodys tangled in each others auras, pelvic energy lighting up the skys, conscious and subconscious thoughts taking over, lost together in a swerl pool of passion, held together by an inner knowing, lost in time and space, a week of shear bliss for all consound.

It's there right in their eyes, the knowing of what their inner soul desires if only someone could share it with them, and let it out.

Take it from me gentelmen, snap C——— up pronto. Or this phoenix will rise from the flames again and pop to you an even hotter letter asking of questions of you of your miss handeling of an goddess. "Or something to that effect." Don't let her slip through your fingers. Keep me posted OK.

Oh! And perhaps you would be so kind; that's if its possible to let me have an address to where I can send a "Look them in the eye and stamp yer foot, don't let them pass you by, congratulations for aquiering your new post of fantasy girl in ——— —" letter.

O.K. I'll shorten that, "A Fan Letter" to C———.

Next post please, pritty please, O.K. she's got it. And so as C———.

Oh! And let me know if she is in any other mags that I could ogle in a nice way of course.

Sorry if this letter seems long...

Its mean to be...

O.K. best go now, look out for me in other mags, cartoon wise, under the pen name of...

That's right, you've guesst it...

Juicy

And your post box... of course. "Will I never." Oh! And gives my loves to J–... pass it on. Three'sms a comming up, for the four of us. Well I meen I wouldn't go out without Jimbo now would I...

CORRRRR!
SORRY! BUT I'VE JUST SEEN IT.
IT'S OFFICIAL
THE
BIGGEST
DIRTIEST
MAG
OF ALL
TIME!......Hmmm?WHAT?
CORRRR! YOU DO MAKE ME
LAUGH!!!
HA! HA! HA! HA! HA! HA! HA! HA! HA!
HOO! HOO! HOO! OH! OH! HA! HA! HA!
HA! HA! HA! HOO! HOO! HOO!
WATCH OUT!
THE PHOENIX HAS ARISEN FROM THE FLAMES
And where's that C——— got too?
You have been awarn'd
Contact her NOWWWWWW!
Don't let her slip through your sticky fingerssssss:
She is a GODDESS in the making...
Goddess APHRODITE her self.
Take another look at her, and you will see for your self.
Take if from one who knows, and don't be blind.

JUICY

Dear Editor,

Can you be of any assistance? Recently I have written to S—— G——, ———, T— F——, ——— magazine and a C———— A—— of ———. Also to J—— – S——, commercial director of ———. Basically I've asked the three models to go to bed with me. I've to date received no replies.

The reason I wrote to them is because I'm a 33 year old gentleman who has never had a girlfriend. I'm a nice looking man and have a nice personality. For the last 8 years I have not been left alone by an individual(s) who I think have rich, powerful friends or connections? They have been making my life – how shall I say – unhappy to say the least. They have been doing things to upset, annoy, humiliate, provoke, threaten, lie and make fun of me so as to force me to do what they want.

There are two older women who are in love with me and perhaps its them who are behind all this. I don't want either of them and haven't been near them since 1987. But its been going on over the years since then. I didn't go with either of them but they've hurt me so much I've been unable to get near/go with any other girl/woman in all this time, ie I've been made afraid of kissing, touching and sex itself or even going near some girls or women sometimes.

I think they're trying to take over my life and control it. I'm trying to get away from them, if I managed to go with a girl it might help me do it?

A final point – they know what I'm thinking, so whenever I try to do something they're aware of it, at least I think that could be happening. You'll have to bear that in mind – LOVE'S involved and, – well strange or unexplainable things can happen sometimes perhaps.

Take an interest, things have happened over the years. If rich, powerful people are involved who knows what could happen in the future?

I'm asking for a girl, can you find me one?

Yours faithfully,

G.H.L.

I have been wanting to write you this letter to explain a unique situation that I have engaged in. First, I have been purchasing ——— and ——— ——— for nearly three years after being exposed to them in the US Navy. We used to have 'porn lockers' to hold our stash of mags and continuously found myself choosing ——— over the rest. The reason? You have the classiest looking babes in the raunchiest positions possible. I would expect to see nearly all of them at a church luncheon, not baring their all in the pages of your magazine. I definitely prefer the latter though, because just looking at them makes me want to grab my dick and go into a cum frenzy.

This leads me to the small story I need to tell you. I have been purchasing your mags through a convenience store. Every time there are women that are so beautiful but so raunchy and wet that I find myself with my hand on my dick rubbing to ease the tension that occurs. I end up getting so damn horny I have the urge to come here and now. Since it is hard to pull off into someone's driveway and get myself off, I found that if I hold my magazine and steering wheel with one hand, and my dick with the other, I can climax while still driving*!!!* It's actually quite a rush. I first found after a climax, my speed was way over the limit, but now I can keep it under control. Three years and no accidents.

Don't try this at home...

Dear Editor,
    Heres a little taste of poetic side; Hopefully you will decide to print this in one of your edditions.

> *When I see you standing there*
> *I wanna lick your body everywhere*
> *I want you to push me up against the wall*
> *and fuck me till we both fall*
>
> *I get wet thinking of you*
> *and all the kinky things we can do*
> *So when your feeling blue*
> *Come to me and I'll show you what I can do to you*
>
> *I wanna sit on your big hard cock*
> *Pump you up and down nonstop*
> *Oh God, I wanna fuck your knee*
> *Uummm, I can feel you pumping, pumping me*
>
> *I want to make my juices flow*
> *I want to have multiple orgasms in a row*
> *And when were done having fun*
> *I'll kiss you then run*

Dear ——————
    Hi my name is d— I just like to say that your reading meatirell is the best I hav ever read in a long time and just want you to know that from one of your biggest fands in a long time.
    Also I want to know if you ken pleas send me an autograph pickjer of M—————— and if you cant I will under stand.
    I have a store to tell you once my gril frend and I were going on a trip wen she started to get vere horne so said way dont you suck my dick and so she did then it got me horne so I poled over and she sat on my face and let a big jusie orgazem in my mouth. and it was very jucie then I let her sit on my lap as I wase figer banging her then she started to rub my big hard cock intell cum bursted all over her face and she loved evre bit of it.
p.s. m—————— is on pag 41 also if you print this store pleas keep my name confidential

Dear Editor:
    I have been a subscriber to —————— for several years now and a disturbing trend has recently come to my attention. I have reviewed all the issues of —————— for the past 4 years and have noticed that the number of pictorials featuring men has increased from 14% (5 of total pictorials of the year) to 30% (14 total pictorials in 1991 to 35 in 1994). Over this same time span the number of pictorials featuring two or more women has decreased from 14% to 10% (total of 14 in 1991 to 12 in 1994).
    This observation is very alarming to me. The reason that I subscribe to —————— is because I enjoy looking at beautiful women – <u>not</u> another man's penis! I understand that magazines change their formats and contents periodically in response to customer requests. The inclusion of pictorials featuring a man and woman/woman are most likely in response to a certain section of ——————'s male audience as well as

it's female audience. I, however, do not belong to that section which appreciates this. I would never expect you to entirely eliminate pictorials which feature men. I understand that your goal is to try to satisfy the largest audience possible. However, by more than doubling the number of men pictorials and reducing the number of girl/ girl pictorials in a relatively short time you are satisfying some of your audience while making others very disgruntled. I am one of the latter and I feel I must voice my opinion concerning this trend. Put simply, I would like to ask that a reduction in the number of pictorials featuring men be initiated. Otherwise I will have to reconsider my subscription renewal.

I would appreciate a response to my letter as soon as possible.
Respectfully yours,

B.S., Rochester

MY VOTE FOR 1994 'GIRL OF THE YEAR' GOES TO L——, THE RED-HAIRED LITTLE LOVELY YOU USED TO FEATURE, PLEASE COULD YOU REGISTER MY VOTE. IN YOUR JOURNAL YOU USED TO HAVE A TOP TEN – HERE IS MY ULTIMATE TOP TEN OF ALL TIME. PLEASE SHOW L—— AGAIN*!*

1. L— (PORN SLUT) – WHO ELSE – EVERY DEPARTMENT OF HER IS BETTER THAN ANY OTHER GIRL – BEST BUM, BEST FIGURE, BEST LEGS, NICEST HAIR, PRETTYEST FACE, LOVELYEST EYES, JUICYEST, NEATEST CUNT – THE ULTIMATE PERFECTION – SPUNKORAMA*!*

2. S—— (PORN SLUT) FROM ——— – A NEW UNBELIEVABLE SPUNK SLUT – FUCKING WOOR*!*

3. K——— I—— (PORN SLUT) – GORGEOUS BEAUTY – PROBABLY THE BEST LOOKING WOMAN IN BRITAIN (IF L—— IS AMERICAN).

4. ISABEL AJARNI (ACTRESS) – SULTRY, WANK-MAKING FRENCH WONDER TART.

5. EMMANUEL BERT (ACTRESS) – 'FACE OF AN ANGEL, BODY OF A WHORE'

6. CLARE GROGAN (SINGER/ACTRESS) – THE SECOND PRETTYEST GIRL IN THE WORLD – NEXT TO L——*!* A FACE TO SPUNK OVER*!*

7. B——— (———/——— PORN SLUT) – BRILLIANT BUM, SECOND BEST IN THE WORLD – NEXT TO SUPER SLUT L——*!*

8. CLAUDIA SCHIFFER (MODEL) – BEAUTIFUL SUPERMODEL – SIMPLY LOVELY*!*

9. SHANNEN DOHERTY (ACTRESS) – REPUIBLY NASTY ACTRESS, BUT FOR FUCK'S SAKE WOULDN'T YOU LOVE TO STUFF YOUR COCK IN HER GOB*!* AND WHAT LEGS*!*

10. CINDY CRAWFORD – O.K. VERY PREDICTABLE, BUT FUCKING GORGEOUS.

YOURS, *C.S.*

HOOKERS FOR JESUS!
The Strange Saga of the Children of God

Chris Mikul

THE CHILDREN OF GOD WERE A FAMILIAR sight on the streets back in the late-Seventies, handing out their cheesy little cartoon illustrated leaflets and asking for donations. They particularly liked to accost passengers on trains, and it was on a train that a couple of them presented me with a full-colour comic book with the eye-catching title *The Green Door! – A Dream of a Polished Hell!* After a while they seemed to disappear, and I had virtually forgotten about them until I came upon a copy of *The Basic Mo Letters*, an awesome compendium of cult leader Moses David's messages to his followers – over 1,500 pages of doomsday prophecy, heavy-handed political satire and sexual perversity. What sort of crazed genius could have come up with this little lot, I wondered.

A BRIEF HISTORY
David Berg, later to be known as Moses David, was born in 1919 into a heavily Christian family. His father was a pastor, his mother a radio evangelist, and following in their footsteps he became a travelling preacher. He married and settled for a while in Arizona where he built a small church, but was forced to leave this after allegations of sexual misconduct. He tried teaching for a while, but was soon back in the Jesus business, working for Texan televangelist Fred Jordan.

Along came 1968. The Vietnam war was raging and the 'beautiful people' (most of them, judging by the available documentary evidence, about as beautiful as my backside) were flocking to California. And who should be moving among them, dispensing old-time religion and free peanut butter sandwiches, but David Berg's elderly mother, Virginia. She was soon joined by her son, his wife and two of their four children. The family took over a coffee shop on Huntington Beach and Berg began to acquire followers. With his anti-authority, anti-parents stance, long hair and beard, and ability to speak like he had just stepped out of the pages of the King James Bible, he proved an irresistible figure and was soon dubbed 'the original hippie'. He initially called his group 'Teens for Christ' but when a local journalist coined the phrase 'Children of God', Berg liked the name and it stuck.

From the beginning Berg's group were more radical than the other 'Jesus Freaks' of the time, with members encouraged to recruit aggressively and disrupt the services of regular churches. When the Californian police began to make things difficult for the growing cult, Berg decided it was time to, in his words, split. Having announced that California was about to suffer a massive earthquake and slide into the sea, Berg left with about 50 followers. They broke up into several groups which, after many travels, converged some months later in Texas, where Berg persuaded his old evangelical mate Jordan to let them stay on one of his properties. By now, Berg, having spent his time in the wilderness, was calling himself Moses David – MO for short – and in order to keep his often dispersed followers together had begun to issue weekly newsletters. These became known as MO letters.

When he started Teens for Christ, Berg's teachings were pretty basic biblical fundamentalism. These were the End Times, Berg was God's End Time Prophet, and his followers would be the 144,000 the Bible foretold would remain faithful during the imminent reign of the Antichrist. He had enforced a strict code of morality among cult members – no dating allowed – but after Berg's mother died things began to liven up in a hurry. Berg took as a mistress a young follower, Karen Zerby, who had changed her name to Maria (it would soon become common, as in many cults, for members to adopt new names). Maria encouraged Berg's messianic beliefs and his teachings grew more bizarre. He started speaking in tongues, claimed to be in touch with the spirit of a Gipsy king called Abrahim, and talked of having sex with succubi. He also announced that free love was sanctioned by the scriptures.

After a while even the rather stupid Jordan realised something odd was going on and kicked the cult off his land. They scattered across America, making recruits and raking in money by 'litnessing' – the name given to handing out leaflets and asking for a donation of 10 cents or so. New members were expected to give everything they owned to the cult and sever relations with all members of their family (at least the ones from whom there was no chance of getting any money). In 1971, one of Berg's daughters went to England to start the first overseas ministry. By 1975, the Children of God had reached most of the countries of Western Europe and some of the communist ones too. Worldwide membership was estimated at around 10,000.

Berg himself had left the US in 1972, following the re-election of Nixon, whom he despised (at least he got something right). He settled in England for a while, making his headquarters in Bromley, Kent, before moving to Tenerife. Increasingly reclusive, he was also becoming sleazier by the second. Incest, group sex, lesbianism, one by one they received the MO seal of approval. (At one point he sanctioned homosexuality, too, but quickly changed his mind when there was an outbreak of it among cult members.)

His most notorious idea, one which became synonymous with the Children of God, had come to him in England in 1973. Maria had picked up a man on a dancefloor, seduced him, and later converted him. A lightbulb lit up over MO's head, or maybe a giant hand came out of the clouds with a thumbs up. So was born the ministry of 'flirty fishing'. Female cult members were urged to cruise nightclubs and bars for men, have sex with them, then while lying in bed afterwards talk to them about Jesus. They were to be 'Hookers for Jesus', and were depicted in the letters as cute little hippie chicks impaled on fish hooks. Many of Berg's followers were appalled by the developments and left. Others, numbed by the hundreds of MO letters which they had come to believe had the authority of the Bible, went along with them. Not surprisingly, there were suddenly an awful lot pregnancies among the women. David Berg was nothing if not a man who could rise to the occasion. In 1979, he issued a letter called *My Little Fish* which advocated sex with children.

By the late-Seventies, word about all of this was getting out and the authorities in many countries were cracking down on the cult, despite a name-change to the 'Family of Love'. Many cult members went underground while others moved to countries like India and the Philippines. In 1977, Berg and Maria, forced to leave Tenerife, disappeared.

FISHERS OF MEN!

TAKE A LETTER , MARIA
Even before his departure from the US, Moses David had become a distant figure, seen by few of his followers and rarely photographed. The sole point of contact with him for most cult followers, and his only way of maintaining authority over them, became the MO letters. The cult's growth and expansion to other countries during these years make these little leaflets some of the most successful pieces of propaganda ever conceived.

The Basic MO Letters leaflets is divided into sections covering spiritual beliefs, politics and economics, love and sex, prophecy and so on, with questions at the end of each section to ensure the disciple had absorbed the salient points. Much of the impact of the letters derives from their illustrations, with a full-page graphic starting most of them off and cartoons scattered liberally throughout. Some of these cartoons are horribly cute, reminiscent of those vile 'Love Is...' cartoons from the Seventies. Others are quite effective. The best are those done by someone calling themself Eman Artist, who draws in a classic, spare comic book style. Moses David is depicted as a big, bespectacled, anthropomorphic lion, often with Maria hanging off his arm. While some of the letters are written in pseudo-biblical babble – especially the ones presented as prophesy uttered by MO in a trance and taken down by Maria – the majority are folksy and controversial. MO comes across as your kindly, concerned dad, though a lot funkier than the one you probably just ran away from. The letters are rambling and extremely repetitive, full of all sorts of weird little digressions and anecdotes from Berg's private life. What they have going for them is a sort of flippant, off-the-cuff feel which makes them unique among the religious writings I have encountered. MO is quite open about his desire to be an enigmatic and distant figure to his followers.

> I LOVE BEING A LEGEND – A MYSTERY*/* I always wanted to be a ghost when I was a little boy. I loved characters like Dracula and Frankenstein and Tarzan. And I would have added Space Man to my list, but it was too early for him then.

I suspect it is this peculiar mix of authoritarianism and apparent innocence which made the Moses David persona so attractive to hippies.

Some of the imagery MO uses is quite startling. In *I am a Toilet – Are You?* he compares his former life as a conventional preacher to being "a beautiful vessel sitting on the mantlepiece". Now that he's mixing with the hippies, however (and "there is hardly anything that one of our dirtiest hippies have done that I haven't also done!", he candidly admits), he is like a toilet, taking the dirt of society, the hippies, and purifying it with a divine flush.

I AM A TOILET, I GET MY INSPIRATION FROM ABOVE: SOMEBODY

PULLS THE CHAIN AND DOWN COMES WATER TO FILL ME UP AND
FLUSH ME OUT! Down comes the water from Heaven, and it carries
everything with it. Pretty noisy too! – Makes a lot of racket!

The letters dealing with prophesy are mostly predictable, the sort of sensationalist stuff fundamentalists have been cranking out for years (MO's particular timetable had the Antichrist appearing in the late-Seventies, the Time of Tribulation beginning in 1989, and Jesus popping down in 1993). America is the Great Whore, the Arabs are going to unite under Gaddafi (with whom Berg was for some reason fixated), etc. When MO gets onto the subject of communism, however, a note of ambivalence creeps in. He is forced to regard communists as tools of Satan – but whenever he discusses Marx or Lenin you can't help but notice a feeling of envy and admiration for their revolutionary achievements. MO constantly refers to his own movement as a revolutionary one and peppers his writings with rhetoric derived from the Left – yet another element certain to go down well with the youth of the day.

The most interesting MO letters are, of course, the ones dealing with sex. MO's ideas on the subject are laid out in *Revolutionary Women*, *Revolutionary Sex*, and *Revolutionary Love-Making*. The first of these goes into obsessive detail about what women should wear – a subject to which he has obviously devoted a great deal of thought. As usual, MO pronounces on this thorny problem with authority.

ON THE WHOLE, A WOMAN SHOULD WEAR AS LITTLE AS POSSIBLE,
so as to both partially reveal and yet at the same time partly and
provocatively conceal her natural beauty and charm.

Net stockings are highly recommended, as are see-through blouses, halter-neck tops and other Seventies fashions (MO was certainly a man of his time). Women must be careful not to reveal too much, however, lest "familiarity breed contempt". This latter point eventually leads him, in his usual rambling way, to a spirited defence of polygamy.

Revolutionary Love-Making is MO's sex manual, complete with anatomical diagrams, and apart from a few old wives' tales it's actually quite a good one. MO boasts of his own sexual exploits, and sees no conflict between his roles as God's prophet and ageing stud. As he points out, the Bible records that after 120 years, several wives and quite a few children, Moses still had "sexual juices". MO's view of sex is a straightforward one – God made it so you should enjoy as much of it as possible – and, if you disregard for the moment his later penchant for child abuse, it's a pretty sensible one, certainly preferable to the fierce repression which has been the norm for Christianity. It was undoubtedly this aspect of the cult which led to both its early success and persecution.

In *Come on Ma! – Burn your Bra!*, MO chides a female disciple who has found these letters on sex a little hard to take. If she balks at these latest revelations, he asks, how can she possibly hope to enjoy "the coming orgasm of the spirit... the very wonders of total intimacy with a sexy naked God Himself in a wild orgy of the spirit as his totally surrendered bride". How indeed? And what's more, there are "even heavier letters on the way". He wasn't kidding. Less than a week later, in January 1974, came *The Flirty Little Fishy* and MO's recruiting brainstorm. There's something incomparably sleazy about the unctuous, pseudo-biblical manner in which MO, turned God's wimp, exhorts his female followers to go fourth and pick up men.

> ART THOU WILLING TO BECOME MY BAIT. To sacrifice thy life upon my hook and be devoured of others that they may live and be caught by Me to feed men. Then yield thyself therefore to be pierced through with many sorrows...

> YOU'RE SUCH A CUTE LITTLE FISHY, SO PRETTY! You roll those big eyes at them and you peck them with that pretty little mouth and you flirt all around them! – You wrap your pretty fins around them and you wiggle your little tail between their legs!

> MAY GOD HELP US ALL TO BE FLIRTY LITTLE FISHIES FOR JESUS to
> save lost souls for this creel! – Amen? – God bless and make you a flirty
> Little Fishy for Jesus.

David Berg had achieved a remarkable transformation – from itinerant preacher to the biggest, best organised and most successful dirty old man in the world.

WHERE ARE THEY NOW

David Berg's whereabouts have been a mystery since his departure from Tenerife in 1977. Over the years he was rumoured to be in many countries including Switzerland, Mexico and more recently, Greece. In 1981, Berg's daughter, Deborah, left the cult and wrote a book about her experiences, which included being crowned 'Queen of God's New Nation' and being raped by her father. According to some reports Berg is now dead and control of the organisation has been passed to Maria, while Berg's ex-wife has started an off-shoot called the 'Star Family'. The cult carries on in many countries, generally operating under the names 'Family of Love' or 'Heaven's Magic', with members living in small groups in 'safe-houses' and keeping a low profile. They still make headlines occasionally, as in England in 1990, when a school they were running was discovered in Hertfordshire; while a January 1991 article in *Truth* – 'Weird Cult Steals Oz Kids' – claims the cult was 'thriving' in Australia, had hundreds of members, and was responsible for the disappearance of a dozen children each year. Such claims seemed to be vindicated when, in dawn raids on 15 May 1992, police seized 140 children from houses in NSW and Victoria, claiming that their parents were members of the Children of God, and that they had been subject to sexual abuse. The cult was on the front pages for the first time in years, with some papers reporting that Berg is in Japan. A week later all the children had been released and the legal battle for their custody was on. Slowly, the facts emerged. The children, it seemed, belonged to a sect that called itself 'The Family', most members of which admitted they had once been the Children of God, but in interviews they emerged as rather a dull lot, mainly intent on keeping their children away from TV and other manifestations of the Twentieth Century. The evidence for sexual abuse, which they strenuously denied, doesn't seem to go any further than a few old MO letters found in the houses. Indeed, the Department of Social Services and the police seem to have done very little preliminary investigation. (It was suggested that the police had been urged to make the raids when they did because of the TV programme *A Current Affair*, which was preparing an exposé on the Children of God. This was duly aired on the Monday following the raids.) The whole affair seems to be a sort of Christian version of the more common Satanic ritual abuse scare. The situation was probably best summed up by one sect member who, when asked by a reporter how his sex life was, replied, "Not as varied nor as interesting as when we were in the Children of God."

The cult again made the headlines two years later, in Great Britain, when the Channel 4 television series *Witness* aired the programme 'Children of God' (27 July 1994). The documentary focused on the Padilla family who had quit the group after 18 years, detailing instances of 'Flirty Fishing', free love, child sex abuse, and pornographic videos made for the edification of cult leaders.

IT MIGHT SEEM STRANGE BUT. . .
Fetish, Obsession and Cool-Whip

A Miscellany of Correspondence to Various Porn Magazines, Pt V

DEAR SIR,
I realize that in these 'politically correct' times I have very little chance of success with my letter, but I am finding it increasingly difficult to obtain satisfaction from the current magazines on sale. I therefore have written to not only your publication, but to several of your competitors. I'm sure you will understand that my reading (and purchasing!) habits will be greatly affected by how you respond to my request.

My problem is the almost complete non-availability of magazines featuring women in Nazi uniform. Before you throw away my letter and think I am a racialist or in the KKK let me say it is only the uniform I find arousing. I am not an admirer of Adolf Hitler or of anything he did. In fact, I voted Democrat last time around! However I, I like I think many men in America, am most turned-on by blonde women dressed this way.

Many years ago in a bookstore I purchased a magazine which featured a theme concerning women in Nazi uniform. There were two girls, both perfectly suited to wear that sexy outfit. The pictures concerned them interrogating a captured soldier using torture. He was whipped severely but overcame his tormentors by screwing both. I cannot remember the title (it was a long time ago) but the images have been vividly imprinted on my mind ever since. I have searched in vain for the magazine without success and in my frustration I turn to ———— in the hope you will see fit to allow we enthusiasts of such uniforms to see our desires fulfilled.

I did once hear of a dominatrix in LA who specialized in this kind of thing, but it was too far away and besides I am not turned on by pain very much.

If your magazine could fulfil my wish you will have a loyal reader for life. If not, who knows?
respectfully,

Dr D———— P————————

Thanks very much for your last two issues. It was the only magazine that had photos of girls with balloons!!! And you did it on the last *two* issues. I'm impressed. Last year's Christmas magazine has balloons in it too. Also as far as I know your magazine is the only one that had a party girl balloon bursting romp – it was great. The trouble is that I'm wearing out my copy of ————, so is there any chance of doing another one, not the same, if possible with some different girls?

My wife and I both enjoy balloons and I'm very lucky to have a wife that knows how to tease me with them. Sometimes she will blow them up until they burst whilst giving me a blowjob – as in suck blow, suck blow... bang. Sometimes she will make me blow them up until they go bang. She won't let me touch her until this is done. This is a bit painful as she knows I am frightened of them, but to get my leg over it is necessary. Is she a sadist or am I a masochist? She also sits on them and bounces up and down on them until they burst. There is nothing quite like a balloon stretched between a girl's tight bum and a chair seat. Thanks ————, as you are the only magazine that has catered for us balloon fetishists this year. More balloons please!

Dear Sir: I wish to thank you for, and congratulate you on, the fine pictorial in the July 1993 issue of ————. Although I've been a regular reader for years, I have yet to see much coverage of my favorite fetish. You see, I have a strong fetish for women who smoke. So I was very happy to see sexy L—— smoking a long cigarette on page 46.

I first got the chance to indulge my fetish while in college. I was dating a beautiful hot French girl named N———— – she had blonde hair, green eyes and a killer body. One night on the way to the movies, our conversation somehow got around to smoking. I mentioned that I found women who smoke elegant and sexy. N———— agreed and my dick instantly began to swell. "Shall we stop and get some?" she asked. I could only nod and my cock was straining against my pants. We stopped and N———— bought a pack of 120 Slims. I couldn't believe my luck. In the parking lot, she began to massage my cock through my pants. "Ooh," she cooed, "I'd like a cigarette now."

She lit up and blew a plume of smoke in my face. I was in heaven. Right there in the parking lot she yanked open my fly to expose my dick. N———— bent down, took a deep drag and blew a puff on my cockhead. Soon she was giving me the blowjob of my life, sucking the cock deep into her throat, nibbling on the head and pausing only to smoke her cigarette. Before long I came into her hot mouth and she swallowed hard. Needless to say, we blew off the movie and spent the rest of the night sucking and fucking. All the while N———— was smoking her cigarettes. It was the best night of sex I'd ever had!

Since N————, there's been sexy A———, who liked to impale herself on my engorged prick while puffing away, and beautiful D————— who let me fuck her delectable tits while she smoked hot pink cigarettes.

I realize this is a strange fetish, but give it a try, folks – you'll like it! And to the people at ————, more pictures please! Come on, props are cheap – do me and all your other readers a service and show more pictures of sexy women smoking!

Sir,

I feel I must put pen to paper and share my experience with your readers, hopefully someone out there may be able to advise me if they have had a similar thing happen to them. I like to wear my wife's underwear when we make love; bra, knickers, stockings and suspenders. In fact my wife used to dress me up and tell me how nice

I looked as she touched and fondled me. She would make me lie on the bed and pull up my stockings before clipping them to my suspenders. Then make me stand up and pull on my knickers, often asking me to walk around the house while she followed me, playing with my nipples as we walked around. Very horny, I can tell you!

Just last week we went for a drive and underneath my normal clothing I was wearing a g-string and teddy as well as my stockings. We had a kiss and a cuddle but nothing more as it was quite busy where we had parked. We decided to return home for a good fuck. We went upstairs and I laid on the bed as my wife began fondling me and rubbing my cock outside my jeans. As we gradually removed each others' clothing my wife realised what I was wearing and she was none too please. Asking what was wrong she told me that she did not want me to wear anything apart from knickers, which incidentally we always buy together. I was most disappointed, not to mention embarrassed and removed the offending teddy, stockings and suspenders. She told me leave on my knickers as she liked me to wear them, but I do not know what is wrong with the rest of my undies. We made love with me still wearing my white knickers, they slide up my bum and allow me to pull out my cock and shag my wife, still a great turn on for us both.

You may think, so what's your problem? Well, I still like to wear my full repertoire of undies but do not want to do so if my wife does not want me to. Now I have started to dress up as I used to only when my wife is at work, and I can wear what I like. She knows I do this, because she has asked me so and I have told her I do, and she does not seem to disapprove. However, I wish it was the same as before.

Only yesterday she asked if I would like to go and buy a pair of knickers – to which I agreed like a shot. We always look through the display of knickers together but she insists that I select the pair I want and then go pay for them myself. She stands in the aisle and watches me pay for them and we rush home to try them on. I strip off naked and she pulls them on over my throbbing cock and we have fantastic sex sessions. But I feel I am missing out on the rest of my undies.

Should I be happy with what I've got or is there a solution that is not obvious to me.

Regards

B——, Sunderland

I have a weird fetish and I wonder if any of your readers have found the same desire. I love to fuck celebrity lookalikes. I've had quite a lot of success in my quest and to date I've been to bed with 'Sherilyn Fenn', 'Madonna', 'Liz Taylor', 'Farrah Fawcett' to name but four. There's something incredibly horny about the thought of having your cock sucked by someone 'famous' that I actually find it difficult to get worked up about anyone who doesn't remind me of a star.

That's the downside, but when you get to make love with a lookalike, then the sex is so damn good that you wouldn't believe it.

My Madonna was actually called N——, but she knew she looked like the singing star and was into her too.

Back at her flat we put some Madonna music on, plus a video of some of her raunchiest dance numbers and N—— acted them out precisely. She even put on a black basque identical to the one in the video. My cock was starting to rise and N—— – flashed me her delightful pussy as she danced, making me even hornier.

By the time she decided to let me enter her my balls felt heavier than they had ever done before and the amount of spunk I unloaded into her gaping hole was enough for half of it to come cascading out again! Not that N—— seemed to mind; she was bucking and writhing and coming just the same as I was.

So Madonna. If you're reading this, I hope it gets you wet just to think of our sexy fucking session; it was all in your honour!

G.K., Newcastle

What makes me buy a magazine when there are dozens to choose from in the store? It's more than just a pretty face or body – ALL MENS MAGAZINES HAVE THAT. What I look for are photos that completely include the woman's high heels. Yes, like a lot of men I know, we really get off on high heels. They are really sexy and feminine and make the difference as to when I buy a magazine.

There is nothing more frustrating to me to pick up a magazine and then see a hint of a beautiful high heel on the model and then see they are cropped out of most of the pictures, or partially cropped. Why have the models wear high heels if you are going to crop them out of the photos?

One last observation – if there are photos in your magazine that do not crop out the high heels, they are usually white heels. Believe me, I keep track. How about more photos of black high heels (or red, or blue)? And if you do, please do not crop half the shoe out of the picture.

C.T.R. Clearwater, FLA

Sir: man, you guys at ——— really hit the spot on my dick with the November 1994 issue! Yeah!! Tit-fucking is where it's at!! Man, my dick can't get enough of fucking a lady between her soft, hot, jiggling jugs and rubbing all over her gorgeous big nipples!! And cumming – YES, CUMMING, CUMMING, CUMMING ALL OVER A LADY'S NIPPLES AND BETWEEN HER BIG, SOFT TITTIES is the ULTIMATE sexual experience! My cock agrees, tit-fucking is the greatest, no doubt about it. It's the most fun thing to do with tits, and it's the 'breast' way to cum!

You guys ought to think about doing a special issue on tit-fucking, with a lot of tit-fucking letters, stories and pictures of guys going wild tit-fucking beautiful, bug-titted babes! Man, that would make me cum and cum and CUM!! I'll bet it would really sell out quick, since so many guys love and worship womens' breasts! Think about it, OK?

Man, that gorgeous C——— is just too much! I don't usually get off on African-American ladies, but she is incredible! Her skin looks like cafe au lait. Her pussy is totally succulent, and her tits W-O-W!! I could spend months with my aching, throbbing, drooling boner wedged so lovingly between them, fucking her gorgeous titties until I exploded all over them!

And her nipples – they're absolutely incredible! I would never tire of sucking on them, rubbing my drooling boner on them, and squirting my hot creamy cum all over them. They are perfect cum-targets! I've imagined pressing and poking my dripping dick-slit against her nipples and fucking them, and rubbing the underside of my cock all over them, and then having her squeeze her tits together so that I could fuck both of her nipples at once until my cock creams all over both her nipples. That would satisfy my nuts, big time! Man, I'm sure there are some lucky guys who've done that with her!

Please tell her that, if I had her, she'd have the most frequently-worshipped and fucked breasts, and the most frequently semen-soaked nipples, of any woman on earth! I beat my meat off three times yesterday, imagining the ecstasy of what it would be like to tit-fuck that gorgeous lady and cream all over those fantastic nipples! man, she's fantastic!

And that sweet, sexy lady N—— in ——— is so sexy! Her titties look so soft and inviting, and her pretty pink nipples drive me wild! To say I could spend as much time titty-fucking her and cumming all over her gorgeous nipples as I would with C—— ——— is totally obvious! Many times, I have whacked off dreaming of reaming and creaming N——'s sweet titties, too! I love her sweet pink pussy lips, too – I could spend months with my mouth and my tongue on her pussy, driving her out of her mind with pleasure! And, of course, I've imagined what it would be like to be tit-fucking both N—— and C——— together! What a fantastic cream-dream that makes!

Please tell N—— she's a really special woman and that she's given many men a lot of intense sexual pleasure! Of course, you guys have featured many other beautiful, sexy ladies that I would love to do that titty-fucking, pussy-slurping, cunt-fucking thang with as well!

I also want to say how much I enjoy reading all of those hot, horny, nasty sex letters in your publication. They're a real blast, especially the ones on the topic of – can you guess? – TITTY-FUCKING!!!

Yeah, you guys know what gets America off all right! Keep up the great work!

S.H., Maryland

Dear L—— I am writing to tell you that I love your pussy and I what to eat your pussy I saw you in the ——— magazine you are buteful you got some big tits I what to suck on I wish you where my girlfriend I will eat your pussy all night and I will put some cool whip in our pussy and suck it I will like it when you cum in my mouth. When I see you in the magazine I cum all over you – And your Ass is nice and big I will put my tongue in your Ass hole and lick it clean and play with it. I am crazy over you <u>plese</u> write me back. And plese send me some hair from around your pussy so I can lick it. And plese send me a nude picture of you or some pante's you <u>cum</u> in you will make my day.

Love C——

Dear ——— girls,

I've been a big fan of yours for years. I really love to check you out. <u>Your Super Extra Fine</u>!! I fantasize about eating your slicky shaved cunt and sliding my tongue deep into your perfect ass! I've kissed and licked your entire body from head to toe and I've even done this while masturbating. I always like your tight butt-hole in the magazine while I'm pushing a big fat dildo in and out of my butt. I pretend it's you that is controlling those mighty hard pushes deep inside me and pulling the 15" of latex cock real slow, then w/o any hesitation you bury the 3½" cock to the max! You dildo fuck me while I tongue fuck your sweet, butter-sweet tasting butt! It's only a fantasy that I'm always eating you up, every last drop of pussy juice and your ever so tender and tastey butt. I always lick up every last morsel, every last drop of liquid your lovely body produces. Keep up the killer work. <u>YOUR TOO FINE</u>! Thanks x

G.E.S.

DEAR J———,

I AM A BIG LOVER OF FANTASY SEX, AND AN EVEN BIGGER LOVER OF YOU: EVERY TIME I SEE YOU ON THE FRONT COVER OF A MENS MAGAZINE, I HAVE TO BUY IT. YOU LOOK SO BEAUTIFUL AND NEAT, WITH THOSE CHILD LIKE WOMANLY FEATURES, THOSE INNOCENT BROWN EYES, THOSE SEXY BROWN NIPPLES, AND THOSE LEGS OF YOURS REACHING STRAIGHT UP TO YOUR DELICIOUS AND WELL GROOMED LOOKING FANNY. VERY ELEGANT AND ARISTOCRATIC: SO WHEN I SAW YOU IN THE LATEST ISSUE OF ———, ACTING OUT FANTASIES BY REQUEST, I COULD'NT RESSIST; IN TELLING YOU MINE?

YOU SEE I LIKE FANTASISING ABOUT WOMEN IN DANGEROUS SITUATIONS OF A FEMME-FATAL BASIS, BASED ON A PERIOD OF HISTORY. FOR EXAMPLE MARIE ANTIONETTE; AND THE FRENCH REVOLUTION. YOU COULD ACT OUT A FANTASIE ON THIS BASIS. YOU ARE A DECETANT YOUNG ARISTOCRATIC COUNTESS. THE PERIOD IS 1793 IN PARIS. THE TIME OF THE TERROR. WHEN ARISTOCRATS ARE ROUNDED UP, PARADED THRU THE STREETS OF PARIS AND GUILLOTINED IN PUBLIC: YOUR CAUGHT BY REVOLUTIONARIES, AND PLACED IN A DARK DUNGEON, AWAITING YOUR TIME OF EXECUTION? SUDDENLY A GUARD COMES IN THRU THE CELL DOOR. YOU DO NOT RECOGNISE THAT THE GUARD IS A BEAUTIFUL WOMEN REVOLUTIONARY. BEING OF LESBIAN, TOMBOYISH, NATURE, THE GUARD MAKES HER PRESENCE KNOWN. SHE TAUNTS AND PLAGUES YOU AND ORDERS YOU ABOUT. THEN SHE GRABS THE BACK OF YOUR HAIR AND ORDERS YOU TO LICK HER BOOTS MORALLY DEGRADING YOU FROM THE HIGH AND MIGHTY PERSON YOU ONCE WAS. THEN SHE GETS CARRIED AWAY! SHE ORDERS YOU TO STRIP NAKED. YOU ARE EMBARASSED BY THIS. LOOK AWAY AND CLOSE YOUR EYES AS YOUR GUARD STRIPS OFF ALSO. SHE THEN LIES YOU ON THE DUNGEON TABLE WERE SHE LICKS YOUR PUSSY AND SUCKS YOUR NIPPLES OPEN MOUTHED AND SHOCKED YOU TRY TO RESIST, BUT SHE HOLDS YOU DOWN AND POINTS TO THE BARRED WINDOW WHERE YOU CAN SEE THE GUILLOTINE! NERVOUS AT THIS AND WHAT COULD HAPPEN TO YOU YOU RESIST NO MORE. YOU GIVE IN AND TEND TO SUDDENLY ENJOY IT, WHERE BY YOU LICK AND SUCK THE GUARDS TITS AND PUSSY, FULLY CARESSING AND FONDLING, AND FINGERING EACH OTHER TO AN EXHAUSTABLE CLIMAX... YOU THEN WANT TO SHOW THE GUARD SOME GRATITUDE? YOU DRESS HER IN YOUR SILK AND SATIN FRILLY DRESS AND JEWELLERY, WHILE YOU DRESS IN HER REVOLUTIONARY RAGS AND HAT. BESOTED BY THE FACT SHE AS ATTAINED YOUR FINERY, SHE DOSE'NT RECOGNISE THE GUARDS COME IN, AND SEEING HER IN YOUR CLOTHES AND FINERY TAKE HER INSTEAD TO THE GUILLOTINE! AND YOU ARE SAVED! AND THE BITCH GUARD IS TAKEN OFF SCREAMING AND STRUGGLING – AND

YOU JUST SMILING, AND WAITING TO SLIP OUT UNOTICED.

I HOPE YOU LIKE MY FANTASY, AND CAN PUT IT INTO YOUR MAGAZINE. WITH THAT VERY PHOTO-GENIC STYLE YOU HAVE. CAN'T WAIT TO SEE YOU AND YOUR NEXT ADVENTURE IN ———

LOVE,

S

My Question

The sight of cum squirting from the end of my hard dick and splattering on soft, tan skin is exciting to me and to those who watch me and/or masturbate with me. I masturbate in varying places and in front of, along with, and onto a variety of people. My question relates to the theme of my masturbation: The spurting of my cum.

I always thought my dick shot cum a fairly good distance. After stroking my dick (usually covered in Vaseline), after slowly stroking my hand up and down the length of my dick, the feeling of cum ready to burst from my dick would be too much to resist and I would squat in front of a mirror and continue to stroke my dick until its head swelled and gushed thick white cum everywhere. The creamy stream would usually travel 6-8 feet. When I aimed the milky fluid at my open mouth the force of each spurt was substantial and soon covered my waiting mouth and face.

The first time I received "acclaim" from others who observed this was in an outdoor setting. I often go to a park known as a meeting place for gay sex. When I go, I wear intentionally enticing clothes. I usually wear very skimpy, thus revealing, shorts along with an opened-to-the-waist shirt. The resulting bare skin reveals my suggestive dark tan-lines. I walk through the park pretending not to notice the stares my dress elicits. While I walk, I am looking for a secluded (actually semi-secluded) location that will allow me to toss my shorts around my ankles and my shirt over my head onto a limb or similar hangar and start to masturbate.

The spot I have chosen offers a one-way view of anyone approaching, while at the same time being exciting enough to start my dick dripping pre-cum. As a person who appears interesting approaches I turn away so as to pretend not to see their arrival. My eyes averted, after my "walk-n-strip", I try and give the impression that their arrival is unnoticed. As such, I continue to masturbate while the observer comes closer (much to my apparent "surprise"). As the "voyeur" reaches a point deemed "close enough" I "suddenly" notice that I am being watched as I (with my pants to my ankles) masturbate to my dick's content.

As the person arrives at the point where they can clearly see that I am jacking-off they stop and watch for a moment before usually moving in for a closer encounter. By the time I have been aware of their presence and "suddenly" notice/acknowledge my company. Acting slightly embarrassed at being "caught" wildly masturbating openly in a park, I, nevertheless, continue to jack-off in front of my guest. Most stop and admire/gaulk at this naked and masturbating, sex-crazy person but eventually continue and join the Cum-A-Thon.

When I finally do "notice" my guest, I explain that I am only into "safe-sex" but ensure them that they are welcome to stay and watch me spurt or join me in cumming over our faces and/or chest (yes, I always check for scratches, etc. so as to be as safe as possible).

One memorable day I encountered two fortyish guys and the wife of one of them. After some chat, the wife wanted to see which of us could squirt the furthest. As

incentive, she unbuttoned her blouse and offered her taught (somewhat tiny) tits as our target. The three of us started to stroke our dicks and strained to cum at nearly the same time. Standing only inches away, first one, then the other guy, splashed cum over her very enticing breasts. Realizing my opportunity I stepped back several feet and proceeded to sensually stroke my shaft until I squirted what must have been 7-10 feet. I still managed to send enough spurts onto her then somewhat slimy tits to totally cover her rose-colored nipples and their remaining tanned tit-flesh with a thick layer of cream. As I came, the wife sighed with surprise at the distance, as did one of the guys.

Lately I've been using a dildo when I masturbate (or have others masturbate for me). At first, the feeling of a hard shaft sliding in and out of my ass was delicious. However, eventually, even after sessions where I would squat in front of a mirror, Vaselined-dick in hand (with a long dildo sliding in and out of my butt) I'd get to the point where my cum could no longer be contained and I'd send it flying everywhere, BUT, only within a short distance (usually 2-3 feet). I can still cover my face (or my partners face) with gooey cum but only from 2-3 feet away, not the previous 2-3 yards. This brings me to my question.

Lately I've noticed that since fucking myself or being fucked with a dildo (usually 7-inches long and 3-inches circumference) that my cum-squirting distance has rapidly diminished. Does filling my ass with these plastic cocks diminish my capacity to shoot large and/or long loads of cum? Does my ass-fucking weaken muscles that are key to cum-squirting?

The women who watch and/or join me love to see cum blasting out of my shaft from nearly across the room, landing on their faces and/or tits. I love masturbating with them any way they may desire. Will my squirting distance return if I restrain from shoving these greased dildos up my ass?

S——

Enclosed is postage (SASE) Please send me xerox of article if it appears in your magazine. You may use my initials "S.P." Please do not use my name. I really would like an answer to my question. If it is in the published article that is fine. Thanks for your stimulation.

Dear Editor

I have never written to a magazine like ———— before but after viewing the pictures of L—— in the recent issue I have been inspired to write and tell you about what turns me on the most.

L——'s pictures were an especial turn-on for me because she was extremely heavily made up, with lots of blusher, eye liner, lipstick, eye shadow, mascara etc. What a doll! I think that a painted face is a wonderful thing and the more cosmetics a woman wears the sexier she becomes. I love to see women with very heavily made up faces. When I see one like L—— I develop an instant hard-on, that can only be relieved by sex of masturbation.

In recent years the trend has been toward women wearing little or no make up at all, the so-called 'natural' look. To me, it is <u>unnatural</u> for a woman to not paint her face. They always end up looking like boys and I'm sorry but boys don't do anything for me. I guess they think not wearing make up gives them 'equality' but it certainly doesn't make them sexy.

Seeing a woman paint her face is another big turn on. I always adore watching my girlfriends put on their make up and always insist on them doing so before we have sex. To put it another way, I am sexually inoperative unless my partner wears make up.

Lips are central to my obsession. Nothing is as sensual or provocative than a woman's mouth lined in deep red lipstick and highlighted with lip gloss. In L——'s pictures we had many wonderful poses in which her marvellous full and generous lips were parted sensually and her red-colored lips glistening provocatively. I was in heaven imagining myself receiving oral sex from a mouth like that. I work in an office where there are many female co-workers and every day I am very watchful when they check their make-up before going to lunch or leaving work. I always have a tremendous hard-on as the women around me put on more lipstick. If she has an especially sexy mouth or uses an attractive shade it gets so bad sometimes I have to visit the rest-room and masturbate. As our rest-room is some way from where I work I get some strange looks on the way!

I constantly fantasize about women painted this way. Once I had a sex doll which I would make up before proceeding to fuck its mouth. My climaxes were always highly satisfying and to observe my hard-on smeared with red lipstick only added to my sensual pleasure. Sometimes I purchase lipsticks and smear them on myself before masturbating. This too is extremely pleasurable.

I currently am without a regular sex partner and consequently very frustrated. I know there are hookers who would wear as much make up as I desired but I would worry too much, being in a powerful position at work and very vulnerable to embarrassment. In the meantime there is L—— and the rest of the wonderful women in your magazine.

G.P.L., Chicago

TOTAL WAUGH
Do we yet know the Full Truth about the Twentieth Century's Greatest English Speaking Novelist?

Simon Whitechapel

LITTLE OVER A QUARTER OF A CENTURY AGO Evelyn Waugh died on the lavatory from the cumulative effects of excessive drinking and drug-taking. If he is at this moment peering exophthalmicly down on the earth from the traditionalist Roman Catholic heaven he espoused in his lifetime, he would not be pleased by any comparison with the death of a rather more famous American; and yes, such a comparison would be most unjust. Waugh's excesses were in "bromide and chloral and crème de menthe";[1] he did not eat hamburgers, nor did he wear satin jump-suits, nor was he a cretin who happened to have a pleasant negro-effect singing voice; and *his* point of departure for the hereafter was a very English country house in Somerset called Combe Florey. But his death was, like Elvis Presley's, an undignified and more than faintly ludicrous one.

And perhaps also a just one. Death in Evelyn Waugh's novels very often takes undignified and ludicrous forms: in *Decline and Fall*, a prison chaplain is butchered with woodworking tools; in *Black Mischief*, the daughter of an English diplomat is served up to an ex-lover at a cannibal feast; in *A Handful of Dust*, an English lord of the manor finds a living death imprisoned by a jungle patriarch with a taste for readings from Dickens; in *The Loved One*, a semi-literate American mortuary cosmetician commits suicide by injecting herself with cyanide, and is disposed of in an animal crematorium. Waugh was a cruel man, a bully and a snob, and what happens to his characters very often reflects his character. The works of the Marquis de Sade are partly, in a literal sense, masturbation fantasies of gross sexual power; the works of Evelyn Waugh are partly, in a literary sense, masturbation fantasies of gross social power. They are, for example, full of ironies and barbs and sniggers at social upstarts or outsiders. Trimmer, Beaver and Atwater, the great triumvirate of Waughvian *untermenschen*,[2] are detestable because they are not gentlemen and do not know how to *behave* when they try to be. Nor, of course, would the working classes: they however are not detestable, merely ludicrous, because they at least know their place.

Given that Waugh was a snob and a bully, the fact that he was also a reactionary Roman Catholic is perhaps not surprising. Given that he was also a very intelligent man, with an acute sense of the ridiculous, this fact perhaps is surprising. Waugh took very little seriously. He disliked and distrusted (temporal) authority and those who exercised it

> many of the motives which make us sacrifice to toil the innocent enjoyment of leisure... are amongst the most ignoble – pride, avarice, emulation, vainglory and the appetite for power over others.[3]

and satirized it and them (he was certainly a conservative, but more in an aesthetic and economic sense than in a political). He disliked and distrusted modernism and modernists

> His strongest tastes were negative. He disliked plastics, Picasso, sunbathing, and jazz – everything in fact that had happened in his own lifetime.[4]

and satirized it and them with gusto. Perhaps he also disliked and distrusted himself, for he took himself as little seriously as he took almost everything else, and satirized himself mercilessly in *The Ordeal of Gilbert Pinfold*. He seemed to take only two things seriously: the English language, and the Roman Catholic Church.

I can understand, and am profoundly thankful for, his attitude to the former; his attitude to the latter once puzzled me. The Roman Catholic Church is not now, and never has been, a humane or intellectually coherent institution. I would call it and many of the things it teaches at best grotesque and at worst evil. Mother Teresa of Calcutta, for example, one of its chief propaganda weapons, is perhaps in herself a worthy, even a saintly person. She believes, however, that it is infinitely preferable for human beings to be born and starve to death than for them to be aborted or prevented by contraception. Perhaps this sort of thinking comes easily to a mind trained, as young Roman Catholic minds were before the Second Vatican Council, in the doctrine that eternal damnation can be yours for the price of a small mortal sin. The death-camps of the Nazis, overseen by a hierarchy of which a startlingly high proportion were brought up as Roman Catholics,[5] endured some dozen years; Hell, the death-camp of the Roman Catholic God, endures for ever. The Roman Catholic Church still teaches this doctrine of infinite punishment for finite transgression with other uncouth absurdities; many, in some countries most, of its professed adherents no longer apply its teachings in everyday life; in time it will succumb to the decadence that is already rooted in it (and that is now in full, glorious flower in the Church of England).

But it was not decadent for most of Waugh's life, and Waugh seemed to accept all of its traditional doctrines fully. He converted in 1930; in 1935, he wrote a biography of the Jesuit martyr Edmund Campion[6] in which one learns a great deal about the cruelties practised by the youthful Church of England on those who refused to renounce Roman Catholicism, the age-old faith of these islands. During the period covered by the book, the St. Bartholomew's massacre took place in Paris.[7] This is noted in passing

> He [William Cecil, chief adviser to Elizabeth I] had not foreseen the massacre of St. Bartholomew's Day, 1572, which had broken the supremacy of the Huguenots...[8]

The supremacy of the Huguenots was broken by the killing, with great savagery, of thousands of men, women, and children. On hearing the news, the deeply pious King of Spain, Philip II, was seen to smile for the first time in years, and the Pope, Pius V, ordered a medal struck in celebratory commemoration.[9] None of this, and none of the semi-genocidal activities of the Spanish army in the Netherlands over the period, is mentioned in Waugh's book.

The concept of double-think is perhaps useful in explaining these omissions. In *1984*, Orwell wrote

> "It [a Newspeak word] means also the ability to *believe* that black is white, and more, to *know* that black is white... This demands a continuous alteration of the past, made possible by the system of thought... known in Newspeak as *doublethink*".[10]

A further example of doublethink would perhaps be to believe that the persecution of Roman Catholics by Protestants proves that Protestantism is wrong, while the persecution of Protestants by Roman Catholics proves that Roman Catholicism is right. Orwell, who recognized the Roman Catholic Church for what it was, almost certainly drew on the psychology of the religious as well as the political believer in formulating the concept. It is not, however, the only or even a necessary means of explaining Waugh's apparently irrational religious beliefs. It may not be, as I shall try to demonstrate, the true means.

The first step I made towards discovering what possibly were Waugh's true motive for becoming a Roman Catholic was not a literal one. On holiday in the Seychelles last year, I was re-reading his collected journalism and came upon a passage, a notice from the Oxford university paper *Isis*, that had not caught my attention before:

> LOST, LOST, O LOST: Mr Evelyn Waugh regrets to announce he has lost a walking-stick made of oak, preposterously short with a metal band around it. It is a thing of no possible value to anyone but himself; for him it is an incalculable loss. If it should fall into the hands of any kindly or honest man or woman, will he or she bring it to the *Isis* office, and what so poor man as Mr Waugh is can do, shall not be lacking.[11]

For some reason, on this occasion, my attention was caught – and held. I read the passage through several times, not quite sure why I did so. I was conscious of only one strong impression, which was that in spite of its jocular air the notice seemed to indicate a very strong desire on Waugh's part to be re-united with his stick. The stick is mentioned again in Anthony Powell's Oxford memoirs, *The Infants of Spring*:

> Evelyn Waugh... was excluded from [the Hypocrites' Club[12]] at this period for having smashed up a good deal of the Club's furniture with the heavy stick he *always carried* [London, 1976, pg 154; my italics]

Why was a stick heavy enough to smash pre-war furniture "always carried" by its owner? Unless he was joking about his own lack of height, why should Waugh describe a stick that was "preposterously short" as a walking-stick? What was the significance of the metal band?

One possible, absurd answer is that the stick was a magic wand. The term immediately conjures up laughable Tinkerbellesque or Enid-Blytonian associations. If one tries to purge one's mind of these and take the term in an austere, occultic sense, it has to be admitted that the equation "stick-magic wand" answers all the questions raised by the *Isis* notice and extract from Powell. It remains, nonetheless, absurd. What possible connexion is there between Evelyn Waugh and the Black (or even the White) Arts? None, surely? A passage from his part-autobiography, *A Little Learning*, proves that this is not so. Waugh is describing his life immediately after Oxford:

> I also wrote some pages of a novel I had begun... it was named *The Temple At Thatch* and concerned an undergraduate who inherited a property of which nothing was left except an eighteenth-century classical folly where he set up house and, I think, practised black magic.[13]

This slight doubt about the plot is not found in a letter he wrote in 1925, shortly before beginning the novel

> I am going to write a little novel... "The Temple At Thatch"... about madness and magic.[14]

Waugh did what he had written he would. He sent the manuscript for comment to Harold Acton (1904–94), a friend whose aesthetic judgment he trusted. Acton was not enthusiastic and Waugh

> took the exercise book in which the chapters were written and consigned it to the furnace of the school boiler.[15]

The school was in north Wales, at Llanddulas, where Waugh was working as an assistant master and where, from his own words, his first attempt at a novel seems to have been drawing on the experience of his days at Oxford. A great deal has been written, by Waugh himself, by his contemporaries, by his later commentators, about those days, but some important evidence is lacking. Waugh kept a diary for part of his time at Oxford, but it is no longer available to us:

> I have been living very intensely the last three weeks. For the past fortnight I have been nearly insane... My diary for the period is destroyed... I may perhaps one day... tell you of some of the things that have happened. It will make strange reading in the biography.[16]

Christopher Sykes's biography of Waugh describes his going through an "extreme homosexual phase [at Oxford]... unrestrained, emotionally and physically".[17] Were entries pertaining to this period what prompted Waugh to destroy the diary? Quite probably yes – in part. But there may have been something more, something that would later provide material for his first novel: some kind of involvement in the occult.

That the extremity of this period may have taken in more than homosexuality is suggested by another letter Waugh wrote at the time to Dudley Carew, an old friend from Lancing, in which he said

> St. John has been eating wild honey in the wilderness. I do not yet know how things are going to end. They are nearing some sort of finality. One day I will tell you things to surprise you and sell an edition of the biography if faithfully recorded.

St. John's "eating wild honey" is a playful reference both to Waugh's less well-known second Christian name and, very likely, to homosexual practice. However, the remaining lines are not so easy to interpret as references to homosexuality. How can sexual indulgence be regarded as "nearing some kind of finality"? On the assumption that St. John's "wild honey" refers to the pleasures of non-penetrative activities like fellatio and masturbation, these words may refer to an impending decision as to whether or not to indulge in full homosexual intercourse, and yet they seem rather hyperbolic to bear this interpretation – particularly in the light of what follows. Why should Dudley Carew, a contemporary and great admirer of Waugh at Lancing, be surprised by Waugh's participation in homosexual activity? Because Waugh had not, like so many others, indulged in it at Lancing? If so, why should the circumstances of Waugh's participation at Oxford help to sell the biography Carew had long intended to write? That many young men were homosexually active for a period was taken for granted by those of Waugh's or Carew's public-school upbringing; that those same young men should make public admission of this fact in later life was certainly not. Homosexual practice was illegal at the time, and would remain so for decades; in the minds of the vast majority of those who would form the market for Waugh's putative biography, it would surely have been regarded as sordid and shameful, as Waugh himself must surely have recognized.

Yet the strains evident in the interpretation of these words as references to homosexuality disappear when one assumes that they refer rather to participation in the occult. Among the book-reading public of the day, and of many days to come, the occult was very popular: the novelist Dennis Wheatley enjoyed enormous success with books like *The Devil Rides Out* (1935), in which a black mass is celebrated near Stonehenge and there is a euphemistic but unambiguous description of black magicians pissing into a chalice containing pieces of holy wafer. Such things were sordid, certainly, but also fascinating, and one could easily imagine a biography containing details of Waugh's undergraduate dabbling in the occult provoking great interest. The dabbling need not be taken seriously, neither would news of it be an admission of participation in illegal activities: it would seem perversely sophisticated, rather than simply perverse. Given the hedonistic cynicism he was cultivating, if Waugh was aware of, and being invited to join in, occult practice at Oxford, he might very well have expressed himself in the words given above.

The assumption that he did see some participation in the occult bears exegetic fruit then, not only here but also in explanation of the plot of *The Temple At Thatch*, his destruction of his diary and even his concern at the loss of a heavy stick. It may also be usefully applied to his conversion to Roman Catholicism, which can now be seen as a reaction to, or even a flight from, memories of his involvement, which may have been a far more frightening or intense experience than he had anticipated. That he chose to enter the Roman Catholic church rather than resume the practice of Anglicanism, in which he was born and brought up, adds weight to this possibility. A reaction against a mildly affecting involvement in the occult might send one into a mild faith but defecting Satanists, like defecting communists, seem more naturally to become Roman Catholics than to become Anglicans. Nonetheless, it must be remembered, particularly in the case of an imaginative and aesthetically sensitive person like Waugh, that to be affected by an experience is not necessarily to have been a direct participant in it.

Evidence for Waugh's involvement in the occult nonetheless remains. More can be added to what has already been presented: the most direct (and least known) available to date is perhaps best approached through a more famous work. In *Brideshead Revisited*, the flamboyant, stuttering, homosexual aesthete Anthony Blanche is described as having practised black art in Cefalù.[18]

Cefalù, a small town in Sicily, is a shorthand for Aleister Crowley's infamous Abbey of Thelema, which was based nearby. Elsewhere, Waugh referred to Crowley directly. In *A Little Learning* he speaks of his election as secretary to the Hypocrites' Club[12] and continues:

> My predecessor in the office, Loveday, had left the university suddenly to study black magic. He died in mysterious circumstances in Alistair [sic] Crowley's community and his widow, naming herself "Tiger Woman", figured for some time in the popular press, where she made "disclosures" of the goings-on at Cefalu."[19]

Later he speaks of the hostess of many of the parties he attended in London after leaving Oxford:

> There was Mary Butts, a genial, voluptuous lady of the *avant-garde* who wrote short stories and at the time consorted with a man who had been in Alistair Crowley's black-magical circle at Cefalu.[19]

It is possible that his acquaintance with Crowley was not entirely third-hand. In 1933 he wrote a short story called 'I Step Off the Map'. Waugh's short stories are not particularly good, for the most part, and 'Out of Depth', as 'I Step Off...' was later renamed, does not stand out even amongst them for its literary merit. It is however of extraordinary interest from the point of view of this article, for it describes a dinner party encounter had by a lapsed American Catholic with a man called Jagger (later renamed Kakophilos),[20] who is unmistakably based on Crowley

> an elderly, large man, quite bald, with a vast white face that spread down and out far beyond the normal limits... a little crimson smirking mouth

The American, Rip, is introduced to the bald man

> "Do what thou wilt shall be the whole of the law," said Dr Kakophilos, in a thin Cockney voice.
>
> "Eh?"
>
> "There is no need to reply. If you wish to, it is correct to say, 'Love is the Law, Love under will.'"
>
> "I see."

Rip does not take Kakophilos seriously, but finds himself unable to resist the force of his personality and becomes involved in an occult experiment that projects him five hundred years into the future, to a London in which "[g]reat flats of mud, submerged at high water, stretched to his feet over the Strand". Europe has reverted to barbarism; Rip is treated almost as a zoological specimen by the savages inhabiting the ruins of London, and is eventually presented to a party of black African anthropologists for study at a coastal military base. He finds only one sane and familiar thing in this new world: a Roman Catholic mass conducted in Latin by a black priest at the base. Somehow he returns to the Twentieth Century. The story ends with him speaking with another Roman Catholic priest

> "Father," said Rip, "I want to make a confession... I have experimented

in black art...”[21]

The story is not well-known. According to Martin Stannard’s study of Waugh’s life to 1939,[22] it is now out of print. It was substantially revised for inclusion in Waugh’s short story collection *Mr Loveday’s Little Outing and Other Sad Stories* [Chapman and Hall, 1936] and

> Waugh did not include it in Penguin Books’ *Work Suspended and Other Stories* (Harmondsworth, 1947)[23]

Did its autobiographical elements become embarrassing to him as time passed? Margot Metroland and Alastair Trumpington, characters from his early *romans à clef*, appear in the story, and though Rip is named from Rip Van Winkle, is it entirely fanciful to see a resemblance between this harsh and somewhat violent monosyllable and that of Waugh’s own surname? Perhaps not. But on more prosaic grounds his neglect of the story is not inexplicable: it is not very good, and seems to have been written partly as emotional catharsis following the break-up of his first marriage – “a period of considerable anxiety”.[23] However, this latter fact may point again towards autobiography. Perhaps Waugh found this period of anxiety bringing to mind a similar at Oxford, and perhaps the story drew on relevant memories. The link between Crowley and Oxford has already been presented in the extract from *Brideshead Revisited*. The exegesis of this extract is, however, incomplete. Anthony Blanche was based, by Waugh’s own admission, on Harold Acton,[24] to whom, as has already been described, Waugh sent his first novel for comment. We are now in a position to see rather more in this fact. Was Waugh interested merely in Acton’s aesthetic judgment, or also, and perhaps more importantly, in Acton’s occult expertise? Was Waugh’s introduction to the “black art” made through Acton? Was Acton’s unenthusiastic response to *The Temple At Thatch* based less on the book’s artistic demerits than on the fact that it perhaps revealed too much, was too indiscreet?

An obvious way of trying to answer such a question would be to consult the letter in which Acton passed judgment on *The Temple at Thatch*. Part of this read: “Too English for my exotic taste. Too much nid-nodding over port. It should be printed in a few elegant copies for the friends who love you.” Or so Waugh gave the world to believe. The letter itself cannot contradict him, for it seems to be no longer extant. Christopher Sykes, discussing it in *Evelyn Waugh*, suggests that Acton’s judgment was

> a hard blow and it may be significant that, though Evelyn kept all his letters from Harold Acton, this particular letter is missing from the collection.[25]

Significant certainly, but precisely how? Is it likely that Acton had participated with Waugh in occultic practice, and so should be consulted by Waugh on a literary fruit of this? Evidence that strengthens the case for the participation of them both is found in Humphrey Carpenter’s *The Brideshead Generation*, which presents a far more detailed picture of the Oxford of Waugh’s day than any biography devoted specifically to Waugh:

> Emlyn Williams [an Oxford contemporary of Waugh’s]... records that lurid gossip was circulating about the Hypocrites, such as ‘they’re supposed to eat new-born babies cooked in wine.’[26]

Acton was the leading light of the Hypocrites, Waugh a prominent follower. And yet there is no need to assume that this gossip is literally true, for it is typical of the hyperbole associated with such aspects of the occult as Satanism, whether serious or pretended. It is in fact reminiscent of the gossip that circulated two hundred years before about Sir Francis Dashwood's Hell-Fire Club, another group of hedonistic, dissolute, and aristocratic young men. In those days, however, when non-attendance at church, let alone religious heterodoxy, was regarded as shocking and devilish, the gossip was likely to be have been nourished by rather less than its equivalent in Waugh's day. The Hypocrites would have had to do rather more to excite gossip, and so it was likely to contain more truth, without, of course, necessarily being entirely true. One may dabble in the occult without worshipping the devil, and one may worship the devil without eating new-born babies cooked in wine. But if one is rumoured to have done the last in a period in which the occult was attracting increasing participation, the likelihood of one's having done the first is not nugatory.

I believe that I have by now established that the imputation of some involvement in the occult to the reactionary Catholic novelist Evelyn Waugh is not so ludicrous as it might at first appear. This involvement nonetheless remains speculatory, and that it may have extended to the point of participation in satanic ritual or devil-worship can only be more so. And yet if it is, for the sake of argument, taken as a donnée of Waugh's experience, much light is cast on aspects of his adult character, and certain references made both by him and his acquaintances assume new significance.

As his brother-in-law Auberon Herbert recognized and said, Evelyn Waugh could be "an awful shit". Waugh recognized this himself, and would claim, on being taxed with the gulf between his behaviour and the demands of his religion, that if he had not been a Catholic he would have been far worse. The phrase he chose was "scarcely human". Catholicism was for him a defence against the malevolence he knew to be within himself. Cyril Connolly had made a similar observation. In an article he prepared on Waugh but never published, he said that

> Waugh's Catholicism was a force that saved him from... this "demon of destructiveness"... "which might otherwise have destroyed him"[27]

The metaphor chosen here need not be seen as of particular significance, and yet it occurs elsewhere in reaction to Waugh's behaviour. At one period, Waugh made strenuous efforts to persuade John Betjeman to become a Catholic, warning him again and again of the literal damnation that awaited him if he remained *extra ecclesia*. Betjeman's wife Penelope told Waugh that his propagandizing had affected her husband badly: "[he] thinks you are the devil and wakes up in the middle of the night and raves."[28] Again jocular, but again a diabolic metaphor. Such metaphors are not exhausted. There is a curious passage in Christopher Sykes' biography describing how

> Evelyn had long been an admirer of Hilaire Belloc [and] asked Duff [Cooper, husband of Diana] if he would introduce him to the great man... When the appointed day came around, Evelyn arrived neatly dressed, in a state of perfect sobriety, and on his best behaviour... [After the lunch was over and Waugh had left for an urgent appointment,] Duff asked Belloc what he thought of his brilliant young friend.
> "He is possessed," replied Belloc.
> How, Duff often asked, how, except by supernatural means, did Belloc know?[29]

On its own, any of these references can be taken as jocular: together I believe they are not insignificant support for the claims of this article, not least for what some will call the most extravagant of these. Involvement in the certain forms of the occult is known to be dangerous, and whether one accepts a literal or a psychological interpretation of them, the realities of demonic possession cannot be dismissed. Evelyn Waugh may have participated in satanic ritual at Oxford and been possessed by a "demon" in one or another sense for the rest of his life. The supernaturalism he espoused as a Roman Catholic may have pre-dated his conversion and been based on terrifyingly personal experience. He described possession once in his novels, in *Helena* [Chapman & Hall, 1950], a literary treatment of the story of St Helena, the discoverer of the true cross. The novel is set between the Third and Fourth centuries and makes use of "certain wilful, obvious anachronisms which are introduced as a literary device".[30] They do not, it has to be said, meet this end very successfully, either in such passages as

> "What a spread!" said Princess Helena, when she had guzzled. "What a blow-out!"[31]

or in an extremely interesting scene in which Waugh describes the Emperor Constantine and his wife Fausta witnessing a prophecy made by a young African witch who has been possessed by a devil:

> Music, unheard to the watchers, was sounding in the girl's heart, drumming from beyond the pyramids, wailing in the *bistro* where the jazz disc spun. She had stepped off the causeway of time and place into trackless swamp. [She begins to speak:] "Zivio! Viva! Arriba! Heil!"... [32]

Writing in 1950 of a ceremony taking place in 327, Waugh draws on imagery from the 1920s and 30s. He re-uses elements – blacks, travel in time, swamp – that he had first used in 1933 in 'Out of Depth' (see above). Is the link between such incongruent things, the ultra-modern and the ultra-primitive, to be found in the occult, encountered by Waugh both in England and in Africa during his extensive travels there in the early 1930s?

Anyone answering this question in the negative must still, surely, see the need for an explanation of the way such things occurred not once in Waugh's work but twice, separated by more than a decade and a World War, and of the way they find echoes not only in the remainder of his fiction but also in his correspondence, in his life-story, and in the reaction of his friends and acquaintances to his personality. Waugh has always been recognized as a complex and tormented man whose work is full of darkness and the macabre. I would suggest that the true extent of his complexity and torment and the true roots of his obsession with darkness and the macabre have never been recognized. Does Waugh deserve a place among the greatest writers in English this century? Undeniably. What were the obsessions and influences that prompted him to that place? This is a question that I have tried to answer fully for the first time here. Time may never tell, but I believe that at the very least I have shown that the full truth about Waugh's life and religious beliefs may still wait to be confirmed. Waugh as occult practitioner. Waugh as worshipper of the devil. Waugh possessed. Impossible things? Implausible things? Or, as Waugh himself may have predicted, simply "things to surprise"?

NOTES

1. Evelyn Waugh, *The Ordeal of Gilbert Pinfold*, ch. 2.

2. In *Men at Arms*, *A Handful of Dust* and *Work Suspended* respectively. If Hooper and Mulcaster from *Brideshead Revisited* and Corker from *Scoop* are added to the list, the ergative suffix "-er" can be seen to be of great importance in Waugh's nomenclature of contempt. The first person narrator of *Brideshead*, Charles Ryder, is perhaps shielded by his patrician "y", perhaps reflects Waugh's anxieties about his own social status: he was once described to his face by Duff Cooper, the husband of Waugh's longest-lasting and most aristocratic correspondent Diana Cooper, as a "common little man... who happens to have written one or two moderately amusing novels" [Philip Zeigler, *Diana Cooper*, Hamish Hamilton, 1980, pg 266].

3. Evelyn Waugh, 'Sloth' in *The Seven Deadly Sins*, ed. Raymond Mortimer, London, 1962. Reprinted in *The Essays, Articles and Reviews of Evelyn Waugh*, ed. Donat Gallagher, London, 1983 [pg 572].

4. *The Ordeal of Gilbert Pinfold*, ch. 1, 'A Portrait of the Artist in Middle Age.'

5. Hitler, Goering, Goebbels, Himmler (who based the organization of the SS on that of the Jesuits), Heydrich and Eichmann, *inter alios*. This over-representation of Catholics was found also among the smaller cogs of the Nazi machine. It is true that Catholics tended not to vote for the Nazis in elections but then communists tended not to vote for the Nazis either: I don't think anyone could regard this latter fact as rehabilitating Stalinism.

6. *Edmund Campion: Scholar, Priest, Hero, and Martyr*, re-published by Oxford University Press, 1980.

7. Campion was born in 1540 and executed in 1581: the massacre took place on the 24th of August, 1572.

8. op. cit., pg 96.

9. Pius V was canonized in 1712. Waugh's biographer Christopher Sykes, himself a Catholic, commented of one passage in Waugh's treatment of Pius: "This is to evade by rhetoric the fact that Pius V was a persecutor who went to extremes considered shocking even by the standards of his time, and that he never seems to have scrupled to support his principles by the use of atrocity." [*Evelyn Waugh: A Biography*, Penguin, London, 1977. pg 208.]

10. Taken from the appendix to *1984*. In formulating the concept of doublethink, Orwell was perhaps thinking of precept 13 in Ignatius Loyola's *Spiritual Exercises* (1548): "That we may be altogether of the same mind and in conformity with the Church herself, if she shall have defined anything to be black which to our eyes appears to be white, we ought in like manner to pronounce it to be black." Loyola founded the Jesuits, the "intellectual shock troops" of the Roman Catholic church.

11. *The Essays, Articles and Reviews of Evelyn Waugh*, pg 18.

12. The Hypocrites' Club was "notorious not only for drunkenness but for flamboyance of dress and manner which was in some cases patently homosexual". Evelyn Waugh, *A Little Learning*, W.J. Mackay & Co., Chatham, Kent, 1964, pg 179.

13. ibid., pg 223. Waugh's eldest son Auberon Augustus would later write in *his* memoirs [*Will This Do?*, Century, London, 1991] of a schoolfellow called "Brenninkmeyer who shopped me for trying to hold a Black Mass in the chemistry laboratory" [ch. 4, pg 69].

14. *Evelyn Waugh: A Biography*, pg 87.

15. *A Little Learning*, pg 228.

16. *The Letters of Evelyn Waugh*, ed. Mark Amory, Weidenfeld & Nicolson, 1980, pg 12.

17. *Evelyn Waugh: A Biography*, pg 78.

18. *Brideshead Revisited*, ch. 2, pg 47 of the 1984 Penguin paperback. The extract is taken from a description of Anthony Blanche's travels and experiences that falls in a section called ET IN ARCADIA EGO. The occult associations of this Latin tag are well-docuented: see, for example, Baignet, Leigh and Lincoln, *The Holy Blood & The Holy Grail*, Jonathon Cape, 1982.

19. pg 180; pg 211.

20. Greek for "lover of evil".

21. The extracts are taken from the revised version of the story, which was reprinted in *The Fifth Mayflower Book of Black Magic Stories*, ed. Michael Parry, Mayflower, 1976.

22. *Evelyn Waugh: The Early Years, 1903–1939*, JM Dent & Sons, London, 1986.

23. Reference(s) to pg 345 of *The Early Years*.

24. "There is an aesthetic bugger [= homosexual] who sometimes turns up in my novels under various names... 2/3 Brian [Howard] 1/3 Harold Acton," Waugh wrote in a letter of 14 March, 1958 to the Earl Baldwin [*The Letters of Evelyn Waugh*, pg 506]. In his discussion of Anthony Blanche in *Evelyn Waugh: A Biography*, Christopher Sykes argues convincingly that the proportions are reversed in this particular character. Brian Howard (1905–58) was a flamboyantly homosexual Old Etonian poet whom Waugh had first known at Oxford.

25. *Evelyn Waugh: A Biography*, pg 99.

26. *The Brideshead Generation*, pg 79.

27. ibid., pg 377.

28. idid., pg 395.

29. op. cit., pg 181.

30. Introduction, pg x.

31. op. cit., ch. 1, pg 18.

32. ch. viii, pg 187.

MICHIGAN AVENUE AFTER DARK
Reflections on the Vexed Issue of Race and Sexuality in Modern-Day America

A Miscellany of Correspondence to Various Porn Magazines, Pt VI

DEAR SIR:
After this annual note, I'm not going to subscribe to your magazine because of these reasons:

Although most of your models are curvacious and "beautiful" (or rather "homogenized") like most Caucasian women they are a little too beautiful – "fake beauty". Everyone who knows the score and whose been around knows African women are generally better in bed than Orientals and most definitely better than Caucasians. Why? It has something to do with the way they strut their stuff. My ideal woman would be around 55-60% African, 30-35% Oriental, and 10% Caucasian. That's pretty much how I rate their sexiness.

Anyway, what's so daring and bold or important about 2 women doing it together. How about 2 guys and 1 girl. Also, all your guys seem to fit into only 2 categories: the artificially muscular (usually short), long-haired, glassy-eyed, rock or country musical band type, or the lean, haircut-trimmed, bespectacled, 3 piece suit, office worker type. It's almost like your magazine is published in and comes out of some university town with bars and offices around.

I'm getting off much better with films these days anyway – it seems like magazines have all gone the way that Playboy Magazine did decades ago: $100,000.00 centerfolds (is this financial approach designed to intimidate or emasculate the suseptible – I think so: sort of like "Queen For The Day" – everybody hide behind the fairy-godmother: who really cares who publishes a magazine anyway, or who owns it?), That is: $100,000.00 centerfolds who look like nuns with their habits off and an attitude with a schoolteacher-type mentality which assumes the reader is an asshole!

I'm a Caucasian male and nothing personal, but I'll take 2 Africans in bed anytime (or maybe 1 African and 1 Oriental) – in a triangle-arrangement, or maybe 4 people in a square-arrangement: 2 guys and 2 girls.

Like most sex publications – your magazine isn't creative enough.
Sincerely,

A—

The Aryan Brotherhood gave the word – prison war. They did not direct it to the BGF or the Chincanos but everyone in prison began to survive on the weapons they could get smuggled in or the gasoline they could obtain at work in small engine school. Whatever weapons could be gotten, warfare survival would be the ultimate weapon. It was easy for a black man to get burned in his cell with gasoline as it would be for some petty embezzler that didn't have a friend in prison, but if a black got burned the war would go on because some white man would have to pay for it with broken fingers or a world of hell created out of terror and fear. But the petty embezzler might put an end to the war for both sides. He was a man that had all the money and prosperity he needed to succeed in the system and all the prison gangs knew it was a rare chance to meet him at all and an evil miracle to find him in prison. They have him as bad as the slickest snitch because people like him were the cause of their prison time and they could take out a life of hate with a certain intelligent method. He was what they hated and it put reason to their hate when it finds its source. Just like blacks hating whites, they all seek that thing they hate. That embezzler was such a freak in prison it seemed almost like they had put a woman in a mens' colony. It was a privilege to be in the same prison as him. As a matter of fact, he might be as lucky as they were just like the women who are as lucky as the men in a co-ed prison. Sure, he may never leave the prison alive, but it could save him from a life he had already decided to think was at least as bad as prison to him. How bad could the life of rock and roll troupe Nirvana be? It led to suicide, did it not? Well, some people who look like they could or seem to have a dream come true in real life wind up in prison and so it was for the embezzler. Maybe this was the case for many people, but some people go to prison just because they have to kill others and prison is as good a place as any to do it. Even a better place than most because they can't be punished for it. What punishments they have in prison for someone who kills there only makes that man more respected than he was. You see, death in prison works like an evil machine. Nothing changes, someone is dead and the machine keeps turning. If you know how the machines runs or how to operate it, you can kill in prison with no fear of punishment. The body of a human in prison runs on a certain diet, a certain daily routine and certain social functions. Anything alien to that prison life can kill that prisoner. If the police knew what it was they would prevent that death, but the irony is that the inmates know what it is and use it on some inmate just to kill. Some guy thinks he got some crank and instead he gets chemical that is deadly. The problem is that one cannot obtain an antidote in prison. The brain needs oxygen to survive. The blood takes it to the brain. Also the brain works like a muscle. It has a central body organ like all the muscles in the body. If one part of the brain is damaged, the entire brain becomes affected. Imagine the brain as several coordinated muscles serving thought, glandular and some unknown reflex muscles. They all respond to a central muscle control factor, blood or oxygen. Say the brain perceives a sensation that slows its reflex, possibly a sensation of self-awareness, possibly the awareness that its asshole is under its yes or no response direction. Or possibly that there are other brains just like it, five and a half billion of them to be exact. When the brain muscles cease to function correctly there is a self-destruct mechanism built right into the cerebral cortex.

But for a certain embezzler in our prison, the brain was not an abstraction but a real honor in his cell for every inmate and every corrections officer there. For you see, several white power gangsters entered his cell one evening and extracted his brain from its safe haven in his skull. Parts of his brain wound up in the commode, parts of it spewed into the corridor and one white power member even ate part of it. The guards witnessed much of the atrocity, but could not make an ipso facto arrest. The brain emenated a noxious smell before the prison guards stopped the white supremacy group with mace and billy clubs. The toilet in that embezzler's cell was more conscious than his once-living brain. It might even have been conscious of a brain being flushed down its pipes with the rest of the shit.

But there are those who would waste a million dollars on a brain in a shithole, because they have shit for brains themselves! One such man and his faithful queen, Cleopatra of the porno screen, used to spend his money at an exact quality level above his competitors, which gave him a whole lifestyle with his queen Cleopatra Cricket. It caused a few heads to boggle, but there was most times to do it in. So he combined his lifestyle to a computerized system which led to one calculated error. He soon ran out of money and became the victim of a crueller profit war! The game he wanted had only a few days to it and he used it for only one week or so. But anyway Cricket had men galore and only four of them were the right quality. So when they moved it was only safe to assume that Cricket went with them. They never returned, but Cleopatra did. She was not with them. The four of them moved to Bodega Bay with no Cricket. She had seemed to vanish. What happened at Bodega Bay? Well, they went in search of women or young girls that they could exploit. They found some and used them for porno pictures and distressing movies.

But Cricket missed her opportunity with them. She had gone to Boise, Idaho. Why there, of all places? To seek the golden rule Covanity Club. There she could meet people her own age or younger, which she could not do with those four militant mf's at Bodega Bay. One night they split up the card game and began to patrol the blocks for signs of life. There were none except a barking dog. All four of them began to bark like a pack and promptly robbed a Weinerschnitzel for $2,500 in cash. With that amount of money they could operate trafficking in various fields. They travelled out of the state of California into Mexico where they lived for two years on the money they had stolen. Chicanas, marijuana, bullfights and good coconut juice made their lives heaven. They would have stayed three years, but they all had to see Cricket one more time. In Boise, Cricket had left them a calling card. When they got together again, she showed them how she really was when she was hot and she was wanton and unbusinesslike when four men took their turns with her in one wild night. The only reason she did not have all four of them was because one of them went to the other bedroom with her roommate. But three of them got the suck and fuck of their lives and the more it had the appearance of a gang rape the more Cleopatra would respond with delight. She would suck one of them while she jacked a second one's dick and squealed as the hot cum spurted into her mouth. They knew that her chubby butt would get a third before the night was over and she was not disappointed when the three of them entered her ass in a train. She just rolled over, spread her legs and showed why men loved her so much, her sweet and tender cunt. It was a long night of sex and Cricket was a satisfied woman when it was all over. They got in their car and drove to a gay bar and they were all happy as they made wisecracks to the fags there and Cricket was secretly amused to watch her boyfriends bully this one gay, because she knew he wanted to suck as much as she did, but could never fulfill his desires without the risk of some blood on him. So they went for a month or more, each taking their time with her on successive nights, and days, too. And so they all proceeded into a life of pleasure that set the town of Boise talking. But no one had a bad thing to say about her or them because the people in Boise are a good natured lot and like to see young people have fun.

There is an old warehouse in Chicago that is long on the decline in Chicago business and industry, but the old building on Michigan Avenue still serves a purpose for the remaining gangs that inhabit Chicago who also have little purpose nowadays except to take their enemies into that warehouse and keep them for days and subject them to any torture that their wicked minds could devise without any police interference. It was easy in the 1980s Chicago to carry the body of their victim to Lake Michigan just as Al Capone once did in the 1920s. It was especially easy from that warehouse on Michigan Avenue as it was only a short walk to the lake.

Well, it was a shock to imagine Cleopatra Cricket in that warehouse. She had met the Southside gang in the same way she had met all her men, through a sex game. But these men had taken her to their warehouse. Maybe because after the sex game was over they were still black and she was still white and black people in Chicago still hate white people and vice versa. Cricket thought she was going to see some poor grocery store clerk tied up in the warehouse and she had her own way to torture men that was part of her sex game. Well, her screams were never heard outside of the warehouse, as she was on the third floor and few people strolled Michigan Avenue after dark. But there she was, nude and tied to a beam with black men coming from long distances to see her suffer. How she got there was a long story which could be rather boring, but suffice it to say that her four boyfriends knew where she was, but did not know that she had a secret life with the black gangs on the Southside of Chicago. But their ears were keenly tuned to her screams which she claimed could bring a hundred men running to her aid if she ever did scream. Well, she was screaming now and these four men were conscious of her agonies. It seemed hard to be here, but they were able to gravitate towards that warehouse where she was falsely imprisoned and on hearing at the entrance it gave them the clue they needed to establish that she was indeed inside and screaming loudly. The warehouse was locked but they were able to gain entry by tearing the plywood off the lower window. The first thing they confronted when they were inside was a lone black man with a silk bandana around his forehead, gold earrings and an assault weapon in his hands.

"What have you done with Cricket?" they said. But one of them had sneaked back out through the window while this conversation was taking place and had brought the gun arsenal from out the trunk of their car and came back in through the window the same way. Before they could learn the whereabouts of Cricket from the ugly black, the guy with the guns had cold-cocked him and he was now only one dead nigger. The gunshot in the warehouse echoed through the three stories and several blacks appeared, all armed and dangerous. A fight ensued that looked like the street wars of France under German occupation. The only difference was that it mattered who died here on Michigan Avenue. They had to kill every black man in the warehouse to save Cricket from some pain that would never go away because even the memory of it was painful.

Two blacks went easy because they attacked our four heroes Zulu style. Just a bullet in the head was enough to stop the ambushing blacks. But the rest of them, six or seven, it was not certain, became more canny and took defensive positions around the warehouse. Our four white friends stayed behind some crates and the gangsters held various spots behind boxes, posts or wherever they were safe from the silver bullets. The shootout lasted about a half hour with still no sign of police, although half the population of Chicago knew it was happening all the way to Cicero. What finally brought an end to the fight and became the decisive weapon of the battle was the two-way wavelength that served as a long-distance walkie-talkie. The blacks had it and the signal could call in any number of their people from the Southside. When ten blacks arrived in their cars it was only a few minutes before three of the Cricket savers were dead and the fourth one was naked and tied up beside Cricket in the back of the van which was headed for Lake Michigan.

Suddenly the driver of the van got the brilliant idea to take the Cricket and her boyfriend to Detroit instead of drowning them in Lake Michigan. It was not a smart decision, but it was a necessary one because anyone might see them throwing the bodies off the wall into Lake Michigan to be swept downwards in the undertow. But an unexpected thing happened to the van on the way to Detroit. Right on the highway fifty miles out of Detroit the van suddenly burst into flames and crashed head-on into a tourist bus leaving Detroit for Gary, Indiana. Four blacks, Cricket and her faithful lover all met with a fiery death and a few tourists suffered minor cuts and bruises. What seemed like a miracle was actually a premeditated bomb planted by a white Chicago socialite who knew that a race war was happening in that warehouse on Michigan Avenue. He had carefully placed a night flare used by the train crews in the drive train of the van and the heat from the moving vehicle had caused the flare to ignite, exploding the gas tank and the whole rear end of the van. I suppose he was the hero of the race war, but even he could not make Cricket come back to life again. She was gone forever and no one in Boise will ever know what happened to her. Her body was burned so thoroughly that no identification could be made and the coroner assumed that she was a black woman for that reason did not waste a lot of his time in trying to establish her name, age etc. But she left a token to remember her by. She was only 26 years old.
The End.

DEAR EDITOR,

THANKS FOR C————!

MMMMMM!

IN MY OPINION SHE IS THE MOST BEAUTIFUL QUEEN I HAVE EVER SEEN IN YOUR MAGAZINE.

YOUR MAGAZINE SHOULD SHOW MORE LATINAS AND I DON'T MEAN BLEACH BLONDES.

AND IT SHOULD SHOW MORE BLACK LADIES

I THINK THAT THE EDITOR PREFERS BLONDE WOMEN

BUT ANY PRETTY BOW OR BLACK LADY WHO WANTS A PUSSY AND ASS LICKING FROM ME GETS IT BEFORE A BLONDE WHITE WOMAN

SO IF I HAD A PRETTY BROWN OR BLACK LADY WHO WANTED TO SIT ON MY FACE AND

WIGGLE

AND

A PRETTY WHITE BLONDE LADY WHO WANTED TO SIT ON MY FACE AND WIGGLE

I WOULD PICK THE BROWN OR BLACK LADY

IF YOU NEVER EXPERIENCED IT, YOU DON'T KNOW WHAT YOU'RE MISSING.

TRY IT

THOSE BEAUTIFUL, SPECTACULAR, IRRESTABLE BUTTS ON PRETTY BROWN OR BLACK LADIES

THOSE SWEET JUICY PUSSYS

THEY ARE THIS PUSSY AND ASS LICKERS FAVORITES!

SO JANET JACKSON CAN SIT HER ABSOLUTELY PERFECT SWEET ASS ON MY FACE AND PARK IT THERE!

THE NEXT TIME YOU PUT AN ADD IN YOUR PERSONALS SECTION IN THE BACK OF

YOUR MAGAZINE ABOUT

"REAM JOBS"

SHOW A NICE BROWN OR BLACK FEMALE ASS!

I'LL REAM IT!

AND THERE ARE A LOT OF THEM THAT LOVE HAVING A HANDSOME WHITE MAN LICK THEIR

BEAUTIFUL BROWN AND BLACK ASSES

A PERFECT MATCH!

AND I HAVE PLENTY OF DICK POWER. DOING THEM GETS ME HARD. A TREMENDOUS TURN-ON.

TO ME!

NOW I KNOW THAT IT UPSETS BLONDE WHITE WOMEN

THEY SHOULD KNOW THAT THE OTHER SIDE OF THE RACE MIXING COIN EXISTS

ONE OF THE MOST FAMOUS MEN IN YOUR COUNTRY,

WHO IS ALSO A SEX SYMBOL,

JUST TOLD YOU THAT HE LOVES DOING REAM JOBS ON BROWN AND BLACK FEMALES

AS YOU SAY, FANTASY BECOMES REALITY FOR THOSE WITH THE GUTS TO GO FOR IT.

YOU'RE RIGHT!

HOW RIGHT YOU ARE.
AND NOW THAT <u>THE TRUTH ABOUT ME</u> IS OUT I EXPECT THERE WILL BE A
LOT OF BROWN OR BLACK WOMEN WANTING THEIR PUSSYS EATEN
AND
**A NICE REAM JOB FROM THE BEST PUSSY AND ASS-LICKER
IN THE WORLD**
BROWN AND BLACK WOMEN ARE MY FAVORITES.
PUT THAT RIGHT OUT THERE FOR ME
I'M ADVERTISING AND YOU HAVE HELPED ME A GREAT DEAL
WHEN I HIT IT BIG, WHICH I WILL
YOU GET $100,000.00
FROM ME TO YOU
IF YOU WOULD LIKE I'LL DO A LAYOUT WITH THAT QUEEN FOR
YOUR MAGAZINE
FANTASY BECOMES REALITY FOR THOSE WITH THE GUTS TO GO FOR IT
YOU'RE RIGHT!
Love, L— E———
PS: THANKS FOR BEING MY FRIEND.

IT WAS 6: AM SATERDAY MORNING. I HAD PLANNED TO STAY IN BED ALL
MORNING SINCE I HAD REALLY DID MY THING WITH THE LADIES AND GUYS
LATE LAST NIGHT. MY HEAD WAS REELING AND ROCKING AND I COULDN'T
CALM DOWN. DAM THAT SHIT IS STRONG! FUCK ME DADDY FUCK ME, DADDY
FUCK ME. I BEGAN TO GAIN MY SENSES AND REALIZED WHAT WAS
HAPPENING TO ME. MY NEW WHITE NEIGHBOURS IN MY APARTMENT
BUILDING WERE FUCKING LIKE IT WAS GOING OUT OF STYLE. AND IT WAS
GOOD! THE NASTY SEXY ASS SCENT OF HER PUSSY WAS FLOODING THE
BUILDING. GOD SHE WAS FUCKING NASTY AND GOOD AND I COULDN'T WAIT
TO MEET HER NASTY SEXY WHITE ASS. OOOOO BABY FUCK ME FUCK ME. I
HEARD HER MOANING AND FUCKING. THEY WERE IN AN APARTMENT NEXT
TO MINE AND I COULD HEAR HER MAN FUCKING HER BETWEEN HER BIG
NASTY ASS SEXY THIGHS. SMACK SMACK SMACK SMACK SMACK. HE WAS
SMACKING HER BETWEEN HER FILTHY ASS WHITE THIGHS POWERFULLY
AND RHYTHMICLY. FUCKING HER NASTY PUSSY WITH QUICK SHORT
STROKES. HER PUSSY WAS LOUD TO MY SENSES. UNNNNNN. UNNNNNN.
FUCK, FUCK ME, UNNNNN BABY! I SWEAR I NEVER KNEW FUCKING WAS SO
GOOD AND NASTY. I AM NO PRUDE BUT BEING FROM THE SOUTH I AM ONE
THAT HAS NEVER BEEN BLESSED WITH HER EROTIC SEXUAL ENDOWMENTS.
I WANTED TO FUCK AND SHE WASN'T DOING GOOD FOR ME. I COULDN'T
TAKE IT ANY MORE AND MY HAND FOUND MY BIG NASTY NIGER DICK AND
STARTED TO CARESS IT SLOWLY. I COULD SMELL HER SUCCULENT ASS SHIT
CAKES AND HER HOT JUICY WIDESPREAD WHITE THIGHS AS SHE FUCKED
AND FUCKED. MY 8 IN. DICK HAD SWELLED ANOTHER INCH FOR HER HOT
FILTHY WHITE ASS. I HAD TO FUCK A SEXY ASS WHITE WOMAN AND SHE
WAS THE SEXY WHITE WOMAN THAT I HAD TO FUCK. I SKINED MY BIG NASTY
DICK FOR HER AS SHE FUCKED. I COULD ALMOST VISUALIZE HER PLUMP
SHIT JUICY WHITE ASS THIGHS AS I SKINED MY FILTHY BIG DICK FOR HER

DICK BACK AND FORTH. I PISTONED MY BIG NASTY NIGER DICK HARD IN TO PUSSY LIPS WHICH HAVE A SUCKIN IN SOUND AS I WORKED IT DEEP INTO THE GLOVE OF HER HOT JUICY WHITE PUSSY. YES, FUCK ME NIGER, NASTY FUCK ME BABY. DO IT TO ME BABY. FUCK MY PUSSY. PLEASE FUCK MY PUSSY GOOD BABY. SHE WAS HUGGING ME AND I WAS TONGUE KISSING HER SENSUAL MOUTH AS WE FUCKED. SHE HAD HER BIG FINE LEGS PULLED UP AND SPREADED WHILE HUGGING WITH THEM AS WE FUCKED. I FUCK HER PUSSY FROM SIDE TO SIDE AND AROUND AND AROUND HARD AND DEEP BETWEEN HER GOOD PUSSY LIPS. HER PUSSY BEGAN TO SMACK AS CUM AND AIR PRESSURE ESCAPED AS WE WORKED DICK AND PUSSY TO EACH OTHER FUCKING. WE FUCKED UNTIL I RAN CUM TO PUSSY THAT SOAKED THE SHEET WE WERE FUCKING ON AS HER OWN NASTY CUM TOO COAT MY BIG NIGER DICK AND HER THIGHS AND ASS CHEEKS AS WE FUCKED IN AND OUT AGAIN. HER PUSSY POPING FUCKING AS SHE AND I FUCKED. MY BIG DICK POPING INTO HER PUSSY DEEPLY AS SHE WHIPPED HER JUICY ASS GOOD PUSSY ALL THE WAY TO THE LARGE BASE OF MY HUGE NIGER DICK. FUCK FUCK FUCK FUCK FUCK HER HOT JUICY ASS NAKED PUSSY WAS POPPING AS WE FUCKED, SHE WORKED NASTY JUICY SHIT CUM TO MY DICK AGAIN AND COATED THE FULL SIZE OF IT AS WE FUCKED. I KISSED HER AS WE FUCKED AND ROLLED SLIGHTLY TO ONE SIDE AND MESSAGED HER NASTY SEXY WHITE THIGH AND ASS CHEEKS. I BACKED MY DICK OUT OF PUSSY HALF WAY AND FINALLY SLIPPED MY BIG DICK OUT OF HER PUSSY BUT I DID NOT RELEASE HER. I WANT SUCK YOUR BIG NIGER PENIS SOME MORE BABY SHE SAID. SURE BABY I WANT TO SUCK NOW HONEY. I LAYED BETWEEN HER LUSCIOUS BIG WHITE THIGHS AND MESSAGED HER ASS CHEEKS AND THIGHS AND LAYED MY BIG NASTY PENIS BETWEEN HER WET STICKY NAKED WHITE ASS CHEEKS. I MESSAGE HER SEXY WHITE TITTIES AND HER HIPS AND THIGHS AND PUSSY AND GENTLY WORKED MY PENIS TO HER BIG FINE STICKY ASS CRACK AND MESSAGED HER PERT YOUNG TITTIES AS I OPENED MORE OF HER FILTHY FINE ASS CHEEKS WITH THIS BIG DARK NIGER PENIS. I MESSAGED HER FILTHY JUICY SHIT ASS CHEEKS APART AND WORKED A FINGER INTO HER SENSUAL HONEY SHIT POT AND FINGER FUCKED HER SEXY WHITE ASS UNTIL HER FINE HONEY SHIT CHUTE WAS JUICY LOOSE. I KISS HER THIGHS AND MESSAGED HER SEXY WHITE NAKED LUSCIOUS ASS CHEEKS. I BIT HER BIG FINE ASS CHEEKS AND LICKED HER NASTY SEXY ASS CLOSER AND CLOSER TO HER LUSCIOUS HONEY SHIT POT. I LICKED INTO HER NAUGHTY ASS CRACK AND SPREAD THEM APART AND LICKED AROUND HER HONEY SEXY NAKED ASS SHIT CHUTE. I WET HER HONEY ASS SHIT CHUTE LUSCIOUSLY WITH MY HOT NASTY NIGER SPIT AND WORKED MY TONGUE AROUND HER TASTING HER SUCCULENT SHIT JUICE. I LICKED DEEP INTO HER HONEY SHIT CHUTE AND RAN MY TONGUE AROUND HER HONEY SHIT HOLE TASTING THE HONEY SHIT HER NASTY SEXY WHITE ASS MADE. BABY I LIKE YOU. I LIKE YOUR BIG FINE NASTY SEXY FILTHY LUSCIOUS WHITE ASS. I LICKED OUT HER LUSCIOUS SEXY WHITE ASS AND KISSED AND LICKED HER ASS CHEEKS AND HER NAKED WHITE FILTHY FINE ASS THIGHS. NOW I WANT TO SUCK YOU BABY SHE SAID. I WANT TO SUCK THE PISS OUT OF YOUR BIG NASTY NIGER PENIS. SHE PUSHED ME OUT OF THE BED AND SIT ON THE SIDE OF IT AND PULLED ME IN FRONT OF HER. I'M GOING TO GIVE YOU MY MOUTH BABY, BE GOOD TO ME, PLEASE, FUCK THE

PISS OUT OF MY MOUTH WHILE I SUCK YOUR BIG BLACK PENIS DRY. SHE TOOK MY NASTY BLACK BIG PENIS AND STROKED IT SLOWLY. SHE WAS SO PETITE HER HAND COULD NOT ENCIRCLE ITS THICKNESS. SHE LOOKED AT IT AND LOOKED UP AT ME AND SMILED WICKEDLY, YOU KNOW I CAN'T GET ENOUGH OF YOU FUCKING ME DON'T YOU? I LIKE IT BABY, IT'S SO GOOOOODDD. I WANT YOU TO PISS IN MY MOUTH WHILE I SUCK YOU BABY, WILL YOU DO THAT FOR ME BABY? YES I SAID, YES BABY JUST SUCK ME I'LL DO ANYTHING YOU WANT ME TO DO TO YOU BABY, JUST SUCK ME BABY. IF I SUCK YOU NASTY ENOUGH WILL YOU FUCK ME AND SUCK ME AGAIN. YES BABY SHIT YES, JUST SUCK MY NASTY BIG DICK HONEY SHIT BABY. O-K GIVE IT HERE. SHE PULLED THE SKIN BACK TO THE BASE AND WET HER ALREADY WET LIPS AND BEGAN TO RUB HER HOT JUICY TONGUE AGAINST MY PISS HOLE. SHE RUB HER TONGUE AGAINST MY PENIS HEAD AND LICK IT AND WET IT WITH HER JUICY SALIVA AND RUB IT BACK AND FORTH ON HER MOUTH. YOU LIKE IT BABY? IS IT GOOD ENOUGH FOR YOU? YES HONEY IT'S GOOD AS IT CAN BE, SUCK ME YOU FINE NASTY SEXY ASS BITCH, SUCK ME GOOD. SHE STROKED MY BIG DICK AND RAN SALIVA FROM HER MOUTH ONTO IT'S BIG NASTY BLACK HEAD AND LICKED ALL THE WAY TO MY BLACK BALLS AND STROKED IT AS SHE SUCKED MY NASTY BLACK BALLS. I WANT YOU TO PISS CUM INTO MY NASTY MOUTH BABY AND FUCK MY NASTY WHITE PUSSY SOME MORE. YES BABY, AND I WANT SUCK YOUR DELISIOUS SHIT CHUTE AGAIN BABY IT'S SO GOOD AND NASTY. YES BABY I'LL FUCK SOME MORE BUT FIRST I WANT YOU TO MAKE MY PENIS CUM IN YOUR SEXY MOUTH. YES BABY I'LL DO IT FOR YOU JUST GIVE IT ME IN MY MOUTH NOW BABY PLEASE GIVE IT TO ME IN MY MOUTH AS SHE OPENED HER WET NASTY MOUTH AND SLIPED IT DEEP INTO IT AND BEGAN TO SUCK NASTY. MY NASTY BLACK BIG DICK STARTED OOZING FILTHY CUM MIXED WITH PISS INTO HER WAITING MOUTH AS SHE SUCKED AND WHIPPED IT WITH HER HAND IT'S GOOD BABY SHE SAID AS CUM AND SPIT AND PISS OOZED OUT OF SEXY FILTHY WHITE MOUTH AND RAN DOWN HER CHIN AND THROATH. CUM AND PISS WAS DRIPPING FROM MY BIG NASTY BLACK DICK AS STROKED AND LICKED IT. SHE HELD HER TONGUE UNDER THE PISS HOLE SO SHE WOULDN'T MISS ANY OF IT. IT'S GOOD BABY, GIVE IT ALL TO ME, IT'S NASTY GIVE IT TO ME BABY, POUR IT TO MY MOUTH. SHE SLID HER SEXY MOUTH OVER MY BIG FILTHY DICK AND SUCKED. CUM AND PISS AGAIN FLOWED FROM MY BIG NASTY BLACK BALLS AND PENIS INTO HER HOT NASTY SEXY MOUTH GUSHED OUT OVER MY NASTY BIG BLACK DICK AND BALLS ONTO MY THIGHS. I PUSHED HER BACK, DOWN ONTO THE BED, MY EJACULATION SHOOTIN ALL OVER BIG FINE NASTY SEXY NAKED WHITE HOT LUSCIOUS FILTHY GOOD PUSSY ASS. I SPREADED HER LEGS AND LICKED HER THIGHS DOWN TO HER BIG FINE NASTY HONEY SHIT ASS CHEEKS. SPANKING HER WONDERFULLY SEXY WHITE NAKED LUSCIOUS ASS CHEEKS FOR NOT LETTING ME SUCK AND FUCK FOR ALL THESE YEARS. I SUCKED THE NASTY SEXY SHIT OUT OF HER BIG FINE FILTHY BLONDE NAKED ASS HOLE. I KISS HER FILTHY SHIT ASS CHEEKS AND LICKED HER FILTHY FINE BLONDE WHITE ASS CLEAN.

J——

A GREAT AND DREADFUL GOD
Plague Years

Steve Green

SEX, RELIGION, DEATH: ONE ABSOLUTE, preceded by two ineffectual stabs at immortality. But to a Europe in political and ecclesiastical turmoil, where plague stalked the shadows and a terrified intolerance cost the lives of many spared from the pestilence, even the intangible promises offered from the medieval pulpit demanded to be given weight, notwithstanding that their failure to be fulfilled would eventually strike at the very roots of the social hierarchy they empowered.

It begins, if we adopt the conceit that such chains of events have a quantifiable point of origin, off the coast of Sicily in the October of 1347. Reports of the virus which has left vast areas of Asia devoid of human life are already a year old, but the Genoese trading ships which dock at Messina that autumn bring the holocaust into the very heart of civilized Europe: dead and dying sailors, their armpits and groins seeping pus and blood, oblivion a welcome end to days of excruciating pain. To twist the knife, the landing has coincided with an earthquake which has shattered communities from Naples on Italy's western coast to Venice in the north, traumatizing the population at the moment it has greatest need of inner strength. "Almost everyone expected death," wrote one observer in Siena,[1] where the town's cathedral remains half-constructed as testament to the tide of human tragedy. "And people said and believed, 'This is the end of the world.'"

It was by no means an entirely inaccurate assessment, certainly not from that period's perspective. Within four years, at least ten million Europeans would have died – approximately one-third of the continent's inhabitants – and the process of social evolution be left so badly damaged that the historian J.J.Bagley judged the Twelfth Century in many ways more advanced than the Fourteenth.[2] Fewer than one in ten of those who fell victim to the first wave of plague survived, entire villages disappearing as it passed across the English Channel during the summer of 1348 and swept west from Hampshire and Dorset towards Cornwall and northwards into Oxfordshire. During the three centuries which followed the Norman invasion, the English population had grown from two million to approximately five million; by the close of the third outbreak in 1369, more than two million of these may have perished, a demographic disaster from which the country would not recover until well after the coronation of Charles II. The young were particularly vulnerable, the contagion of 1361 soon cursed as "the pestilence of children".

Nor were the disfigured corpses dragged from those Genoese vessels the sole portent of apocalypse. Europe's background temperature had dropped since the turn of the century, the damaged harvests during this "little ice age"[3] resulting in widespread chronic undernourishment and reduced resistance to infection; sheep and cattle plagues from 1313 onwards had forced farmers to hitch horses to their ploughs in place of oxen; huge floods between 1315 and 1317 echoed the Biblical deluge and fuelled the atmosphere of impending cataclysm.

Such omens were not lightly ignored. Astrology had risen in prominence to effect the status of a rational discipline, with both the scientist John Ashenden and Bishop William Rede later credited for predicting the bubonic slaughter from their studies of lunar eclipses; the arrival of plague-ridden crews from France in 1348 was also attributed by certain astrologers to the planetary conjunction of Jupiter, Mars and Saturn in Aquarius three years earlier.[4]

That such 'theses' could rest hand in glove with the established doctrines of the Christian Church without conflict is indicative of a period when the spread of non-traditional beliefs was underpinned by the increasing literacy of the middle-class laity, now exposed to such views as those of the philosopher John Duns Scotus, who before his death in 1308 had reduced the then-intrinsic philosophical truths to a shortlist of those which could be proven through pure reason, and fellow Franciscan William of Ockham (1280-1350), who rejected his contemporary's perhaps didactic distinction yet shared Scotus' embrace of Aquinas' division between faith and reason.

Attempts to check the splintering of the theological landscape was meanwhile undermined by the vicious internecine wars raging between the established religions. Even as late as 1591, Johann Georg Gödelmann's *De Magis* would brand the Catholic rite of exorcism as a ceremony of enchantment and the Mass as a magic ritual, whilst Martin del Rio's *Disquisitionum Magicarum*, published eight years later, responded by linking sorcery and witchcraft with the growth of Protestantism, claiming they were as interdependent as the body and its shadow. It is little wonder, then, that many of the peasant class reacted to these confrontations by reverting to more ancient faiths and fears; as J.B.Russell observed,[5] "Deprived of the old securities, people responded in panic that at that particular time found vent in terror of witchcraft." It was surely no coincidence that the second major outbreak of witch-hunting in England would coincide with the dawn of the Fifteenth Century, coming, as Pennethorne Hughes noted,[6] "after the Black Death, the long-drawn Hundred Years War and the development of nationalism had brought another period of disillusion and questioning."

Such debate demanded extension into the sociopolitical arena. The Peasants' Revolt had occurred a mere three years prior to the plague's introduction to British shores, and just one year before Edward III's forces had crushed the French and Scots threat to his throne at Crécy. The son of Edward II, whose murder in 1327 had forever shattered the belief in regal indestructibility, he courted a personal apocalypse; it was, David McDowell concluded,[7] "surprising that the English never rebelled," given "an expensive king at a time when many people were miserably poor and sick with plagues".

Many landowners had already found their profits dented during the early

When the plague struck in Britain in 1348, doctors took to wearing leather gowns and masks with a spice-filled nose piece. A wand enabled them to feel the pulse of a patient without having to touch them.

Fourteenth Century's trade slump, seeking to restore their commercial status by abandoning hired labour and once again enslaving those "villeins" whose thraldom had previously underwritten their social protectionism; it would not be until 1351 and the Statute of Labourers that salaries and rents would be fixed, thus alleviating exploitation at a stroke. The landowners' cash crises had in turn intensified pressure upon the soil, which could no longer be allowed to lie fallow for one year in three, in turn damaging the harvest and increasing the chance of crop failure.

The vacuum which began to replace the position traditionally occupied by religious and bourgeois authority fostered the evolution of numerous fringe movements as the plague took its toll, such as the gangs of flagellants who now roamed from town to town, atoning for imaginary sins by scourging their own flesh with leather whips, tipped with iron spikes. Forbidden to change clothing, sleep in beds, bathe, talk or fornicate without the express permission of their lay master, they stoned those priests who attempted to restore papal control and attacked Jewish communities, accusing them of deliberately spreading the contagion. Pope Clement VI had issued a papal bull in 1348 which sought to prevent anti-semitic persecution, but the local leaders swiftly caved in to public pressure and allowed such atrocities as the seige at Mainz, where as many as six thousand Jews burned themselves to death rather than submit to the crazed mob without.

Faced with spiritual and political anarchy, Clement ordered the dispersal of the cult members and the arrest of its leaders; their claim to divine inspiration rejected by scholars at the University of Paris, these "masters of error" were rounded up and hanged or beheaded. He was less successful preventing the spread of unorthodox views such as those of the reformist John Wyncliffe (1324-84), who converted several of the leading teachers at Oxford to his belief that salvation could be earned individually and not solely through the communal vehicle of the Church, rejecting the concept of a "state of grace". As holy figures proved as susceptible to the plague as the laity, Canterbury's newly-ordained archbishop dying within two days of his arrival in the capitol, such arguments rapidly gained ground.

In many ways, this would be the longest-lasting legacy of the Black Death. In a world robbed of order, the individual had begun to shake free from the shackles of feudal serfdom and spiritual brainwashing, and to move slowly towards the enlightenment and challenge of personal responsibility. An event which many had seen as signalling the end of humankind would instead usher it into the dawn of a new age.

NOTES

1. Quoted by Barbara W. Tuchman, *A Distant Mirror* (1978)

2. J.J.Bagley, *Life in Medieval England* (1960)

3. Asa Briggs, *Social History of England* (1983)

4. Richard Cavendish, *A History of Magic* (1977)

5. J.B.Russell, *Witchcraft in the Middle Ages* (1972)

6. Pennethorne Hughes, *Witchcraft* (1952)

7. David McDowell, *An Illustrated History of Britain* (1989)

BANNED, TORN & QUARTERED
The Story of Savoy

David Kerekes

MANCHESTER POLICE SEIZED MORE THAN *350 copies of the novel two years ago, and last week the magistrate, Mr Derick Fairclough, declared it likely to "deprave and corrupt" under Section Three of the Obscene Publications Act.*

History has a habit of repeating itself. The above excerpt isn't a reference to charges brought against the novel *Lady Chatterley's Lover* in 1960, *Last Exit To Brooklyn* in 1968, or *Inside Linda Lovelace* in 1976, but to *Lord Horror*. And the source, the *New Statesman & Society*, is dated 27 September 1991.

Lord Horror is a fictionalised life of the wartime traitor William Joyce – 'Lord Haw-Haw' – who broadcast propaganda messages from Germany to Britain during the Second World War. He was hanged for treason on his return to Britain in 1946. In the novel, Lord Horror searches for Hitler, who has survived the war and taken refuge in a sea-bunker off the Malayan coast. What seems to have upset Magistrate Fairclough is the virulent anti-Semitism expressed in the book. However, the publishers declare that the work itself is not anti-Semitic, only shocking and amoral. And they have their own theory as to what lies at the heart of the furore. *Lord Horror* has a peripheral character called 'Appleton', obviously based on James Anderton, the former Chief Constable of Manchester. God's Cop. In the novel, Anderton's speeches are put into Appleton's mouth – but substituting "Jews" where Anderton referred to gays.

Manchester-based Savoy is the publishing house responsible for the *Lord Horror* novel. But *Lord Horror* isn't the be-all-and-end-all of Savoy. Far from it. Over the years, Savoy have been in constant pursuit of the esoteric and the imaginative. Their history of independent and controversial publishing claims such luminaries as Michael Moorcock, Harlan Ellison, William Burroughs, and Jack Trevor Story. Not only that, Savoy are responsible for taboo-breaking forays into the realm of comics: Their adaption of Moorcock's *The Jewel in the Skull* stands as the first UK-originated graphic novel, while issue No.1 of their title, *Meng & Ecker*, has become the first comic to be banned in Britain. As well as Rock 'n' Roll picture books on the likes of Led Zeppelin and Ted Nugent, Savoy were behind *Sinister Legends*, the first published work on The Cramps. They remain uncredited for *Here To Go: Planet R101*,

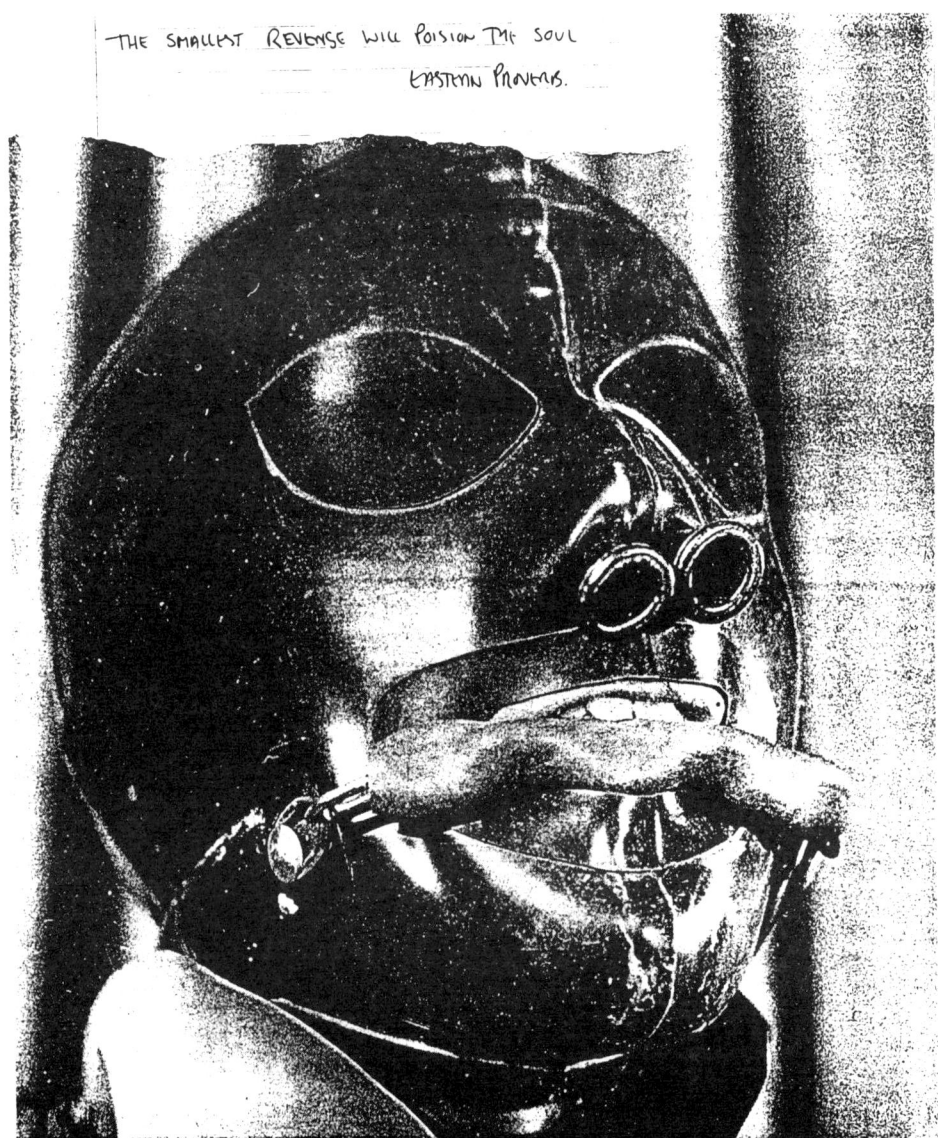

Mock-up for endpaper in Reverbstorm No.2

the celebrated volume on painter, poet and philosopher, Brion Gysin (which, ultimately, came out as part of the RE/Search catalogue). More recently, they have been involved in the production of peculiar dance-sleaze records, 'rediscovering' Sixties pop idol PJ Proby, and getting him to record TS Eliot's 'The Waste Land' over an Edgard Varese electronic backing.

It was Man Ray who said, "The Public? I think they must accept what comes to them... People who don't create have no right to make a choice in Art." With each freshly excavated idea, so, it seems, must come the inevitable CONFRONTATION WITH THE ESTABLISHMENT. And Savoy are no strangers to such confrontation. The *Lord Horror* debacle doesn't herald the first police bust for Savoy, nor the first obscenity prosecution. Savoy can barely put the proverbial foot out the door without receiving a summons. Their retail outlets are the butt of constant police 'interest', having received something in excess of 60 raids over the years. They have been busted for everything from selling bootleg vinyl, to stashing pornographic literature "behind a secret wall".[1]

In years past, Savoy admit that it wasn't so much the publishing house that bothered the police, but more the Savoy shops. A combination of shrink-wrapped pornography and a sound system playing "tapes pressured up high to limits of aural tolerance" was simply too public a profile for the police to ignore. Now it's different. Now it *is* Savoy itself and the work they produce that is the focus of attention.

The Greater Manchester Police don't hold a monopoly on being pissed at Savoy, however. At some point or another the company has managed to rub the wrong way: United Features Syndicate Ltd, The Arts Council, a Manchester restaurant, Rough Trade, WH Smiths... But we run ahead of ourselves. All and more will be revealed in good time in this, a tracing of the most glorious history of the Savoy empire. In speaking with Michael Butterworth, one of the founding members of the company, we shall be party to some dastardly deeds and notorious Savoy artifacts. Here, then, follows the years and circumstances preluding the declaration of the 'Savoy Wars'.

THE SKY BEGINS ON THE GROUND [2]

Independent to one another, Michael Butterworth and David Britton were busy in the early-1970s producing small press publications. For Britton it was *Weird Fantasy*, *Bognor Regis*, and *Crucified Toad* – all A4-sized, litho-printed fantasy-meets-surrealism magazines covering some film, but mainly artwork and articles by or about such exponents as Poe, Aubrey Beardsley, Mervyn Peake, Alan Garner, early Ramsey Campbell, Brian Aldiss, Clark Ashton Smith, and Manchester artist Ken Reid.

By contrast, Butterworth's *Concentrate*, *Corridor*, and *Wordworks* – A4 litho, colour covers – were not at all art nouveau, but more original fiction; imaginative writers on the small press scene of the Sixties and Seventies, such as Heathcote Williams, Thomas M. Disch, psychologist John Clark, playwright J.Jeff Jones, Trevor Hoyle.

Recalls Butterworth, "We were introduced to each other by our printer, John Muir, who later ran Babylon Books, but at that time had a press called WHITE LIGHT on Upper Brook Street. He was printing my magazines and Dave's, but both of us wanted a more mainstream look and to do paperback books."[3]

So the two got together, sometime in 1974, with Britton working as Art Editor on Butterworth's *Wordworks* and *Corridor* magazines. But another seed of the Savoy empire had been sown in 1972, when David Britton and friend Charles Partington opened the shop HOUSE ON THE BORDERLAND on Port Street, near the Crown & Anchor. Says Butterworth, "That was the shop with the brothel upstairs, where, out of good neighbourliness, the ladies running it offered us free wanks. House On The Borderland was the first Savoy shop because it established the formula on which all the others were based, selling a mix of Rock 'n' Roll, cinema, fantasy, comics, sci fi, art and whatever was streetwise at the time. It was a variant of the formula Bram Stokes pioneered with his London shop Dark They Were And Golden Eyed, from which Titan Books and Forbidden Planet later grew."

ORBIT BOOKS, adjacent to the Wheatsheaf pub, Whittle Street, became the second Savoy shop. "From these premises, Charles and Dave published James Cawthorn's adaptation of *Stormbringer*. Charles dropped out of publishing almost immediately."

In 1976, Savoy entered the world of publishing with SAVOY BOOKS LTD and *Stormbringer*, a 30-page illustrated version of Michael Moorcock's fantasy novel (measuring in at a lowly 427mm x 305mm!). *Stormbringer* was the first in a series of four adaptations of Moorcock's works by artist Cawthorn. The other (sizably modest) titles are: *The Jewel in the Skull*, *The Crystal and the Amulet*, and *The Sword and the Runestaff*.

A tie-in with NEW ENGLISH LIBRARY in 1979 meant that Savoy was able to reissue the best works of artists and writers like Henry Treece, Harlan Ellison, Jack Trevor Story and Ken Reid, and distribute them around the world.

"In those early days, we were mainly reprinting work we thought was being neglected. We did some original titles: *The Savoy Book*[4] was an anthology, and we published an original Moorcock work, *My Experiences in the Third World War.*[5]

"The thing was Dave and I had tastes which overlapped. We're miles apart in personality, but in terms of interests, we both liked Captain Beefheart; we both remembered Ken Reid's Fudge and Speck strips in the *Manchester Evening News*..."

In 1938, a young and hopeful Ken Reid approached the *Manchester Evening News* with several layouts for a strip called *The Adventures of Fudge the Elf*. It became a regular feature and soon was appearing every night. With only a few brief absences, *Fudge the Elf* ran right up until 1962, and even as late as 1974 reprints were appearing in the paper.

Reid's strip chronicled the escapades of two elves, Fudge and Speck, caught within the landscapes of Tummy-Ache, the Land of Nowhere, the underwater kingdom of Bubbleville, and the sugary planet of Plum-Duff. Inhabitants here had similarly peculiar names and preoccupations. 'King Bong', for instance, was the invisible owner of a pair of magic gloves.

Savoy published a total of six volumes of Reid's work. "We have always tried to push against the grain one way or another," admits Butterworth, "even when we were bringing people back to public attention. Ken Reid's strip in the *Manchester Evening News* was stopped because it was getting too way out, and frightening kids. We regret we didn't get out as much of Reid's work as we wanted to."

I THINK THAT WAS THE CATALYST [6]

"FUCK*!*" chanted the nuns. "FUCK, FUCK, FUCK*!* FUCK, FUCK, FUCK, FUCK, FUCK, FUCK, FUCK*!*"

"Oh, no*!* " moaned the priest. "Oh no, no, no*!* "

The Gas, pg 84

Amid this flurry of publishing activity, unbeknownst to Savoy, their retail premises were being 'Moonbeamed' by undercover agents in the BRITISH PHONOGRAPH INDUSTRY.

'Britain's recording industry has cracked a bootlegging syndicate!' screamed the tabloid press. *'Undercover agents working on an investigation code-named OPERATION MOONBEAM have carried out raids in London, Manchester, Newcastle and St. Helens.'*

Beneath familiar mug-shots of Bob Dylan, David Bowie, and Elton John (*'BOOTLEGGED!'*), the reports went on to stipulate how, in April 1979, a telephone tip-off had set into motion the greased wheels of Operation Moonbeam.

'Inquiries led to Manchester where stocks of bootleg records were being imported from America.' The ingenuity of the Moonbeam agents was such that *'One investigator posed as a manufacturer to infiltrate the network'* while *'Suspects were trailed all over the country by BPI investigators with long-range cameras'.*

" Let's see what it says." Together, they plodded across to the decaying sign-post and slowly read its disheartening message. " Well! " moaned Fudge, " at least we know where we are now."

"I don't see any point in going on now," wailed Speck. "If there's nothing but nothing everywhere, there's no sense in searching for civilisation." "And there's no sense in sitting here to sizzle in the sun," argued Fudge.

Both Orbit Books and BOOKCHAIN (the third Savoy outlet, Peter Street) were hit by the operation. David Britton found himself in the High Court in London, agreeing to pay the BPI a sum of £7,250 for damages and costs, as well as to a permanent injunction not to make, sell or offer for sale any bootleg recordings.

"We were two days late making the first payment of £1,000," says Butterworth of the fine. "They sent the cheque back and instructed the bailiffs to move in straight away and stuck further costs on top. This was our second bust... at Orbit Books we had been done over by the BPI as early as 1976."

Although to this point their output remained relatively catholic, Savoy's publication of works by sci fi authors Samuel Delaney and Charles Platt was soon to cause considerable unrest.

Of Delaney's novel, *Tides of Lust*, one reviewer said that it "might be described as a pornographic picaresque; it's a chronicle of various sorts of sex, hetero and homo, but lingering on rather down-&-dirty black/white S/M of a sort that would be automatically labelled racist (among other things) if the author wasn't black". The book follows a group of people in an uncompromising search for erogenous gratification, every other page providing the reader with a fresh sexual twist.

Platt's *The Gas*, on the other hand – a novel of sci fi eroticism, perversion and insanity in which an accident at a secret germ warfare laboratory causes a deadly aphrodisiac to be released over England – despite having been Savoy's most consistently requested title, has yet to elicit a review. Neither were Savoy able to secure an English distributor bold enough to release it, and potential readers had to purchase the book direct from the publishers.[7]

In November of 1980, thousands of pounds worth of retail stock was seized by police. Savoy offices and all the Savoy shops were raided in a coordinated swoop. Butterworth elaborates, "*The Gas* was first published by OPHELIA PRESS in the States. Savoy gave it its only UK publication. The police seized it, as well as copies of Samuel Delaney's *Tides of Lust* – and one copy of Jack Trevor Story's *Screwrape*

Lettuce! – but did not get the full print run. The main problem was not so much the police but the booktrade – no one except us would sell *The Gas*. Our only outlets for it were our own shops."

(By this juncture, Savoy had opened STARPLACE on Oldham Street – it no longer exists – and BOOKCHAIN LEEDS LTD. About to open was CHAPTER ONE in Liverpool.)

Savoy Books Ltd was forced into voluntary liquidation in February of 1981. Was this a direct result of the raid?

"The collapse of New English Library and, since 1976, continual police harassment. New English Library were getting our books out, but TIMES MIRROR in America – who own New English Library – pulled the rug from under them, and our distribution collapsed, too. We were getting a lot of raids; Anderton raided our shops about 60 times, acting as a constant heavy drain on our financial resources. We just couldn't survive as Savoy Books Ltd anymore, and went into liquidation."

Raids of the frequency to which Savoy were now accustomed began in 1976. James Anderton took over as Chief Constable of Greater Manchester Police on 1 July 1976. Between the years 1977 and 1981 the Chief, in an annual report to London, detailed that he had obtained a total of 1,010 search warrants from magistrates, issued for the purpose of raiding under the Obscene Publications Act (meaning that, on average, at least one Manchester high street shop and distributor was being raided every two days).

The confiscation of the novels *The Gas* and *Tides of Lust* was just part of a major raid on Savoy that ultimately resulted in the prosecution of both Britton and Butterworth, and landed David Britton in prison (albeit a full 19 months later). Britton and Philip Bunton (shop manager) at Orbit Books were charged with selling obscene material for gain in an operation utilizing about 25 police officers and vehicles, as well as an unknown amount of plain-clothed officers who had been observing stock movement for about a week before the raids.

The obscene material took the form of seven paperback novels: *No Place for a Lady* by A. DeGranamour; *Something for the Boys* by Kenneth Harding; *Mama Liz Drinks Deep*, *Mama Liz Tastes Flesh*, and *Secret Sisterhood*, each by Howard Rhinegold; *Cruel Lips* by Marcus Van Heller; and, *Two Suspicious Girls* by Katy Mitchell.

Charges were brought under Section Two of the Obscene Publications Act. More serious charges than these it is difficult to get, yet the novels in question contain no pictorial matter and their authors, Rhinegold in particular, are erudite and often comical. In the well-plotted *Secret Sisterhood*, a spy called 'Jerry Cornelius' makes a cameo appearance, which can only be a reference to Michael Moorcock's ironically conceived character. "It's a rip-snorter of a book," says Butterworth. "Cornelius is a hapless aviation cop who loses his job after being spiked with LSD. Just in time he manages to implant a microscopic surveillance device into his semen!"

The novels were already widely available in bookshops and newsagents around the country, such as the London-based WORDS AND MUSIC chain, who initially supplied Savoy.

Of the relatively innocuous nature of the books, says Butterworth, "If the police and courts are determined to get a conviction they will use anything to get one."

Long after the trial several of the titles were reprinted by an English publisher.

Published in the Seventies by the prestigious American outfits, GROVE PRESS and VENUS FREEWAY PRESS, Savoy picked the seven titles up at remainder prices in

1978 (meaning that they must have been freely imported into the country, in spite of HM Customs censorial powers). Furthermore, these same books had already been seized from Savoy on numerous occasions and returned by the police because they did not merit prosecution.

In *Savoy Dreams*, the second volume in a proposed trilogy of anthologies, Butterworth addresses an open letter to the reader with regard this "puzzling" case. In the piece, entitled 'Under Seige', he claims that the trial of Britton and Bunton was not altogether *unbiased*; that the judge was out to make an example and "nail Dave". Also, because the raids had cost many thousands of pounds to execute, to bring the men to trial was, in some measure, a justification of this vast expenditure of public money. Of the trial itself, Butterworth stipulates how Judge Hardy's "*manner* (for example the tone of his voice) frequently gave otherwise fair and just pronouncements an inflexion". Of Hardy's summing up to the jury Butterworth has transcribed the speech and made references to a total of 11 points which "until that precise moment had not been brought up in court; which might refer to parts of the law which nebulously remained unexplained; which appeared to me to be opinion; which appeared to be biased interpretations; which appeared to be denials of points raised by our barrister".

As a result, and after much deliberation, the jury found the men guilty. Philip Bunton received a one-month suspended sentence. David Britton was sentenced to 28-days imprisonment (of which he served 19). Inexplicably, the case against Butterworth, who was to have been tried separately, did not come to court. Britton later recounted to Butterworth that the guards who escorted him to the cells afterwards threw up their hands in disbelief.

There followed widespread press denouncement over the imprisonment.

On the morning Britton was released from Strangeways, one of the Savoy shops was again raided and relieved of 'obscene' material.

Seasons greetings from Savoy, Christmas 1993

LIFE DOESN'T GIVE A RAT'S ARSE WHO LIVES IT [8]

"They were like the bottom market," says Michael Butterworth of New English Library (NEL). "They weren't well regarded in literary circles."

Interesting titles, though.

"They were good for us because they were on rocky ground and they wanted more titles to boost their list, you see, especially titles which would give them credibility."

Immediately following the liquidation of Savoy Books, SAVOY EDITIONS LTD was formed, preparing books for publication by companies like MUSIC SALES and PROTEUS BOOKS. Among these were the large format Led Zeppelin *In The Light*; the AC/DC biography, *Hell Ain't No Bad Place To Be*; a *David Bowie Profile*; and *The Legendary Ted Nugent*. The original cover of the Nugent work was deemed too far over the top for wholesale distributors WH Smith. Says David Britton, "The final design by OMNIBUS PRESS, like all their Rock jacket designs, achieved the required condition of muzak."

A paperback volume on American shock Rock band Kiss, sporting the legend 'The Savoy Kiss Of Death' on the jacket, remains to this date the company's biggest-selling title.

Butterworth: "Savoy commissioned, originated, conceived and performed every function except *shit* these books. *The Bernard Manning Blue Joke Book* – the *only* Bernard Manning joke book – was a Savoy book which we packaged to our former distributor, NEL, who had re-emerged as part of the HODDER & STOUGHTON group."

On the subject of packaging – though "not really in the realm of 'packaging' but more a labour of love" – Britton edited and assembled *The Life and Times of Captain Beefheart* (1977) for John Muir's BABYLON BOOKS. He was partly responsible for Babylon's *Frank Zappa* book. "Dave also gave Morrissey quite a lot of information that Morrisey, as author, eventually put into Babylon's *James Dean* book."

A major disappointment for Butterworth and Savoy are the titles that "got away". UK paperback rights for William Burroughs' *Cities of the Red Night* were purchased by Savoy but had to be relinquished following the demise of Savoy Books Ltd. Michael Moorcock's novel *The Brothel in Rosenstrasse* was originally commissioned by Savoy but, again, had to be relinquished. Ironically, it eventually came out through NEL with an authorial credit to Savoy.

Savoy Books Ltd were also set to publish the collected works of Gerald Scarfe, having assembled, with the assistance of Scarfe, 90% of the artwork which was to eventually appear in THAMES & HUDSON's book, *Gerald Scarfe*. At the time, complications that arose over the exact ownership of Scarfe's work for Pink Floyd's film, *The Wall*, precluded use of that cartoon work in Savoy's book. This was later resolved and the work was used in the Thames & Hudson edition.

Contrary to the pre-publication advertising for Nik Cohn's definitive Rock 'n' Roll novel, *Johnny Angelo*, the book was six years late coming out. It tells the story of a young Rock 'n' Roll singer, the eponymous Angelo, from his unhinged and hedonist lifestyle to his inevitable demise and consequent legendary status. Interestingly, Savoy were scheduled to publish not one but two versions of the novel. The first – to have carried the slightly but significantly different title, *I Am Still The Greatest Says Johnny Angelo* – was to have been a reprint of Cohn's *revised*, more formal, less powerful 1970 PENGUIN edition. This, because Savoy felt that both versions together told the full story of Johnny Angelo.

Author Cohn – who went on to write *Saturday Night Fever* – had created in Angelo an iconoclast not a million miles removed from that of disgraced Sixties star PJ Proby. Little wonder Savoy should be so interested. More later.

Another work that "got away", a recollection that rifles the slightest pique for Michael Butterworth, is Brion Gysin's *Here To Go: Planet R101*. Gysin, interviewed by Terry Wilson, gives a travelogue of his ideas, theories, adventures and philosophies. He relays how William Burroughs came to improvise new meaning from the newspaper cut-ups he experimented with; mirror staring, the first step in personality-switching; the machineries of joy; drugs, sex and space travel without rockets ('Here to go' being a reference to the 'meaning of it all' – mankind is *here to go* into space).

Explains Butterworth, "RE/Search published that. The book was my idea. I myself originated it, though I was never credited in it. I commissioned Terry Wilson to do it and William Burroughs to write the introduction, and after Savoy Books Ltd got into its difficulties Terry took it off me and gave it to RE/Search. They've done a very good job, but he's just taken it as his book. If it wasn't for me he wouldn't have that book. You stole the keys, Terry."

GROWN-UPS IN A TEENAGE WORLD [9]

The eve of 1984 saw the publication of Savoy's second anthology, *Savoy Dreams*; the first book under the new imprint, simply SAVOY.

"We were back paying for the printing ourselves," says Butterworth, "but from that date have done without a distributor, and our print runs – once in their tens of thousands – are now in single 1,000 units. The police raids and the rise of the censorious Politically Correct made things very difficult, but coupled with this was our refusal after our dealings with NEL – who often pushed their own titles to the detriment of ours – to consider a straightforward distribution deal where we ended up paying for everything."

September of 1985 heralded SAVOY RECORDS and the first PJ Proby single release for the company, 'Tainted Love'. Sylvie Simmons wrote of the record in *Kerrang!*

> Single of singles! The song Soft Cell made a hit gagged and chained in
> some leatherette-lined sewer deep below the earth's epidermis. Sounds
> like a motorway pile-up in Hell. The band just go for it and P.J. sounds
> gloriously bad and sleazy. As he says on one side, "It's a tasty world."

Born in the United States, PJ Proby made demo discs for Elvis Presley in the late-Fifties and early-Sixties, and appeared in several B-movie Westerns. He came to Britain after being discovered by TV producer Jack Good, who first displayed him on a Beatles TV spectacular in 1964. A flamboyant character, Proby wore his hair long and in a ponytail, and dressed in tight velvet trousers, fancy shirts and buckled shoes. His strong, throbbing voice perfectly suited the image.

Over the next four years he had numerous hits, and his debut album in 1965 was a commercial success. However, Proby was always a controversial figure, and trouble dogged him throughout his career. He would upset theatre managers by refusing to take the stage without first being paid. On a 1965 tour with Cilla Black, Proby was given the benefit of the doubt when he claimed that his trousers splitting mid-performance was an accident. But then the 'accident' occurred again in other shows. Of one concert, the *Record Mirror* reported that Proby

Focus - Dutch Rock Band built a following with singles and albums. One of the most musically talented groups over the last decade. P. J. Proby A singer who needs no introduction and has never been involved before with this type of group.

Left. **Proby in the Sixties.** *Right.* **Proby teaming up with Dutch progressive Rock band, Focus, in the Seventies.**

leaped about, covered his right ear with a hand, splayed his legs and executed a series of grinds as performed in a number of outlawed burlesque houses in the States. Ecstatic teenage girls, beside themselves with desire, hurled themselves like human bullets at the line of commissionaries guarding the stage.

That's not all. Later in the show, largely composed of screaming pre-pubescent girls, Proby

saw fit to introduce into his act a gesture which I personally considered in extremely bad taste. He very carefully put one hand on the top of his trousers and slowly pulled down the material to reveal some inches of flesh at the top of his leg. [From then on] the act developed into an erotic display. One which many people will agree was not fit to be put on in front of young girls... Again, his hand was run from knee to knee, via his stomach. His behind was massaged and his trousers were torn from the knees to the top... with one hand, he ripped one leg all the way up from the knee... the Texan crawled across the stage, ripped the other trouser leg and did the splits revealing a wide expanse of flesh. After a series of gymnastics, Proby placed a hand between his legs and did another grind. This was not a man going just far enough, this was a man going too far.

The RANK/ABC organisation agreed and promptly banned Proby from performing at their venues. So, too, did the BBC and ITV television networks.

Proby publicly declared that Tom Jones – who made his name as Proby's replacement on Cilla's tour – was "rubbish" and challenged him to a singing match. The contest never took place and, by 1968, Proby was bankrupt. He appeared in a couple of Jack Good stage productions in the Seventies (a rock musical version of *Othello*, and as the elder Elvis in *Elvis On Stage*), but for the most part was out of favour with the press and public. Like this things remained. He made the headlines when charged with assaulting his girlfriend and again, when at the age of 45, he wedded Alison Hardy, a girl of 15. Not long after, recording with Savoy in 1986, Proby confessed that Alison had left him and that this particular recording – a cover of David Bowie's 'Heroes', which Proby sang as a straightforward love song addressed to his young wife – would be his last. He intended to shoot the girl and then join his father in the sky. In an interview with *i-D* magazine, David Britton said of Proby, "He's a man who's deteriorated a lot since I've known him. When he's sober he's nice and sweet and when he's drunk he's angry and bitter and wants to die. His liver's shot and he's got all the problems that come with being an acute alcoholic. I'm told he's lost all sensation in his feet for instance. He's too ill to perform... he can't learn new songs sufficiently well to do on stage."

How did Savoy get involved with Proby?

Butterworth: "Well, we started doing his biography (in 1982). We went interviewing him, got miles of cassette tape which we hoped to turn into a book, but we decided what he needed more than anything else was a record deal. He hadn't done anything serious for about 16 years."

What's the arrangement?

"We originate the songs. His voice is fed through audiofile, edited, rearranged. Nothing is simple about these songs and they aren't the sort that Proby would willingly do. To be honest, he hates them. But he likes something about us – probably recognises us as fellow musical anarchists."

Of the singles that Proby has recorded for Savoy are covers of contemporary anthems such as 'Love Will Tear Us Apart', 'Anarchy In The UK', 'Sign O The Times', 'In The Air Tonight', and 'Garbageman'.

"The B-side of 'Love Will Tear Us Apart', the live version," recalls Butterworth, "was recorded in an old schoolhouse on the Rippenden Road, near Oldham, a block away from the church where Joy Division recorded the original. We went there just to get a sense of history, simply for ourselves, recording on the doorstep of the original. One week after our recording was made, kids from the nearby Sholver Estate burnt the school to the ground – a fucking good omen! The out-of-tune backing is deliberate. We de-tuned the synth so it would sound like inept Velvet Underground."

Press reaction to Savoy's recordings was mixed. "Reeks of insanity" wrote *Melody Maker*. "Hideously fascinating" admitted *Creem*. *Hot Press* denounced Proby as "a very, very sick man in every sense of the word", while CHANNEL 4's talk show *The Last Resort* categorically refused to feature the singer in its line-up of guests. "The only way Proby will ever get on our show is when he's dead."[10]

In an original composition, 'M97002: Hardcore' (being Dave Britton's prison number in Strangeways), Savoy claimed a team-up between PJ Proby and Madonna. Against a crushing, primordial backbeat, the unlikely duo delineate a succession of surrealist episodes. 'Telly Savalas uses his bald head as a phallus/He leaves vaseline everywhere he sits/What a knob.'

On 22 September 1987, London's *Evening News* carried the frontpage headline: MADONNA IN PORN RECORD ROW. The following morning, the *Daily Mail* reported, MADONNA TO SUE OVER 'PORN' DISC, stating that, "Despite the fact that the female voice on the record bears no resemblance to Madonna's, Proby yesterday insisted that they teamed up after her debut UK concert at Leeds on August 13."

Of Savoy's recordings in general, Butterworth says, "They occupied a great deal of our time as producers in the middle and late-Eighties. We were consciously trying for an ironic juxtaposition between the old and the new, so that there are lots of Fifties Rock 'n' Roll references in the records, as well as literary ones. On 'Anarchy In The UK', we sampled the voices of TS Eliot, William Burroughs and Harlan Ellison."

For their version of 'Blue Monday', Savoy introduced one 'Lord Horror' on vocals.[11] The backing track on that record uses the same samples as the New Order original, borrowed from Peter Hook's files, "only we well warped it."

Savoy's 'Blue Monday', released October 1986, gives credit to 'The Savoy-Hitler Youth Band'. The sleeve depicts the head of a bearded gentleman, brains exploding through the top of his skull, around which the words 'White Natzi Cunt-Scum... Fucking Suckarse Nigger Jew' are scrawled. The figure is attired in a black uniform, displaying the emblem 'J.A.' and '1976-1986 – A Decade of Service and Protection, Greater Manchester Police'. On the reverse of the sleeve is a backdrop comprising scenes at the liberation of Dachau. The record never got further than press review copies. No distributor would touch it. More later.

THERE AIN'T NO SUCH THING AS RAPE WHEN YOU'RE WEARING A SUPERMAN CAPE [12]

> Horror reared back up and slipped the bloodied razors carefully into his own mouth and sucked them, sliding his thick tongue over and over the keen blades. Stretching his pop-eyes, Horror pulled the blades free from his mouth and jumped from the man's shoulders, landing solidly in front of him. He turned around and heaved his frame upwards, catching the Jew in mid-fall. He ran his twin razors up the full length of the man's exposed chest, completely parting the neck and splitting the anguished face. The Jew finally collapsed, and amongst the infra-sound of roaring blood Horror dipped his head into the open chest, laying still for a while in the soft ooze within. He shuffled, swallowed a mouthful of the blood. Edging further inside the gash he gripped one of the man's organs, knotted with veins, between his horse teeth and tore it away. He stood up, letting the organ trail in the wind, and then dashed it against the back window of the terrace house, where it clung like a piece of red afterbirth on a glass slide...
>
> *Lord Horror*, pg 94

In May of 1989, Savoy published the David Britton novel *Lord Horror*, the first book to fictionally explore Auschwitz and the Holocaust without the utilisation of sympathetic characters.

Later, in June, Savoy launched its no-holds-barred comics line with the first issues of *Lord Horror*[13] and *Meng & Ecker*.

July brought the Meng & Ecker 12" vinyl release, 'Shoot Yer Load/Golden Showers', another slice of sleaze Hi-NRG dance (the B-side opening with, 'Open your mouth let me piss in it/There's more to sex than a pair of tits').

In September 1989, copies of the *Lord Horror* novel, and *Lord Horror* and *Meng & Ecker* comics and records, were seized from Savoy offices and retail premises by Manchester police.

Left. Lord Horror novel, cover. *Right.* Lord Haw-Haw, "a Bertie Wooster type" – David Britton. Art: Kris Guidio

First of all, how did the character 'Lord Horror' come about?

"Lord Horror is very loosely based on William Joyce, the so-called 'English traitor'. He's also got albino blood in him, from characters like Zenith the Albino, in the Sexton Blake magazines of the 1930s, and Elric of Melniboné, Michael Moorcock's antihero of the Sixties. But the culture of the *Fifties*, the era in which Dave and I became teenagers, was dominated by three things – Rock 'n' Roll, the atomic bomb, and the Second World War. They had a powerful effect. There were times when, as kids, we went to sleep not knowing whether we would wake up, because of a hydrogen bomb war. All my first published work in Moorcock's *New Worlds* magazine in the Sixties, was set in post-atomic war landscapes. In the Eighties I started to explore the Nazis, and the Holocaust. By the time I met Dave, who *was* Rock 'n' Roll, he had got together a series of characters for a novel, which didn't include the Lord Horror character and therefore lacked a focus.

"I started writing a novel featuring a fictionalised Adolf Hitler in South America; I wanted to use a symbolic exotic setting to attach to Hitler. I portrayed him as an inane, very ordinary person – and found, as of course others have, that the contrast potentised him in a very bizarre way.

"It sparked Dave to start writing – though obviously he didn't also want to write about Hitler. He was looking around for another character and eventually hit on William Joyce, Lord Haw-Haw. That's how it came about in literal terms."

What happened to Hitler in the South American swamps?

"I stopped writing mine because I was getting bogged down with it. I decided Dave's was *the* book, and helped him get it into shape instead. It took four years to write."

Here follow the events surrounding the seizure of the *Lord Horror* novel and comics: **SEPTEMBER 15 1989** *Jewish Telegraph North West*, on receiving a copy to review, run a front page story about the *Lord Horror* novel. The piece highlights those parts of the book containing Chief Constable of Manchester James Anderton's pronouncements on gays, pornographers, anti-churchgoers, and left-wingers. In one of the speeches, Savoy substitute the word 'gay' with the word 'Jew' to draw the comparison between Anderton's speeches and those of 1930s political anti-Semitism.

SEPTEMBER 19 1989 *Manchester Evening News* run the same story next to a photograph of Anderton. Like the *Jewish Telegraph*, it announces that the Police Chief is "investigating" *Lord Horror*.

UNSPECIFIED DATE Posing as members of the public, police officers purchase copies of the *Meng & Ecker* and *Lord Horror* comics from Savoy shops. This enables them to obtain seizure warrants from Stipendiary Magistrate Derick Fairclough.

SEPTEMBER 26 1989 Police simultaneously raid Savoy offices and three of their retail outlets in Manchester, seizing, as well as non-Savoy material, all copies of *Lord Horror*. So too all copies of *Meng & Ecker* comic issue No.1 and *Lord Horror* comic issue No.1. The cover artwork of the former depicts the decapitated head of James Anderton/Appleton.

OCTOBER 17 1989 Greater Manchester Police Headquarters: Acting under orders from superiors, Detective Inspector Malcolm Wood conducts separate hour-long interviews with David Britton and Michael Butterworth. The interviews focus on the contents of the *Lord Horror* novel and *Meng & Ecker* comic No.1.[14]

JULY 1990 Summonses dated 19 July 1990 are served on Britton and Butterworth under Section Two of the Obscene Publications Act.

SEPTEMBER 10 1990 Britton and Butterworth appear before Stipendiary Magistrate Fairclough. To get a quick sentence it is usual police practice to bring defendants before the same magistrate who issues the seizure warrants. Fairclough makes it plain that as far as he is concerned a prison sentence is inevitable. To obtain a fairer hearing – before a possibly unbiased judge – Savoy elect to go before a crown court, enter a plea of not guilty, and are remanded on bail until a court date can be secured.

OCTOBER 1990 Fingerprints of Britton and Butterworth are taken at Bootle Street police station. Under new police laws, defendants have to give their fingerprints when charged.

Elizabeth Young, reporting in *New Statesman*, said of the novel, "*Lord Horror*, unlike *American Psycho*, is a work that outrages current taboos on racism: taboos so strangulated that no one may transgress them."

Almost two years after it had been seized, at a hearing on 28 August 1991, Magistrate Fairclough upheld *Lord Horror* as obscene. It was described as anti-Semitic, while passages of the novel were read out loud in court. David Britton defended his work, stating that the passages had been read out of context. The novel itself, he said, was not anti-Semitic, but Lord Horror, the character, was. "That is what it is all about... If you are going to do an anti-Semitic character, then you have to do it to the one-hundredth degree," said Britton. "It does concern me that some Jews might find it upsetting, but others would accept it for its reality. There is no point pretending that these sort of people do not exist... I wanted my book to go over the top, to be taboo breaking. Even then, I could not possibly hope to measure up to the reality of the Holocaust."

Britton told the court, "My father was Jewish."

Butterworth: "An interview in *The Observer* with frustrated anonymous Manchester police officers made it quite clear that they recommended a prosecution under Section Two (hardcore pornography), but the Director of Public Prosecutions (DPP) declined to act. The police therefore pressed ahead with Section Three, actually a more oppressive law than Section Two. Although Section Three doesn't carry a criminal penalty, under it magistrates are empowered to destroy the stock without a jury. Magistrates like Derick Fairclough, who prefer to handle the obscenity cases, do so with great regularity, working in tandem with the police. Also, in the event of a Section Two being brought, all past Section *Three* offences are dragged up to prove you have been warned, and that you are a persistent flouter of the law.

"Because the police had got a Section Three, we found we couldn't go to Crown Court to defend it in front of a jury. We had no choice but to have it judged by Fairclough. Despite protestations from our barrister that *Lord Horror* was not obscene under the terms of the Obscene Publications Act, Fairclough decided otherwise and upheld his own charge. Nobody, except us, seemed to find the result quite amazing!

"The procedure the police took is a replay of what has gone on before, when they prosecuted us ostensibly for pornography but actually for *The Gas* and *Tides of Lust*. The DPP won't let the police prosecute us for the Savoy material because they know that before a jury we'd win hands down; even if we lost we'd win, because of the precedent that would be set of a work of art or literature being found obscene; whereas with 'backdoor' censorship they win something every time. The appeal we are making at the moment, we made as a result of the destruction order brought about by Fairclough."

IT'S LIKE BEING IN A LUNATIC ASYLUM WITH PERMISSION TO MASTURBATE FOR THE REST OF YOUR LIFE [15]

> Garfield is perceived as a wholesome and endearing character, with a hint of childlike rebelliousness, with whom all the family can identify.

So said prosecution witness Ausbert DeArce (managing director of a Dutch company owned by UNITED FEATURES SYNDICATE) of Savoy's usage of the lovable feline rogue in one issue of their *Meng & Ecker* comic series.

Meng and Ecker are offshoot characters from the *Lord Horror* novel. They are Lord Horror's "obsequious psychotic" sidekicks (bearing the slightest facial resemblance to Britton and Butterworth?), carving a trail of blood and frivolity through urban society. Pertinent to Savoy's circumstance at the time, each issue sees artist Kris Guidio planting Meng and Ecker firmly in a crazed celebrity curdle. As integral as the (satirical) narrative itself are the familiar faces and arcane references; anyone from Judge Dredd to Charles and Di, from Salman Rushdie to Divine, is liable to show up in the strips. In one episode, Fudge the Elf claims that Meng is his alter ego. Meng, at the time, happens to be moaning that his shafting of a dry "old granny" (cunningly disguised as Margaret Thatcher) will require him to undertake a foreskin transplant. In *Meng & Ecker* No.3, the doppleganger of a certain bearded ex-Chief of Manchester Police – in full riot-gear regalia – can also be seen on the receiving end of Meng's pork baton. No one is spared. Tank Girl and Ramsey Campbell are in there.

"Campbell was in there," notes Butterworth, "because he asked to be in there. So we put him in. But we genuinely spelled his name wrong. We apologized and inadvertently spelt it wrong again some other time! Tank Girl, we put her in because she is one of the few comic characters that we actually like. The others we were lampooning because we felt the artwork was inferior... and these were the characters that the media were putting forward as examples of excellent."

Non-excellent characters get flattened or fucked. Because Tank Girl holds her own, she is portrayed as a chick with a dick and gets one up on Meng.

Meng & Ecker No.3. Art: Kris Guidio

In 1991, Savoy paid around £20,000 on court costs and fines. Not surprisingly, that was a year in which the company brought nothing new out, embroiled as they were in the *Lord Horror* scandal and an out-of-court settlement of a 10-month legal battle with United Features Syndicate (UFS).

UFS had shown an interest in *Meng & Ecker*. In particular issue No.4 and an eight-frame sequence where a cat, not unlike Jim Davis' comic strip creation, Garfield, is featured. Meng is seen to masturbate and ejaculate over the animal. Defending their copyright, UFS initiated extensive investigations of Savoy's activities. This resulted in UFS solicitors and agents, and the covert use of an ex-Vice Squad officer, forcing a seizure of all copies of the comic and relating artwork.

"Even a faint suggestion of obscenity would destroy Garfield as a marketing tool," said UFS. But, speaking in the September 1991 issue of *Comics International*, Michael Butterworth argued that "for all United Features' thoroughness in the business of detection they were unable to apprehend the most obvious fact about Savoy – our tiny status relative to their own".

Meng & Ecker has a circulation of 2,000.

So, then, does the whole UFS issue have more to do with Savoy's legacy of controversy than it does with the possible 'destruction of a marketing tool'?

In the heart of Manchester town centre, in a place just on the outskirts of St Anne's Square, resides a pleasant, if modest, coffeeshop by the name of MENG & ECKER. Offended by the alleged use of their name but without sufficient funds to do anything about it, the lawyers of the coffeeshop saw an opportunity present itself when Garfield looked to get a creaming. They contacted the UK licensees of Garfield, who passed their letter on to UFS.

Was the title *Meng & Ecker* taken from the coffeeshop?

Butterworth: "I could never say that on tape (laughs)*!* Meng is short for Mengele; Ecker is short for Eckart, the Nazi poet. You can make up your own mind from that*!* Well, according to the Meng & Ecker restaurant, we have ripped off their name, and they touted this to United Features."

How do you manage to cope with all these problems and prosecutions?

"You just get used to going from one crisis to the next. If you set out to do something radical it's inevitable that the machinery is going to catch you."[16]

The police have a file labelled 'Savoy', perhaps?

"They probably have. Shout 'LORD HORROR*!*' to a policeman, see if he knows*!*"

COMPREHENSION IS ONLY A KNOWLEDGE ADEQUATE TO OUR INTENTION[17]

On 31 August 1991, *three days* after Magistrate Fairclough found *Lord Horror* obscene, police raided Savoy again and seized over 4,000 comics, including their Lord Horror mini-series *Hard Core Horror*. Issue No.5, the final instalment of *Hard Core Horror*, opens with publicity photographs of Jessie Matthews, 'England's favourite sweetheart', who married 'Lord Haw-Haw'. The full-page panels that follow depict the satanic machinations of the Nazi death camps, putrid smoke rising from chimneys, skeletal bodies and architecture mortified as one. An intense blackness – the shade of caked blood – John Coulthart's artwork had never been more harrowing. (So harrowing, in fact, the text set to accompany the artwork was deemed impotent and not used. Hence the empty white spaces throughout that issue.) The issue closes with another set of photographs, only this time it isn't Jessie Matthews, but rather anonymous corpses, beaten, battered, and torn. One can scarcely imagine what

Double page spread, Hard Core Horror No.5. Art: John Coulthart

ugliness must have befallen the woman whose innards erupt from fissures the size of a football, or the man whose hands lie at some distance from the mangled, bloody stump of each arm. These are truly wretched creatures.

In police interviews, Britton and Butterworth were questioned on the 'meaning' of the more esoteric references in John Coulthart's artwork, as well as fending the "very strong" objections to the photographs at the close of *Hard Core Horror* No.5. In a scenario comparable to that of some cliché-ridden Hollywood thriller, the police, says Butterworth, "had the comics examined by experts who 'deciphered' many of the really quite elementary references. They had also shown the comic to one of their forensic experts who examined the photographs."

The conclusion?

"That we may be fascists attempting to spread Nazi propaganda in secret code language to children. Fantastic as this sounds, they told us that they intended to attempt prosecution under the Corruption of Children and Minors Act."

At Manchester Crown Courts, 30 July 1992, Savoy successfully managed to overturn magistrate Derick Fairclough's ruling that the novel *Lord Horror* was obscene. However, the ruling against issue No.1 of *Meng & Ecker* was upheld. The appeal between Michael Butterworth and the Department of Public Prosecutions, was made on the publisher's behalf by Geoffrey Robertson QC (previously defending *Oz* in the Seventies and *Niggaz With Attitude* in the Nineties), and supported by international

"This is the record that did it" – Michael Butterworth

freedom group, ARTICLE 19. Author Michael Moorcock and Home Office child psychologist Guy Cumberbatch were among those to take the stand in defence of the works. Flanked by two magistrates, Judge Gerard Humphries read passages from the book and leafed through the comic, deliberating as to why, in *Lord Horror*, Hitler might have a freethinking penis named Old Shatterhand, or the 'point' of the vaudevillian singsong that opens *Meng & Ecker* (doubly ironic is irony lost). Proceedings came to a temporary halt when it was discovered that the two magistrates had been supplied with documents of which neither the defence nor the Judge had been made aware. Following a brief adjournment, not wishing to postpone to a later date, Robertson and the defendant agreed to continue.

Judge Humphries, in reaching his verdict, said of the novel, "The true meaning of obscenity is that a book or comic is obscene if and only if it depraves or corrupts a significant proportion of likely readers. The book is not obscene under that definition." Contrary, with regard to the comic, he concluded that it "could be read – and possibly gloated over – by people who enjoyed viciousness and violence. It had pictures that would be repulsive to right-thinking people". From an original print-run of 500, the 150 copies of *Lord Horror* impounded by police in 1989, were relinquished. Issue No.1 of *Meng & Ecker*, on the other hand, the first comic to be banned in Britain, would be the focus of further appeal.

The objection levelled at the novel was that of anti-Semitism. Lord Horror kills Jews.

There was little mention in court of the book's *other* harbinger of ill-tidings: Chief Constable James Appleton (and his similarity to Manchester's own James Anderton). But Savoy maintain that this, indeed, is the source of the contention.

Is the use of the 'Appleton' character some sort of retaliation against the police?

"It's not retaliation. He's given us the ideal character – himself. How could we not use him*!* It's him who's got the bee in his bonnet about raiding shops instead of doing... er... whatever police are supposed to do."

Did it not make matters worse, though?

"It did. But his men had raided us 60 times and put Dave in jail. Then all those ludicrous pronouncements he was making. With all this happening we just had to record it. The pronouncements he made early in his career about interning young people in camps, for instance. We actually brought out 'Blue Monday' by the 'Savoy-Hitler Youth Band' as a result of that proclamation. The sleeve shows scenes from Dachau on the back and it's got what looks like James Anderton's head on the front in his uniform. Actually, it's a doctored still from a horror film [*The Stuff*]. It was an *anti*-authoritarian statement we were making. It was this record that put the new wave of Politically Correct people against us. And it's one of the reasons we haven't been able to get any distribution, and coined the term 'Savoy Wars'. People think we're fascists. The so-called 'alternative' people decided they would have nothing more to do with us at the retail and distribution end. We were getting raided, that made them nervous, too. And other people, who didn't mind what we were doing but didn't want to get involved in police raids. We were ostracized and alienated by everybody."

Further repercussions in the *Lord Horror* debacle were felt on 27 April 1993, when author David Britton was found guilty for non-Savoy material (pornography) confiscated in August 1991, and sentenced to four-months imprisonment. This was the raid that came three days after magistrate Derick Fairclough had initially ruled *Lord Horror* to be obscene, and in which 4,000 copies of the comic *Hard Core Horror* were seized.

Ironically, it was while Britton was doing time that *Reverbstorm*, the much-anticipated, much-delayed follow-up to *Hard Core Horror* finally saw the light of day.

Says Butterworth, "*Reverbstorm* is an eight-part Rock 'n' Roll phantasmagoria set in an alternate *Stürm-und-Drang* city world. Dave sees the comic as a fugue, with its characters – Jessie Matthews, Lord Horror, James Joyce, the Ether Jumpers, Blue Blaze Laudanum, the Ononoes... even the city, which has a palpable presence – as musical components."

Continuing on from Coulthart's death camp images in the final, controversial issue of *Hard Core Horror*, *Reverbstorm* opens to vertiginous structures set against a bleak and foreboding skyline Except this time it isn't the death camps of a Nazi Germany.

"The city, Torenbürgen, is a cross between New York and Auschwitz... Torenbürgen means the House of the Dead." It is where Lord Horror – when not broadcasting on the radio or engaging in groupie sex – takes to the streets with fellow countryman James Joyce, making short work of anyone careless enough to stand in their path. It is where Seurat's *La Grande Jatte* becomes as volatile as Central Park after dark. And it is where the emancipated soul of superstar Jessie Matthews, gnarled and twisted, allows itself to be penetrated by the soul of the Virgin Mary.[18] Of course, things promise to get more twisted from here on in.

"The similarity between our work," says Butterworth, "and the so-called 'apocalyptic' culture or much of the literature arising from the current interest in death and sex, the serial killer, is coincidental."

But for how long do you want to argue 'what it all means'?

"I've never seen it as an argument... what I mean is, there's two aspects, eg. the obvious, where we show scenes of Dachau on the 'Blue Monday' sleeve, or have Meng hoist Anderton's severed head on a pike or fillet Billy the Fish with a dagger; those might have to be explained to people who don't know the references; and there's the sublime aspects, which draw from the nature of life in the Twentieth Century – Picasso, James Joyce, Auschwitz. If you read *Reverbstorm* now, and could come back in 30 or 40 years time you'd see that what we're dealing with has already become the everyday literature of the future. Auschwitz will be the subject matter of fiction far more than it is today. Picasso, Joyce and Auschwitz are the three touchstones of this century – they're all peaks in their own way that cannot be surpassed. The trend is already distinct. It has been said that it is almost *de rigueur* for an author to write a death camp novel. Well, *Lord Horror* started the trend, our novel appearing well before Martin Amis' *Time's Arrow* or the current spate of death camp films."

There stands a difference, however, in presenting a story in the form of a novel and that same story in the form of a comic book. Many people – as evidenced by Judge Humphries' dismissal of *Meng & Ecker* as having "pictures that would be repulsive to right-thinking people" – cannot accept that comics might be anything but a medium for juveniles.

"One of the things that triggered *Reverbstorm* – this probably needs explaining – was our reaction to the low standard of so-called 'adult' graphic comics heralded by the comics industry and press over the last 15 years or so. There's only been two graphic books that have lived up to the promise – Alan Moore's *Watchmen*, and Burne Hogarth's *Jungle Tales of Tarzan*. The rest have been various degrees of dire. Adult

This page. Jessie Matthews, Reverbstorm No.1. *Next page.* Lord Horror, Reverbstorm No.3 Art: John Coulthart

comics in the Eighties and Nineties have become the platform shoes and flares of their generation. Adult comics were far more adult in the Thirties and Forties.

"People who want the simple-mindedness of X-Men or Judge Dredd will do better to look elsewhere. But if you want something sublime, that will stretch reference points in artistic and philosophical terms, then look no further."

THE SMALLEST REVENGE WILL POISON THE SOUL [19]

History has a habit of repeating itself. With the ban on *Meng & Ecker* No.1, Savoy were quick to release the latest instalment of that series, issue No.7, which has on its cover... a bearded gentlemen in uniform, surrounded by disembodied, pink and mottled, wildly ejaculating male members. The whole issue is a kind of fond farewell to the ex-Chief Constable.

In 1992, Savoy published *Michael Moorcock: Death Is No Obstacle*, Colin Greenland's booklength interview with the celebrated author. Not focused primarily on Moorcock's fiction, but covering also his writing of comic strips for Fleetway in 1960 and, later, *Look and Learn*, *Death Is No Obstacle* comes with an introduction by Angela Carter. "She was another author of the imaginative sort," says Butterworth. "Not part of the realistic novel movement; not the 'University of East Anglia' types who've been holding sway for years."

On a musical front, *Savoy Wars* is a CD compilation album of several of the company's rare 12" single releases.[20] As an added bonus, it includes PJ Proby deconstructing the traditional folk ballad 'The Old Fenian Gun' (which, in his drunken stupor, Proby pronounces 'Finnegan'; 'That old *Finnegan* gun'). 'Reverbstorm', the song, is the posthumous anthem of Martin Flitcroft, ex-Savoy Press Officer who, one day, placed himself quite deliberately in the path of a moving train.

In March 1995, the company was filmed for BBC 2's *The A-Z of Horror*. On the horizon is the imminent release of *PJ Proby: The Savoy Sessions* CD LP. The bad boy of Rock made a surprise appearance on ITV's chat show,

Barrymore, aired 30 April 1994. Successfully fielding questions levelled at his drink problem (he hasn't touched a drop since 1992), Proby avoided mention of Savoy and finished on a song from *West Side Story*. The appearance marked the singer's self-reclamation in the mainstream. An extended interview with him appeared in the August 94 edition of *Record Collector* magazine. In July, Proby told *Hello!*, "I can't find Proby any more. The things he did, I can't do."

The police still have in their possession over 4,000 copies of *Lord Horror* and *Meng & Ecker* comics seized back in September of 1989. For the hearing – pending as of writing – Savoy intend to challenge the current procedure that, under Section Three of the Obscene Publications Act, police can seize controversial material, hold it for an unlimited period of time, and then seek its destruction before a magistrate. It will also be argued that the publishers should be allowed to have their trial before a jury. Under a 1964 amendment to the Act there is a non-statutory provision for a trial if the publishers ask for one. Savoy *have* asked for a jury trial, and been refused. If Savoy win their case they may set favourable precedents for future publishers. If they don't win in the magistrates court, they have plans to take the case to the divisional courts for judicial review. If they *still* fail, they will answer the charge of obscenity.

For the first time in over a decade, *The Gas* has a national distribution.

The Savoy office is reached through a locksmith shop and up a staircase which falls back on itself, its rickerty handrail of little comfort in the darkness. A coffin is set to oneside. A floating head, painted on hardboard, eight-foot tall and baring razor-teeth greets the visitor at the top – a backdrop from UKCAC, a comic convention which Savoy attend annually to the chagrin of many. There is a bathtub full of books to the left, and on the right an assortment of old metal toys and archaic filing system. The view from the windows is of busy Deansgate, the business heart of the city. For a surreal moment in the not too distant past, there was talk of turning the Savoy offices into a huge pirate ship with sails billowing down the side of the building and the Jolly Roger on a flagpole spanning the congested main street. Unmissable, unavoidable. The kind of madcap brainwave that Savoy would once have leaped upon and goaded into harsh reality. One in the eye of THE ESTABLISHMENT. But now it's a little different. Now the insanity is tuned to work *into* the system as opposed to up against it. It takes the form not of illicit vinyl recordings, bagged pornography, or music pressured high and forced out the door, but of Savoy product. Slivers of *otherness* wedged into that irritating rash called Reality. It is societal bigotry as portrayed in Meng and Ecker; the urban despotism of Lord Horror and Reverbstorm; the immolation and resurrection of PJ Proby.

What of the future?

Says Mike Butterworth, "There is quite a lot to get out. Readings of 'The Waste Land' and *Lord Horror* on CD – we've got the recordings, we just need to edit and press up. A *Meng & Ecker*, large format, best-of collection. After we get this product out, if we still can't make any breakthrough we'll probably call it a draw."

Are you saying no new Savoy product? The closure of the shops?

"Since we've started Lord Horror we've paid scarcely any attention to the shops, anyway. Today, all the shops are just dumps; they're nothing like they were in their heyday, when they were the first *and* the best. I'd like you to mention that."

NOTES

Throughout the main text the company's imprint as it stands to date, simply 'Savoy', has been used. Only where historically pertinent have the past imprints — Savoy Books Ltd, Savoy Editions Ltd — been introduced.

1. In a raid on the Bookchain shop in October 1980, police removed 1,833 obscene books and magazines, "The large majority of which," said Gordon Smith, prosecuting, "were hidden behind a secret wall."

2. Heathcote Williams, *The Savoy Book*.

3. An 'interesting' aside: Sitting outside Sinclairs pub in Manchester town centre, during the warmer months of 1991, the author was exchanging talk with a friend over a few beers. When the conversation got round to Frank Zappa and his Studio Z recording studio, a bearded guy, somewhat dishevelled in appearance, made his way over. "Studio Z? Frank Zappa?" he said, drunkenly. It turned out the guy *was* drunk, but he also knew a lot about the subject at hand. Telling us he was fresh back from the hippie trail in India, he introduced himself as John Muir, Mr Babylon Books, and told us he now lived in Todmorden where the locals referred to him as "Mad Jack" and Hell's Angels were after him.

4. *The Savoy Book* (1978) was the first in a proposed trilogy of anthologies. A collection of *belles lettres*, faction, fiction, art and Rock 'n' Roll, it was intended to fill the gap after *New Worlds* temporarily suspended publication. The second anthology was *Savoy Dreams* (1984), which Angus Wilson called "a super dip". The third in the trilogy, *Savoy Sword & Sorcery*, has yet to appear.

5. The Moorcock connection goes back beyond Savoy. Butterworth had been a regular contributor to Moorcock's *New Worlds* magazine; Moorcock to both Britton and Butterworth's respective publications. Later, Moorcock lent his name to Butterworth's novel, *The Time of the Hawklords*.

6. Michael Butterworth, *The Sunday Telegraph*, 10 October 1993.

7. *Tides of Lust* had also been unavailable in the US since 1973, when the paperback edition went out of print.

8. Heathcote Williams, *Savoy Dreams*.

9. Colin Greenland, *Michael Moorcock: Death is no Obstacle*.

10. "As you suggested, if Jim *does* die in the near future, which seems likely, Savoy will certainly make every last effort to bring his corpse to *The Last Resort* office — though we cannot guarantee he will say much." Letter from David Britton to John Flemming, producer of *The Last Resort*, 29 September 1987.

11. In actuality the voice of Bobby Thompson, singer with Kingsize Taylor and the Dominoes, one of the first Merseybeat groups.

12. Opening lyric, 'M97002: Hardcore'.

13. The *Hard Core Horror* mini-series is actually an offshoot of another proposed series. Two issues only of a *Lord Horror* comic appeared. These proved a working drawing-board for the character and, come issue No.3, the series switched to become *Hard Core Horror*. (Hence the reason the fifth and final instalment in the *Hard Core* series carries on its cover, 'Issue No.7'.)

14. **DAVID BRITTON** "That's four lines from the novel you have just encapsulated there. There's not long descriptions of that. As you have read it out that's exactly as it is in the book."
 MALCOLM WOOD "On page 57, 58 and 59 there is a scenario that describes Jews coming out of a synagogue and the young Jew being slashed open and disembowelled and a Rabbi intervening, various other atrocities involving the killing of Jews in various sadistic manners. Is it true that on these pages that scenario is

described in the book?"

BRITTON "With the qualification that again you're reading the book out of context, taking isolated bits out."

WOOD "On pages 93 and 94 again a scenario describes where Jews are being attacked with a razor, the Jew's tongue is pinned by the razor to his chin. His body slashed open displaying his organs and even the central character delving into the body gripping organs in his teeth either to eat or to do whatever you would describe his actions. Is that again another scenario within the book?"

BRITTON "Again you have taken it out of its text. Out of what surrounds. But that scene is in the book."

WOOD "I put it to you again that that scene and the others I have described would tend to show a racial discrimination attitude couched in that book."

BRITTON "No certainly not, certainly not."

WOOD "In certain quarters the reading of the book, would you not think that it was racially inflammatory."

BRITTON "No I would not."

Transcript – in part, out of context – of interview with David Britton conducted by Detective Inspector Malcolm Wood, Obscene Publications Dept., Manchester Police, 17 October 1989.

15. Henry Miller.

16. Savoy threw a spanner in the works when, on its covers, *Meng & Ecker* began to carry the tag 'Arts Council Funded'. Over a period of several weeks, the London Arts Council entered into correspondence with Savoy, querying as to what it was the acknowledgement related. Their first letter noted, *'Colleagues here and at North West Arts have been unable to trace any record of having offered any assistance.'* In their reply, Savoy thanked the Arts Council for their *'offer of financial assistance'*. A hurried missive from the Council emphasised that their previous letter *'did not as you must realise, offer financial assistance'*. But, Savoy wrote, *'Christina at North West Arts supplied funding for our involvement in 1987 in a visual prospectus aimed at the teaching profession.'* The London Arts Council came back, *'assured by North West Arts that they have no Christina working for them and have never supplied funding for your involvement in a visual prospectus... '*
Previous to all this, Charles Osborne, ex-Arts Council, was quoted in the *Daily Telegraph* as saying, "Savoy's *Meng & Ecker* comics do more for racial harmony than all the Arts Council Funded community centres from Brixton to Moss Side."
In 1994, *Meng & Ecker* announced that it had landed not one, but *five* Eagle Awards. That would make it just about the country's favourite comic book.

17. Immanuel Kant.

18. Jessie Matthews' legendary status can be measured by Savoy's decision to release *Monoshock*, a one-shot publication devoted entirely to the wartime sweetheart. Little more than a collection of pin-ups by artist Kris Guidio, *Monoshock* was not entirely successful. Mike Butterworth denies the caricatures in *Monoshock* to be based upon Jessie Matthews, however. "All Guidio's women tend to look the same."

19. Eastern proverb.

20. The *Savoy Wars* CD comes complete with a 24-page booklet which chronicles Savoy music. Contrary to Mike Butterworth's wishes, the decision was made *not* to put a copyright date on the package and, in effect, leave it "timeless". Come the day the package was to go to the printers, Butterworth made an impromptu change to the copy, adding a date. This amendment came to light only when the print run had been completed. *Savoy Wars* was now indeed held to a copyright date, but one mistakenly noted '1984' as opposed to '1994'. "Rather fortuitous, though, isn't it?" Butterworth later recalled. "1984? That was also roughly when we first started doing records. 85 to be precise, but we were certainly preparing work in 1984."

Savoy can be contacted at 279 Deansgate, Manchester, M3 4EW.

EVERYTHING WAS CHANGED*!!!*
Sexualis In Excelsis

A Miscellany of Correspondence to Various Porn Magazines, Pt VII

EVERYTHING WAS CHANGED*!!!* This is MY STORY for ———— magazine.
3 years a go I was good at giving head to men. I make loved to a woman on several ocassions but men was the thing for me. Men in bars men in Burger King even I all gave them head and loved to do this.
BUT EVERYTHING WAS CHANGED.
I found I could give head to GOD and make him cum. Now I dont sleep with women I just give head to GOD and make him cum. I bet you never know it is possible? But he is the best*!!!*
When I give head to GOD he always has a lot of sperm. Cum tastes good. GOD sperm is best*!!!* I suck for a long time and always there is a lot of cum and this is what has changed my life.
You should try it as well your models could do it GOD has enough for them all to give him head. TRY IT AND IT WILL BE CHANGED*!!!!* I like your mag it has the best girls but none of the know what it is like to give head to GOD.
You should try it.

H—— S———, Kansas

Dear Sir:
I urge ———— to organize a real estate company with models, ex-Playboy bunnies, ex-Penthouse playmates, etc that give a free fuck with every sale. Further, I urge ones organization to become Rosicrucian philosophers and black belts in judo. Lastly, I urge ones organization to memorize days three and four of Genesis in the Bible in order to eliminate opposition in ones lifestyles.
Peace Profound

J—— S———, US Judo Association

Dear ———— magazine,
I am a 53 year old Catholic priest who reads your magazine regularly and gets great enjoyment from doing so. I understand that reading ———— is a sin but more priests than you think do this. In NYC I know of many such priests who are fornicators etc, and I have had many carnal adventures over the years as well.

Among my congregation is a lady named S——— G———. She is 28 and married but I know she frequently has affairs outside of her marriage vows. It is one of my dutys to hear her confession and frequently I am startled to hear of her sexual feats. The priests I work with all say the same. Mrs G——— is an extremely attractive woman and dresses in a sexy way so it is no surprise this happens as much as it does. I have to say I look forward greatly to her visits to the confessional here.

Yesterday I was hearing confession when who should arrive but S———. I have often thought she derives enjoyment from telling these stories to me and other priests and going into much detail regarding the sins she has committed. When she yesterday told me about how she had been seduced by a friend of her husband it was particularly exciting to hear. The friend F——— had arrived at her house while her husband was at work. He had started to kiss her and fondle her breasts. This made her excited and she responded by touching his private parts through his pants. He raised her skirt and began to touch her private parts as well. This made her even more excited and she could no longer resist. She took his penis in her mouth and ran her tongue all over his penis.

At this point I was becoming excited from listening. I started to touch myself through my clothing. My penis was very hard. S——— admitted she had wanted F——— to climax in her mouth. He however wanted to fuck her. They went into the living room and he fucked her on the couch. She had a number of climaxes. He then fucked her in the ass and S——— found this very exciting. I myself was now close to my own climax and found talking difficult. I asked S——— whether she considered sodomy a sin? She replied she found it exciting and enjoyed being fucked in the ass very much. At this point I could not prevent myself from climax even though I had only been touching myself very slightly. I believe S——— knew I had because I heard her laugh.

She then left and it was some time before I regained my composure. It had been a very exciting experience.

I wonder if S——— would really like to fuck a priest. Perhaps if she reads this she would make her desires more clear. As you would understand I would wish my identity to remain unknown. Please take measures to do this if you decide to print my story in ——— magazine.

Yours Sincerely

N——— F———

Dear ———— Magazine,

I am a long time and loyal reader of ———— Magazine and get a lot of pleasure from the women and information you have in your pages so I am writing you in the hope you can help me with the trouble that I am having.

Until five months ago I had a great sex life with my wife C————————. We are both 26 and married four years and we both read ———— Magazine and enjoyed all the sex and fucking there was in there. We were adventurous in sex and tried many things even a threesome with a friend of C————————'s from work on one great occassion but that was before C———————— became a christian and began to attend a local church here. Now she says that what we used to do was a sin and refuses to do it any more. C———————— will have sex with me but refuses to indulge in things like oral sex or anal sex as that is a sin she says. I am very unhappy she refuses to now give me head as C———————— is a wonderful cock sucker but now she just says no when I ask her to perform fellatio and wont even let me lick her pussy. As a result I am very frustrated of course. I looked up in the bible where it says that sodomy is forbidden and I could not see any where that it says fellatio isnt allowed. But when I told C———————— she said her minister said it was not allowed. It made me mad as I knew she had told this man about our sex life. He also said reading magazines like – ———— Magazine was sinful too and she threw all the magazines in the trash and now I have to purchase your magazine and read it in secret. You might think Im crazy to stand this but I love my wife, she has a great body and I enjoy making love to her even if it is not like it used to be. I hope she will one day change and be how she used to be but for now I am thinking about visiting a prostitute to get head because my wife refuses to do this. I would like to know what you think about this situation and if there is any way I could get her to see how she is hurting my feelings.

G.S., Tulsa

IF MASTERBATION IS AGAINST GODS LAW THEN WHAT ARE YOU
PEOPLE DOING*!!!*
YOU PEOPLE MAKE ME CUM*!!*
WHEN I SEE ———— MAG I CANT NOT MASTERBATE AND CUM AND
CUM
BUT I KNOW IT IS AGAINST GODS LAW AND IT IS A SIN*!!!!*
YOURE HOT BITCHES SHOW THEIR BODIES & I AM FORCED TO LOOK AT
THEIR WET PUSSEYS AND THIS MAKES ME MASTERBATE & CUM*!!!*
IT IS AGAINST GOD BUT I CANT NOT DO IT EVER TIME I GET ————
MAG
BECAUSE THE BITCHES SHOW THEIR PUSSEYS AND HAVE MEN FUCK
THEM IN THERE PUSSEYS I HAVE TO MASTERBATE
I WONT TO FUCK YOURE BITCHES BUT I CANT BECAUSE I KNOW I
WOULD BE DAMNED IF I WERE TO DO THIS
YOU PEOPLE ARE DOING THIS TO ME*!!!!*
ARE YOU PEOPLE FREINDS OF GOD
OR THE DEVIL*?????*
WHEN I SEE ———— MAG I KNOW YOU PEOPLE WANT ME TO
MASTERBATE & PROVOKING ME TO MASTERBATE
BY SHOWING PUSSEYS AND ASSHOLES TOO
THAT MAKE ME NEED TO CUM

I MASTERBATE & CUM ON THE PAGES WHERE THOSE BITCHES ARE
SHOWING THERE PUSSEYS
I KNOW THIS MAKES ME DAMMED & I CUM ON ALL THE BITCHES IN
YOURE MAG
IF THERES ONE BITCH WHO SHOWS A LOT I WILL MASTERBATE & CUM
MORE THAN ONE TIME
MY CUM IS ALL OVER HER*!!!!!*
SHE GETS IT BECAUSE SHE HAS MADE ME MASTERBATE

O.L.

I AM PRAYING FOR YOU ALL AT ——— MAG

Sir:

When I married my husband I knew he had very strong religious beliefs, but this did not overly concern me as I too was brought up in a God-fearing family environment where my sexual education was conducted within a very strict religious framework. As a young girl I was taught to avoid fornication and preserve my virginity for my wedding night. I did this and surrendered my purity to R——— on the night we were married. It was not what one could call a memorable experience. As any woman can relate, there was a lot of pain and mess and very little actual pleasure. However, in the weeks to follow sex became more pleasurable and two months later I actually achieved an orgasm – my very first*!* However, I noted that R——— was not overly pleased that I came, he believed sex to be strictly for procreative purposes. I though was confused, unable to see why one should feel such intense pleasure during sex if it was not meant to be enjoyable.

I soon fell pregnant and gave birth to a daughter, followed the year after by another. Throughout this time I was experimenting with the pleasure I could gain through masturbating. I had not done this prior to marrying, not even in my adolescence, the reason being I shared a bedroom with my two elder sisters and my grandmother, but also because I knew masturbation to be wholly unclean. But now I became addicted to the pleasure I could derive from teasing my clitoris and would often do this when R——— was at work and the kids were at school.

I cannot stress too much how much confusion this made me feel. Even when I was enjoying an orgasm I found it difficult to see why something that felt so good could be deemed as unnatural or unChristian. In some barbaric cultures I know that female circumcision is practised in order to prevent the woman experiencing sexual enjoyment, but I lived in a civilized society and this part of my body was something that made me complete as a female and therefore I didn't understand why such enjoyment should be forbidden.

This caused me so much confusion and guilt that finally I confessed to R——— what I had been doing. He immediately told me to talk to Mrs G———, who was the wife of our pastor. Mrs G——— agreed to meet me at her house and she was extremely understanding as regarded my problem, suggesting that I return one day during the week to discuss the matter in more detail.

The following Wednesday I arrived at her house and she made me welcome. We drank coffee and discussed my 'problem'. After an hour or so she suddenly startled me when she declared that, in her opinion, the church law regarding masturbation was unnecessary and ridiculous.

I asked her what she meant by that and she replied that she regularly sought enjoyment by doing this. "It is a relief to know I am not the only one," she said. I was astonished! At the time I was 29 and Mrs G—— was 38 and suddenly I began to feel very much at ease in the company of this older woman, who like me, derived secret sexual satisfaction from masturbation. But what happened next really took my breath away!

"Would you like to do it right now?" she asked me. I hesitated, because I actually did want to, but I certainly could not imagine masturbating right here in the pastor's house, in front of the pastor's wife!

"I would like to, A——," said Mrs G——, "We could both do it together." Then she smiled at me and raised the hem of her dress high enough that I could see she was not wearing any underwear. My heart was pounding as she opened her thighs slightly and brought her hand down to caress her naked pussy. "Please watch me, A——," she said, "It would make me very happy indeed."

I was so amazed I couldn't move at all and simply stared between her thighs as Mrs G—— began to caress herself with more urgent strokes, her fingers parting the lips of her pussy and actually inserting a finger. As startled as I was, I did find the sight extremely exciting. I had never witnessed anything on a par with what was happening now and wasn't at all certain how I should react. However, I did suggest we move somewhere more private if we were going to continue as the drapes were wide open and we were in plain sight of any callers to the house there might be.

Mrs G—— agreed and led me upstairs to her and her husband's bedroom. As we entered the room she reached up and unzipped her dress, letting it fall to the floor so she was clad only in her underwear. "The fact you suggested coming here must mean you are excited," she said, and I couldn't argue with her logic. If I had been shocked or affronted I would obviously demanded to leave the instant she bared her sex to me.

All the same, I was still confused as Mrs G—— walked toward me and began to unbutton the front of my dress. "This has to be wrong, Mrs G——." I said, hardly able to comprehend what was happening. "It isn't wrong, A——," she replied, "And please call me L——."

By this point my dress was fully unbuttoned and I was standing there in only my brassiere and panties. That was when L—— pulled me close to her in an embrace and kissed me fully on the lips. Even R—— had never kissed me like that before! Now I was no longer in control of my passions and I responded eagerly to her kiss, thrilling to her touch as she unclipped my brassiere and tenderly took my breasts in her hands, fondling them and lightly stroking the nipples until they were erect and tingling to her touch.

Still locked in a passionate kiss, we fell on the quilted counterpane. L—— removed my panties and then took off her brassiere so her large breasts fell forward, milky-white and marbled with light blue veins around her large nipples. When she pressed her breasts into my face it seemed wholly natural to take the nipples between my lips and suck on them. I was gratified by L——'s response. She moaned gently and told me how wonderful it felt.

Again it crossed my mind that this was not proper, that it was utterly sinful in The Lord's eyes. But when L—— placed her hand between my thighs and tenderly caressed my pussy I once more experienced that pleasure I knew so well, only now it was increased twicefold and becoming steadily more intense the more her fingers probed and stroked between my thighs. In what seemed only a matter of moments I was in the throes of a huge orgasm as L—— teased my clitoris with her fingertip. I was gasping for air, but she was not letting me off that lightly! Her face went between my thighs and as I felt her tongue touch my clitoris I exploded in orgasm so intense it frightened me. All I could feel was the wet warmth of L——'s tongue pushing me into a frenzy where any notion of what was wrong or right seemed utterly irrelevant and meaningless. Only later did I realize that what I had experienced was my first multiple orgasm.

As I regained control of my senses I heard L—— talking to me. She asked if I had enjoyed what she had done. I could only reply that it had been the most thrilling moment of my life and that I had no idea you could feel such things. Then, without warning, I found myself bursting into tears as the guilt of what we had just done overwhelmed me. L—— cradled my head against her breasts as she consoled me, telling me we had done no wrong in the eyes of God. I asked her how she could justify saying that and her reply was that The Lord loved all his creatures and his love meant that they should not close themselves away from the pleasures for which they were made. Any union that gave pleasure was blessed, she said, if it meant that his creation were being fulfilled. If we failed to be fulfilled we were not using that which he had given us in the first place. Her words were very soothing and the guilt I had felt greatly lessened. I was especially relieved when L—— suggested she visit my house next week to see whether I was still feeling upset about our liaison.

With hindsight, everything she told me was simply an excuse for her to seduce me. But I didn't see things that way then and I was still confused, having several sleepless nights agonizing over what I had done. I even contemplated telling R——
—, but that would have been insane and would have caused a massive scandal in such a small town! I was delighted when L—— came over the following Wednesday and we again made love. This time it was even better as I was learning how sexual anticipation heightens one's enjoyment of sex. Afterward, L—— informed me that she would be attending a church conference in Atlanta the weekend after next and asked me if I would want to accompany her. Of course, R—— was delighted I should be pursuing religious work so enthusiastically and even volunteered to drive L—— and myself to the airport. I felt such a hypocrite as we prayed together for a safe journey, knowing what was likely to happen when L—— and I got to Atlanta.

It was during that weekend in Atlanta that I finally lost my faith. For three nights in succession I shared a bed with L—— G—— and became adept at pleasuring her orally, her guidance proving invaluable as I fumbled nervously in the arts of lesbian lovemaking. However, I think the moment that I really realized the hypocrisy of religion was upon encountering a prominent church leader (and a married man!) who had only that afternoon given an address on the Scriptures in an elevator accompanied by a woman who was clearly no child of God! He pretended not to know the woman as I stepped into the car but from her appearance and the prominent erection clearly visible in his pants I knew exactly what he intended to do with her. From that moment on, I knew I could never have any respect for such figures again. This man would have undoubtedly condemned L—— and I, yet he was consorting with hookers! When I informed L—— of what had witnessed, she replied that there was nothing unique in this and that she knew of many church leaders who were fornicators and worse. Some of the stories she related that night made the 'sins' that we had committed appear minute by comparison.

To say that I returned from Atlanta a 'changed woman' would be an understatement! My faith was completely destroyed and I have not been the same since. No longer could I follow blindly everything R—— demanded and more and more I began to perceive subtle things in those religious people in the community. I saw men looking at women with obvious lust and became aware that I was surrounded by people who said one thing yet when they thought no one could see them did the complete opposite.

However, R——— was unable to see this, so strong was his faith. In many ways I admire him for that, but unfortunately, I still feel he is blind to the truth, even though he knows in his heart I was right. Eventually, we parted company, though I still see him when visiting the kids. He has remarried and found a woman far more to his liking. I even attended the ceremony and was delighted to see L——— there! We talked about why she continues to remain with her husband, the church and all that goes along with

that, but I can understand her wishing to be with her husband, much as I miss the passionate liaisons we once had.

I am 34 now and living in Milwaukee where I have started a successful catering concern. Though no longer in the full bloom of my youth I feel I am still reasonably attractive and enjoy the company of many male admirers and several female too. Making up for the lost years, you might say! In fact I was going to write and relate an especially exciting experience I had this weekend which involved a married couple I met through my business, but as I sat down to write I found myself more inclined to tell the tale you have just read. I must apologize for the length of this letter, but I hope that you are able to find space in your splendid magazine to print my story as I feel that hopefully it might encourage any readers who find themselves in a position similar to the one in which I was to know that you can escape the background into which you were born. In other words, it doesn't always have to be that way!

With love from Milwaukee,

A.R.H.

GOD IS FOR LOSERS

I am a SATANIST for 2 yeers. SATAN has give me sex powers. Wen I see yor mag I do magic and fuck yor girls. I fuck them any way I wont. I rape them. They do things I comand. SATAN helps me do this.

SATAN tells me fuck young girls. Young is teen aged like girls in yor mag. SATAN tells me to have power over them there bodis are mine. Wen I fuck them it is a worship to SATAN. Wen I fuck there pussys I fuck for SATAN.

I wont to fuck yor girls in church. I wont to cum on the † it piss me off.

ABADDON LUCIFER BELZEEBUB SHAITAN EBLIS SATAN SATAN SATAN SATAN SATAN

RAXCUU FEAAT JHEALLIS IN NOXAH I FUCK THE GIRLS IN YOR MAG EVER DAY

A FATAL ATTRACTION
Suicide-Homicide

Douglas Daniel Clark

BEFORE GREAT BRITAIN OPTS TO ENTER into the select club of nations which put citizens to death as just one more civil service function, it behoves you all to carefully consider ramifications beyond the emotional urge for vengeance and the outrage at the horror of crimes in your midst.

Within the latter half of this century, in the United States, the death penalty and murder rates have taken great strides. Locked in a dance of ever more frantic steps, the entwined legal and illegal slaughter seems destined to pale the body-counts of all wars this nation ever fought.

With evolving data, however, there are disturbing conclusions one cannot easily ignore. The worst aspect involves the broadly ignored phenomena of suicide-homicide. As is often the case this inverted self-destructive goal within perpetrators' unstable minds explodes outwardly, in a frightening kind of murder: serial killings.

England is not unfamiliar with serial murder. Possibly the most internationally notorious of all, Jack the Ripper, was not only undeterred by the threat of the gallows, but went unexposed into history's dusty tomes.

What is known now, after just a few decades of mass and serial murders in the US, is that a great many of the most prolific killers have been quite obviously not a bit deterred by the threat of death at the hands of police or subsequent judicial processes. In fact, many of the most lethal seemed clearly to have sought self-destruction by their acts. There have even been cases where the killers emulated previously-executed killers' acts.

Carol Mary Bundy duplicated almost each detail of Theodore Bundy's string of murders in Washington state. The Hollywood area's Hillside Stranglers executed their many victims by using every method of 'legal execution': gas, injection, hanging, electrocution. Gary Gilmore actively sought the fame and notoriety of the death sentence. Gerard Gallego, the son of a man himself put to death by electrocution, committed a string of capital murders and ended up sentenced to death in both Nevada and California.

Yet more chilling, even death row guards are not 'deterred' from capital murder by their very duties of confining those already sentenced and due execution. In a most amazing case, a California guard regularly tried to engage men condemned for serial sex-murders of young women in conversation. Officer J.W. preferred to whisper these chats with a man who is said to have kidnapped, tortured and murdered several girls in his van. When the officer was caught (wearing his uniform, nametag and badge), after abducting and raping a young woman at knife-point, there was little doubt that he had been taking her to the remote hills to commit capital murder when she escaped, naked, and ran for her life. He could not have more perfectly duplicated the horrific crimes committed by the prisoner he spent his days guarding if he had followed a script.

The facts are ever more conclusively proving there are many fatal attractions for these unbalanced persons who contemplate either their own destruction with the government as the instrument, or seek to emulate those who have gone before up the gallows' steps. One need only look to the public's fascination with the entire topic of fiction or nonfiction murder, to realise this goes beyond mere passing curiosity. Consider Ted Bundy, who escaped from prison after asking a journalist which state would *surely* put him to death if caught there, then went to that state, committed inescapable capital crimes, and got himself caught and finally executed.

One cannot help but envision a moth and a flame. The girls who lost their lives were a tragic aside to the dance of death, individuals who just happened to live in the wrong place – Bundy passed through states which had no death penalty and committed no violent acts. Yet he killed in states which employ each kind of legal execution: gas, hanging, firing squad, electrocution and lethal injection. His was a death march which left an estimated 100 or more murdered women in its wake. Any serial-homicide detective will admit these killings are the most difficult to solve. The series will often reach double-digit victim counts before the slaughter ends. While 'mass-murders', such as a man killing a score of people with an assault rifle in a suicidal act, are easily 'solved'; that kind of crime is encouraged, not deterred by death laws. Death is the object, not a dreaded consequence, as far as these killers are concerned.

Society may demand executions to ease their fear and feeling of helplessness spawned by these atrocities. But for a nation, which used to execute children for as little as petty theft, to rush back into the arena of governmental killings without first knowing there are fatal attractions for potential killers in such laws, would be folly. America has just begun to reap the rewards and assess the damages of these laws. The enormous legal costs alone are a topic for debate. But one must face the future steadfast, prepared to apologise to the families of victims killed *because* of these capital laws. For surely, as has occurred a hundredfold across the Atlantic, there will be victims who died solely because of the Fatal Attraction these laws hold for a number of future killers in your midst.

"IT'S FUN TO KILL PEOPLE!"
The Sunset Strip Murders

David Slater

MUCH HAS BEEN WRITTEN ABOUT THE *series of murders which happened in Hollywood during the summer of 1980. Previous articles, references and books have all been based on the testimony of Carol Bundy (as was the trial), convicted murderer and accomplice of the so-called 'Sunset Slayer'. This article is based on the account of Douglas Clark, currently awaiting execution on San Quentin's Death Row following his arrest for the crimes in August 1980. Clark insists he is not guilty of the six murders he was convicted of. He maintains that Carol Bundy and her illicit lover John Murray (whom she later murdered in a most brutal manner) were the real perpetrators of the serial killings. Clark also affirms that Carol duplicated the crimes of her namesake Ted Bundy in a bizarre copycat homage.*

Marnette Comer was only 17 years old when she died. A regular runaway and juvenile delinquent, she had been disappearing from her Sacramento home since the age of fourteen. After absconding for the last time in January 1980, she attempted to survive the rigours of independence in an unfamiliar town by renting her vagina to any Joe Shit who could afford it. She reunited with her sister Sabra, who was two years older and also a hooker, and together they prostituted themselves on the streets of Anaheim, California for a wise-ass pimp named Mark Benton.

Around May 21, Marnette went her own way, travelling up towards Hollywood where she believed trade would be better. Moreover, she hoped she could work without some parasitic pimp ripping her off.

Sabra was concerned about her sister's safety, preferring her to go back home and make up with her mother. Better than standing on the street corners of some screwed-up town fucking and sucking half-a-dozen strangers a day. But Sabra was well aware that Marnette could fight like a bitch if any punter got too rough. And anyway, her sister had a preference to pull doubles – two females to one male – as a safety precaution when hooking, so that consideration put her mind at rest. Somewhat.

Marnette made it to Hollywood – the glitz and glamour evidently a derelict myth – and found herself slap-bang in the same situation she'd endeavoured to break from: working for another rapacious hustler. Going it alone, she concluded, was pretty much impossible. The pimps controlled the whores and the turf they worked. Any independent hooker trading on someone else's territory was liable to have her face sliced off or cunt sewn up, either by rival whores or predatory pimp. The only solution was to enrol in the syndicate and be part of a one-sided, uneasy, bad-paying alliance. Nothing had changed. The streets looked the same, the pimp treated and cheated her the same, the punters' dicks felt and tasted the same, and the co-workers squawked and bitched the same. It was as good as it gets.

On Saturday, May 31, Marnette's overseer placed her for a night's work on Hollywood's notorious Sunset Boulevard. The Strip was a veritable streak of diseased asphalt cutting through the centre of Hollywood. It functioned as a meat-market for hookers and punters, junkies and dealers, dykes and faggots, pornographers and paedophiles. It was the road to Hell, or Heaven, depending on individual perspective and decorum. Marnette, a naïve street-corner whore, forever smiling in an attempt to conceal her general unhappiness, fitted in with the social misfits. Her only real grudge about the situation was handing over her earnings to the bloodsucking pimp and being palmed back an all but insignificant sum. Just enough to survive a day or so and ensure she'd be back dealing with another anonymous hard-on in the back of a car or stinking hotel room complete with piss-stained mattress. But at least this arrangement offered her an assurance of protection in a neighbourhood with which she was yet to become acquainted.

When it came to tricks, Marnette preferred the older guys. They couldn't hold back their juices like the younger guys, who'd often make you suck till your lips blistered. They could be stiffed for extra cash, and lack of regular sex ensured speedy ejaculations. Some would shoot their load as she spat a gob of lubricating spit on their dicks prior to a warm-up jerk-off. That was best of all. No need to peel off her pants; no seed spraying in her mouth; no lingering aftertaste that only seemed to pass away just as another guy squirted his stuff on her tongue. Five minutes work. Eight dollars for Mr Pimp, two bucks for herself.

As the late hours slipped into June 1 a punter came along, pulled up to the kerb where Marnette posed, and struck a deal with the coffee-breathed kid. She ducked into the vehicle, already allowing saliva to collect in her mouth: a practised preparation to help dilute the bitter taste of semen she'd agreed to take. The vehicle pulled away and rolled down the Strip that still sparkled with neon sex-shop and cinematic promises despite the hour. Marnette wasn't listening to the prerequisite chat her punter nervously waffled, just watched the lights blur by. The nocturnal activity on the Strip was consistently entertaining. She saw a flagrant transvestite sporting a comical dislocated wig, a bloody nose, and a grinning cop on either arm being bundled into the back seat of a black-and-white. A wretched vagrant lay either sleeping or dead in a shop doorway and someone, somewhere, screamed profanities so loud everyone in the immediate vicinity figured it was directed at them, "*Hey, you! Dirty muthafucka. Fuckin' sonvabitch, al fuckin' kill ya... you fuckin' lisnin' to me?... Hey, YOU!*"

The punter wasn't listening to his own patter, let alone the threatening patois filtering in from the sidewalk, just sensing the pressure in his stiff, curved dick. Stiff as the barrel of the gun tucked in his belt. Curved as the blade of the knife hidden in his well-polished cowboy boot.

As Marnette Comer was driven away, totally oblivious to the violent, lingering murder that awaited her in the hills, she was trying to calculate how many guys' cocks she'd have to suck to buy some decent clothes for the winter. But she wouldn't see the dawn, let alone some forthcoming season. Within the hour her mutilated, naked body would be tumbling down a mountainside scattering rocks, crushing shrubs and spooking the wildlife. Beside her, the last dick that would ever pass her lips strained and ever-so-slightly leaked in the pink, silky panties that enclosed it.

Thursday, June 12th, 1980. The sun mercilessly burned down on the blacktop surface of the Ventura Freeway: a vital road that skirted the Santa Monica mountains and functioned as a main route for affluent Californian suburbs such as Glendale and Beverly Hills.

It was around mid-day when a streetcleaner parked his van near the freeway off-ramp close to the Disney film studios and proceeded to collect rubbish left by careless travellers. The only sounds came from the buzzing insects, the scuffing of his broom, and occasional vehicle commuting to or from Hollywood. The perimeter of the off-ramp dropped sharply to a steep, gravelly ravine over which spiralled an occasional dust-devil. The twisting air currents did little to alleviate the 90° heat that baked the hillside; only made the labourer's work more arduous by scattering wrappers and other debris from hand's reach. Crushing a coke can beneath his heel, the last thing he expected to see dumped down the ravine was the body of a young girl. But there one was, partially hidden beneath undergrowth several metres down the slope. He stared for a while, wafting a curious fly from his face and dabbing a bead of sweat that ran an irritating trail from his brow to his cheek. Heat-shimmer made the form ripple as though it shivered with life. Perhaps she *was* alive. But closer examination showed not the slightest movement; no indication of breathing; nothing. Still as the stones on which she lay.

The girl was naked, save for a pink jump-suit pulled down around her legs. Slight traces of blood and minor abrasions were visible on her body. Flies scurried over her lily-white flesh, dabbing their probosci in search of seeping post-mortem fluids. Others shifted out of sight under her hair, feeding, and eager to deposit egg-clusters around and within the neat little bullet hole that led to, and through, her brain. Several metres along the slope lay a second female corpse nourishing the insects in a similar manner.

The cleaner reported his find and within 30 minutes Los Angeles police officers and detectives outnumbered the flies. Their uniforms the colour of carapace, the constant bursts of radio static fuzzing the air with insect-like drone. The area was cordoned off with yellow tape, intermittently printed with a 'DO NOT CROSS' warning, and a serious-crime team set to work on the bodies and surrounding terrain. The distance between the bodies suggested they had probably been thrown from a moving vehicle. Lividity on one of the bodies indicated she had been dead over 12 hours. Anything was sought on or around the girls: a bullet case; a blood drop; a flake of dried semen; a cigarette butt; a hair from head or groin; a fibre; a boot print; a beer bottle; any clue that might help identify a future suspect. After the preliminary photographs and examination, the two girls were wrapped in plastic sheeting, strapped into aluminium gurneys and hauled up the slope, then loaded like animal carcasses into the back of the coroner's van. They were taken away for thorough forensic scrutiny.

So began the task of tracking down a particularly brutal serial killer. A familiar, almost prosaic routine for the Californian cops. The previous year Ken Bianchi had been arrested in the Hillside Strangler case. A mild-mannered family man, Bianchi, allied with his cousin Angelo Buono, had raped and murdered at least 10 women. Their naked bodies were dropped in sexually provocative poses on the grassy slopes of LA, legs akimbo, labias crusted with give-away semen samples. In that case the media had labelled the killer pertinent to the location of the dumped corpses. In this circumstance, the moniker conceived by the press related to the killer's stalking

The bodies of Cynthia Chandler and Gina Marano as discovered off the Ventura Freeway. The distance between the bodies indicated they had been thrown from a moving vehicle. Lividity was evident on the upper-surface of one body suggesting it had been lying for some hours elsewhere before being dropped in its present location.

ground: Sunset Boulevard. So, as the Hillside Stranglers awaited trial, the hunt for the Sunset Slayer began.

On Friday, June 13th, the dead girls were identified as 16-year-old Cynthia Chandler and 15-year-old Gina Marano. They were stepsisters from Huntington Beach, and despite their ages both were allegedly involved in drugs and prostitution. The girls had recently been staying with associates in Beverly Hills where Gina had been drugged and raped at a pool-side party. The day before they died, they had been offered a lift by removals man Henry Brigges and his partner. Cynthia had handed Brigges the telephone number of the Beverly Hills home where they could be contacted. Brigges reciprocated and gave the girls his business card. They were dropped off and spent the night with two men they had met at the Colorado River the previous week. Cynthia allowed the men to film her naked for money and the girls ripped off the house before leaving. The following day they were picked up by their killer or killers.

Marano had two gunshot wounds through her head. One entered the left side of her head and exited near her right eyebrow. The second bullet had entered the back of the head and exited slightly lower than the first. The diameter of the holes indicated a bullet calibre of 6mm or .25 inch. Chandler also had a gunshot wound to the back of her head. There was no exterior exit wound. The bullet had emerged from her skull but failed to penetrate the flesh of the scalp. Its location was evident as a small raised bump beneath her hair. The slug had shed its copper jacket which remained like a shrapnel fragment within her brain. A second shot had penetrated Chandler's lung and heart which plausibly indicated the head-shot had been non-fatal. Tissue damage on her chest, caused by muzzle flash and escaping discharge gasses, revealed the weapon had been pressed tight against her bare flesh when fired. The bullet was found inside her chest cavity. Abrasions on her body had been caused after her death and probably occurred during the roll down the bank from the freeway. Traces of semen were found around her external vulva area. This was analysed and proved to belong to a secretor type blood-group A person.[1]

Ballistic experts studied the signatures left on the two slugs retrieved from Chandler. Microscopic examination of the lands and grooves[2] identified the weapon as a .25 Raven automatic, a cheap, toy-like weapon easier to buy than a bottle of beer. The fact that neither of the bullets had remained in Marano's head suggested perchance a second weapon being used and thus the possibility of two killers operating as a team such as in the Buono/Bianchi and Bittaker/Norris cases in 1979. Furthermore, the notion that the bodies had been thrown from a moving vehicle would also suggest at least two people being involved, one driving, the other pushing out the bodies. Having identified the weapon used on Chandler, investigators began checking recent gun purchase records around the area.

Detective Leroy Orozco, working from another division, contacted the detectives investigating the double homicide and informed them that they may have a copy-cat killer on their hands. He pointed out that only yards from where the girls where found, the body of Yolanda Washington had been dumped by the Hillside Strangler the previous year. Orozco would eventually take full charge of the Sunset case.[3]

On the evening of Saturday, 14th June, two days after the girls had been found, a telephone call was made to the Van Nuys police department. A woman, calling herself Betsy, was speaking from a call-box and claiming to know the person likely responsible for the murders of Chandler and Marano. Before she gave any relevant information the call was abruptly terminated, but within two hours she phoned back. The reason for the sudden cessation of the last call was, she explained, because a police officer had approached and caused her to panic. This time she called herself 'Claudia', concerned that the bogus name she had previously used would be recognisable should it be publicised by the media. 'Claudia' indicated to the detectives handling the call, Heinlein and Westbrook, that someone she knew had admitted killing the two girls. The reason she was speaking to them now was to "ascertain whether or not the individual that I know, who happens to be my lover, did in fact do this. He said he did". She indicated that the man she was referring to was apt to fantasise, and his claims of murder may be just that. However, she explained, if the police could confirm details, corroborate what he claimed he did, and give any possible witness details that would verify her lover's guilt, then she would give his name immediately. It was evident from what she told detectives that this was indeed someone with knowledge, perhaps first-hand, of the crimes. The excuse she used to retain identity of the man, that he may be fantasising and taking credit for a crime he didn't commit, didn't make sense. 'Claudia' told detectives that she found female clothing, saturated in blood, stashed in her lover's car, and she had washed them clean. The informant also admitted to hosing out blood from the vehicle. She confirmed locations of the bullet wounds in the girls, details which hadn't been made public and were known only to the police and the killer. The only hints she let slip which could help identify the ostensible killer was his name: 'John', and his approximate age: 'early forties'. She also told them he drove a Plymouth. The call was unintentionally terminated by the operator.

The conversation was recorded and labelled as either the killer or someone who knows the killer. Oddly, the transcript made from the tape was actually *longer* than the recording, indicating editing of the tape by the police. The reason for this discrepancy, they explained, was that the call was only recorded some time after it had commenced. The unrecorded dialogue was written from memory later. This explanation doesn't resolve how the transcriber remembered each "eh", "hmm", or "uh" uttered during the opening of the conversation [*see Appendix 2 for full transcript of call*].

On Monday, June 16, a woman named Laurie Brigges received a phone call at her husband's removals company. The caller claimed to be an LAPD detective. He spoke of the Chandler/Marano murders indicating that a business card with the company telephone number and Henry Brigges' name had been found on the bodies. He asked if Henry had blond hair, indicating they were looking for a blond-haired man. When the police were contacted they confirmed the call was a hoax. Henry admitted to picking up the two girls on June 10th and exchanging contact numbers with Chandler. Laurie Brigges told detectives that the call had come in around noon and the man had called himself "Detective H-something", but she couldn't recall his name fully. Henry Brigges was not a suspect.

This same week the police had amassed a series of vital clues from their investigations into the Sunset murders. They had the tape recording of a female caller whom they knew was either involved or at the very least knew the killer. They were aware that the call had been made on a pay phone in the Van Nuys area, thus denoting she probably lived in Van Nuys. Chandler had been killed with a .25 Raven automatic, and Marano had been shot with, if not the same gun, one of a comparable calibre. The police now had a list of recent buyers of that particular weapon. There were about 30 names on the list, one of which was a woman who lived in Van Nuys: Carol Bundy. The record indicated she had bought two Ravens on Friday, May 16th, 1980, just four weeks before the double murder occurred. It also contained her name, address, age, physical description and car registration data amongst other personal details. A simple phone-call to Bundy would have given the police a voice sample to compare to the Betsy/Claudia informant. The police however, where looking for a male Caucasian, mid-twenties to mid-thirties as proposed by FBI profiling techniques, and ergo Carol Bundy was not investigated.

Sunday, 23rd June. 19-year-old Mindy Cohen received a telephone call from a man claiming to be an LAPD detective. Like the call to Laurie Brigges, he talked about the murders of Chandler and Marano. Cohen knew the girls, although she was unaware they were dead. After the call, which she was worried about, she phoned her boyfriend Mark Gottesman, a lawyer living in Beverly Hills who subsequently called the police. When Cohen told police of the call, like Brigges she couldn't remember the name the supposed detective gave but she knew it had two syllables. It was suspected that the killer was making the calls.

Using the superficial information obtained from the vague memories of Brigges and Cohen as to the bogus detective's name – beginning with 'H' and containing two syllables – the caller was possibly using 'Detective Heinlein', the recipient of the June 14th call from 'Claudia', as an alias. Although the transcript doesn't indicate that Heinlein gave his name to the informant, it must be remembered that the beginning of the transcript has been 'written from memory'. It is therefore plausible that 'Claudia' had told her lover 'John' a Detective Heinlein was working on the case. 'John' had then dialled numbers found on the bodies of the two girls and used that detective's name.

Monday, 24th June, 3.05 AM. A police officer discovered the fully-clothed body of a girl lying in the gutter of a Burbank street. She was sprawled in a manner that suggested she had been thrown from, or hit by, a moving vehicle and her face was considerably bloody. However, closer examination revealed the presence of a small-calibre bullet hole in her left temple. The victim was later identified as Karen Jones, a prostitute last seen on Sunset Boulevard seeking tricks only hours before her murder.

That same morning, some miles away in Studio City, an even more grisly find was made. At 9.30 AM, Donald Clark pulled into the parking lot of the Sizzler restaurant which he managed. Behind a waste-skip to the rear of the premises he discovered the remains of a young woman. She was naked, lying in a vast pool of congealed blood. The excessive haemorrhaging was the result of her decapitation. A search of the waste-skip and surrounding area failed to trace the head. The killer had apparently taken it away to retain as a grisly memento of the crime. Later, detectives would remain speechless when told of the use the severed head was put to.

Fingerprint tests showed the decap victim to be another frequently arrested prostitute. Her name was Exxie Wilson and post-mortem examination confirmed the alarming fact that she had been decapitated while still alive. The frayed appearance of the neck stump, cut close to the shoulders, suggested a fairly short knife, used in a rough sawing manner. Wilson, like Jones, had been working the Sunset Strip the night she died.

The remains of Karen Jones and Exxie Wilson, both found close to Carol's Burbank apartment.

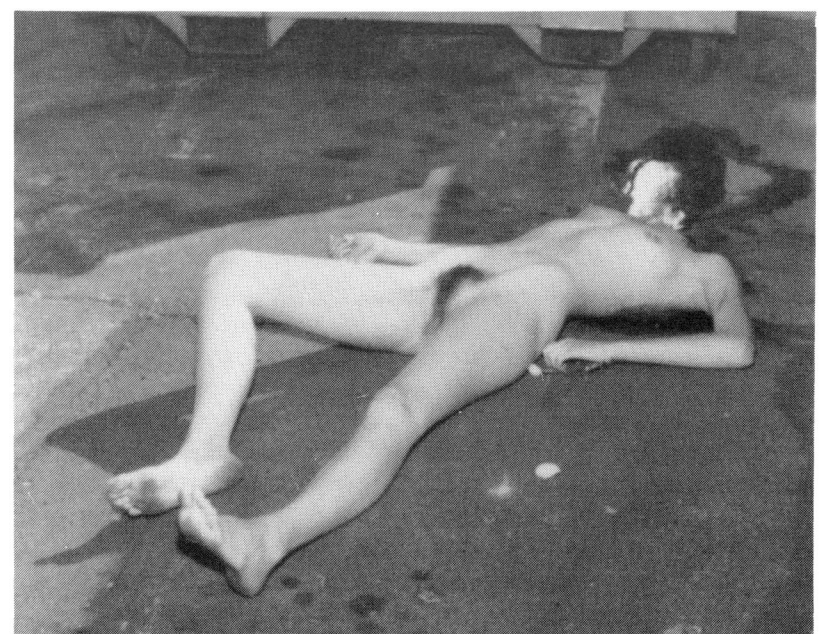

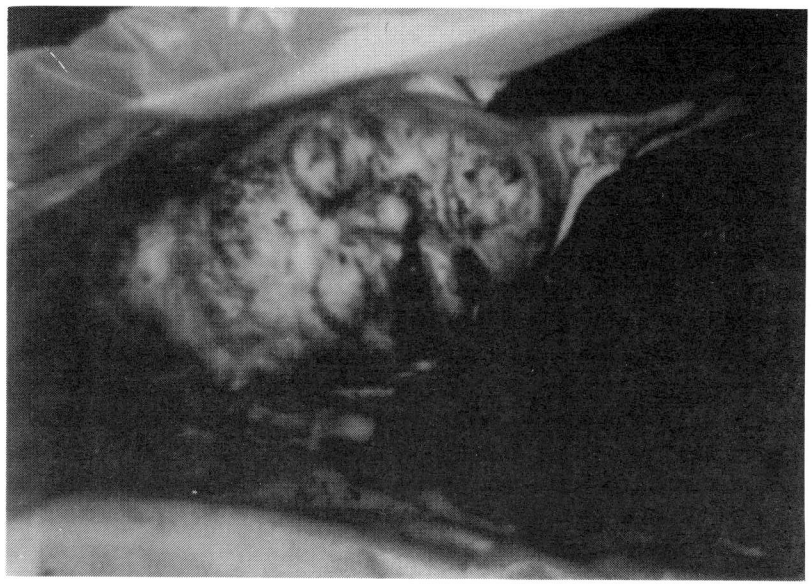

On Thursday that same week, at around 1.00 AM, motorist Jonathan Caravello found a wooden chest obstructing access to his driveway. He left his car to move the box which appeared slightly damaged on the upper corner. Lifting the object, its weight suggested it contained something. He opened the hinged lid to reveal bundled T-shirt and jeans. Shifting the clothing exposed a severed female head. Its wax-like face appeared asleep, the lips slightly parted offering a glint of upper teeth.

Pathologists confirmed the head was that of Exxie Wilson. The face, for some purpose, had been scrubbed and cleaned with a detergent. Furthermore, it was

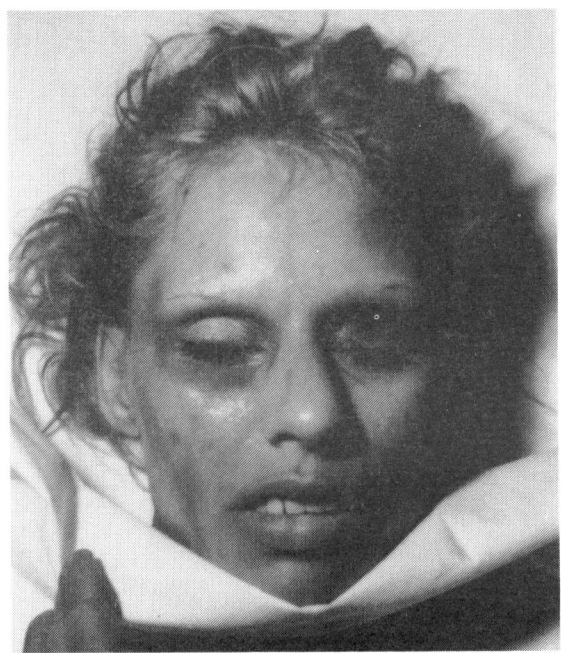

The ornate wooden box and it's shocking contents. The box was bought specifically for the disposal of the head the day before it was left in the road.

unusually cold and when the cranium was opened the brain was found to be icy. Exxie's head, it seemed, had been refrigerated.

A single gunshot wound was observed at the back of the head with no exit damage. The slug removed from within the skull matched identically those taken from the previous victims. Semen traces were found in the throat. The sample was analysed yielding a possible blood-type of the killer. It proved to belong to blood-group A, like the discharge found around Chandler's vagina. The T-shirt that had been wrapped around the head was quite distinct. It was pink in colour and had the logo 'Daddy's Girl' emblazoned across the chest. Holes in the material appeared to be knife-inflicted, although the body of Wilson had no such wounds. The jeans, too, were of a size that didn't match Wilson's dimensions.

The box that had contained the severed head was a vital clue and a search was made for stores that stocked similar chests. Such was its distinct design that tracing its origins was relatively easy, it had been bought in a Newberry's store in the Reseda district. The shop manager recalled the sale and gave a description of the buyer: a short, fat lady with very thick glasses and black gloves. It was the fact that she wore gloves on such a hot day that had drawn her attention. Even though the description matched that of the female on the gun purchase record, detectives still declined to pursue further.

The following Sunday, June 29th, walkers reported finding a body in the hills surrounding Foothill Boulevard. An attempt had been made to hide the corpse beneath scrub. It had lain there for some time and the summer heat had rendered it dehydrated and mummified, although it was still identifiable as a young female.

Death was a result of three gunshots to the chest. One bullet was found inside the body-cavity, wedged in the spine, the other two had passed clean through. The stomach wall had been sliced open and some internal organs were missing. The slug

The mummified remains of Marnette Comer who disappeared on June 1. Her body lay in the hills for almost a month before discovery. She is believed to be the first victim of the Sunset Slayer.

removed from the spine was linked to the .25 Raven used in the other Sunset murders.

The girl was identified as Marnette Comer. The duration of time since her murder suggested that Comer was likely the Sunset Slayer's first victim. The death toll of related homicides was now five. Police, still ignoring all the evidence that pointed towards a female participant, pursued the notion that the killer or killers may be rogue pimps, particularly as Comer's hustler had gone underground and Exxie Wilson's pimp had once served time for second-degree murder.

On Sunday, August 3rd, Carol Bundy, a 35-year-old nurse, arranged to meet her lover in the parking-lot of the Little Nashville Club in north Hollywood. John Murray, who was 45 years old and trapped in a marriage of convenience with two children, was waiting for her in his Chevrolet van.

The unlikely pair had met the previous year at Valerio Gardens, a near-slum apartment complex managed by Murray in Van Nuys. Murray, who was born in Scotland, came from Australia and resided in the US as a green-card alien. He liked to call himself the "Australian Tom Jones", and would frequently sing at the Little Nashville. His good looks, good voice, and ability to verbally seduce any bimbo that strutted into the Nashville led him to fucking around five different girls each week, excluding his wife. Despite his high sex-drive and urgent need for submissive women, Murray was a cruel misogynist. Sex, pain and humiliation were regular constituents of his brief relationships and one-night stands. He would smooth-talk a woman into the back of his Chevy then push her as close to rape as he thought she would allow without actual rape charges being brought later. This pseudo-rape often took the form of violent anal sex and culminated in the humiliation of his partner by forcing her to orally clean his penis after the event.

On several occasions John beat his wife, one time breaking her arm, other times just leaving her sporting embarrassing bruises or black eyes. On another occasion he assaulted a girl with a coke bottle, driving it repeatedly into her rectum. But his hard-man attitude balked at any male to male confrontation, despite his recurrent tall-tales and fantasies about Vietnam heroics and being a hired killer.[4] He was better known to wait outside the club until an adversary within had left, then swagger in insisting "he better not let *me* catch him in here!" Basically, John Murray was a crooked, violent, chicken-shit coward who cheated just about everyone he knew, even stealing cash from a charity collection he helped organise.

Green-card status made it illegal to purchase or possess a firearm, but Murray openly flouted this rule by owning several pistols. Van Nuys was in such a state of deterioration that it was as much a matter of personal safety as intent to commit crime to carry a weapon. Murray was often seen with a gun tucked in his belt or down his cowboy boot. He also carried a false police badge: feigning official authority just another of his devious abilities.

He became acquainted with Carol Bundy as she sought a new place of residence and drifted into Valerio Gardens in January, 1979. She arrived with her two sons in tow. The boys were probably the product of Bundy's failed marriage to, as she described her spouse, "a screaming faggot", however, their paternity is by no means certain.

Bundy, who was an overweight, legally-blind, bisexual diabetic, was temporarily financially secure due to the settlement she received following her marital break-up. Murray's fingers itched as much as his dick when he became aware of Carol's money, and a relationship soon developed. Bundy found sexual gratification with Murray. She liked to be dominated by men, and this sycophantic masochism coupled with Murray's testosterone-permeated sadistic cravings made the two ideally compatible. However, if Carol was having sex with a female partner, then she preferred to adopt the aggressive, domineering role.

Murray, as well as deriving satisfaction from the kinky sex offered by the portly woman, exploited the added attraction of her healthy bank account. It wasn't long before he had lightened it by $18,000, half of which was used to pay off the loan on the Chevrolet, more accurately described as his mobile sex-den.

Carol Mary Bundy, "It's fun to kill people!"

Bundy didn't mind Murray's use of her finances, she had developed a serious, if confused, love for the man, despite him on one occasion levelling his gun at her son's head and threatening to shoot him. Around Christmas of 79 she approached his wife and offered her $1500 if she would leave her husband. Furious, she insisted Carol vacate the complex and Murray agreed that she go.

Bundy moved to Lemona Avenue, approximately three miles from Valerio Gardens. Murray helped her transport her belongings and vowed to keep in touch, the money and dirty sex too alluring to abandon. Their relationship continued, but in a more discreet manner. In a letter dated January 26th, 1980, Carol wrote:

John Robert Murray, a violent erotomaniac.

I know who my master is, and I'll follow your lead. Why I want you to control me, I don't know. But it feels good when you take command... I don't know if it's just a game, but it is a good feeling... Will you give me a pet name?

Adapting to her new surroundings, Carol became acquainted with her neighbour's daughter, 11-year-old Shannon. She was a well-developed child, both physically and mentally, and the two established communication by trading adult jokes. As trust ripened, Carol invited Shannon into her apartment regularly, and soon their rude talk and touchy gestures developed into full sexual contact. Shannon, it seemed, was eager to learn and ready to please and pose for Carol's often-used Polaroid camera. On one occasion, Carol bought the child a black suspender-belt, stockings and lurid panties, and often tarted her up with make-up giving her the appearance of an infantile whore.

The carnal activities performed between John and Carol continued despite their apparent separation. Murray, by now, had his eye on Shannon, paedophilia being just another avenue to explore and assuage his jaded sex-drive. An attempt was made to deflower her on one occasion as the three of them cruised around in the Chevrolet. Carol prevented the act for fear of discovery by Shannon's parents. Carol also wanted to photograph John and Shannon together but he had no intention of allowing that.

On June 22nd, Carol moved again. This time renting an apartment on Verdugo Avenue in Burbank. However, Bundy remained unhappy in general and on July 29th she attempted suicide. Sitting in her Datsun she injected herself with insulin and Librium, and swallowed a handful of pills. The endeavour failed, despite her medical knowledge, indicating it to be an attention-seeking stunt rather than a serious attempt on her life and she fully recovered following a day in hospital. From her sick-bed, she telephoned John who drove to the hospital to take her home. On arrival, Bundy saw that Murray had brought along Nancy Smith, a dancer from the Little Nashville. He was also carrying his gun. Suspicious, Bundy declined the ride and walked home.

On Saturday, August 2nd, Carol took Shannon to a child psychologist and explained the sex situation. The doctor asked Shannon whether she was concerned about what was going on and she admitted the situation didn't bother her. The psychologist, indicating his unwillingness to moralise, sent them both away. Following the meeting, Murray, Bundy and Shannon indulged in mutual oral sex in the back of the Chevrolet.

In the late hours of Sunday, August 3rd, it was only Carol and John who sat in the back of the Chevy. They had driven several blocks from the Little Nashville to Barbara Anne Street. Murray placed a false disabled-driver card in the window to evade parking regulations, and climbed into the back of the van, eager to get down to some kinky sex.

He lay belly-down on the plush red bench-seat and Carol tugged down his trousers and pink, turquoise trimmed panties. She crouched behind him, sucked on his protruding balls then parted his buttocks and licked at his anus. As he moaned with pleasure, pushing his rear into her face, Carol reached into the waistband of her trousers and retrieved her Raven automatic. She touched the muzzle to the back of his head, inserted her tongue in his anus, felt the muscle clench, and fired a single bullet into his brain. Murray gasped and jerked and shivered. Carol moved back and watched his saliva-sheened arsehole twitch and spasm. He looked stupid now with his big white butt sticking in the air, blood and cerebral fluid mixing in his hair. She checked his pulse. Tell-tale life-signs prompted a second bullet into the head. Despite massive trauma to the brain, Murray still refused to die and gargled and snotted into the cushion under his face. His hard cock, never to enter another orifice, gradually softened as his blood pressure vented through the holes in his head. Bundy reached for the bag and took out a large boning knife which she drove into her lover's back repeatedly. Murray succumbed to the brutal stabbing assault and finally expired.[5] Nevertheless, Carol wasn't satisfied. "It's fun to kill people," she would later confess to detectives. But fun could also be had with the dead. She gleefully continued to drive the blade into his body, then sliced open his buttocks, cutting off a portion in the process, and slid the blade into the anus mutilating the sphincter. She checked the pulse again, made certain the heart had ceased beating, then pushed the blade into Murray's neck close to the shoulders and prised apart the spinal vertebrae. With both hands she sawed and cut until his head was completely detached.

Carol cleaned herself up with the home-like facilities the van provided, collected her weapons, and placed Murray's head in the bag: an article she liked to call her "kill-bag". Before leaving the van she took Murray's gun and keys. She walked back to the Little Nashville where her Datsun had been left, and put the weapons and her lover's head into the car. Before driving home she telephoned her tenant and one-time sex-partner Douglas Clark.

Douglas Clark had met Carol at the Little Nashville sometime around mid to late January, 1980. Neither can agree on an exact date, and Bundy claims most recently that they met on December 28th, 1979.

Says Clark, "Carol admits we met and moved in instantly, but into the Lemona apartment. She and everyone else agrees I never set foot in Valerio. She moved into Lemona early January. I met her, fucked her, moved in all in one day. She went to great lengths to pretend she met me a week or two before I laid her and moved in... that is crap. I met Carol, laid her, she agreed to let me 'crash' there as a renter."

Clark was 31 years old and worked as a plant engineer at the Jergens soap factory in Burbank. He was a sexual hedonist and appreciated nothing more than a varied choice of eager girlfriends: those who liked to fuck and those who offered accommodation. He talks freely of his sexual encounters and was known amongst his associates and friends as 'King of the One-Night Stands'. Clark's lifestyle was sleazy to say the least. He bought and sold Super-8 pornography, spent a good percentage of his income on whores and go-go dancers, and following his association with Bundy, sexually molested a minor.

After moving into the Lemona Avenue apartment, an oblique friction developed between Clark and Murray. Although they rarely met, only occasionally bumping into each other at the Nashville, John was obviously anxious that he may lose his sex partner and personal financier to this other man. It was also apparent that they both shared virtually all the same women. Clark says, "I was not the least bit nervous about Murray, knew he was a punk, and often told his buddies I'd kick his ass if he ever fucked with my car or bike – he liked to cut tyres and sneak away." When Clark's Pacer was discovered a burned-out wreck at the plant in February he reasoned the arsonist was Murray. It is likely that Bundy kept this antagonism on the back burner. It gave her a feeling of importance, two men squabbling over her.

Like Murray, Clark had been drawn into involvement with the underage Shannon and Carol had photographed him in compromising positions with the girl. Unlike Murray, however, Clark wasn't interested in full sex with the girl and all the photographs depicted simulated sex poses. Molestation of the young girl occurred on and off over the period of time Clark knew Bundy.

"Carol knew with me and Shannon she had to coax, go slow, step by step. From hair-brushing her on my lap, to back-rubs, to petting through clothes over a period of four months or so to get to sexual activity. Carol knew I was really negative, but when I gave in it was on the wrong theory that Shannon was aware of what she wanted. Why not play? But not intercourse of any kind. Even on August 2, at night,

Douglas Daniel Clark, unrepentant hedonist.

after they were with Murray (though I didn't know it) Carol pushed hard for me to have intercourse with Shannon and she had coached her to demand it. I realised Shannon was not aware of the consequences, so I gave in partly, nudged her hymen and said, See, you don't want this yet... wait a few years. Carol then pushed Shannon's face into her grotesque vulva and forced her to perform oral sex against her will." But before this phase had developed Clark had moved out of Carol's Lemona Avenue apartment "to get away from temptation" around the first week of May after finding another willing partner and landlady.

"I moved in with Linda Hendricks after I left Carol. Linda said I lived with her three weeks to a month. I met her at Playtime or Nashville, took her to her house, fucked her and rented a spare room." Hendricks was a single mother living with her twin 13-year-old daughters and later Clark discovered she was one of Murray's ex-lovers.

Alleges Clark, "She'd get drunk, fuck anyone around, then sober up and be mad that she was out of control. She used to rub herself almost to orgasm on her brothers' legs in the Nashville when she got bombed. Her twins never got touched by me but they slept with their mother in a small bed while an empty room was furnished with a double bed, and they nursed milk from her, she admitted. She also admitted to incest with her own brothers, but had made a threat on one of her brother's lives for messing with one of her girls. Her older daughter was moved out and living with a black lesbian.

"While I was there I left to take a girlfriend to my parents' home over the Memorial holiday towards the end of May. When I got back she was ticked off. Sex became a problem and I was told she was not there for that. I agreed, Hey, my door is open, come in if you want it, if not, no big deal. She said no, her mother was coming to live in my room so I had to leave." It transpired that Carol Bundy had informed Murray of Clark's relationship with Hendricks, and they both challenged her as to why she allowed Clark to live with her. The tale of her mother moving in was a ruse. Clark believes she wanted him out so Murray would cool off, which indicates Hendricks saw Murray as a potential threat to herself.

"Around May 29/30 she tells me I have to leave, so I go to the nearest country bar, The Viking, that weekend. I score and bed a broad, if you will, by laying Cissy Buster that Saturday.

"The band had just started and I met Cissy and Carol La Doux. I was going to try out Carol but Cissy was so fat, with a huge set of thighs, I just had to see what a 350-pound pig like her would be like in bed. It was a mistake. I nearly expired under her in a '69'. When she came, I came, and then I tried to get her off but could not get her attention. Her double bed was a huge valley in the centre. I had bravely coaxed this enormous hog up on top and got her going. Well, as we both came I could not inflate my lungs. I was trapped in that huge valley in her broken-down bed and could not budge her fat body off of me. I wish I had gone with her friend who was equally ready to get laid and made it clear she thought I was nuts to pick Cissy over her. The next day Cissy told Carol La Doux I was moving in and the sex was great."

Clark stayed with Cissy until Sunday, June 22 when an argument terminated their relationship.

"She said, Leave if you don't wanna live with me, meaning, Your cock is mine, as if I had something going on with Carol or any other person. I finally said, Fuck it, and lugged my stuff down to the Buick. I forgot my suit, cowboy boots and a few shirts. Came back for them later. I put the stuff in my garage which I used like a big junk-bin and closet."

Clark had earlier made arrangements to move back in with Carol, strictly as a tenant, once she moved into a bigger apartment. She had found a new place in Burbank and asked Clark if he would help with the move. After leaving Cissy, he drove the Buick back to the Lemona Avenue apartment and waited with Carol for the removal men.

"The movers came about 3.00/4.00pm and moved her into Burbank in two trailer and pick-up truck loads. I rode with them, she had a slew of kids help her put kitchen shit into the Buick. At the other end we moved it all up, and after one effort to help I strained an old back injury and left early. They finished alone without me and I rode the bike back to Van Nuys." As a week's rent was still paid on the Lemona Avenue apartment, Clark stayed there until Friday 27th when he finally moved in with Carol with certain concessions. "I made Carol agree to terms on the new place – no Shannon, no sex, no nothing. And I can move a girlfriend in if I wish. Separate baths, kitchens, bedrooms, bills and no fucking with my friends."

It was the early hours of Monday, 4th August, when the phone roused Clark from his sleep. Nancy Smith, the dancer from the Nashville was staying in the apartment. The ringing woke her too. Clark, barely half awake, answered the phone and listened to Carol muttering through the receiver.

"I tried to wake up and figure what the fuck she was whispering and giggling about. I saw Nancy drooling blood and moaning as she stood shaking, leaning on the wall of my room." Smith, an epileptic, was having a seizure, probably brought on by the trauma of the abortion she'd had that day, and Clark needed to phone for an ambulance.

"I told Carol, 'Will you just shut up and get home,' and hung up on her." Clark then phoned the hospital. A team of paramedics arrived and while they were still in the apartment treating Nancy, Carol came home. Being a qualified nurse Carol offered her assistance, but the medics declined, not noticing the crescents of blood behind her fingernails and crimson flecks on her glasses. When the medical crew had left with Nancy, Carol led Clark outside to the Datsun. Lying in the well in front of the passenger seat was the head of John Murray, its ragged neck-stump poking from the plastic bag. Clark was stunned and he turned and vomited on the grass verge. Carol insisted he help her dispose of the head. She wanted to skewer it on a fence post but finally decided against such a public display and, as Clark drove the car, she tossed it from the window into a rubbish pile awaiting collection. The head was never seen again. Clark drove to the Jergens factory to start his early shift and Carol took the Datsun back home.

Clark was confused, worried. He considered calling the cops but knew his messing around with Shannon was a criminal offence. Not only that, but he had now helped dispose of Murray's head, an act which could be considered accessory to murder. "I went to work to get away from her because I needed time to think about going to the police. But I couldn't bring myself to commit legal suicide over the Shannon pictures, and feared I would get framed over Murray's death as Carol promised. I asked Al Joines to come in early and cover my shift so I could skip work the next day, Tuesday, and he said he would."

On Tuesday he phoned in work feigning sickness. He needed time to sort himself out, to get his thoughts in order. "I was too freaked out to think and to this day I have no idea what I did all Tuesday. Joey [Lamphier: Clark's one-time girlfriend] reported to police that I called her, drunk and depressed, said I was in a lot of trouble and was probably going to jail for Carol killing her boyfriend." But if Clark thought he had problems at this moment in time, by Thursday night he would be up Shit Creek without · a boat, much less a paddle.

On Thursday 7th August, Clark recounts, "Carol was pestering Tammy Spangler, one of Murray's prior lovers he treated rough, to come out and meet us for dinner, her treat. And, it is hinted, for three-way sex. Tammy comes over, not at all interested in

The Datsun outside the Burbank apartment.

Carol... Tammy and I hit it off. I want her away from Carol the minute I discover she is related to Murray. Eventually Tammy leaves for the graveyard shift at work. Carol insists we go to Hollywood." Although Clark was reluctant to go, he felt in no position to argue considering what she had done to Murray. Not only that, Bundy frequently threatened him with the photographs she claimed to have hidden of himself and Shannon.

They took Carol's Datsun, Doug driving, Carol seated in the front passenger seat. She wanted a hooker to replace Tammy Spangler and she would foot the bill. Clark was nervous, unsure of Bundy's odd behaviour and dubious of her intentions. The last man she'd had sex with was rotting headless in his Chevrolet. He attempted to bluff his way out saying it would cost $500 to get a whore to do a three-way. Bundy countered with the suggestion that she would buy him a blow-job as a late birthday present.

They drove to Highland Avenue, saw an available hooker and pulled into a parking lot. Doug parked the Datsun with the passenger door by an empty vehicle, got out and called the girl over. A deal was agreed and the girl climbed into the cramped rear of the car. Carol paid the girl, who called herself Cathy, and the whore made it clear that she didn't do three-ways, "I don't do nothing with no women." Doug squeezed in the back, leaving the driver's seat up against the steering wheel. Carol watched from the front through her thick spectacles.

Explains Clark, "We were in the back, me on the left, her on the right leaning over me and twisted around with only her left buttock on the edge of the seat." Cathy began working on her client's penis as best she could considering the cramped area. As her head bobbed up and down Clark noticed Bundy fidgeting in her seat. "Carol had begun heaving herself up and down and craning her neck to view the area around the car." When he saw her hand reach around the seat he thought she was about to grope Cathy. But then he saw the gun. For an instant Clark thought he was the target, about to be executed like Murray had. Instead, Carol placed the pistol to the back of the prostitute's head and pulled the trigger. The bullet went clean through the girl's head and struck Clark in the lower-left side of his stomach leaving a bruise. Blood flooded over his shirt and soaked through to his T-shirt beneath. Doug, stunned and freaking out, climbed over the body and out of the car and Carol moved into the back with the dead girl. She remained calm and cool and instructed Clark to drive as she began removing the girl's clothing. As Clark drove in search of a drop-point he heard Carol muttering and giggling in the back. Glancing over his shoulder he saw the cute girl's face, the mouth and chin dark with blood that frothed from her nose, and observed Carol's activity as she roughly inserted her hand and wrist deep into the whore's lifeless vagina, "all the while ranting she was sure the girl liked it."

On Saturday, 9th August, the Van Nuys Police Department received a call complaining about an unattended Chevrolet van that had been parked on Barbara Ann Street for several days. The caller also reported a foul smell that hung around the vehicle. A squad car was directed to investigate and the officer was able to distinguish a prone body in the back of the van. It looked like a possible suicide but a call was put out to the homicide division anyway.

Detective Pida was the one who had the task of entering the vehicle. As he opened the rear doors the stench was overwhelming. A semi-naked man was lying belly-down, wedged between the bench seats. He wore cowboy boots and a shirt rucked up under his armpits. Around his ankles were his trousers and a pair of pink and turquoise panties. It quite evidently wasn't a suicide for the dead man had no head and his back was perforated with several knife wounds. The sealed confines of the vehicle and high temperatures had promoted the beginnings of decomposition. The body was swollen and dappled with vast, blood-filled blisters. Unfortunately for those who had to prise the corpse from between the seats, it was also infested with maggots. The mutilation of the buttocks and anus and the feminine underwear indicated a possible homosexual crime of passion. Documents found in the victim's wallet identified the man as John Murray. He had been reported missing by his wife three days earlier. When the body was cleared from the vehicle a thorough search commenced of the interior. Pornographic Polaroids and sex toys were found scattered on the floor. Caught in the overhead vent hatch was a sliver of human scalp. It was about two-inches long and covered in long blonde hair. It seemed that Murray wasn't the only person to have died in the Chevy.

Word hit the Nashville that Murray had been found murdered in his van just around the corner. Doug Clark was there with Tammy Spangler. Doug already knew he was dead, Tammy didn't. Carol Bundy was on the dancefloor and feigned disbelief and shock when she heard the news. She asked Clark to take her home. Outside, on the parking lot, Bundy took a bunch of keys from her handbag and handed them to Clark. He looked at them, puzzled, and she told him they were Murray's. Struck with paranoia, particularly with the police activity in the vicinity, Clark hurled them onto the roof of an adjacent building. Doug and Tammy drove Carol back to Verdugo Avenue. There, when Tammy was out of the room getting ready to leave with Doug, Carol thrust a make-up bag into his hands. "Right fucking *now*, go ditch these where they will never be found," she insisted. The bag contained the pair of Ravens she had purchased back in May.

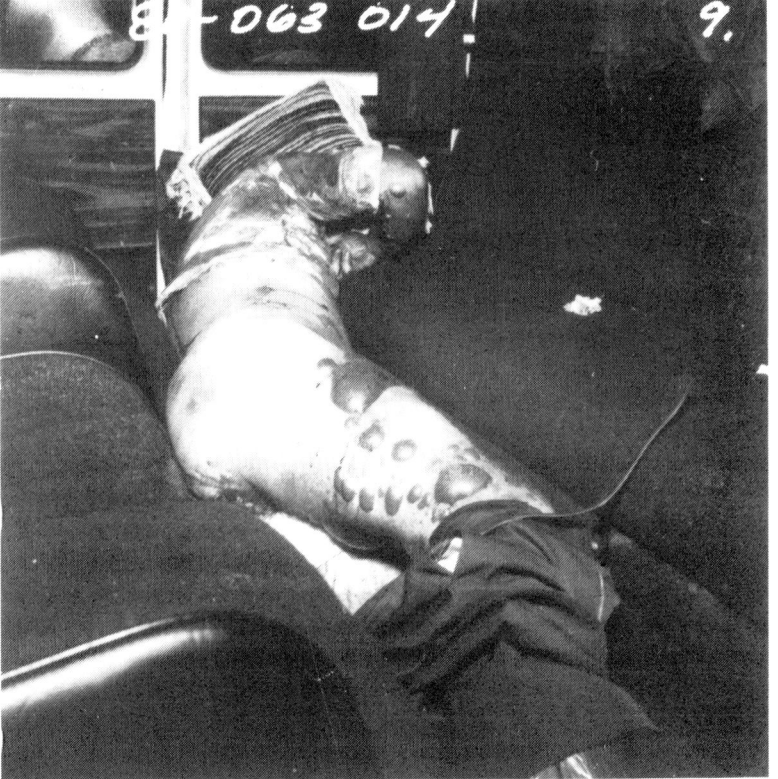

Above. John Murray's Chevrolet van as foun Barbara Ann Street a blocks from the Little Nashville Country Clu

Left. Murray's mutilate remains first thought be a possible suicide, then a homosexual cr of passion.

John Murray's body still wearing pink feminine panties, similar to those taken from the victims of the Sunset Slayer.

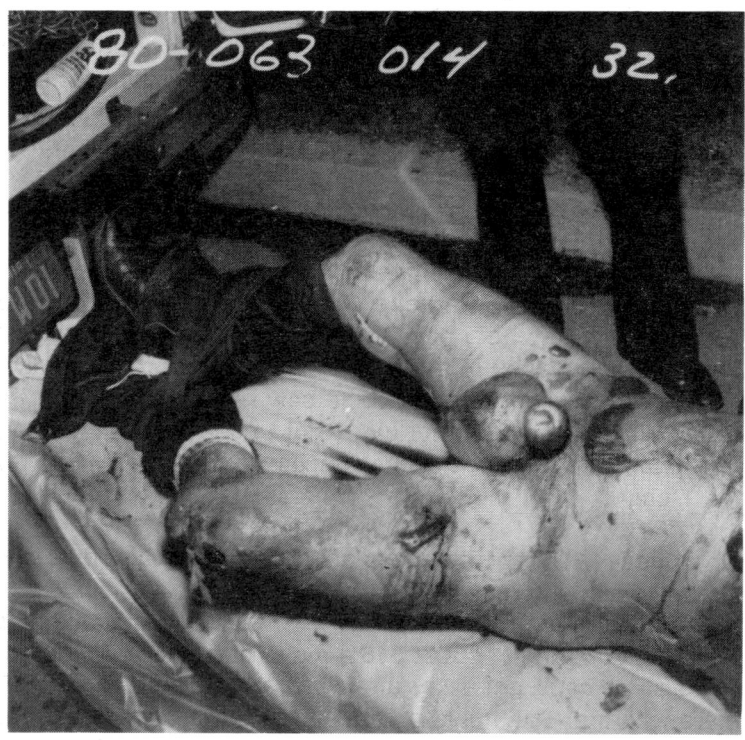

Recalls Clark, "Here they are, in my hands, *the guns*, one of which I *know* killed Cathy, one, maybe the same, maybe not, killed Murray. I'd been scared she was going to use the guns on me and was possibly toying with Tammy as a Cathy-style killing. So, hell, I was stunned to finally have them both securely in my grasp. But, I was so freaked out at this turn of events – having wondered where they were, not daring to act too nosey into this crazy cunt's murderous events – I left, walked, tried to think, but could not figure what to do and could not commit myself to do anything *permanent*. I decided to keep the guns, just until I could think what was best. I ran to the plant a block away and tucked them behind the typewriter in my desk. Carol had calmly told Tammy she sent me to get her some marijuana, which I never knew she smoked and knew no one to get any from if she *had* sent me for it." When Clark returned to the apartment he left with Tammy and they spent the night in a motel.

Detective Mike Stallcup, who was working on the Marnette Comer homicide, interviewed Marnette's sister Sabra on August 9. At this time homicidal pimps were still suspected as the most likely perpetrators of the killings. When Exxie Wilson's head was found by police, efforts were made to identify the jeans and the pink 'Daddy's Girl' T-shirt wrapped around it. The garments were not a suitable size for Wilson. Attempts were made to match the holes in the shirt with wounds on Comer's torso. When a photograph of the T-shirt was shown to Sabra Comer she recognised it as that worn by a hooker named Toni Wilson who worked for a pimp known as 'T'. Sabra identified Wilson from a mug-book. Stallcup wrote her comments on the interview report sheet. Such information could be used to back up the killer pimps theory. Conjecture suggested the possibility that Marnette had left one pimp (Benton) without his consent and she was subsequently murdered; clothing identified as worn by another hooker (Toni Wilson) controlled by another pimp ('T'), was discovered with the remains of a third prostitute (Exxie Wilson) whose pimp was a convicted killer. With such information a tenuous link with insubstantial motives is established between two victims and three pimps. But of course, with the arrest of Clark and Bundy two days later, and the pimp conspiracy theory thus becoming redundant, none of this was necessary. Any mention of Toni Wilson now would simply complicate matters.

When the Stallcup report was later typed up, the name Toni Wilson was erased and substituted with Marnette Comer. The hand-written report was surreptitiously disposed of. However, prior to its disposal, the report had been found by a clerk, Xeroxed, and placed in a file of a similar but unrelated case. Later, in court, Sabra Comer swore under oath that she saw her sister wearing the T-shirt she originally stated was worn by another girl. Prior to her court appearance she must have been instructed that it was no longer necessary to identify Toni Wilson as the wearer of the T-shirt.

On Sunday, August 10th, Clark and Spangler returned to Verdugo Avenue for clean clothes and a shower.

"We showered there in my room," recalls Clark, "because the motel bathroom was a mildew jungle, but at $16 a night, no wonder. I mean, we were both broke and it was all we could get. I was afraid of Carol, so I did not want Tammy to stay overnight there with me. She may have been her target on August 7th. I needed to see what she was up to because I dreaded what she may do next." While they showered together two detectives arrived and Bundy was asked to return to the station with them for questioning about John Murray. Clark and Spangler offered to accompany them in order to give any assistance and to bring Carol back home as the policemen insisted she rode with them.

At the station Clark told police that Bundy had been with him constantly on the night that Murray had died. This was what she had told him to say in the event of any interrogation by detectives. Bundy, however, admitted to being with Murray for a short time on the night in question. She also told them she had owned two Raven automatics but had sold them to a man named Mike Hammer, late in May. Tammy Spangler, meanwhile, spoke of a girl named Avril who was also seen with John Murray at the Nashville on the night of his murder.

Police released Bundy then sought and questioned Avril Roy-Smith that same day. Roy-Smith gave a verifiable alibi, but she said had been with Murray that night and he'd been carrying a gun. While they were in his van he had been trying to raise someone on his CB radio. She also added that the last time she had seen Murray he was returning to the van with Carol Bundy.

On Monday 11 August, detectives, suspicious of Bundy's story, were preparing an arrest warrant. At the same time Bundy walked off her job at the hospital after confessing to colleagues that she had murdered and decapitated her lover. She told them that she was going to "clean out evidence before Doug gets home". Instead of going directly to the apartment, she stopped off at the Jergens factory and asked the security guard for Douglas Clark.

Meanwhile, Clark already knew the game was up for Carol. His main concern was the possibility of her accusing him of murdering Murray, and maybe Cathy, even though there was no indication that the cops knew of her death. He reasoned she would keep quiet about Shannon and the photographs as Carol herself was pictured molesting the child. At work he tried to telephone Detective Pida but was unable to contact him. "I called Pida soon as I got to a phone with no Carol hanging around with an extension in her room. I called several times but he would not talk to me." Later, he was summoned to the gateshack by the guard and saw Carol was there waiting for him.

Clark says, "She said, I told them everything and they are coming to get you... you can have all my money, take your bike and just leave. I said, Get the fuck away from me, you crazy cunt. I went back in to keep calling Pida, leaving messages for him to call me. He never did, he was being real cagey and sneaky... dumb as a brick, but sneaky. I was going to tell him *everything* but Shannon." Detective Pida was already on his way over to arrest Clark.

When Bundy arrived at her apartment she phoned Detective Kilgore, offered to turn herself in, and gave detailed information on the recent Sunset Strip killings. She admitted, "the honest truth is, it's *fun* to kill people... it's kind of fun like riding a rollercoaster. Not the killing, not the action that somebody died, because we didn't kill them in a way that hurt them... " The conversation was being recorded, not by the detective, but by Bundy herself. She begged the detective not to come and arrest her at her apartment but to meet her later, after she'd had time to get the evidence together. She suggested meeting at a diner at 2pm. Kilgore agreed.

That meeting was not to take place because other detectives from another division were already on their way to arrest Carol. When they knocked on the door, Bundy, somewhat confused as to their early appearance, held a cardboard box that contained several pairs of panties, other items of clothing and a handbag. All these articles belonged to murder victims. Not those already found, but others whose skeletal remains would not be discovered for almost a year, and who would remain unidentified, tagged with the names Jane Doe 18 and Jane Doe 28. She gave police a spent bullet which she kept in an Excedrin pill box, tablets specifically for headaches. She told them the slug had gone through the head of Gina Marano. Inside her bedside cabinet detectives found several rounds of .25 ammunition and a pair of handcuffs.

As the officers continued to search the apartment, Bundy retorted, "Want to see what kind of guy Doug Clark is?" She reached for her handbag but was stopped by a wary officer concerned that it may contain a pistol. Opening the bag he retrieved a key-ring holding several keys, one of which was newly cut. This fitted a filing cabinet in the room Clark rented. Inside was a personal photo album filled with pictures of Clark and his many girlfriends, including those of Shannon in sex poses with himself and Carol. They also found a fake gun-sales receipt that Carol had written and secreted amongst Clark's tax return forms.[6] As the search of the apartment continued, Detective Pida had taken Clark in for further questioning.

Says Clark, "They took me to Van Nuys, no food, no water or toilet for 10 hours from when I got to work. They held me without reading my rights because I wanted a lawyer. They finally read me my rights after eight hours in custody and when I asked for a lawyer they said they had all gone home for the day and it would take hours to get one back. I gave permission to search the house, my bike, job, everything. I gave them my boots, saliva and blood samples, the works. They asked if I would take a lie-detector test and I eagerly agreed. They then refused to do it."

In custody, Clark was asked if he knew what he had been arrested for. He believed it was for involvement in the murder of John Murray. The police then produced the

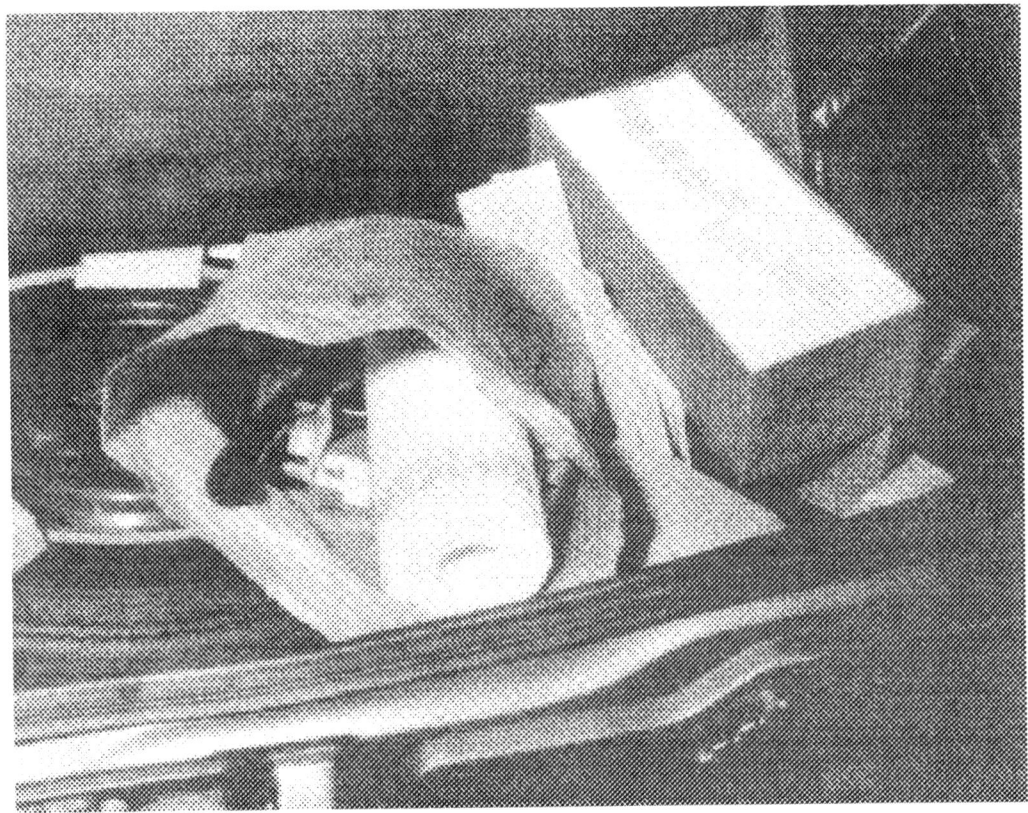
The Kill-bag in the boot of the Datsun.

photo album they had taken from his locker and confronted him with the Shannon pictures. Clark was also handed photos of Gina Marano and Cynthia Chandler, the latter whom Clark recognised as a hooker and admitted seeing on occasion. He told the cops he had once had her telephone number and had seen her last around mid-May. When the questioning switched from child abuse to murder Clark's response was to shout out, "Someone is trying to lynch my ass, and I have a hunch I know who it is." But Carol had asked the cops not to tell him she was feeding them information and she'd also wanted to know how she could benefit her own situation. In order to detain Clark he was charged with child molestation.

Someone had recognised Carol Bundy's voice and identified her as the source of the Betsy/Claudia call on June 14th. Things began to tie together, and they didn't look good for the detectives. One predominant dilemma for the police was the fact that they'd had Bundy's full details on record only a few days after the Chandler/Marano murders and hadn't investigated her. In that phone call she had told detectives her 'lover John' had committed the crimes and Carol's lover, John Murray, was now dead. The police had found the scalp in his van, and he was wearing feminine panties, like those taken from other victims and found in Bundy's hands when she was arrested. The detectives must have realised they'd had enough information to close the Sunset murder case only days after that phone call.

Bundy began to talk about the murders. Not just those killings the police were aware of, but others crimes whose victim's bodies lay hidden in the hills. Murders she *now* insisted had been committed by Douglas Clark and not John as previously claimed. She told of sex with the dead. She rattled off grisly details about shooting girls through heads, and slicing open stomachs, and playing with frozen heads.

She told detectives how Doug had murdered Marnette Comer on June 1st and dropped her body in a ravine along Foothill Boulevard. She said he had sliced open her abdomen to hasten putrefaction, to allow in "all the wiggly-squirmies".

She told of Cynthia Chandler and Gina Marano and how Doug had picked them up in her Buick on Sunset Boulevard, June 11th, and paid the blonde for a blow-job. The dark haired girl, Gina, was in the back and Clark asked her to turn away while her step-sister performed the sex act. While her head was turned, and Cynthia was bobbing in his lap, he raised his gun and shot Gina twice through the head. Quickly, he turned the gun down and shot Chandler in the head, then raised her up to fire again into her chest. He covered them with a blanket and drove to his basement garage across town. The dead girls were dragged bleeding from the car and into the lock-up where Clark had vaginal, oral and anal intercourse with both corpses. He drove back to Bundy's apartment and left a note on the kitchen table indicating he had something special for her. But when it transpired that Clark didn't have a key to get in the apartment at that time Carol changed her mind and said the note was pinned to the door. Later, he returned to the garage, put the girls back in the Buick and dumped them off Ventura Freeway. She went on to explain how she needed the Buick that night and had driven to Cissy Buster's apartment in the Datsun to get the larger car. In the back of the Buick, she claimed to have found a duffel bag filled with bloody clothes and towels which she took to the launderette and washed. The police were eager to examine the garage where the girls had been temporarily stored, but Bundy told them not to expect to find any trace evidence as herself and Doug had scrubbed the garage clean.

She told how Doug found three hookers on a street corner, June 22nd, and lured one into the Buick. It was Exxie Wilson. He drove her to a parking lot and shot her in the head as she performed oral sex. She was pulled from the car, stripped naked and decapitated. He put the head in the back of the Buick, returned to the pick-up point, and lured her co-worker into the vehicle. Karen Jones was driven around, shot in the left temple, then pushed from the car. He once more returned to the pick-up point but failed to find the third hooker. Clark took the head home and put it in the freezer. Carol claimed he phoned her at Lemona from the Burbank apartment and was on the line for several minutes but she cannot recall the conversation.

Later that week, she claimed, Clark had sex with the frozen severed head, sliding its open mouth over his penis in the shower. And Carol played around with it too, covering the face with garish make-up. Seeing the head, she claimed, was her first real evidence that murders truly were happening. On Thursday, after Carol had scrubbed it clean of make-up, they dropped the head in the alley, neatly packaged in the box she had bought the previous day. She said when she dropped it from the Buick she didn't throw it far enough and the rear tyre went over the corner of the box causing damage.

Bundy told the detectives a hooker was murdered "two weekends ago", indicating the weekend of July 28th, but insisted Doug gave her no details whatsoever of the crime and she could therefore tell them nothing about it. When the police moved on to other things, abruptly, she began to give a full description of the event and an indication where the body was dumped: by a large water tower in the hills, hence the dead girl's nickname 'Watertower'. He had, she said, placed the girl's body on the bonnet of the Datsun, squeezed the urine from her bladder, and had sex while the engine was idling, giving the body movement and the illusion of life.

'Watertower' was discovered on August 26 by a walker in Canyon Country near the San Fernando Valley. Scattered around the base of a large oil-storage tank were the girl's skeletal remains. The bones were collected together and the coroner removed a single bullet from the skull. It had been fired from the nickel-plated Raven. 'Watertower' was officially christened Jane Doe 18.

Carol even informed police of a planned attack on a fast-food restaurant which never transpired. They had, she told them, intended to storm a McDonald's, both armed with shotguns and communicating through her walkie-talkies, and massacre the customers within.

Carol's description of the killings seemed to indicate she wasn't just feeding back information that had been narrated to her, the grisly details and sound effects she imitated were more evident of first-hand experience. The Sunset murder suspects at this moment in time were Carol Bundy, John Murray and Douglas Clark.

Meanwhile, police were trying to find the murder weapons.

During the Memorial holiday weekend on May 24th, Clark had made arrangements to travel up north to visit his parents with his girlfriend Tomi. He was intending to make the trip on his motorbike but, in case Tomi was too nervous to ride, he phoned Carol to see if he could borrow the Buick should he need it. During the conversation Carol told him she had recently bought two guns and asked if he would check them over for her. He agreed to, and asked if he could borrow one. She had bought the guns on Friday, May 16, two days before Murray's birthday.

Says Clark, "I had nothing but a huge shotgun and the state's biker gangs were doing a run up the same route we were going, to Yosemite Park. I felt nervous with Tomi on the bike among hundreds of rough bikers for over 300 miles of open road." Carol, however, refused to lend him a gun but when he arrived to get the Buick to fetch Tomi from the airport, she changed her mind and gave him both pistols; a shiny, chrome-plated Raven and a dull-finished nickel-plated one. Neither gun was loaded and Doug intended to buy a box of bullets but found no time. He picked Tomi up from the airport and they spent the night in a motel.

The following morning they drove back to Carol's apartment where he'd left his bike. Before they left for Yosemite he asked Carol whether she had any ammunition for the guns and she handed him a box that was two-thirds full.

When they returned from the trip, Tomi flew back to Indiana and Doug took the guns back to Carol. He told her that the chrome-plated one jammed and caught the empties. Carol said she already knew that and he could keep it as a gift.

On June 16th, he gave the pistol to Joey Lamphier, a girlfriend who was concerned about the recent murder of a woman at the place she used to work. He told her it was liable to jam and demonstrated how to clear it should it catch the empty cartridge.

Sometime in early July at the Burbank apartment Carol demanded to know where her gun was. He told her he had lent it to a friend and she immediately assumed it was Joey.

"She started to rant and rave about giving away a gift. I offered to pay her for it, she got madder. I said, Okay, fuck you, I will give it back, I never wanted the fucking thing in the first place. I went over, got it, told Joey flat out, the person who gave it me wants it back. No problem, and I left." The pistol was promptly returned to Carol and the next time Clark saw it was when she fired it at the head of Cathy on August

Top. The nickel-plated Raven identified as being the weapon that killed most of the Sunset victims. *Below.* The chrome-plated Raven said to have been used on John Murray and Jane Doe 28.

7th. Clark saw the guns again when Bundy panicked over the discovery of Murray's body and she asked him to dispose of them.

They were eventually found at the Jergens factory by a worker, still inside Carol's flowery make-up bag. Clark said he had put the guns in his desk. "A guy stole them after my arrest, then returned them when he discovered they were the precise reason for the search coming soon." They turned up elsewhere in the factory after a court order threatened to close it down to conduct a thorough search should the weapons not surface. Ballistics confirmed that of the two, the nickel-plated Raven was the one used in the shootings of Marnette Comer, Cynthia Chandler, Exxie Wilson and Karen Jones. Bundy told police the nickel gun belonged to Clark and hers was the chrome-plated one which she used to shoot John. With Murray's head missing, and therefore no ballistic evidence, it could not be confirmed that the chrome gun had been used on him as Carol claimed. In fact there was only Bundy's word to suggest he had been shot at all. When what was believed to be Cathy's skeleton was discovered the following year, no bullet was found in the skull, which confirmed Clark's statement that the slug passed clean through her head, striking him in the stomach. Although no exit wound was detected, the bullet may have exited nasally, leaving no detectable route following disintegration of the soft tissues.

John Murray also had at least two illegally owned guns. One was a 9mm-calibre model, the other a small calibre pistol. As Murray was a suspect in the crime, police searched his house and found the guns. The smaller of the two was described in a police report as a '6-millimetre Perfecta'. Although the smaller pistol was of the same calibre used in the murders, only the 9mm gun was taken. The Perfecta promptly disappeared. The person responsible for searching Murray's house was Detective Stallcup.

Eighteen days after her arrest, on August 29, Carol was taken out for the day by detectives. They went in search of murder scenes. But that wasn't all. Says Clark, "She goes out to chat, eat lunch, go clean out her and Murray's safe deposit box, illegally, no reports, all hidden. She talked them into flashing a badge at a postal clerk and giving her my post box mail. Then they went to the apartment – cops had her sales receipt marked 'paid' showing I owned all the furniture – they let her arrange to sell it. They let her have all her lingerie (in all sizes of these girls!) and jewellery boxes filled with junk." Later Carol was caught attempting to furtively dispose of a watch from within the Correctional Institute. It was believed to belong to a victim. Clark continues, "They let her have her car back untested by us, and she destroyed the evidence. They never let murder cars go back, *never*. They let her steal $3000 out of a bank box in her and Murray's name, without even noting what else she took out of it. Smell a dirty under-the-table deal? For two years they swore this trip never occurred, until we proved it, then they claimed it was done without a single question or answer to her."

Following Carol's claim that a bloody necrophile orgy had taken place in Clark's garage, a forensics team went to investigate. Carol insisted they wouldn't find anything because she and Doug had both scrubbed it clean of any evidence. Nevertheless, aware of the difficulty in eradicating bloodstains completely, the team set to work on the garage.

In the centre of the lock-up was a dark stain measuring about two by eight feet, instantly contradicting Bundy's clean-up statement. The investigators theorised the long stain was caused by dragging the bodies across the floor. The squared-off end of the mark suggested a mattress or sheet had been there and the bodies pulled on to it. A boot-print of a similar substance was also found. The stains were tested with orthotolidine, a chemical spray that eliminates certain substances and endorses a confirmative blood-test should it yield a positive result. The spray verified the blemishes were organic in nature, but samples of the stains would be required to establish the true identity of the substance. However, the corroborative blood-test, which necessitates microscopic observation of the cellular structure and chemical analysis of the pigments of the material, was not made. The police decided to rely on the positive result of the presumptive test.[7]

Explains Clark, "There was a track, where my bike went in and came out over a period of six months, right down the middle of the garage. I stored raw wood, ply and particle boards there. There were four woodworking shops in a 50-foot radius that directly dusted the area. The door allowed leaves and dust to blow in, around and under it. This, they guessed was a drag-mark, then admitted it was as likely a roller item marking it over time.

"Carol told the cops this fable about this orgy because at the time of Cindy and Gina's murders she knew I had no place to have sex with two dead girls. At that time I was living with Cissy in an upstairs apartment. I had no van, only a bike. She told them this story to cover the fact that the girls may have had sex and she needed a place for Doug while they had Murray's van. The cops perked up their ears and wanted to go see the garage. She *instantly* and *frantically* began to insist, 'You won't find any evidence there, we scrubbed it out.' *Why this lie*? The garage had obviously not been scrubbed out, not even *swept* out. It was to explain why the cops would not find a trace. She assumed testing would prove no blood was there. She didn't know how incompetent or sleazy the cops' handling of the testing would be. Bingo! They create 'proof' to back up the story she was backtracking off of." The fact that the police had discovered a boot print on the garage floor bemused Clark, "What the fuck am I supposed to do," he points out, "*levitate* around my garage?" The soles of the boots in question were thoroughly examined and tested but failed to show even the minutest blood-traces.

While in jail awaiting trial, Clark received a letter from a female admirer. Her name was Veronica Lynn Compton and she was in custody for attempted murder: a failed, lunatic scheme to help free Ken Bianchi, the Hillside Strangler. Compton, a playwright, was working on a play about a psychopath and wrote to Bianchi in order to gain insight into the mind of a deranged sex-killer. At length, Compton 'fell in love' with Bianchi and the two devised a method of freeing him. If it could be established that the real Hillside Strangler was still at large, they reasoned, Bianchi could claim false imprisonment. To achieve this, Bianchi passed Compton a sample of his semen, deposited inside the cut-off finger of a rubber glove and hidden in the spine of a book. Compton was to strangle to death a female stranger then smear the semen in and around her vulva. Forensics would analyse the discharge which would match identically that found on the bodies of the first Hillside victims and conclude that Bianchi, in jail and therefore with the perfect alibi for *this* crime, must be innocent. Of course the plot failed, and Compton was duly arrested and convicted after attempting to kill Kim Breed on September 19, 1980. Compton was placed in the Sybil Brand Institute where she met Carol Bundy.

Says Clark, "Veronica Compton wrote to me because Carol Bundy was in a cell near her, telling her they (she and Veronica) were both framing someone for killings committed with their lovers (Carol Bundy/John Murray, Veronica Compton/Ken Bianchi). See, Veronica was lying about being Ken's partner... She had just met him after he was arrested for the Hillside Strangler case. Now Compton wrote and begged me not to front her off as a person telling about other prisoners, but Carol says she is framing you and that she and Murray did the crimes. Then, after several letters back and forth, we realised Compton was a coke-freak and weirdo. To keep her 'on the line' I went along and played the game of sex letters to her, catering to her ego as some kind of super sex-kitten.

"She kept wanting to know about this case. I sent her over 30 photos, from police extra prints we had, which included apartment shots, cars, odds and ends, locations, victims, the works. These were crime scene numbered police prints. They were accompanied by detailed and lengthy documents explaining each photo's relevance to the case. They were sent to appease her interest and all were to be returned. She stole one photo of Exxie Wilson's body."

Compton had a necrophile fixation, a desire made evident in her letters to Clark, and, because Carol no doubt had told Compton that Clark was a practising necrophile, presumably the reason she contacted him in the first place. In order to retain her as an ally he wrote similar letters back to her. The prosecution heard about the correspondence and ordered the search of Compton's cell. There, officers seized the letters written by Clark and the photo Compton had refused to return. The material was used during trial to show that Clark had an interest in necrophilia.

He continues, "The DA admits he faked the context of how Compton got the photo. He admitted he knew she had lifted *one* from *scores* of photographs." However, Doug was hoping to use Compton as a witness for the defence, one who could testify against Bundy. But, "we lost the pull, the edge... the *magnet* to draw her into court. See, she faced a dreaded informer label in prison, and *worse*, she had to beg these men in the 'prosecution brotherhood' to grant her parole. The DA in this case, illegally, *on record*, threatened to try her for perjury, *without even knowing what it was she would tell*. Yet, in the next courtroom, the same DA office was using her as their own witness to try to [secure a conviction against] Angelo Buono in the Hillside case. In *my* court she is a total liar and in the *other* she is god's own sainted seer? Hogwash!"

With Bundy operating as a police agent and seeking a deal to avoid the death penalty, she agreed to testify in court against Clark. At one stage she considered blaming Clark for killing Murray to get herself off the hook completely, but Clark's alibi for that night was too strong. Investigators began amassing as much evidence as they could to link him with the murders. All they had at this time was Bundy's word and an unidentified stain in his garage. The weapons and vehicles linked to the Sunset murders belonged to Bundy and John Murray. Clark's former girlfriends were questioned and a roster was produced to establish where he lived at specific times. Telephone records were collected from the phone companies and these showed calls had been made from the Jergens factory to Brigges' number around 3 o'clock in the afternoon of June 16th, and from Verdugo Avenue to Mindy Cohen on July 24th. These calls, reasoned the police, were the ones made by the bogus detective, and Clark had evidently made them.

He explains, "About 3 PM, I called Laurie Brigges per Carol's request to try to locate a cheap mover and make her a good deal, but Laurie could not quote prices. Carol gave me the numbers she said were from the paper, on the phone about 11.30 AM that day. She also asked me to turn on the electricity and water at the new Burbank apartment." Clark insists John Murray must have made the early call to Brigges probably imitating his voice, something Murray had a talent for. The evidence of the false police badge carried by Murray also backs up the suggestion that he faked being a detective. Clark also declares the reason Carol asked him to call was so records would prove he did in fact phone Brigges that day.

He also admitted calling Mindy Cohen early morning on July 24th, proven by phone records showing the call came from the Verdugo apartment. Unaware that Cynthia Chandler was dead, he called the number she had given him as a possible contact location. Cohen panicked, thinking it was the same caller who had phoned the previous month. The conversation was brief, registering only two minutes on the phone company's records.

Under interrogation Clark told police he knew Chandler and had been given her phone number which he no longer had. Investigators found a typed phone list in his wallet. Says Clark, "One detective would claim that after police Xerox-copied a phone number list from my wallet, miraculously, highly damning names and numbers appeared upon it – in *pencil*, out of chronological order, and most curiously of all, alleged to have been added to the list *after* the girl's death. This must have been for contact via ATP – American Telephone and Psychics." The number was that of Mindy

Cohen with 'Cindy, Blonde hooker $30' written by it.

"I frankly admitted knowing a victim shown in the photos: Cindy. I saw her the last time about the next to the last week in May. I saw her thumbing, as I recall, and naturally stopped. We ate lunch and had sex and she kept the key to the motel she rented for the night. She was *alone* and that was that. She gave me a number on a piece of paper and said I might be able to reach her there for a while if I wanted to get together. I gave her about $20 in cash, or less, having paid for lunch and her motel room to trick out of. I had called the number on July 24th seeking Cindy as a companion for the ride on the bike up the coast of California to my brother's wedding that coming weekend. This call was very brief at 7 AM, two minutes logged, but remember, one minute six seconds counts as two minutes on the bill."

Cohen, speaking of that call, told police that the 'killer' had called her again and had said words to the effect, "Remember me, I called before, I killed them, then had sex with them and I want you next. I saw you at the party." Detective Gary Broda visited Mindy Cohen to question her further about the calls. Following the new interrogation she 'recalled' the bogus detective had said his name was Detective Douglas Clark. Broda played a recording of Clark's voice, taped during the police interrogation. Cohen said it was the same man.

Comments Clark, "The cops, after my arrest, needed to gain a voice ID, but flew to Lake Tahoe, over 400 miles away rather than drop in on Laurie Brigges, a *local* businesswoman. Why? Because they didn't have her tit in a wringer, could not guarantee she would ID the one guy, one voice, one name offered. The cops admitted that during this period they were looking at *three* people – Carol, Murray and me. They had tons of tapes of Murray talking, crooning etc., yet, the cop went and held a one-voice line-up, illegal itself, and excluded Murray's voice. Broda pointedly selected the segment he played off the tape of my police interrogation. Cohen swore she heard a segment about producing a film with a "girl sucking off a horse". Broda swears he carefully selected non-prejudicial segments, not *that* one, and he has no explanation why she knew that weird topic was even on his tapes."

The fact that Clark actually *had* Cohen's phone number was used against him in court. It was argued by the prosecution that the only way he could have possibly acquired it was from the body of Chandler or Marano. Clark claimed to have been given the number by Chandler in mid-May. Cohen spoke of briefly meeting the girls at a party thrown by her lover Mark Gottesman on June 1st, and she had given Marano her number. She claimed not to have seen the girls before or after that date so it would be impossible for Clark to have been given the number before then. Clark is adamant that this is a lie and gives this version of events.

"In May, Cindy and Gina met Mark Gottesman's shills Mindy and Dudley. The girls are brought to Mark's home, provided a crash pad, drugs, food etc. Mark and Mindy threw a party on June 1st and later would claim they met the girls there only for a very brief moment. Mark would testify he did not remember *ever* seeing *either* girl. He later recanted and admitted maybe seeing them at the party. Mindy likewise called it 'like ships in the night', and only meeting Gina, not the blonde girl. They now admit the girls were hanging around for weeks. Witnesses say they saw the girls there topless by the pool. One says he saw Gina crying, saying she was drugged and raped by them." Clark claims police coerced false details from Cohen to establish incriminating evidence against himself. He later learned Gottesman was under investigation by the FBI for suspected involvement in a white-slave ring with his associate Richard Lieber. According to FBI reports Lieber was shipping blue-eyed blondes to Lebanon. Alleges Clark, "Cohen lied to keep herself and her lover out of jail."

Cohen wasn't the only prosecution witness to be accused of lying. Around the same time the Sunset murders were occurring, a series of savage knife-attacks and robberies of prostitutes took place. In April, Charlene Anderman, a hooker and junkie, fell victim to one such attack. A punter had her in his car when he pulled a knife and stabbed her several times in the back before she managed to escape from the vehicle. Police eventually arrested a man named Jerome Van Houten for the robberies and assaults. His last victim had grabbed the keys from the ignition, struggled free from his car and ran for her life. Van Houten had to abandon the vehicle. As he scrambled out, his wallet, containing his ID and driver's licence, fell from his jacket and their discovery led to his arrest. Anderman identified him in a line-up as her attacker. However, at the time of the knifing, Anderman was high on PCP and heroin and her recollection was hazy. She said it took place in a motel room, then a car. Because of this uncertainty about specific details the police deemed her testimony unreliable despite her positive ID. Van Houten was allowed to plea bargain and have the Anderman charges dropped. He was jailed for the other identical attacks.

Clark says, "*Two years later* she is bragging in jail about being attacked by the guy in the newspaper at the time (me) and acting like a big shot... but she doesn't tell the cops, she knows who really did it: Van Houten. Carol Bundy hears it and she tells the cops to check it out. She then sends me a joke birthday card saying she just sent the cops on a wild goose chase because some gal was bragging you attacked her. Much later, on the reverse side of the earlier case's Anderman report, Carol wrote in detail how stupid they are to believe her. Anderman decided to use me as a get-out-of-jail-free card."

The police re-interviewed Anderman and showed her a photograph of Clark. She now identified him as the attacker and agreed to testify against him. Bizarrely, Anderman's once unreliable testimony – which specified the attacker's vehicle as having wood panelling, and the attacker a moustache, neither of which related to Clark – was now deemed dependable and valid two years after the event. Following her brief appearance in court she was released from jail. The authorities claimed her sudden discharge was merely a coincidence: "She just got lucky." The use of Anderman as a prosecution witness was evidently a means of predating the killing of Marnette Comer, the first girl to be killed by Carol Bundy's gun. Anderman identifying Clark as her attacker ensured a Sunset murder *attempt* was made a month before Bundy bought the guns. This would not only incriminate Clark further, but also bolster Bundy's defence of being an everyday housewife under the control of an evil man. Anderman's sister said of her, "Charlene is a pathological liar, she would lie readily to get out of trouble ever since she was a kid."

Charlene Anderman wasn't the only dubious witness used to implicate Clark as the Sunset Slayer. Donielle Patton, a go-go dancer from the Outrigger bar on Van Nuys Boulevard, recognised him on television and decided to testify against him. Her account was used to verify that Clark was indeed fixated on necrophilia. She informed the jury how he had told her he'd slit a woman's throat while he was having sex with her to feel her vaginal muscles contract as she died. She also said he had brought some of the victims into the bar where she worked. All this despite the fact that the Outrigger had closed down weeks before the first murder had occurred.

Clark takes up the story: "This broad was a total *nut case*. She said I offered her – a real *dog* – $800 for sex with a girlfriend. I had actually hired Nancy Smith and

Linda Bokros for $40 each, *one-twentieth of that*, and *they* are foxes. She said I showed her two huge knives, begged her to pimp me to *other men* and that I gave her a gold necklace as a tip with a letter on it, 'T', 'J', 'S', 'L', she kept changing the letter. Of course she threw this jewellery away so it no longer exists. She said I told her I dreamed I slit a girl's throat during intercourse to see if her vagina tightened up. In a bar filled with my friends and strict bouncers any freaky shit like that to a hostile dancer would be reported. *No one* ever alleged this crap, not even the prolific Bundy, but she said in court, 'When the police officer told me that had actually happened I realised he did not say he *dreamed* it, but that he *wanted* to do it...' She promptly changed *that* into, 'he told me he just *did* it.' She also had me there in *hour-long chats* the manager disallowed – with her, not the girls I *liked* – and on her *day time shift* while I was at work! Remember, this had to be in April, or the first week of May, because the bar closed down the first week of May where this all allegedly was said. She kept embellishing her tale each time she told it. She added that, in her home area – dunno where – she saw me on a black chopper motorcycle glaring at her in a gas station. I own a huge stock red, full-dress touring bike."

Patton's tale helped the DA to convince jurors of the authenticity of Charlene Anderman's testimony. Anderman's neck had been nicked while she struggled to escaped the knife-attack, and this wound, the DA proposed, was in fact the effort made by Douglas Clark to cut her throat to see if her vagina did indeed tighten. The testimony of Donielle Patton was only made admissible because of the statements made by Anderman; the minor cut on her neck making Patton's story relevant to the case and the proposed necrophilia motive. But the necrophilia aspects of the case were, according to Carol Bundy, achieved by shooting girls during fellatio, not cutting throats during intercourse. The notion of any man firing a gun into the head of a girl while sucking his penis is quite absurd. Not only is there the danger of injury from bullets passing through skulls, as with Gina Marano and Cathy, but the possibility of severe biting during death throes. "Shoot a girl sucking my cock? What if her jaw locked shut?" said Clark.

Clark recalls his most recent 'contact' with Patton while watching television in his cell. "I switched to this other channel running a tabloid show that is utter trash. The split-second the picture came on I saw a close-up of a woman in a trance, talking... I felt I knew her somehow. One second later I saw 'Donielle Patton – Psychic'. That *fucking lying bitch* whose stories grew, changed 180° half a dozen times, and who the court relied upon as *credible*. She is offering her 'visions' to police for attention as a psychic in murder cases. She thinks she was psychic in this case, having made up the 'he cut her throat to see if her vagina tightened up' story. Now she is actively calling herself a psychic, but not one lead she has given anyone has panned out. She is on TV chatting about how important she is, then acts like she got hit by a vision, goes into a 'trance' and begins to mumble her visions as she gets them."

Clark's financial situation prevented him from hiring his own attorney to defend himself against the state. His court-appointed lawyer, Maxwell Keith, opened the proceedings claiming his client was guilty but insane and should therefore be given a lenient sentence. The judge had to remind him that this was the first phase of the trial where they determine whether he actually committed the crimes. Any suggestion of sentence is left to the penalty phase.

Says Clark, "Keith simply walked into court, tried to say the defence would not put on any defence, and try to coax the jury not to impose the death sentence for the

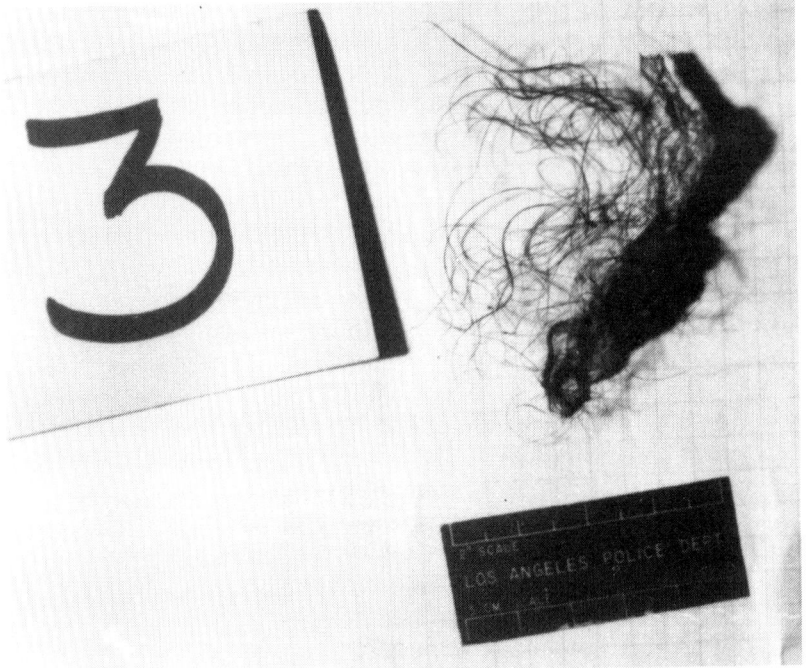

crimes. Basically the case was over before trial began.

"The first day of formal trial my lawyer dared to claim he had not spoken to me in weeks. Yet jail logs and his bills to the court say he was with me for several hour-long visits right before this. He said he wished to change my plea of not guilty to NGI (not guilty by reason of insanity). The judge had to ask him if I approved. He said he had not asked me because he knew I would not allow this change. Then the judge had to tell him what every 1st year law student knows: In this state and nation no lawyer can do this without signed and informed permission of his client."

It soon became clear that Clark's lawyer had a serious drink problem. A condition probably worsened following his declaration of bankruptcy and being charged with legal malpractice and theft of a client's funds.

"Family, friends and witnesses for the DA all say they saw him downing drinks, doubles usually, during early hours before court. The bailiff complained of his alcohol fumes at 10 AM in the morning session. He fell asleep several times while I was on the stand being cross-examined by the prosecutor, so I had to tell him to wake up or inject the legal objections to lines of questions the court had ruled inadmissible. The DA saw he was asleep and tried to slide it past him. It worked, the court said I could not object, only my lawyer could and he was asleep. He swore under oath he was an out-of-control alcoholic and so distracted by his bankruptcy that he paid little or no attention to the case." Even Carol Bundy commented on his incompetence. "Max Keith was not competent to defend Doug," she said, "He came in looking like an unmade bed every day."

As the trial progressed Clark became increasingly aware of his lawyer's inadequacy and requested that he be allowed to represent himself. *Pro se*, the term for self-representation, was denied by the judge. Clark refused to sit quietly and would burst out with angry rants and accusations, usually directed at the judge. To restrain him, the judge ordered he be manacled and tied into his seat. In order to silence his profanities a sanitary towel was pushed into his mouth and fixed in place with a leather strap. When such means weren't sufficient to disable his emotions, Clark was dragged off to a small adjoining holding-room equipped with a loud speaker so he could hear the trial continue without his presence.

In mid trial the judge finally bowed to Clark's demands for *pro se*. Despite it being exactly what Clark wanted things only got worse.

Says Clark, "When I took over I was denied co-counsel, advisory counsel and a law clerk. Judge Torres said the law says you have to go it alone. The law says no such thing. He was required to hire competent counsel who would prepare for trial. He did nothing and kept harassing me severely throughout trial." Clark's primary defence was structured around showing that Carol and Murray were in fact the Sunset Slayers, not himself. He gave the judge a list of items he required as evidence, several of which had been discovered in Murray's van. These items included dildos, handcuffs, home-made videos[8] and the fragment of scalp. The judge blocked all the items. Clark was astonished, "At the bench, on record, I said if we had a colour movie with sound of Carol and Murray committing these murders you would not let us bring it in. He smirked and said, You are right. He refused to let us test the hair and scalp, the Datsun seats and other evidence, saying it was too late, trial had begun."

Clark required a female witness to testify that he was with her on the night that Carol dropped Exxie Wilson's head. He had been partying with friends and a go-go dancer who was shortly to return to her home in New Zealand. Clark had written her a cheque, "It was her *bon voyage* party and said so on the check," bank records showed it had been cashed the following day. The girl offered to come to trial if her air fare would be paid as she couldn't afford it herself. Clark asked for funds to cover the cost. "Any attorney can fly in scores of witnesses. The DA got several, including a totally unwarranted FBI man from Virginia just to say a boot-print was my boot which I stipulated to all along. He spent over $10,000 on travel for his witnesses. I got $20 in dimes, once, for the phone. That was the entire defence funding for my efforts." Now that there was no possibility of his witness appearing in court he requested she be able to testify by phone. This is a legal procedure if the witness is identified and sworn in at a local court. Notwithstanding, the request was denied.[9]

The 'Daddy's Girl' T-shirt and jeans, despite being redundant evidence, were used during the trial by the prosecution. Speaking of Marnette Comer in his opening statement, the DA said, "She was wearing a white sweater and a pink shirt. The pink shirt, which is particularly significant, was inscribed with the words "Daddy's Girl". And later, "I told you earlier the shirt worn by Marnette Comer was particularly significant – the shirt that she was wearing when she disappeared. That's the shirt that says, "Daddy's girl" on it. It is significant because when Exxie Wilson's head was found, it was wrapped in Marnette Comer's shirt." Further into the trial Sabra Comer took the stand and was asked to identify the clothing.

Q. Showing you the jeans marked People's 33 for identification, Ms Comer, do you recognise these jeans?
A. Yes.
Q. Whose jeans were they?
A. My sister's.
Q. Marnette's?
A. Yes.

Q. I show you the white sweater marked People's 28 for identification. Do you recognise that?
A. Yes.
Q. Was that your sister's sweater?
A. Yes.
Q. Was she wearing it when you last saw her?
A. Yes.
Q. I show you the pink shirt inscribed, "Daddy's Girl", People's 29 for identification. Do you recognise that?
A. Yes.
Q. Is that your sister's shirt?
A. Yes.
Q. Was she wearing that when you last saw her?
A. Yes.
Q. Have you ever seen her since May 21, 1980?
A. No.

As the defence had copies of the original interview that Stallcup conducted with Comer there arose an opportunity to challenge the credibility of the witnesses and Stallcup himself.

On the stand Stallcup stated, "I had one homicide that I had the entire investigation on. That was for Marnette Comer." The Defence asked, "At anytime during that investigation did you falsify any witnesses statements?"
A. Never.
Q. You have never done that?
A. I have never done that.
Q. When you take notes of an interview and later caused them to be typed up, are they usually verbatim from your notes, the typing portion?
A. Depends.
Q. Would you ever take a statement and turn it around 180 degrees between the time you took the notes and the time that you typed it up?
A. No. I would put myself in a very, in a very bad spot of jeopardy there. The crime for doing such – something like that if it ended up to be a capital case, I would be under the same problem you have got sitting right over there.
Q. What you are telling us is that for a police officer to falsify evidence, to commit perjury on a capital case offence, is a capital offence, is that correct?
A. That is correct.
Q. Referring to Sabra Comer, you interviewed her, didn't you?
A. Either myself or my partner did.
Q. 7/9/80, 1600 hours?
A. I did an investigation with her in Sacramento. I don't recall the date.
Q. You took written notes?
A. Pardon me?
Q. You initialled them R.M.S?
A. I probably did.
Q. And she told you, in effect – this is offered for another cause here – did she tell you – in your typewritten form, are these the words she told you: "I've seen my sister wearing a white long-sleeve sweater, V-neck. She also wore T-shirt, pink, with lettering 'Daddy's Girl' on the front. Witness shown picture of recovered T-shirt, and

she identified it as probably same worn by victim" ? Do you recall that?

A. I recall something to that effect, yes.

Q. And that typewritten page is dated 7-9-80, 1600 hours, just like your notes are, aren't they?

A. I don't know.

Q. Let's put it this way: If your name appears on a typewritten form at 7-9-80, that's 7 – July 9th, 80, 1600 hours, and your name appears on hand-written notes of the exact interview more or less –

A. Should be the same.

Q. – should be the same. Do you recall her telling you during that interview in your hand-written notes, "There was another girl named Toni Wilson, female Caucasian, 19 years, blond-blue –" meaning blond and blue eyes, I assume, "thin built, five-foot-seven, freckles, natural blond hair, initial T was her pimp, I saw Toni wearing a T-shirt, pink in colour, with the words 'Daddy's Girl' on the front. Witness I.D.d photo of 'Daddy's Girl' on T-shirt. Toni and T were working –" And she told you that Toni was wearing the T-shirt and you typed it up as Marnette was wearing the T-shirt?"

A. No.

Q. Would you like to look at it?

A. I can look at it all you want. Bring it up here and let me look at it. That is not what she told me.

Q. I'd like you to compare those, see if they are accurate.

The Court: Wouldn't do any good, Mr Clark. He's told you –

The Defendant: I know what he's told me, Your Honour.

The Sacramento Police Department report that confirms Detective Stallcup did indeed change the name of Marnette Comer to Toni Wilson in the Sabra Comer interview.

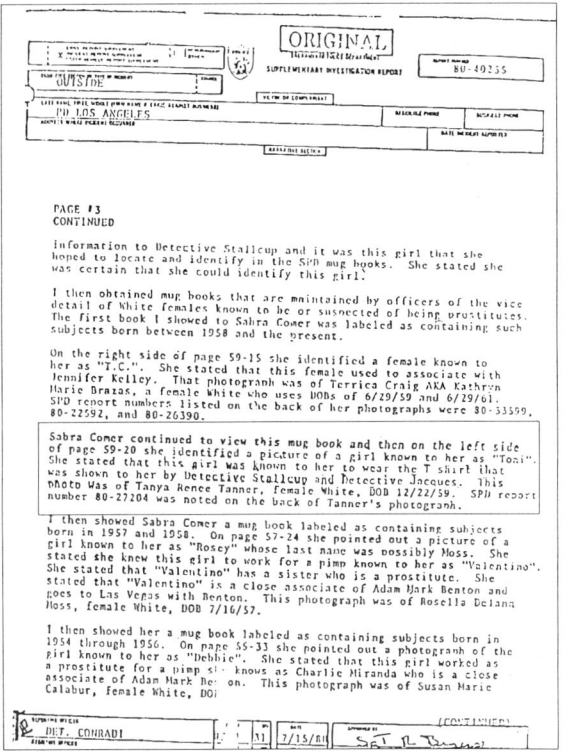

The Court: You can sit down with your paper Miss Sarkis.

The Defendant: I'd like to mark this.

The Court: It is not going to be marked. Let's proceed.

The Defendant: I'd like that in evidence as next in order.

The Court: It is not going to be marked.

Later Clark attempted to bring in the report again and get Stallcup, who was still on the stand, to identify it. "Do you just want me to see if it's my handwriting?" he asked.

Q. Well, yes, in reference to a report you testified to here earlier today. Have you got it all? Yeah, that's all of it. May I approach with this, Your Honour?

The Court: Yes.

Q. By the way, while we are waiting on that, may I ask another question?

Mr Jorgensen [Prosecutor]: Excuse me, Your Honour, I can't read it and listen to the witness's questions.

The Court: Yes, Mr Jorgensen can't do both at one time, Mr Clark. You'll have to wait.

The Defendant: I'll have to remember that.

The Court: Unless you want to withdraw that having him look at those documents.

The Defendant: No, I'll wait. We are not looking at this for content, Your Honour, we are only looking at it as a display.

The Court: Mr Jorgensen can look at anything he wants to look at, Mr Clark.

The Defendant: I was just referring back to when I wanted to read all those massive sets of letters and was denied the privilege.

Mr Jorgensen: Thank you, Your Honour.

Detective Stallcup: This is my writing.

The Defendant: What date did you write that report?

A. It's partially blocked out. It could be – it's possibly 7-9-80.

Q. And is there a time on there as well?

A. 1600 hours.

Q. Now, do you see a typewritten report up there as well?

A. Yes, I do.

Q. Does that purport to be the typewritten report made from those notes of yours?

A. I'll have to read it.

Q. Would you read that also?

A. Okay.

Mr Jorgensen: I object to the pending question as irrelevant, Your Honour.

The Defendant: For credibility of the witness, Your Honour.

The Court: Sustained. It's irrelevant.

Despite the defence having the evidence that Stallcup's report had been altered, the judge simply brushed it off as irrelevant. It was instances like this that led many people to remark that the trial was overtly biased in favour of the prosecution.

Douglas Clark was found guilty of six counts of first-degree murder, those of Marnette Comer, Cynthia Chandler, Gina Marano, Karen Jones, Exxie Wilson and Jane Doe 18, and the attempted murder of Charlene Anderman. He was sentenced to die in the gas chamber at San Quentin. Carol Bundy was found guilty of two counts of first-degree murder, those of John Murray and Jane Doe 28. She was sentenced to two terms of life imprisonment.

While incarcerated, Carol Bundy wrote to Douglas Clark indicating she wasn't pleased the way the case was going. They weren't getting the media attention achieved by the likes of Ken Bianchi, Lawrence Bittaker or Ted Bundy. The letter also suggested that Clark get hold of a specific book pointedly intimating he would find it very interesting. The publication, by Steve Winn and David Merrill, was entitled *Ted Bundy – The Killer Next Door*.[10] Clark acquired the book and noted many similarities in the text to the Sunset murders scenario. So strong were the links that it appeared this case was a virtual duplicate of details in the Winn/Merrill report. Carol Bundy had shown an interest in Ted Bundy when he appeared on television news in the months prior to the Sunset murders beginning. It was evidently the same name that drew her interest, particularly when Ted married a woman named Carole. Her son once asked if they were related.

Ted Bundy was arrested for the third and final time on February 15th, 1978. Six days before his arrest he had abducted and murdered 12-year-old Kimberly Leach. On January 15th he had infiltrated the Chi Omega sorority house wielding a hefty wooden club. Stalking from room to room he bludgeoned, mauled and raped three co-eds, killing two girls in the process. So brutal was his assault that one victim's skull was split apart, exposing the brain. Parts of the bodies were bitten off and teeth-marks incised in the buttock of one girl would seal Bundy's fate. During his final arrest, Ted re-established communication with a female friend named Carole Anne Boone. A relationship developed and she stood by him throughout his trial and the two were married on February 9 1980. Ironically, the date was the second anniversary of the killing of Kimberly Leach, Bundy's last victim. Three days after the ceremony, Ted was sentenced to death.[11]

This bizarre and highly publicised incident may have triggered some affinity between Carol Mary Bundy and Carole Anne Bundy, formerly Boone. Consequently, a similar cerebral alliance evolved between Carol and Ted. Despite their gender differences, the two share remarkable similarities in their formative years.

As a child, Carol was generally rejected by her mother and school peers, and as a result slipped into delinquency at an early age. By the age of eleven she was regularly shop-lifting and made what was to be the first of several non-too-desperate suicide attempts by ingestion of poisons. One occurrence in her childhood dismayed her to such a degree it remained embedded in her mind: Carol had watched in horror as her father chopped the heads off live chickens and allowed their headless bodies to flutter about. That was her first exposure to violence and death: decapitation.

When her mother died Carol was 14 and her father took her as a surrogate wife. On the night of her mother's funeral Carol was summoned to her father's bed to perform oral sex.

Less than a year after his wife's death, Carol's father re-married. Some months into the marriage he made a confused decision to wipe out the entire family with his shotgun. He only got as far as the cat which Carol found when she returned home from school. Carol shortly thereafter became a frequent masturbator, a night-stalking voyeur, and would parade herself naked in the streets. Furthermore, she had developed lesbian tendencies and a desire to sexually dominate other females.

When she was 17 she met and married a man almost 40 years her senior. He was a hopeless alcoholic who pushed her into prostitution to provide funds to sustain his addiction. The marriage didn't last, but Carol's trading sex for money did. Shortly after the marriage break-up she met a 32-year-old man named Richard Geis. Geis was a writer, and his work mainly consisted of science fiction and pornographic narratives. He also edited a small publication called **Psychotic** which won him several awards.

At 19, Carol's father committed suicide by hanging himself. The behaviour of both her parents indicated severe mental instability, a condition which Carol inherited genetically or absorbed through the social conditioning of her mother and father. She attempted to escape from reality by fantasising, and occasional half-hearted suicide attempts. To make matters worse her body also rebelled against her: she was severely overweight, an insulin-dependent diabetic and, to cap it all, began to lose her sight. Her lesbianism indicated a higher than normal testosterone level, a condition prevalent in many female killers. Her eventual marriage to a homosexual would ensure she remained existent within a dysfunctional lifestyle. By the time she was 30, Carol Bundy was a latent psychotic on the threshold of eruption.

Perhaps her two children stabilised her mental status for a period; maternal instincts overriding other more wretched desires. But when she finally separated from her homosexual husband and met John Murray the children became inconvenient hindrances and she shipped them back to their father. Her predilection towards suicide had transposed into a murderous instinct. Throughout the crime period, Carol alternated between two boyfriends: John Murray and Douglas Clark. With these men she became active in paedophilia, indulging in sex with an 11-year-old girl. Masses of pornography were found in her home along with sex toys, weapons, rounds of ammunition and handcuffs.

Ted Bundy was born illegitimate. He grew up believing his mother was actually his sister. In his formative years his grandfather acted as a required father-figure, but his violence towards others initiated Ted into brutality at an early age.

He began to fantasise and steal when he was a teenager, and after getting a brief glimpse of a girl undressing beyond an open door he became a recurrent Peeping Tom. Masturbation became a daily fixation and his onanistic behaviour isolated him further from the real world.

His first true sexual encounter occurred when he was 'raped' by a friend's mother while he stayed at their house sleeping off an evening's drinking. The fact that Bundy said it was rape indicates he found it a disturbing, possibly unpleasant experience. Moreover, because it was a friend's mother, the episode was quasi-incestuous.

Pornographic magazines and books became shopping-list necessities. Bundy developed an interest in necrophilia and sexual domination. Such urges are indicative of a self-confidence deficiency, usually caused by rejection of the opposite sex or parents, or inability to achieve peer approval. Later, Bundy would only gain sexual gratification by killing his 'sex partner'. A live and autonomous individual was perceived as a threat rather than a cherishable companion. While he followed his predatory instincts of stranger-killing he shuttled between two girlfriends: Meg Anders and Stephanie Brooks. Before his arrest he would practise paedophilia and sexually assault, prior to murdering, a 12-year-old girl. When his home and vehicle were searched vast amounts of pornography and pairs of handcuffs were discovered.

Following his arrest Ted denied the crimes despite irrefutable evidence to the contrary.[12]

Although Ted Bundy's murders far outnumbered those in connection with the Sunset case, parallels can be found in certain individual murders, specifically dates and MOs.

Marnette Comer, the first Sunset victim, was abducted late night May 31st. However, during Carol Bundy's arrest interrogation she said the girl died on June 1. This murder paralleled Ted Bundy's killing of Brenda Ball on June 1, 1974. Georgeann Hawkins was his next target and she died on June 11, 74. The second Sunset killing was the double murder of Cynthia Chandler and Gina Marano on June 11. Carol told police of the unsuccessful attempt to separate the girls and take only Chandler, the blonde. Victim selection by hair-colour and style was Ted's widely publicised MO.

Following the Chandler/Marano killing, Carol Bundy telephoned the police accusing her lover of the murders. Likewise, Meg Anders called detectives naming Ted Bundy as the probable multicide sought by police. Although Anders' information implicated Ted by his full name and was clearly given to assist in his capture, Carol's data was vague and deliberately misleading, evidently not intended to hasten arrest.

When police first placed a request to the public for help in the Ted Bundy case, from the little information they had, the man they sought was 'Ted' who drives a 'Volkswagen'. Carol offered the police matching information: 'John' who drives a 'Plymouth'. In truth this was a combination of information and misinformation; the name being legitimate but the vehicle type was a red herring.

On July 14 Ted Bundy drove to Sammanish Park where, equipped with fake arm-cast (bogus disability was one of John Murray's frequent deceptions), he openly lured Janice Ott to his car on the pretext of requiring assistance with his boat and trailer. Ott was driven away and Bundy returned to Lake Sammanish without her. This time he used the same ploy on Denise Naslund and she too was abducted. Both girls were sexually tortured and killed. Bundy, however, wasn't satisfied and returned to the area a third time that day. Fortunately on this occasion he failed to get another victim. When Ott's remains were found, the head was missing, but the mutilation was as likely caused by carnivorous wildlife as any sustained effort or intention to decapitate by Bundy. Whatever, Ott was in effect murdered and decapitated.

The consecutive murders in the Sunset case were those of Karen Jones and Exxie Wilson. Although the date no longer matched Ted Bundy's Lake Sammanish murder, the *day* did: both occurred on a Sunday. Moreover, there were other remarkable parallels.

As Carol explained to police (by now implicating Clark, not John Murray), the victims were seen hooking together on Sunset Boulevard and Wilson was picked up by Clark. After her murder and decapitation he returned, with Wilson's severed head in the back of the car, and picked up Karen Jones. She was subsequently executed and Clark made a third trip in search of another victim but failed to find one. Of course this account of events is preposterous. Wilson's decapitation was an extremely bloody operation; the perpetrator would unavoidably be covered with blood. To return for her co-worker in such a condition, moreover *without* the original girl, and succeed in luring her into a car splashed with and smelling of blood is evidently not a true interpretation of events. What is important is Carol's rendition of abducting two victims separately and trying for a third – she was telling police how *Ted Bundy* did it at Lake Sammanish. Or at least, how she had *read* Ted Bundy did it.

Carol Valenzuela was murdered by Ted on Friday, August 2, 1974. That same date in 1980 Carol Bundy was with John Murray cruising in his van. With them was Shannon, Carol's 11-year-old neighbour. But no murder occurred, instead Shannon satiated their sexual desires that night. The following night, August 3, Carol and John were in the van again and this time Murray himself was to become the victim, butchered by his lover. Was Carol intending to emulate Ted's August 2 murder the previous night, but Shannon's presence prevented it? Moreover, was Shannon herself to become an eventual victim; a child victim to echo Kimberly Leach, Ted's final quarry?

The Charlene Anderman knifing now takes on a different light. A reason is borne for Carol's initial suggestion to the police that Clark had attacked her: in the Ted Bundy case there was a strikingly similar event. Carol DaRonch was approached by Ted Bundy on 8 November, 1974. Ted posed as a police officer and, after telling DaRonch a man had been seen trying to break into her car, requested her to accompany him to police headquarters. DaRonch, convinced of his authenticity, entered his car and they drove a short distance before Ted attempted to snap handcuffs on her wrist. She managed to struggle free despite being attacked with a tyre-iron and having a gun levelled at her head. Anderman neatly echoes Ted Bundy's escapee DaRonch.

The final Sunset killing was that of Cathy/Jane Doe 28. This occurred on August 7[13] and had no discernible pattern with Ted Bundy's killing spree. Clark believes Carol killed her while he was present to inaugurate him as a new killing-partner following the brutal dispatch of her first confederate John Murray.

On January 12, 1975, Ted kidnapped Caryn Campbell from a Colorado ski resort. He raped and murdered her and her remains were found within the grounds of the resort the following month. Ironically, Carol told police where they could find traces of Gina Marano's blood. It was on the rear of a large ski-lift painting hanging in her apartment. The spots had supposedly splashed onto the painting while it was stored in the lock-up.

While Ted Bundy remained at large and the bodies of his victims began to surface, theories of possible occult connections were being contemplated. In regard to the remains of Denise Naslund and Janice Ott the police report specified that "no occult or witchcraft symbols were found near the scene" which indicates they were looking for such evidence. The same report also referred to the discovery of "a large quantity of immature elk bones" ¼ mile from the location of the girl's carcasses, on Sunset Highway. The notion of Satanic sacrifices was hypothesised, motivated in part by the discovery of mutilated cattle, commonly involving total vaginal excision, around

The Ski-lift painting which Carol told police had blood splashes on its back.

the area.

When Marnette Comer's dehydrated body was examined the lower abdomen showed signs of having been ripped open with a knife and several internal organs were missing, seemingly cut away. A number of pig bones were found in the area. Exxie Wilson's head was packaged in an ornate casket-like box, and Carol had informed police she'd initially intended to place it at the scene of another murder. These idiosyncrasies were perhaps intended to establish comparable cabalistic speculation.

The notion that Carol could have been influenced by the contents of a book is validated by her own comments to police during interrogation. When she was first questioned about the whereabouts of the Ravens she told officers that she had sold them to a man named Mike Hammer, a fictional detective from Mickey Spillane crime novels. When she was arrested, she told detectives her planned strategy of false defence was inspired by the Elizabeth McNeill novel *9½ Weeks* concerning a brief sado-masochistic sexual affair between an average, recently divorced woman and overbearing man. When the police asked her what her real defence was she paused and said, "Ehm... well, that's it really..." Remarkably, the duration of the Sunset murders, from the first victim to the last, was to within one day of nine-and-a-half weeks.

One thing that's clear is that Carol had hoped for a lesser sentence than she actually received. She had admitted the murder of Murray but denied killing Jane Doe 28, and wanted that charge dropped in exchange for testifying against Clark. She also wanted the Murray charges reduced to manslaughter. It is evident that the only thing she could negotiate for was a non-capital sentence.

In the event of Clark having an appeal trial, Carol will only re-testify for freedom or a considerable reduction in her remaining jail term. She says, "If for some reason my case was vacated again, and [Clark's] case was vacated again, if they were to offer me 15 years to life, 25 years to life, or whatever, I would still refuse it. They would have to get way, way, way down before I would even consider it... manslaughter or actually be able to walk out the door. I would have to be certain that I would be free before I make a decision... to sell my testimony in order to buy back my life... they screwed up the last time." Clark is all too aware that his fate is determined by Carol's desire to be free: "Ted Bundy got caught, got put away, then escaped and killed several more people. Carol cannot dive out a second storey window, or wiggle through a vent duct to go kill again."

At the time of her arrest, Carol had told the police that the first time she knew beyond any shadow of a doubt that people were really dying was when she saw Exxie Wilson's severed head. This, she claimed, was her first contact with a victim. Such a claim must put the murder of Cathy, which Carol admits to observing, at a date beyond 23 June. Clark says it happened on August 7, but Carol now says it took place on or around June 20 which places it before the death of Wilson and therefore rebuts Carol's original admission. Her description of the crime is somewhat different to Doug's version.

She says they were cruising for prostitutes in the Buick and they found a girl who was coaxed into the car. Carol was in the back and Cathy sat in the drivers seat while Doug was outside urinating. Carol gave the girl $30. Doug sat in the passenger seat and prepared for fellatio. Carol describes how Cathy positioned herself over the

The false disabled person sign used by Murray.

central gear-shift situated between the bucket seats and that Doug was separated from his gun which was in a well by the driver's door. She says he motioned with his hand and she believed it was a signal to give him her gun, which she did. She described it as the dull-finish, i.e. nickel-plated, gun. Clark then shot the girl in the head as she sucked his penis. The body was pushed on the floor of the passenger side and Carol climbed back in the front then stripped the girl as Doug drove away. As Carol described the vehicle she defined the interior of the Datsun. The Buick had a bench seat and steering-column gear-shift. Carol claims she gets confused because it is difficult to remember exactly how it occurred. Yet, she has no problem detailing every item she retrieved from Cathy's boot: comb, knife, specific number of dollars etc.

On Friday evening Clark had been visiting a girlfriend, Joey Lamphier, even though he was at that time living with Cissy Buster. When he left Joey's he had reversed the Buick, trapping the hindquarters of a cat beneath the wheel. He lifted the still-living animal into the car where it crawled under the passenger seat. Clark, who was renowned for his fondness of cats and had taken in several strays and rescued others from animal pounds, drove to the animal hospital. The cat died before he could reach it so he placed the carcass in a cardboard box and left it by a waste-skip.

On Saturday, after work, he was to return the Buick to Carol who needed it for her move to Burbank on Sunday. Clark told her it required cleaning first. He took Cissy's son Timmy to the carwash where he sprayed cat's blood and excrement from under the car seat and vacuumed the excess water out. When he offered the car back to Carol she complained about it being too damp. Clark promised he would try and dry it out and return it the following morning in time for her move. That evening Clark took Cissy to the drive-in and she objected to the smell which she described as a wet dog type of odour. Later, when Cissy was interviewed by Det. Stallcup, the smell was described as that of blood and raw meat. Doug told her the car had been washed out and Timmy mentioned that they had met Carol. Cissy was furious because Doug had been with Carol that afternoon, and an argument developed which led to Clark moving out the following day.

Says Clark, "This was Saturday, June 21. I had to return the car to Carol so she could move out of Van Nuys the next day. I asked Tim since he was bored, nothing to do, if he wanted to come along. Carol, on June 14, on taped call to cops, said they washed out huge clots of blood with hoses, really swooshed it out. In the week-later Buick wash, we used a car washer sprayer, singular, and soaked the area, then vacuumed out the water since it would not run out of the car floor. But if you know a Chevy van design, hoses (at Murray's apartment house?) can swoosh blood out as she described. Everyone who saw or rode in the Buick said from June 14 to June 21 the car was dry and, right after the only Buick wash job, June 21, it was soaked and damp with steamy air for a week. The point is, what fucking vehicle was she washing out just before her June 14 police call? The Datsun was broken down, the Buick was dry. Yet, police and DA tried like mad to get this clearly later wash to be the one Carol "mistakenly said" was June 14, not June 21. How does she psychically goof on tape and mention a wash not yet to occur for a week?"

Is Clark's attestation that Carol Bundy and John Murray were the real Sunset Slayers true? It certainly cannot be brushed aside as mere fabrication by a guilty man attempting to avert blame, for there is as much, if not *more* evidence pointing towards Murray. The only part of Clark's account that seems suspicious is the claim about the cat. However, it is only questionable when juxtaposed with the crimes. Cats being run over is a more common event than murder, even in the US. And, as Clark states, "If this car wash had a sinister motive, why would I take a mouthy kid along?"

In 1990 Carol admitted to a journalist, "There is no physical evidence linking Douglas Clark to the murders exclusive of my statements." There are also many similarities found in the Winn/Merrill book to back up Clark's opinion that Carol did indeed duplicate the Ted Bundy scenario.

There is the sliver of blond-haired human scalp found in Murray's van.

There is the bogus detective who made the phone calls, which fits Murray who openly posed as a policeman, validated by his carrying a false police badge, and again, reflects Ted Bundy's fake cop performance.

There is the fact that Carol bought the murder weapons only two days before Murray's birthday: an intended gift, perhaps?

When Murray's headless torso was examined by the coroner, he declared the decapitation appeared to have been done by the same skilled hand that cut off the head of Exxie Wilson. Not only were the techniques of decapitation allied in characteristics, but the time and day of the murders were virtually identical. Furthermore, the killer made phone calls following each crime, and Carol, without any doubt, beheaded Murray. The first to be decapitated was Wilson, and the process, as shown by the crime scene photos, was exceptionally bloody due to the fact that Wilson was alive, though comatose, during the cutting. Following such an assault the perpetrator would unavoidably be covered in blood. Carol admits when she cut off Murray's head she ensured his pulse had ceased before she began. Is this an indication of someone being somewhat more careful when carrying out a familiar deed?

When the box containing Wilson's head was found, Carol said the damage inflicted on it was caused when it went under the rear wheel of the Buick. Yet the dimensions of the box were such that it wouldn't fit under a low-slung vehicle of that kind. But if it were dropped from a high-riding Chevrolet van, a mishap as described is more feasible.

When Karen Jones' body was found fully clothed, Carol said it was because Clark

Douglas Daniel Clark, San Quentin, 1994.

hadn't had any sexual contact with the girl because she was too fat. This contradicts the fact that Clark wasn't averse to plump women, as confirmed by his sexual activity with Carol herself and Cissy Buster.

The semen traces found on Chandler and in the throat of Exxie Wilson's head were blood group A, as was Murray's, but not Clark's.

When Murray's body was searched for identification his wallet contained a cheque for $250. It was dated June 11, the day Chandler and Marano died. Why did he keep it uncashed? Was it as potential alibi evidence, to prove he was playing a winning game of poker that night, and not cruising in search of hookers?

Of the two men, Murray was the one who had a reputation of being violent towards women and had once almost bitten off the nipple of Tammy Spangler.

What of the evidence, albeit technically inconclusive, found in the garage? Was it blood, or as Clark declares, merely an ingrained tyre-track composed of oils, grease, organic chrome cleanser, leaves, sawdust, etc.? And, if it was truly the blood of the victims, what must be considered of the fact that Carol had full access to the lock-up, including her own key?

Why did the Sunset murders begin when Clark stopped living with Bundy, and cease when he moved back in with her?

If Carol was as innocent as she claimed, only guilty of killing Murray and present only when Cathy died, what of her statements, like:

"I needed some kind of an out. We were going out almost every night hunting."

"Maybe I psychologically set up the situation with [John], knowing damn well we were going to get caught over it."

"The only thing I could think of, the only possible way, one way or another, [John] was going to get it. I couldn't risk the situation getting out of control, and a decision had already been made that [John] was going to get it. It was just a matter of when."

"The day everything started to go bad was on May 18th, [John's] birthday."

In custody, Carol became acquainted with a petty criminal named Dorothea Puente, who was in jail for fraud and theft, and the two often conversed about their individual crimes. Puente was eventually released and opened up a boarding house for elderly mental patients placed in her care by the welfare department. Over a period of two years, 1986-88, several patients disappeared and subsequent investigations unearthed their remains buried in Puente's garden. The victims had been poisoned with Benzodiazepine and then decapitated prior to burial. Attempts to destroy the remains with quicklime had failed. Puente had continued to cash their social security cheques. Clark believes Carol had taught Puente about specific lethal poisons and the decapitations were a reflection of the mutilation of Murray and Wilson.

In 1994, on an American television talkshow hosted by Sally Raphael, Carol and her son Chris were asked to describe the 'strange games' Doug would play with them. The host seemed somewhat disappointed when the only game Chris could recall was Backgammon. Carol, speaking live from the Women's Correction Center, added Battleships. When Chris was asked about the beatings Clark used to give him he said he couldn't remember any occasion, but he had been *told* they took place.

On the same show, Carol related the events of the night of Murray's death. She claimed to have left her apartment fearful that Clark was going to kill her. Yet this contradicts her numerous statements that she had wanted, even *begged* Clark to kill her on several occasions. She took her guns and a knife, and went to the Nashville to find Murray. "I went there to ask him for his help. Would he hide me for the night till I could decide what I wanted to do?" If Carol was truly seeking Murray's help, why did she go prepared for murder? She went on to say that they got into an argument, "it was very bad, and he slapped me, and I exploded." Again, this explanation doesn't make any sense. Carol had suffered abuse from Murray for over a year, he had taken most of her money and even threatened to shoot her kids, all of which she did nothing about. But on this particular night she tries to claim an *argument* prompted her to kill him. Moreover, this does not explain why she and Murray, if they'd had such a terrible altercation, indulged in sex prior to his murder. The fact that Carol met John in his van equipped with her kill-bag is the most telling evidence of what was to occur that night, even if Murray wasn't the initially intended victim.

Unlike Bundy, Clark was denied the chance to speak live on the show, only edited pre-recorded snippets were used, but by now he is used to biased handling of his case.

Clark is convinced that he will be reprieved if and when he gets a fair trial. He believes he will be released and back in society within the next few years. But perhaps his case has gone beyond mere guilt or innocence. Perhaps the state would rather destroy an innocent man to show that they 'got it right the first time'. During a retrial – which, in reality is nothing more than a legal formality that precedes execution – the prosecution will have the limitless finances, the experts, the best lawyers and determined police officers, as they did in the first trial. Carol Bundy, the main prosecution witness, has already stated she is prepared to sell testimony at the next trial. Her fee is freedom. And is it not fundamentally wrong to offer a killer any self-serving deals in exchange for state-benefiting information or misinformation? And how would a jury respond to a defendant who has been on death row for over a decade? In effect, it will be the credibility of the state that is in the dock at a retrial, and, as the defendant will be represented by a state appointed lawyer, is the outcome not already inevitable?

APPENDIX 1

TRANSCRIPT OF DOUGLAS CLARK'S OPENING STATEMENT TO THE COURT

DECEMBER 2, 1982.

THE COURT: In the case of People versus Clark, the record will indicate that the jurors and alternate jurors are present and in their respective seats. The Defendant is present. The People are represented by Mr Jorgensen. It is now time for the Defence. Mr Clark, you may now make your opening statement.

THE DEFENDANT: Thank you, Your Honour. Ladies and gentlemen of the jury, you've received a lot of the evidence defence will rely on in presenting the defence.

In fact, on June 14, 1980, police officer Heinlein working out of Los Angeles Police Department in regards to some homicides that had been uncovered June 12, two days prior, received a phone call. He received some information during that phone call, but primarily he gave some information to the party that was calling him. He received a code name for that individual. That name was Claudia.

Mr Heinlein will testify, and his partner, Mr Westbrook, as well. You'll hear testimony from those two officers that they, on June 14, were certain that that caller had intimate personal knowledge of the murders of Cynthia Chandler − Cynthia Chandler and Gina Marano.

The caller was asked to call back. The caller did not call back until on June 16 − pardon me, strike that − until August 11 of 1980. That caller called back and talked to Detective Kilgore, also of the Los Angeles Police Department, also investigating these homicides, and that caller again used the code name Claudia and spoke at length with Mr Kilgore about not only two but five or six murders. The list had grown since that caller called on June 14.

Claudia, during that phone call, which you'll hear a tape recording of, gave her name as Carol Mary Bundy. She accused her roommate, Douglas Daniel Clark, of many, many murders, including the murders at trial here today.

Mrs Bundy told Mr Kilgore that I had killed a girl she'd nicknamed Foothill.

Later investigation, and in evidence already presented, we'll prove that Foothill was a nickname used by Bundy and her lover for the murder of Marnette Comer on June 1, 1980.

Further, Mrs Bundy accused me of killing the two half-sisters, Cynthia Chandler and Gina Marano, in that phone call. She nicknamed them the Twins. She indicated where they were found. She described their wounds.

She went on to answer questions of Mr Kilgore. Mr Kilgore will testify. Ms Bundy may testify.

Mr Kilgore asked the caller why she wanted to suddenly roll over on her man and Mrs Bundy told him that things were bad between her and her man and that she had killed one person all on her own.

She went on to describe the murder in detail, which is not charged here today. She described how she decapitated that individual.

She further indicated that this man that she was describing to Mr Kilgore had killed over 50 people and that she had been involved in eight or nine of those.

She indicated that she wanted to turn herself in that day, August 11, to Mr Kilgore, Van Nuys Police Department, Burbank Police Department, possibly Glendale police Department, and that she would meet them at a restaurant called the Gristmill in Burbank for that surrender three hours after the phone call.

Mr Kilgore agreed with that. He was very interested apparently and he will testify that he believed that Mrs Bundy had knowledge of these murders and that he was going to meet her at the Gristmill.

The Gristmill holds some significance in this case in that you'll receive testimony regarding Miss Bundy's suicide earlier a few weeks before the August 11 phone call when she tried to commit suicide in the parking lot of that restaurant after leaving a lengthy suicide note defining me as her lover in the apartment where she and I lived.

Miss Bundy told Mr Kilgore, when he asked her how many people has he murdered, referring to me, she responded that she'd only been involved with the two girls, the one that he cut the head off and she stated, "I played around with the head with him on that one."

She further added that she "had been involved with the fat one that he dumped off near the NBC studios".

Again Mr Kilgore asked the caller, how many people, how many men has he murdered – people – and Miss Bundy said that she didn't know for sure, she only had personal knowledge of 12 or 14 all total.

During that call and on that tape Ms Bundy indicated she was scared to death of the killer. She felt she had to get involved so that the killer would have no reason to kill her.

Shortly thereafter, Mr Kilgore made – took the opportunity to ask the question, "Does that make you feel bad, though, that you've killed somebody?"

Carol Bundy asked him if he wanted to know the honest truth.

"The honest truth is," she said, "it's fun to kill people. And if I was allowed to run loose, I'd probably do it again. I have to say that I know it is going to sound sick, it is going to sound psycho, and I don't really think I'm that psycho, but it's kind of fun. It's like riding a roller coaster."

Mr Kilgore asked if the killer was Miss Bundy's boyfriend or husband. She responded, "He's a boyfriend." She indicated to Mr Kilgore she didn't want the killer arrested yet, "Let him get off work," she said. "Don't bother him on his job right now so he's not humiliated on his job."

After arranging for an interview at the Gristmill, arrest interview with Mr Kilgore, Mrs Bundy guaranteed him that she would be there. Not only would she be there, she would bring with her what she had in her hands right then, one of the bullets that hit the Twins. And she referred to the twin as "the younger brunette sister", meaning Gina Marano.

"This one bullet," Bundy said, "as far as I know, is the one that came out of the younger one's head." And, as Mr Choi has testified – or I should say as the coroner has testified – two bullets passed through the head of Gina Marano.

Bundy continued to tell Mr Kilgore where she thought the guns may be found, referring to the Exhibits 3 and 4, the chrome and nickel guns.

She indicated to Mr Kilgore she had given me the guns and I had disposed of them in one of two places, either the top of the Burbank boiler room at Jergens or under the wash between the apartment and Jergens Corporation.

The same woman, who just moments before had told Mr Kilgore that the reason she was involved in these murders was because she was afraid the killer would kill her, then told Mr Kilgore that the killer knew she was not afraid to die.

She said, "He knows that I've given him ample opportunity to knock me off. I'm suicidal. I do not have any will to live. I don't give a damn. I know I'm facing the gas chamber, and it doesn't freak me out."

This is the woman who was so afraid of her life that she joined in mass murder.

She indicated the killer had threatened her children because she had no will to live, and a threat against her life would be meaningless.

Mr Kilgore accepted that premise by indicating he wouldn't let anyone hit the kids.

When Mr Kilgore finally elicited Carol Bundy's apartment, where she was calling from at 240 West Verdugo, when he finally elicited the address from her, she pleaded with him, "Please don't come arrest me, please let me play this my way."

The call was terminated, and before Mr Kilgore could make that rendezvous at 2.00 o'clock at the Gristmill, other officers from Van Nuys Division of Los Angeles Police Department entered the Verdugo apartment during their investigation of a completely separate murder and arrested Carol Bundy for murder and decapitation of John Murray.

The code name Claudia was not new in any way, shape, or form to the Los Angeles Police Department on August 11, 1980. They had received a call on June 14, and that caller declined to tell them the name of the person she described as her lover; rather she allowed him his freedom. And in the interim period Karen Jones, Exxie Wilson, a girl unknown to anyone other than as a number, Jane Doe 18, Jane Doe 28, and John Murray died, all by the two exhibits you've seen here in court as criminalists and ballistics experts will testify that the only murder linked to the chrome gun is that of John Murray.

All of the girls are practically linked, as you've heard, or will hear, to the nickel .25 automatic that you've seen here in court.

These weapons will be offered, as you know, they're in evidence and they've been tested.

Mr Heinlein, the recipient of the telephone call on June 14, will testify that the voice of that caller on that tape is the voice of Carol Bundy. And from testimony of Mr Heinlein, Mr Westbrook, or Carol Bundy, should she testify, you'll learn that on the 14th of June, 1980,

Carol Bundy called and told the police officers that her lover by the name of John, who is in his forties and who drives a Plymouth and whom she sees regularly and calls daily, her current lover, was the killer.

She indicated on June 14 that she was terrified of her lover; that she was afraid he may be a mass murderer.

She indicated she had washed the bloody clothing of Cynthia Chandler and Gina Marano in a Laundromat near her home. You will hear testimony from the manager of the apartment building that she has in that building numerous washing machines and dryers; but that she used a Laundromat as she indicated on June 14.

She further indicated to – the police would find no evidence in that Laundromat because she specifically had scrubbed those machines down thoroughly to avoid such a possibility.

She indicated the killer had used a plain sheet – strike that – plain white towels, like motel towels, to clean up the blood of the victims that he had killed in her car. She described washing the car out.

She stated that the killer and her on the 15th [14th] of June, 1980, used hoses and washed the blood of the victims out of that car; that there were blankets, paper towels and towels blood-soaked, clothing blood-soaked, and bullets given to her that had purportedly passed through Gina Marano's head, but she told the police she wasn't sure that this man had killed these two girls, and rather than turn him in, rather than turn him in at that time she would wait until she was sure, she said, because she didn't want to, in her own words, screw up a relationship she happened to enjoy.

You will hear testimony from Cissy Buster and others that I was not in any way, shape, or form ever, and specifically in June of 1980, Carol Bundy's lover; that there was no relationship at all between Carol Bundy and I that could even constitute friendship during that period of time; that she alleges the killer brought her car home blood-soaked and full of these bloody items.

You will hear evidence from the widow of John Murray. You will hear testimony from Jeanette Murray that her husband had had an on-going relationship with Carol Bundy throughout 1979 and 1980, up until the day he died on August 4, 1980.

You'll see letters that Carol Bundy sent to Jack [John] Murray indicating that relationship during that period of time.

You will hear testimony from the widow of John Murray that Carol Bundy had attempted to buy Jack Murray from her for $15,00 in – in Christmas of 1979 – at Christmas, I should say, 1979.

You will learn that Carol's relationship with Jack Murray lasted as an intense love relationship up until August 4, 1980 at approximately 2.30 in the morning when Carol Bundy pulled the trigger on my gun and shot him in the back of the head in his van.

Referring again to the June 14 phone call of Carol Bundy's, Ms Bundy indicated that there was only her word, only her word that could convict the killer. There was no other evidence.

She talked to the officers for a lengthy period of time. She tried to gain information from the officers. Mr Heinlein will testify that througout that call, the caller wanted to find out if the police officers were closing in on the killer.

You'll learn on August 11, the police officers who arrested Carol Bundy at 11.30 in the day couldn't stop her from talking when they arrested her. They couldn't even arrest her because she was talking so heatedly and so continuously that they couldn't speak – couldn't get in the words edgewise, so-to-speak, "You're under arrest."

They merely listened to her as she led them from one room to the other of that apartment, gave them evidence, handed them items, panties which she described as the clothing of the victims.

She proceeded with those officers into my bedroom, produced a key of her own to that filing cabinet, that's been testified to here, opened that filing cabinet, gave police officers more evidence, evidence of other crimes.

Evidence of molestation of Shannon –.

She gave them a photo album containing Polaroid photographs.

Evidence will show that Shannon – had in fact had sex with me at the age of 11–

THE COURT: I've previously cautioned you about that subject. I am not going to do it again. I've told you not to mention that subject in this trial. It is not relevant to any of the charges pending. Now let's proceed.

THE DEFENDANT: She proceeded to tell officers Pida – strike that – Officer Landgren, Lieutenant Durrer about the murders of these women.

She indicated to Lieutenant Durrer that she had been along when Exxie Wilson was murdered and that she had played with Exxie Wilson's head.

She later told Officer Broda she put makeup on the head, like a big baby doll. She accused me of using the head in some sexual manner. She told Detective Broda I was living with her at the time.

Evidence will be introduced here, and has been introduced here that will show that I did not live with Carol Bundy until June 27, 1980; that the head of Exxie Wilson was discovered, as has been testified to, and will be further, on June 26, the day before I moved in to that apartment with Carol Bundy.

Carol Bundy's lover from her testimony and evidence you'll see here, is definitely one of the killers.

Carol Bundy's statements to police officers, whether she testifies or the officers testify to them, will show you that she has intimate knowledge of these murders – including the sound effects of the girl dying, which she makes with her own mouth on tape recordings.

In fact this is a case of twos, a case of duplication: two guns, two Raven .25 automatics, which you've seen on the stand here, two cars which you've seen photographs of, a Buick and a Buick – pardon me – a Datsun, two apartments, a Van Nuys apartment of Carol Bundy's a Burbank apartment shared by Carol Bundy and myself. Two double murders: Gina Marano and Cynthia Chandler murdered at approximately noon to 3.00 on June 11, two pocket knives – pardon me – the other double murder, Karen Jones and Exxie Wilson.

You will learn from Carol Bundy's statements to police officers that that was supposed to be a triple murder; that was supposed to be three. They couldn't find – the killer couldn't find the third friend, the friend, a black girl who was with Karen Jones and Exxie Wilson that night that they had gone back to find her.

You'll see telephone records from the Burbank apartment to the Lemona Street apartment at 3.08 AM, approximately 15 minutes to 20 minutes after Karen Jones was shot and killed and dumped in the street of Burbank.

There was a phone call from the Burbank apartment to the Lemona apartment. Evidence will show Carol Bundy was in the Burbank apartment near where Karen Jones was found. Evidence will show that I was in the Lemona apartment, some 15 miles away.

Twos. Two killers. Evidence will show there were two killers.

The scene analysis and testimony of the crime scenes where the bodies were found will indicate to you that the inference has to be drawn that two parties were present and took part in dropping those bodies from a moving vehicle. Specifically Cynthia Chandler and Gina Marano.

You'll hear evidence that Carol Bundy knew that I knew Cynthia Chandler as – no later than May of 1980. And that Carol Bundy hated her, and Carol Bundy told Jack Murray's brother-in-law that she wished Cynthia and I would crash, and that – on that motorcycle we were on – Cynthia and I would crash.

On the subject of twos, two lovers. You'll be shown abundantly clearly through testimony of the widow and friends of Jack Murray, friends of Carol Bundy and myself, that Jack Murray was Carol's gigolo lover up until his death; that she met – he met his death at her hands.

Why? There are too many reasons been given to bother counting them, but you'll hear a few from police officers as Carol Bundy told them to her – told them to them.

But back to twos, there's two Carol Bundys that we have to consider. There are two Carol Bundys that we have to consider in this case. There's a Carol Mary Bundy and there's a Carol Ann Bundy. And Carol Mary Bundy is not quite sure at times, I believe, which she is.

I hope to offer psychiatric testimony, although it would be based solely upon her statements to police and tape recordings, that Carol Bundy is, in fact, two people; that she and her lover – I should clarify that – Carol Ann Bundy and her lover, Ted Bundy, lived in a fantasy world.

Carol Bundy – Mary Bundy, in early 1980 and later 79 followed the news and read a book. By her own statements in her own letters, she's made it abundantly clear, and it will be made clear to you here, that Carol Bundy, that's Carol Mary Bundy, considers Ted Bundy, mass murderer on death row in Florida, an idol of hers. And when Ted Bundy, that mass murderer in Florida on death row, married a girl named Carol Ann, and made her Carol Ann Bundy in early 1980, or late 79, Carol Mary Bundy in California, clear across the continent, launched with her lover, Jack Murray, this string of murders.

June 1, 1980, Marnette Comer died in Carol Bundy's automobile, shot to death with Carol Bundy's gun. June 1, 1,179 miles north of here, Brenda Ball died in 1974.

June 11, 1980, approximately noon to 1.00, maybe 3.00 o'clock, Gina Marano and Cynthia Chandler got into Jack Murray's van with Carol Bundy and died, shot to death with Carol's nickel-plated Raven automatic. June 11, 1,179 miles north of here, Georgeann Hawkins died shortly after meeting her killer named Ted Bundy.

Carol Mary Bundy, here in Los Angeles, knew this all in early 1980 before she launched this murder spree.

June 23, 1980, Hollywood, California, on the Sunset Strip, Exxie Wilson and Karen Jones both got into a van. Evidence will indicate that screams were heard, shots were heard, at the Sizzler restaurant, testimony will indicate the shots were heard and tyre squeals at the Sizzler restaurant at approximately 1.30 in the morning of June 23, 1980. As you've heard, Karen Jones' body, freshly killed, was found at approximately 2.45 to 2.55 AM on June 23, 1980. And in her tape recorded interview with Gary Broda and Mr – Detective Jacques, whom you've met here, Carol Bundy said the killer went back for a third victim and was unsuccessful.

Ted Bundy, as Carol knew, murdered Janice Ott and Denise Naslund and went back for a third and failed. The dates, ladies and gentlemen, of June 1, June 11, match perfectly from the first and second murders of both of these cases. From thereon the dates do not parallel.

But Carol Bundy read that book and every piece of evidence in that case comes from Carol Bundy's hands.

You'll hear testimony from Carol Bundy, from police officers, from myself.

You'll learn that Carol Bundy surreptitiously duplicated the keys to the garage in which was found, with adequate evidence, blood, type-O blood that very well could be Gina Marano's blood.

Carol Bundy told police on August 11 that the killer had taken Gina and Cindy to that garage and had sex with them in that garage, leaving the garage unlocked, the killer would have had sex in that garage with these two deceased girls.

He then took them, put them back in the vehicle, which she describes as being her Buick, and evidence will indicate, as it has and will, there was no O-type blood in the Buick, no O-type blood was confirmed in the Buick.

In fact, you'll learn that Carol Bundy and Jack Murray had another vehicle they used, the same vehicle in which Carol Bundy left the decapitated, butchered remains of her lover on August 4, the same vehicle that contained cheap white motel towels as described by her to police officers on June 14 in the phone call; the same vehicle that contained two tyre irons that didn't match the lugs on the vehicle, wrapped in a cloth, wrapped in those cheap white towels; the same vehicle contained rope, industrial strength deodoriser, plastic bags.

You'll hear Carol Bundy's glee and laughter as she tells police officers on tape about how it feels to cut off the head of a human being.

You'll learn she's a licensed vocational nurse; further, that she's a diabetic and has syringes in her possession at her home.

You'll hear her on tape and here in court tell us that she cleaned the van down thoroughly before she left with Jack Murray's head in a plastic bag.

You'll see photographs of that van and the evidence that she ransacked that van removing things.

You will notice in those photographs and from Mr Pida's testimony, Mr Landgren's testimony, that no keys were found in the van; that Jack Murray's key ring was gone.

You'll hear from Jeanette Murray that his key ring had an immense number of keys on it.

Carol Bundy, after removing those keys for whatever reason, left the scene of the murder, leaving behind what she says in her tape to be two shell casings; however, police recovered only one. But that shell casing matches, without any reasonable error factor, the chrome gun, which you've seen and which you've heard testimony that it was the gun that I carried.

You will hear Carol Bundy tell Rick Jacques of the Los Angeles Police Department and Gary Broda of the Los Angeles Police Department that she had one gun and I had the other.

You'll hear Carol's description of the evening when Exxie Wilson's head, frozen, was wrapped in some clothing and – and put in a box by her, closed the top of the box herself, tossed that box out into the alley and did not see the headlights of an oncoming car because she was in such a position that she couldn't see out the front window. While she was throwing the box out the side door of Jack Murray's van into the alley, she didn't get it far enough out, she said, and as they drove off they ran over a corner of it. You'll see photographs of that box, that it's broken, that there's a tack and some sawdust laying where the box was found, to corroborate her story.

The evidence will indicate from Carol Bundy's own statement and from a witness who worked in a Newberry store, that Carol Bundy came into that store on Wednesday, the 26 – pardon me – the 25th of June and bought a wooden box wearing black gloves and shorts, and other clothing.

You have seen the evidence of the black gloves in a ladies size, that came out of the Buick station wagon when searched from Youngstown, Ohio, by Officer Novol.

Carol Bundy tells officers she bought that box; that she never touched it bare-handed; that she bought it specifically to put Exxie's head in. And she, in the next breath, says that I was with her when all that occurred.

You'll hear evidence from the Jergens Corporation that I was at work that day at that time.

You'll hear testimony that on August 11, when I came out of Jergens Corporation at 11.30 to go to the lunch truck, I was taken into custody by Officer Pida of the Van Nuys Division of the Los Angeles Police Department, taken to Van Nuys station, some seven and a half hours later, down at Parker Center.

I was interviewed, as you've heard testimony here. Lengthily, I might add.

You will learn that from my testimony and Officer Pida, Langdren, Durrer, that they knew Jack Murray had been killed with a .25 automatic, because they had found a .25 automatic shell in his van.

They knew that Carol Bundy had two .25 automatics at one time because on August 10, the day before the arrests, she told them she did.

She further told them that she had sold these guns to a man named Hammer or Hammil, she couldn't recall which.

But that August 10 interview that Carol Bundy had with the Van Nuys Police Department is very important. Because, as Mr Pida will testify, I was in the next room being interrogated by him. Neither one of us under arrest and six days after Jack Murray had died, well over 24 hours after Jack Murray had been found. Six days after the murder, we are in different rooms at Van Nuys station, and these officers are hearing totally contradictory stories as to Carol Bundy's whereabouts on August 4 in the early morning.

Carol Bundy freely admits she was at the Nashville club. Douglas Clark, in the other room, says, "No, she was home all night with me."

That frame-up didn't work.

As Mr Stallcup has indicated from the stand, on August 11 he didn't think I had killed Jack Murray. But for six days – you'll learn that for six days I had the knowledge that Jack Murray had been killed with my gun, a gun that I had carried frequently, the chrome-plated .25 automatic and that Carol Bundy was – had assured me that no one had seen her during her murder of Murray, and that I and her, that the two of us, would have to stand, face-to-face, word-to-word, and that the police would take her word that I had killed Murray and not her.

But that attempt on August 10 to cast the Jack Murray murder around my neck didn't succeed. The officers did not arrest me on August 10.

And down at Parker Center on August 11, having known that Jack Murray was dead – because Carol brought that head of that man home to that apartment in Burbank in a plastic bag the morning of August 4, and I went down to the car, and I saw that head, and I helped her dispose of that head in a trashcan in the Atwater area.

You'll learn that in fear of arrest for Jack Murray's murder, I played right into the hands of the two murderers who did these crimes.

Thank you.

APPENDIX 2

TRANSCRIPT OF TAPE #82051

JUNE 14, 1980. 20.00 HRS.

Detective Heinlein. Detective Westbrook. Carol Bundy.

DETECTIVE HEINLEIN: Hello, Betsy?
CAROL BUNDY: Hello?
H: Yeah, Betsy?
B: Yes,
H: Yeah, how ya doin'?
B: Alright, I'm sorry about that but I, when I was talking a police officer walked in the back door and I got spooked.
H: Oh, you're kidding me.
B: No, I'm not, and that's just exactly what I don't need right now.
H: Okay.
B: Now, what I told you earlier; did it compute? [reference to 2 hour previous call]
H: Well, yeah, part of it did.
B: What part didn't?
H: Well, the clothing was off quite a bit.
B: The clothing was off?
H: Yeah.
B: Huh. Very interesting.
H: So, what, uh, can I get your right name now?
B: If I give you my right name before I'm ready, I won't live out the week.
H: Well, nobody's going to get it from us, that's for sure.
B: Yeah, well, there'll be a strip in the papers, and...
H: No there won't.
B: ..."Betsy" is a code name that's devised between my friend and myself, it was a grave mistake giving it out in the first place. So now what I have to do is negate the value of "Betsy".
H: Okay.
B: So, there can be no "Betsy".
H: Alright.
B: Because if the name "Betsy" comes out he's gonna know exactly where it come from.
H: Okay.
B: 'Cause there's no other "Betsy".
H: Alright.
B: It was stupid of me to do that one.
H: Okay. We'll negate that.
B: Alright, so, ah, this is "Claudia". There's no relationship to "Claudia" to me in any way, shape or form.
H: Okay, when are you going to give me your real name? It's one of these dates? Or eventually? Or...
B: Probably in a day or two when I feel secure enough with the situation. The clothing was off?
H: Yeah.
B: I washed the damn clothes.
H: You washed it?
B: I washed them.
H: Well, what else did they have when you were washing it?
B: Oh, a massive amount of bloody paper towels, for one thing.
H: How did, where did the bloody paper towels come from?
B: Presumably, from the back of the Plymouth... presumably from the car.
H: Okay. Okay, well what other information can you give us that will help us? 'Cause we are really up in the air, we're don't know where to go.
B: Uh...
DETECTIVE WESTBROOK: Can you give us the suspects name or anything?
B: You know I'm not going to do that just this particular time. Mostly what I'm trying to do is ascertain whether or not the individual that I know, who happens to be my lover, did in fact do this. He said he did.
H: When did he tell you that?

B: Uh, Thursday I guess it was.

H: What time of the day?

B: Uh, I was pretty close to getting off work, probably about five/five-thirty.

H: Five to five-thirty Thursday. When was the last time you saw him before that?

B: The last time I saw him before that?

H: Yeah.

B: Uh, Sunday, Saturday or Sunday. Sunday I think it was.

H: So you went four or five days without seeing him?

B: Yeah, but we talk on the phone a lot.

H: Well, okay when was the last time you talked to him, that maybe he could have...

B: Well, I talk to him virtually every day.

H: Did you talk to him Thursday during the day?

B: Well, he called me at work. Or I called him, I don't remember which, we call each other quite a bit.

H: Okay, but, would he have told you right over the phone?

B: Uh...

H: Normally, or, you know...

B: In euphemism, directly/indirectly, and in euphemisms.

H: He would directly or indirectly. Did he, any time Thursday lead you to believe that you know it may have happened? Or was it a complete...

B: He told me to catch the news, that the news was quite interesting.

H: And he told you that what time Thursday?

B: Uh...

H: It's really important that we narrow it down to a time, also.

B: Well, when were the kids actually hit? What are your hours on it, what did you peg down?

H: Well, we're within a couple of days is all. That's why we're trying to pin it down to a time.

B: Hmm... what I'm trying to get from you is enough information that, uh, verifies what Don's told me... uh... anyway, what he's told me, uh...

H: Well, that's what we're trying to get information from you too, to see if, you know, it connects with or, you know, is, is going to be...

B: If the clothing is off, if the clothing is off then it may not have happened in front of him at all.

H: Okay, well how did you wash the clothes? How did you come about washing the clothes?

B: In the washing machine.

H: No, no, no, no, where did he get the clothes to wash them? Where did you get 'em? Did you get 'em from the girls? Or was it...

B: I didn't see the girls. I wasn't with him at the time that this occurred.

H: Okay.

B: What happened... I went out to get the... I went to get the car, I opened the car door and there was this, this big laundry bag, this duffel bag sitting there, and I thought it was dirty laundry. So, I jumped into the car and zipped over the Laundromat. And when I opened it up there was all this damn bloody stuff in there.

H: Like what? The clothes and what else?

B: The clothes, the blankets, the towels, the paper towels.

H: Clothes, blanket, regular... like bath towels?

B: Yeah.

H: Family type bath towels, or motel type...?

B: Hmm?

H: Were they, you know, regular ones, or motel type, or, you know, the towels.

B: Um...

H: I mean, were they probably the guy's, or the girl's or, maybe...

B: I'm not sure where they came from, I never saw them before.

H: But they didn't look like motel towels, not the white, cheap...

B: They were white cheap towels.

H: Oh, okay. That's...

B: There were four of them.

H: Okay, and paper towels too.

B: Oh, yeah, tons of them.

W: Well, why don't you give us enough information so that we can start working on it, and then we can either eliminate him or...

B: Well, because, before I give him to you, I have to make sure that it isn't just a... he fantasises a lot and he comes up with a lot of bullshit. Now, I have to know...

W: If it's not him, we can prove it's not him just the same as...

B: And then I turn around and I've got to deal with him.

W: Well, we're not going to bring you into it.

B: How can you help it? I'm the only damn person in the world that knows, maybe if...

W: I don't even know who you are.

B: I know you don't. And you're not going to for a while unless you trace this damn call, you certainly had enough time for that, we've been over a good half hour here.

H: Well, we're not gonna do that, so...

B: Okay, um...

H: But the other thing that you said, this is the fourth or fifth one that you know of personally. You know, even if it isn't the same one for these... you know, obviously...

B: Like I said, he fantasises a lot and I can't tell what's straight and what isn't. He's come into the house a number of times bloodied up. His clothes have been extremely bloody, he's been extremely shaken, his knife is bloody as hell, and then he says that he's been, um, in a knife fight, in some kind of altercation.

H: Uh, huh.

B: And, uh, one particular incident supposedly, he dropped a male in Griffith Park. It's about six weeks ago. Then he told me that three weeks ago he dropped a male, but he didn't give me any details on that. Uh, uh, he's been telling me that throughout his adolescence, his, his, early adult up into his forties that he was uh, you know, doing these things off and on and that for a while he worked in, as sort of a, well he describes it as, as... what is a menial worker, uh, um, uh...

H: Labourer?

B: No, uh, a low man on a totem pole, a flunky?

H: Oh.

B: He said that he was a flunky hit man, that is he worked for a cheap organisation and that he was a flunky, but that he would do hits when somebody was assigned to him.

H: Is that right? And he's been doin' this for since his teens to his forties?

B: Uh huh.

H: Hmm.

B: I will tell you that right now he's forty-one years old.

H: Okay.

B: Okay.

H: Is he white, black?

B: Yes.

H: Yes?

B: Either one or the other.

H: Come on, which one is he?

B: He's white.

H: Okay, he's white. Hey look...

B: He has (blonde? brown?) hair and blue eyes...

W: ...look

B: ...and that much I'll give you.

H: Blonde hair and blue eyes?

W: We can very easily eliminate him if we get, if we know who we're working with, or either make him or eliminate him, that we have to know who we're working with.

B: When...

W: We're not going to bring you into it. If it...

B: Uh, there's just no conceivable way because there is no way of being able, uh, to do it you can't...

W: Well, there certainly is, the police department is investigating this, you're not. We have certain information that you don't have, that we can put a case together, but we have to know who we're working with to do it. We can either eliminate him...

B: I'm well... I'm well aware of that, but there hasn't been enough information released to the media that jives with the things that he tells me. He tells me that this has occurred under this sort of... under another circumstance. For instance, the newspaper say that these children were hitchhiking to Colorado, and that they were runaways from Huntington Park or something like that. Huntington Beach, wherever their home was. He tells me that they're hooking on sunset, and the one time he got to them before, or got to one of them once before um, and that she gave him a very bad blow-job and it was, uh, not worth the money and her attitude was very bad and he decided that he wanted to hit her. Okay. Now, that's not a rational reason for taking somebody's life.

W: Well I agree with all that, but that is no reason for you to conceal his identity either.

B: I'm going to conceal his identity until I have enough knowledge that he did do it to turn him over. Otherwise, if he didn't do it, I've ruined a relationship that I happen to enjoy.

W: Well, how could you...

B: If he did do it I've got to be extremely cautious, because he will get me.

W: How are you going to ruin a relationship? We don't know who you are, we're not going to bring you into it, and the only way we would even talk to him is if we can prove that he did it, and if he did it you don't want anymore to do with him anyway.

B: Well of course if he did it I don't want to have anything more to do with him. Where am I going to hide?

W: Why do you need to hide?

B: If he did it, he will get to me.

W: Why?

B: He will find me.

W: Why?

B: Alright, look at, look at the legal process we have. Alright, supposing you take (John? Don?) uh, you take him off and, you know, he's arrested, you go through the booking process. He puts up bail, and he's released on bail. Who does he go looking for?

W: Well, why would he go looking for you?

B: Because there is no conceivable way that you are going to be able to find out who he is. What do you know about him, that he drives a 66, uh, never mind. Anyway, you don't know anything about him.

W: Well, you don't know whether I do or not.

B: Hmm?

W: You don't know what information I have. What you apparently know, a good deal of it, is what you've read in the papers. Now, I'm not saying that's right or that's wrong.

B: Well, so put me down as a crackpot.

W: No, no, we're not putting you down as a crackpot. I don't understand why you won't give us his name so we can start working on it.

H: See, we may have information already, about him, that the media doesn't.

W: That may put us on his track.

B: Alright, he has already told me that I'm alright, I'm perfectly safe, as long as I don't say anything. That if I say anything you know...

W: Well, how's he gonna know you said anything if you don't tell him?

B: Alright, there isn't any way that you could put a case together without my testimony. Even assuming that you're able to protect me long enough for the case to go to court, and if he arraigned, and all that stuff.

W: I'm not at all sure of that.

B: Hmm?

W: I'm not at all sure of that.

B: There is just no way.

W: Well, you don't know what evidence I have.

B: What do you have that I don't have?

W: Well, I'm certainly not going to tell you that.

B: Alright, then I guess we're at a Mexican stand-off, aren't we?

W: Apparently, 'cause I'm certainly not going to give you the evidence that I have. It's the police job to investigate...

B: Alright, let me put it to you this way then. Alright obviously you're not going to give me details because it might screw things up. Alright. Do you have more information than what I've contributed? You said that the clothing description is off. Do you actually have more than what I've given you?

W: Yes, we have been working this since...

B: Wait a minute, there's cars going by, I can't hear. Actually this is a bad connection for me. Okay, now you can talk.

W: Okay, I said we've been working this since last Thursday, so we've probably got in excess of 150 pages of information on this thing.

B: Like description of the car, what he looks like and all that crap?

W: We have a great deal of information.

B: Well, for heaven's sakes, whatever you do if you want me to contact you again, don't give this to the media. 'Cause if it hits the papers or the (newswaves?)...

W: Ma'am, there's nothing here that you've said so far that the media would even be interested in.

B: That's good. Okay, then, uh, I'll contact you, let's see, this is Saturday, I'll contact you on Monday if I'm really thoroughly convinced that he's the one, then I'll give you his name.

W: Okay.

H: Is, is there any way... hello?

B: I'm here.

H: Yeah, hey, is there any way that we can get any of that stuff, have you drop off any of that... the duffel bag...

B: Oh, I know one thing else we did today.

H: One thing you did today?

B: Yes.

H: What's that?

B: We washed the car. I mean washed the car. Inside out, scrubbed it down, he took hoses and he shooshed all the clots and stuff out of the car. I mean really soaked the inside of that car down.

H: What, where is the rest of that stuff, the duffel bag, any of the paper towels, uh, the regular towels...

B: Well, the paper towels, the paper towels, the blanket and that kinda crap are pretty awful, I just disposed of them. The clothes are (lost?).

H: Wait a minute, wait a minute, we thought we might be able to find them. They would not lead us to you at all, but it, it, you know, it's more evidence, we could maybe use it and then not connect you at all. An anonymous tip that...

B: Well, hell, that was Thursday night, you couldn't possibly find it now...

H: Oh, I wouldn't say that, anything is possible. You know, it could be there, we might find out who the trash service is, you know, there's all kinds of... at least tell us where, you know, where you threw it away, or what Laundromat type of thing you went to, we, we might be able to come up with it, which could help us a great deal one way or the other and still not involve you at all. Probably 100 people a day go into that Laundromat. But, there may still be something there, and to overlook something like that and not be able to...

B: I washed those machines down very thoroughly...

H: No, no, no, the other items, you know, the paper towels, some of the, uh, regular towels, the, you know, anything could be there.

B: Huh.

H: Could you at least tell us where that's at.

B: Well I'm not sure that's a terribly good idea either.

H: Why? How can we... there's no way we could trace you or him anybody, but if it's some evidence and it may help us in the case, even if it doesn't you know and as many hours as we're putting in, as many people as we have working on it, you're talking about maybe 20 minutes out of our time to go and possible to get the stuff, then, uh, if there's any way at all that it is connected to the case, we might be able to find out through it that, uh, that it wasn't him.

B: Well, how can you relate a green and brown plaid blanket with, with, with murder? I mean, so, okay, there's bloodstains on it. Big deal, now it's just a blanket.

H: Yeah, but it could be traced, the bloodstains you can't get them out of that stuff. Not completely. Neither towels, you know, uh...

B: What was she wearing, that white dress, what was she wearing?

H: Uh...

W: Ma'am, that's been in the paper.
B: Hmm?
W: That has been in the paper, what she was wearing.
B: I know it's been described in the paper, but I also know what was in the bag.
H: What else was in the bag?
B: Well, I already described the clothes that were in there.
H: Right, I know you did, but was there any clothes in there that, you know...
B: Well, there was one...
H: ...because if you washed the clothes and you have it, then it couldn't have been on there, they were partially clothed when we found them. And if you had all their clothes, then...
B: There was one thing that was confusing on it, according to the description in the paper, one of the children was wearing a tube top, okay, a red tube top or something.
H: Mm hmm.
B: One of the girls was wearing pink pants, I presume it was the same one, it didn't say whether it was underpants or whether it was street pants. But I know that the dress that I washed was white with red stripes on it. Little thin stripes, and I think there was yellow stripes in it too, but the red stripes stand out in my mind. Now she wouldn't be wearing a red tube top underneath that dress. She might wear a bra or she might wear no bra. There were no underclothing in there. There was another tube top which was, uh, green.
H: Another green tube top inside that duffel bag?
B: Uh huh.
H: What happened to all that stuff? Did you just throw it away?
B: No, I didn't throw it away.
H: Do you still have it?
B: I gave it to John this afternoon.
H: Jeez...
W: Well, why don't you give us his name and then we can start to work and find out if it's him or not.
B: Oh, listen you couldn't... if I gave you a name now, you couldn't even be sure it would be his real name, at this point...
W: Yeah...
B: ...there's an 85% chance that the things that I'm telling you now, because I'm scared off, are misdirection. You do understand that?
W: No, I don't understand what you're saying at all.
B: Alright, put it this way, put it this way. Whether or not the individual that hit these kids is in fact your murderer, obviously I'm not making this up, I have been told by an individual that he did it, I've taken care of some bloody stuff I'm not making this up.
W: Well, I believe you.
H: ...we believe you, you know...
B: Whether, whether or not John was making it up is something else again. All I know is...
W: That is our job to find out.
B: Right, all I know is this. He said that he hit the two teenage girls, one was about 17 and one was about 19. They were hooking on Sunset Boulevard. He couldn't separate them. He couldn't get one away from the other, and he kept referring to the second one as "the friend". There was no reference to being a sister. But he wouldn't have any way of knowing that as far as he knows, it was a couple of teenage kids hooking for a few dollars. Things got out of hand. There was an argument. There was a disagreement, uh. He didn't state that they were trying to rob him per se...
W: Yeah.
B: ...what he said was they were after his money and that they weren't going to perform. And there was an argument and he shot 'em. He tells me, alright you can verify this or not because the papers do not say this. He tells me that he fired four shots. Two in one girl's head and virtually blew the back of the girl's head away. One shot in the head and one shot in the chest of the 2nd girl. Does that jibe with what you've got?
W: Well, ma'am, that's information that I'm not gonna give out.
B: Well then I can't give you any more. If you're not going to... if you're... listen my life is on the line talking with you, now, if you want me to be straight with you, you can, you can verify that because if... you can tell me yes or no on that...

W: Ma'am...

B: ...because otherwise I'm not going to give you anymore information.

W: ... you see, I have to work in certain ways, I have to hold back certain information, uh, to make my case. There's certain things that only the killer and I know.

B: I am aware of that. But, you have to understand this. Either I know the killer, in which case I may be the next one on his list, and I've heard him (?)...

W: In that case you'd better ask for our help.

B: ...otherwise, if he's on a pipedream, if he heard a newsbreak or something and decided to roll in the glory of that, then there's no point in carrying this on anymore. You can tell me...

W: Well, it was, it could certainly save us a lot of time, we could eliminate him immediately, or make him immediately.

B: You can tell me that much. Is the information on the location of the shots correct?

W: That's information that I think we can't give out.

B: Then I can't give you anymore information 'cause you're not helping me either. I'm not going to go to the newspaper or anything. Then, that'll be screwing up your case and (certain? curtains?) for me.

W: Ma'am, I don't even know who I'm talking to.

B: What?

W: I don't know who I'm talking to.

B: I know you don't. I'll tell you this much. The very fact that you've taken this much time to talk with me, and you haven't cut me off, that you haven't written me off as a screwball, indicates that very much of what I'm saying is of interest to you.

H: Well, certainly it is.

W: Anything in this case is of interest to me.

B: Alright, well, supposing I came on the line and I said hey, uh, uh, I've got some information for you and, gee whiz, you sure liked the information I gave you when I talked about the Hillside Strangler. I could set myself up as a total screwball. You wouldn't take the time to talk to me then.

W: Listen, we have taken in excess of 150 calls on this. And we have written every one of them down, and we have spent as much time on the phone with each individual as they would spend on the phone with us.

B: Oh, I wasn't aware of that. I thought that the ones that were obvious screwballs you cut off.

W: How do I know who's an obvious screwball?

B: Am I a screwball?

W: I have no idea.

B: You're impression, then.

W: I have no impression, you haven't really given me anything so far. You've told me the things that have been in the paper.

B: Alright, there was nothing in the paper about the description of the little girl's dress, and there was nothing in the paper about two bullets in each of those children. The paper said only one bullet in each of those children. Alright, he also stated that he used one of the girls in a sexual manner. And this is one that probably won't come up until you've had an autopsy on the kid. But he... right now his current trip is curiosity about necrophilia, which was how he got started on this, and he wanted to take out an old whore who was giving him a bad time, and the only one he could come up across was the kids. Okay. Uh, anyway, supposedly, at least he says, that he took her deep in her throat. He deep-throated her in other words.

H: Okay.

B: That's something that isn't going to come out until you've had your autopsy completed. I don't even know if he did it to the point of orgasm. Knowing him and his sexual pattern, he probably did not, he probably tried it and then just jerked himself off on her chest or something. Because a lot of his sexuality is masturbation in nature.

W: Well, I don't understand why you're telling us all this and will not give us his name so we can work on it. There's no way in the world that, uh...

B: Right, okay, now...

W: ...I know who you are or anything else...

B: ...if, uh, you said you get 150 calls a day, on...

W: No, I said we've had about 150 calls on this particular case.

B: Alright, you've had 150 calls, okay, so check out your 149 other ones, okay?
W: Well, your information is very interesting.
H: This may be the one. We don't want to overlook anything.
B: Alright, this may be the one or it may be a total pipedream outa a neurotic lady. Right?
W: That's right, it could be, but I can't check it out if I don't have his name.
B: But you're not helping me either, you're not putting my mind at rest –
[*Conversation unintentionally terminated by operator.*]

NOTES

1. Secretors' body fluids – saliva, semen, mucus, urine etc. – contain the same substances as the blood and consequently a person's blood-group can be determined from such secretions. Secretors compose about 86% of the population. Non-secretors' fluids, on the other hand, produce no such chemicals.

2. The barrel of a gun is designed to ensure a gas-tight seal is created between the barrel wall and the bullet. This is achieved by the machining of spiral grooves within the barrel. The slug expands into these channels when the gun is fired and the lands (the raised portion of the grooves) cut score-marks into the bullet jacket. The number, depth, and twist direction of the marks identifies the manufacturer of gun from which it was fired. More detailed examination of the score-marks will identify the actual gun if it is found and test-fired bullets are compared.

3. Detective Orozco's bilingual abilities involved him in questioning witnesses in the Robert Kennedy assassination investigation 12 years before the Sunset case. Paul Schrade, Kennedy's aide at the time of the shooting, and himself also shot in the attack, said of that investigation, "The Los Angeles Police Department suppressed and destroyed evidence, manipulated and coerced witnesses, and failed to pursue obvious leads."

4. Murray's deluded Vietnam heroics were remarkably similar to the stories espoused by survivalist serial killer Leonard Lake. Lake had a similar attitude towards women, he required them only as sex slaves. He committed suicide in police custody following arrest for possession of an illegal weapon. Investigations revealed a secret underground bunker where he murdered several men, women and children along with his accomplice Charles Ng. Female victims were videoed being humiliated, raped and tortured.

5. A total of 22 perforations were noted during the post-mortem. The 11th stab wound, which punctured his lung, caused fatal haemorrhaging.

6. Because this search of Clark's property was conducted illegally, i.e. before he'd been read his Miranda rights, the Shannon photos were inadmissible evidence and the molestation charges were never brought to court.

7. Such a method is a good means of convincing a jury that a bloodstain was present even if it wasn't. It can be legally stated in court that an approved test was applied and proved positive. If there is any doubt that the stain may not stand up to a confirmation test it is best left alone. A jury would be convinced with the results of a non-conclusive preliminary test.

8. Carol had bought a video camera for Murray and the notion was that they had been recording the crimes to produce private porn/snuff movies.

9. Another highlighted case that demonstrates the unethical methods that state courts deploy against defendants who proceed pro se is that of Caryl Chessman. Chessman was arrested on burglary charges and fitted up with abduction and rape charges despite the lack of evidence. Aware of his innocence Chessman proceeded to defend himself against the state. Denied virtually all his requests by the judge, the trial was a one-sided affair and he was found guilty and eventually executed.

10. *Ted Bundy The Killer Next Door* by Steve Winn and David Merrill, Bantam 1980. It

was the first book to be published on the case and has long been out of print.

11. Ted Bundy's claims of individual murders cannot be taken as conclusive. His confessions were vague and murders would be admitted to in order to circumvent his inevitable death by electrocution. Moments before his execution on January 24 1989, he tried to postpone his death yet again by admitting to more unsolved killings. The offer of further confessions was not taken up and at 7.07 AM Bundy's life was terminated.

12. When he eventually confessed, several years after his conviction, he would blame the murders on pornography. This is a typical reaction of the sociopath: Blaming someone or something for his or her failings. In truth, the pornographic material collected by Bundy probably saved other girls' lives. He evidently used the magazines as masturbatory aids when his testosterone levels were peaking and while doing so he wasn't interfering with any individual. Had such material not been available he would have been out prowling for victims on many more occasions.

13. Carol changed the date on numerous occasions, finally settling for around June 20.

Index